GAZETTEER
OF THE
LAHORE DISTRICT
1893-94

BY

G. C. WALKER, Esquire, I.C.S.
Settlement Collector

REVISED EDITION

SANG-E-MEEL PUBLICATIONS
LAHORE—PAKISTAN

954.9143   Walker, G. C.
            Gazetteer of the Lahore District
            1893-94/ G. C. Walker, I.C.S.-Lahore:
            Sang-e-Meel Publications, 2006.
            xiii, 336pp,
                1. History - Pakistan. 2. Lahore -
            History. I. Punjab Government.

2006
Published by:
Niaz Ahmad
Sang-e-Meel Publications,
Lahore.

ISBN 969-35-1866-7

SANG-E-MEEL PUBLICATIONS
25 Shahrah-e-Pakistan (Lower Mall), P.O. Box 997 Lahore-54000 PAKISTAN
Phones: 7220100 - 7228143   **Fax:** 7245101
http://www.sang-e-meel.com e-mail: smp@sang-e-meel.com
PRINTED AT: HAJI HANIF & SONS PRINTERS, LAHORE.

GAZETTEER

OF THE

LAHORE DISTRICT,

BY

G. C. WALKER, Esquire, I. C. S.,

Settlement Collector.

1893-94.

REVISED EDITION.

Compiled and Published under the Authority

OF THE

PUNJAB GOVERNMENT.

———

LAHORE "CIVIL AND MILITARY GAZETTE" PRESS.

1894.

PREFACE.

The first edition of the *Lahore Gazetteer* bears date 1883-84. The present edition was prepared in the cold weather of 1893-94. In this edition the *Gazetteer* has been entirely rewritten except Chapter II, which sets out the ancient history of Lahore district; Chapter VI A, which contains the history of old Lahore city; and those earlier portions of Chapter VI B, which relate to the principal ancient buildings around Lahore. Much information has been inserted in this edition that was not given in the former, particularly in Chapters III and IV, on the people and on the methods and conditions of agriculture obtaining in the district. For the account of the Punjab University and its connected institutions the public is indebted to Dr. M. Stein, Registrar of the University. I have to acknowledge also with thanks the kind assistance given me by Rai Bahádur Ganga Rám, Executive Engineer of Lahore, and Mr. David Johnstone, Municipal Secretary of Lahore city, who supplied me with various notes on some of the buildings and other institutions described in Chapter VI B; and I am indebted to Lála Dína Náth, citizen of Lahore, and at present Head Clerk in the district office of Bannu, for some useful information about the inner life and customs of the people of Lahore city, which has been incorporated in Chapter III B.

G. C. WALKER,
Settlement Collector.

13th *August* 1894.

CONTENTS.

CHAPTER I.—THE DISTRICT.

Section A.—Descriptive—

CHAPTER I.—THE DISTRICT—*concluded*.

CHAPTER II.—HISTORY.

CHAPTER II.—HISTORY—*concluded.*

CHAPTER III.—THE PEOPLE.

Section A.—Statistical—

CHAPTER III.—THE PEOPLE—*continued.*

Section B.—Social—

CHAPTER III.—THE PEOPLE—*continued.*

CHAPTER IV.—PRODUCTION AND DISTRIBUTION.

Section A.—Agriculture, Arboriculture and Live-stock—

CHAPTER IV.—PRODUCTION AND DISTRIBUTION—*continued.*

Section A.—Agriculture, Arboriculture and Live-stock—*concluded.*

Section B.—Occupations, Industries and Communications—

CHAPTER IV.—PRODUCTION AND DISTRIBUTION—*concluded.*

Section B.—Occupations, Industries and Communications—*concluded.*

CHAPTER V.—ADMINISTRATION AND FINANCE.

Section A.—General Administration—

CHAPTER V.—ADMINISTRATION AND FINANCE—*continued.*

Section A.—General Administration—*concluded.*

Ecclesiastical—*concluded.*

Section B.—Education—

PART I.—SCHOOLS.

PART II.—PUNJAB UNIVERSITY AND COLLEGE INSTITUTIONS RECOGNIZED BY IT.

PART III.—SOCIAL AND EDUCATIONAL.

CHAPTER V.—ADMINISTRATION AND FINANCE—*concluded*.

Section C.—Military—

Section D.—Revenue—

PART I.—LAND REVENUE.

PART II.—OTHER SOURCES OF REVENUE.

CHAPTER VI.—TOWNS, MUNICIPALITIES AND CANTONMENTS.

Section A.—Ancient Lahore—

CHAPTER VI.—TOWNS, MUNICIPALITIES AND CANTONMENTS—*continued*.

Section A.—Ancient Lahore—*concluded*.

Section B.—Modern Lahore—

CHAPTER VI.—TOWNS, MUNICIPALITIES AND CANTONMENTS—*concld.*

Section B.—Modern Lahore—*concluded.*

Table No. I,—showing LEADING STATISTICS.

1	2	3	4	5	6
		DETAIL OF TAHSILS.			
DETAILS.	District.	Lahore.	Chúnián.	Kasúr.	Sharak-pur.
Total square miles (1891-92)..	3,602	728	1,163	817	894
Cultivated square miles (1891-92)	1,937	485	569	652	231
Culturable square miles (1891-92)	905	126	302	87	390
Irrigated square miles (1891-92)	1,153	246	390	328	189
Average square miles under crops (1888-89 to 1892-93)	1,440	382	382	522	154
Annual rainfall in inches (1866 to 1892)	19·08	19·08	14·66	16·04	14·01
Number of inhabited towns and villages (1891)	1,522	366	420	352	384
Total population (1891)	1,075,379	430,378	230,897	280,647	133,457
Rural population (1891)	846,621	253,524	217,637	246,927	128,533
Urban population (1891)	228,758	176,854	13,260	33,720	4,924
Total population per square mile	299	591	199	343	151
Rural population per square mile	235	348	187	302	144
Hindús (1891)	271,749	116,535	59,998	66,125	29,091
Sikhs (1891)	152,023	52,123	33,791	58,461	7,648
Jains (1891)	886	339	77	470	...
Musalmáns (1891)	645,083	256,186	136,627	155,566	96,704
Average annual khálisa fixed land revenue collections (1888-89 to 1892-93)	5,96,239	1,48,178	1,46,244	1,92,209	1,09,608
Average annual gross revenue collections (1888-89 to 1892-93)*	14,90,869	...	...	...	...
Fixed land revenue demand as sanctioned by Financial Commissioner for 1893-94	10,23,554	3,70,981	2,14,283	2,98,581	1,39,709

* Fixed, fluctuating and miscellaneous revenue together with Local rates, Excise and Stamp.

CHAPTER I.

SECTION A.—DESCRIPTIVE.

THE DISTRICT.

The Lahore district lies between north latitude 30° 27′ and 31° 54′, and east longitude 73° 40′ and 75° 1′. In shape it is almost a perfect square, the two diagonals of which run directly north-south and east-west respectively : only on the north-west side is the symmetry of the figure spoilt by a slight bulge out to the west. The length of the north-south diagonal is 65 miles and the breadth from east to west is 75 miles. The Sutlej river on the south-east separates Lahore and Ferozepore, the river bed being shared between these two districts. This is the base on which the Lahore district seems to rest, and at right angles to it are the side lines bounding the district from Amritsar and Siálkot on the north-east and from Montgomery on the south-west. The north-west boundary is formed by the district of Gujránwála. The river Rávi enters the district on the north-east side just where the Amritsar boundary ends and that of Siálkot begins, at a point 48 miles distant from the Sutlej and 13 miles from the Gujránwála border. The course of the two rivers in the Lahore district is almost parallel and the length of river line intercepted between the Amritsar and Montgomery borders is about 63 miles.

The total area of the district according to the village survey recently completed is 3,602 square miles ; of this about one-fourth lies on the right bank of the Rávi forming part of what is known as the Rechna Doáb, between the Rávi and the Chenáb rivers ; the remainder is on the left bank, or near side of the Rávi between it and the Sutlej. The Rechna Doáb or Trans-Rávi tract is mostly lowland that has in times past been under the influence of river water ; its soil is hard and heavily impregnated with salts ; the land is sadly wanting in fertility and much of it lies completely waste. Cultivation is carried on by means of irrigation from wells or inundation from the Deg stream which crosses the lowlands in a direction parallel to that of the Rávi and about 12 miles distant from it. In this part of the district there are a large number of Government rakhs covering a total area of over one hundred square miles. Presumably Government took possession of the land at an early period of British rule because the people declined to pay any revenue for it. The trees in these rakhs are small and unimportant ; fair grass grows after heavy rain.

The Cis-Rávi portion of the district is divided into two tracts of completely different level and varying greatly in their physical conditions. To the north is a high upland tract occupying the full length of the Amritsar border on the east side of the district, but gradually contracting towards the west as it approaches the Montgomery border. On the south is a large triangular tract of lowlying land divided from the uplands by a very abrupt and in most parts precipitous bank varying from 10 to 30 feet in height. The upland forms the central and principal portion of the celebrated Mánjha, the home of the Jat Sikh. It is far the most important part of the district and the most interesting from an administrative point of view. It is peopled in the main by a very fine race of men, Sandhu Jats, who played a prominent part always in the contests and struggles which attended the consolidation of the Sikh rule and furnished the flower of Ranjít Singh's army, but who have now under the quieting influence of the British rule gradually settled down to regard agriculture as their natural profession, though always ready to take up military service, if necessary, either as a means of livelihood or at the call of Government. The Lahore Mánjha in its natural condition before the extension of the Bári Doáb Canal presented an almost uniformly level surface with hardly any variety of feature from end to end ; its soil is inclined to be dry, but in parts near the Amritsar border one meets with a good sandy loam ; the well water is for the most part saline and the rainfall is very precarious : until therefore irrigation was imported by means of the canal, there was little natural growth of any sort and the agriculture was mostly inferior. In 1854 the Settlement Officer described this part of the district as a jungle in which only the poorer cereals and pulses could be grown. Also in 1868 it is alluded to as a sparsely populated tract without the means of obtaining good drinking water for man or beast. Now the whole of the Mánjha tract, except a small portion on the south-west, is traversed by branches and distributaries of the canal, their banks lined with trees and the lands near them under good and careful cultivation. All over this upland tract one meets with abandoned sites of villages and a few old forts, relics of the disturbed times which prevailed here from the end of the seventh century when the Muhammadan invasions commenced down to the establishment of the British rule. The history of every village in the Mánjha almost contains references to one, two or more desertions of the villages by the founders who used to return from time to time as matters settled down and usually occupy a fresh site.

The lowlands which lie to the south of the Mánjha are known as the Hithár, derived from the vernacular term *het* (below) ; they were the valley of the river Beás when it flowed through this district separately from the Sutlej. The high bank referred to above as the southern boundary of the Mánjha immediately overhangs the Sutlej and Beás streams,

as they enter the district together at Harike on the Lahore
and Amritsar border; from there the bank takes a westerly
direction and the river flows south-west; the two therefore
gradually diverge further and further apart until, as they both
leave the district at the Montgomery border, they are separated
by a distance of 25 miles. Under the high bank the old
channel of the Beás can be very distinctly traced, and on the
edge of the channel is still standing, though in somewhat
ruined condition, a large Dera or sacred abode of a Sikh Guru
who is said to have dried up the Beás river at that point by a
curse, because it was undermining his building. Along the
edge of the high bank at various intervals are village settlements, including those of Kasúr and Chúnián, the two most
important places in the district outside the Lahore city. The
proximity of the houses to the bank in these settlements shows
how reluctantly the people used to move back to the nearest
unoccupied land as the river encroached. In the Hithár tract between the high bank and the river, village settlements are numerous and the population is fairly dense. Cultivation is
carried on partly by aid of irrigation wells and partly
by inundation from canals which only flow however for
such part of the year as the river remains in flood. The soil
is for the most part a soft alluvial loam yielding readily to
tillage but almost too sandy to be genuinely fertile. There is
much sandy waste in which nothing grows but the *sirkana* or
river jungle reed which is fairly abundant and comes in useful as cattle fodder and for various other purposes. Every here
and there tortuous nallahs or lowlying depressions of land mark
the course of the river and its branches in former days. The
district stands eleventh in order of area and second in order of
population among the 31 districts of the Punjab, comprising
3½ per cent. of the total area, and slightly more than 5 per
cent. of the total population of British territory of the Province.
According to the census figures of 1891 its actual population is
1,075,379 souls, of which only 21 per cent. is urban, the rest
being more or less agricultural. The chief town is of course
Lahore which is also the capital of the Province; it is situate on
the left bank of the Rávi about a mile from its present course:
its municipal population as last ascertained in 1891 was 159,597
souls. Lahore is the centre of a system of railways converging
from all parts, from Peshawar, Mooltan, Ferozepore, and
Umballa. It stands on the Pesháwar and Delhi metalled road,
and another similar road approaches it from Ferozepore passing
through Kasúr. Unmetalled roads approach it from Shahpur
through Gujránwála on the west, from Mooltan through Montgomery on the south-west, from Ludhiána through Harike on
the south-east, and from Siálkot through Shahdera on the north.

The only towns of any importance beside Lahore are Kasúr
with population of 20,290 and Chúnián with 10,389. There are
1,522 inhabited villages, only 227 of which have a population in
excess of one thousand, and only 55 have over two thousand.

The administrative head-quarters of the district are situated at the civil station of Lahore, which is also the head-quarters of the Punjab Government. The district is divided into four tahsíls, of which Sharakpur with 401 estates lies to the north-west in the Trans-Rávi portion of the district. Kasúr comprising 366 estates lies to the south-east, those of Lahore and Chúnián occupying the intermediate position with 396 and 414 estates respectively. The Kasúr tahsíl lies mostly in the Mánjha with about one-quarter of it in the Hithár. Chúnián tahsíl lies half in the Mánjha and half in the Hithár, excepting a narrow strip of Rávi land on the north-west. Lahore tahsíl has 150 estates, with an area of 260 square miles, along the Rávi; the rest of its estates are situate in the Mánjha. The revenue recently assessed on this district is Rs. 9,77,996, of which about one-half is paid by the Mánjha villages, one-fifth by the estates in the Beás Hithár, and the remainder by the Rávi and Trans-Rávi estates. The Sharakpur tahsíl is far inferior to all the other tahsíls in respect of people, soil and revenue paying capacity. Leading statistics regarding the district and the tahsíls into which it is divided are furnished in Table I.

The Rávi is the smallest of the five rivers of the Punjab and from the narrowness of its channel and its numerous windings, is the least useful of them all for navigable purposes. Its name is a corruption of *Irávati*, the name in Puranic mythology of Indra's elephant, and is recognisable through its more archaic form in the *Hyarotis* of *Strabo*, the *Hydraotes* of *Arrian*, the *Adris* of Ptolemy, the *Rhuadis* of Pliny, and the raid of Masudi, the Arabian Geographer. The Rávi enters the district from Amritsar, by the village of Ichogil, and after a course of 63 miles leaves it on the borders of Montgomery close to a village called Alpa Kalán. The stream is nowhere navigable in this district, but deodar timber is floated down from the Chamba forests as far as Lahore. Two bridges cross the river near Lahore, one the railway bridge underneath which is a passage for foot traffic, the other the bridge-of-boats of Shahdera which remains standing throughout the year. Up to the present year the railway bridge was 8,218 feet long and supported on 34 arches; this year it has been reduced by more than half its former length and stands on only 16 arches; this economising of work and material has been rendered possible partly by the large decrease proved to have taken place of late years in the Rávi water-supply, and also because the bridge was originally built longer than necessary. Elsewhere communications across the Rávi are kept open by ferry boats for which 22 stations are maintained at intervals along the whole river's course. Just above Lahore city the course of the stream is carefully directed by embankments designed to protect the railway from injury by floods, and the river which used to throw out several branches between Lahore city and the Amritsar border is now /

kept to one channel. Formerly the river channel was much narrower and its stream consequently much stronger than it is now. People say that 20 years ago it was unfordable at any time, hot weather or cold ; now for at least four months of the year it can be crossed on foot, and often in the cold weather it dries up altogether just after leaving the Lahore district. This is largely due to the extensive widening of the bed consequent on the river having encroached steadily to the north of late years. Also in the cold weather the volume of water is materially decreased by the calls made on it for the Bári Doáb Canal. Still, however, during the rainy season in some years the river has heavy floods with a very strong current; in the upper parts of its course through this district land is often submerged. At present some exceedingly valuable land near Lahore is being destroyed in this way. Lower down stream the channel is too wide for the river to cut away new land in ordinary years ; but during the heavy rainfall of August 1892, nearly two thousand acres near the Montgomery border were transferred by avulsion from one side of the river to the other. The Lahore villages along the Rávi follow the rule of fixed boundaries, one with the other, but for the last eight miles of the river course through this district the villages on the left bank only belong to Lahore, those on the right bank to Montgomery ; and between the villages of the two districts the boundary changes according to position of the deep-stream each year.

The land of the Rávi basin is mostly under cultivation. Its soil varies greatly according to the level of the land. High and lowland occur alternately, the lowland lying principally in depressions of the surface in which the river or one of its branches has rested at some previous time. These always contain more or less clay deposit which is very fertile for wheat crops so long as it gets inundation but if left dry becomes hard and impenetrable, with a strong development of saline matter. Outside these depressions the land varies from high sandy waste, in which only river jungle can grow, to a light loam fairly productive and easy of cultivation. On the left side the Rávi lowlands are separated from the uplands of the Mánjha by an abrupt bank varying from 4 to 20 feet in height ; only in parts near Lahore has this bank entirely disappeared under the process of cultivation. On the right hand side of the river the boundary of the river valley is more difficult to detect. Occasionally the rise from the present alluvial tract to the high ground beyond the river influence is marked by an abrupt bank which however seldom exceeds four or five feet in height; more often, however, the slope up is very gradual and a change in soil or vegetation alone indicates that the land which can claim any recent experience of the river floods has been left behind.

The Sutlej river on the south having been joined by the Beás just before it enters the confines of this district has a

Chapter I, A.

Descriptive.

Area and description.

considerably greater volume than the Rávi and its fall is more rapid. The velocity of the current during the cold weather is about five miles an hour; and its ordinary depth about four feet. It is said that the stream used to be navigable for steamers as far up as Ferozepore (half way up the Lahore district), now however all such traffic has been absorbed by the railway.

The Sutlej road and railway bridge which crosses the river at Ganda Singhwála was opened in 1887; before that the river was crossed by a bridge of boats at the place where the railway bridge is now. This, however, was maintained only for seven months in the year being closed in May and re-opened in October. Ferry boats are maintained at intervals along the river throughout the year. The valley of the Sutlej is of considerable width and the stream is constantly shifting its course to the great injury of villages on either side. Land carried from one side of the river to the other by gradual accretion changes ownership. If, however, it is carried across in a recognisable form by means of avulsion, the former owner can claim it. Of late years the force of the river has been setting northwards, and several large Lahore villages have been ruined as more and more of their land accreted gradually on to the other side. Until very lately the land along the river used to change its district jurisdiction as it moved from one side of the river to the other: now, however, the border villages of the Lahore and Ferozepore districts have been fixed by notification and land only changes jurisdiction when its owners change under the action of the river rules.

The Sutlej bed is a mixture of sand and clay; in the rainy season its floods throw up vast quantities both of deposit and of sand, so that the character of the alluvial land is constantly changing. The bare sand of one year may be a rich deposit soil in the next and *vice versâ*. On the whole there is much more bad land than good along the Sutlej; large stretches of river jungle frequently occur with only occasional patches of cultivation, and in the latter the cropping is indifferent as a rule.

The Deg stream rises in the Jummoo hills. In the Hindu Shastars it is called Deoki. After traversing the Siálkot district and just cutting the Gujránwála district as it passes under the curious old bridge known as Shah Dowla ki Pul, the stream enters the Lahore district at its most northern point, close to where the Lahore, Gujránwála and Siálkot districts meet. Its course through the Sharakpur tahsíl is in the main south-westerly and parallel to that of the Rávi; but 12 miles beyond the Lahore border the Deg cuts into the Rávi just as the latter takes a twist direct to the west. Two very heavy masonry bridges were built over the stream in the time of the Emperor Shah Jahán and Jahángír, one at Pindi Dás, and the other at Hudiála. These are still kept up.

Elsewhere the Deg has always been spoken of as a natural river stream, but here its wonderfully zig-zag course through an exceedingly stiff clay soil gives a different impression ; the channel appears to have been dug out along a carefully selected line of country, its banks nearly invariably commanding the country beyond so as not to be subject to injury from outside surface drainage, while any water that tops the bank in times of heavy flood may extend some distance on either side of the stream ; the twists and curves in its course might well have been designed as a safe-guard against erosion by water action. The breadth of the channel hardly anywhere exceeds 30 yards and is often less. The stream only comes into flood when there is a heavy rainfall anywhere in the plains between Sharakpur and the hills. Then it fills up in a few hours and overflows its banks, carrying with it a small amount of valuable deposit more or less beneficial to land on which the floods are retained for any length of time. On the rain ceasing the water subsides at once, the main body of it passing off into the Rávi through the Gugera tahsíl. Except during the rains no water comes down the Deg channel in this tahsíl, but at the upper portion of its course down to the point where it takes a half turn to the west, there are natural springs in its bed which yield a little water throughout the year unless the season is very dry. Besides the main stream there are three other branches of the Deg of minor importance. The first is the " dry Deg " or " small Deg, " as sometimes called, which leaves the present stream shortly before it enters this tahsíl, and passing through the Sharakpur villages on the north rejoins the Deg when it is nearly half way through the tahsíl ; this only gets water in it when the main stream is in high flood. The second branch, the " Chitrang," which leaves the Deg a little below where the natural water springs cease ; this floods up almost at the same time as the main stream. The third branch is the " Nágwah," a connecting link between the Chitrang and the Deg.

The inundations from all these water-courses, short and unreliable as they are, yet have an extremely beneficial effect on the hard saline soil so common in the lowlands, indeed much of the land without this natural inundation would be absolutely unfertile. When the Deg is not in full flood the water can be raised for irrigation purposes by Persian wheels. Along the upper portion of the Deg's course in this district, where there are perennial springs in the bed of the stream, these water-lifts can work all the year round ; lower down the stream dries up usually in October and the water-lifts are dismantled.

No dams are allowed along the main Deg stream. On the dry Deg there are two masonry works constructed so as to divert water to certain villages which otherwise would get no inundation. Also the villages lying above the first masonry work are each allowed to erect one mud dam about four feet high. Similarly on the Chitrang, below a certain point, each village has the right to block the stream by turn for a fixed number of hours.

In the high lands of the Bári Doáb there occur at intervals drainage lines which are called in the vernacular *rohi*. The most important is the Hudiára *rohi*, as called, which enters the district from the Amritsar border at the Lahore village of Kila Jíwan Singh, about 15 miles south of the Rávi, and passes across the Mánjha in a tortuous course generally parallel to that of the two rivers, ultimately draining into the Rávi shortly before it reaches the Montgomery border. Its channel is from two to three hundred yards broad, and it is so shallow that the casual observer in crossing it would hardly notice its existence unless the floods were out. During the rainy season a considerable volume of water comes down this channel sometimes, mostly local surface drainage. The soil in the channel though stiff is very fertile under cultivation, and except in the dryest years it is safe for a fair spring crop. The next best known *rohi* is that called the "Kasúr nallah" which enters the Kasúr tahsíl from the Amritsar district at the village of Súr Singh about twelve miles to the south of the Hudiára *rohi*. This has a deeper channel than the other and when in flood sends down a more rapid stream. It can be traced back as far as Batála in the Gurdáspur district. Of recent years the flood waters which used to fill it several times in the year have been diverted by canal embankments and cultivation.

The channel of the Kasúr nallah is shallow enough to cultivate for the first 10 or 12 miles of its course as far as the village of Algon. From there it has been recently converted into a canal escape and is now assuming the appearance of a hill torrent. It runs into the Beás lowlands near Kasúr. Similarly the Patti nallah further south has been utilised as a canal escape, two or three miles after it enters the district at Patti.

Both the Kasúr and the Patti nallahs have their course marked by ridges of sand thrown up no doubt by the force of the water when in heavy flood. The Hudiára *rohi* having a much gentler slope has deposited no sand along its banks. These *rohi* drainage lines are important chiefly with regard to the influence they have on the local spring water. The only part of the Mánjha uplands where the well water is naturally sweet is along the Amritsar border on the east and between the Rávi and the Hudiára *rohi* on the west. It is also found to be sweet within the drainage channels and along their banks especially in the case of the Kasúr nallah which in former years probably used to carry down a heavier volume of water than the others. Between the Kasúr nallah and the Hudiára *rohi* the water is universally tainted, more so to the west than the east. Towards the Montgomery border it is absolutely undrinkable, much more unfit for irrigation of land. Beyond the

Hudiára *rohi* between it and the Rávi the water is fairly sweet, becoming less and less tainted as the *rohi* channel drains towards the river. All over the Mánjha, however, the well water is being beneficially affected by the importation of outside water through the canals. During the last twenty years the water level has risen by 8 or 9 feet, and the quality of the local water has improved greatly.

The main branch of the Bári Doáb Canal enters the district from the Amritsar district just south of the large Lahore village of Padhána about half way between the Rávi and Sutlej rivers, and crosses the district, in direction almost parallel to that of the two rivers; after a course of 48 miles it terminates at the Chánga Mánga forest where the canal is intercepted by an escape channel which carries off its surplus water into the Rávi at a village called Alpa Kalán. The Lahore branch of the same canal enters at Wágáh just north of the Lahore and Umballa Railway, passes between Lahore and Mián Mír, and joins the Rávi river at Niázbeg, a large village seven miles south-west of Lahore. Its length in this district is 22 miles only.

The Shálámár branch is the old Hasli Canal which was constructed about two centuries ago by Ali Mardán Khan, in the reign of Shah Jahán, to bring water to the royal pleasure grounds at Shálámár, five miles east of Lahore. This enters the district about four miles north of the Umballa Railway, and goes as far as Shálámár, a distance of about 10 miles. The Kasúr branch enters the district at the village of Moghal and after a course of ten miles finishes in Hurdo Algon, where it joins the Kasúr nallah as noticed above. The Bári Doáb Canal is described at length in the provincial volume of the Gazetteer for the census of 1881.

Not counting the old Hasli Canal, this district began to come under irrigation from the Bári Doáb Canal first less than 30 years ago. The canal now irrigates in this district an area of 455 square miles in 480 estates and the present average income derived from it by the Canal Department is upwards of 10½ lakhs of rupees, the total payments on irrigated land for the use of the water averaging about Rs. 3-9-8 per acre. In addition all land ordinarily irrigated from the canal pays under the new assessments extra land revenue varying from 3 to 8 annas the acre in excess of what it would pay under dry cultivation.

The permanent canals of the Bári Doáb system irrigate the Mánjha uplands only in this district. The lowlands of the Beás are dependent for canal irrigation on the "Upper Sutlej Inundation Canals" which flow only so long as the Sutlej river remains in flood, the usual period extending from the middle of May to the middle of September. The series comprises four canals, only three of which take off from the river within the limits of this district. Their names are Katora, Khanwah and Upper Sohág. The fourth, known as the Lower Sohág, emerges from the river in the Montgomery district. For the Lahore district far the most important is the *Katora* Canal which has its head near Ganda Singhwála just where the Ferozepore Railway leaves the Lahore district, after a course of 17 miles through the lowlands of the Kasúr tahsíl where it irrigates at present about 1,500 acres, it reaches the village of Khudián on the borders of the Chúnián tahsíl ; from here its waters are distributed by three branches which in the Chúnián tahsíl inundate on the average 15,000 acres a year lying within 70 villages or so. The Upper Sohág and Khanwah are old canals which were constructed very early in the present century. The Khanwah has its head at Mámoki, about 16 miles from the Montgomery border, and the Upper Sohág has its head at Salolke, 10 miles from the Montgomery border. Their heads, however, are not quite fixed, they have to be moved occasionally according as the current of the river flood changes from year to year. The area irrigated from these two canals in this district hardly exceeds 10,000 acres, but they irrigate large areas in the Montgomery district. Under recent orders of Government the total canal rates which before averaged slightly under one rupee the acre on all irrigated land have been increased and now average about 1 rupee 12 annas the acre. This calculation takes in crop rates which for spring crops are imposed at the rate of 8 annas an acre and for autumn crops vary from 2 rupees 4 annas an acre for the best to 1 rupee 2 annas an acre for less valuable staples ; and it also includes 12 annas an acre imposed as water-advantage or owner's rate once a year on all land irrigated within the year. The income from this latter rate at present averages about Rs. 27,000 a year.

Rainfall.

Table No. III shows in tenths of an inch the total rainfall registered at each of the rain-gauge stations in the district during the last ten years. The distribution over the year month by month and the number of rainy days in each month, as shown by the rain-gauge at head-quarters, is shown in Statement III A., and the distribution by quarters of the year is furnished for each outlying tahsíl in Statement III B. The average annual rainfall for the district varies from 20 inches on the north-east border to 8 inches on the south-west.

Climate.

Table No. IV shows the average temperature of three months, May, July and December, for the years extending from 1868-69 to 1891-92, these being the months adopted as specimens in all the Gazeteer Series ; June is the hottest month in the year, the temperature in a house not cooled by a thermantidote but kept carefully shut up varying from 96° to 106° and unless rain comes, the June heat lasts on into July. For instance on the night of July 8th, 1892, the thermometer stood at 105° in most houses in the civil station.

The hot weather indicates its approach early in April, and after that camping out under canvas becomes unpleasant and, as the heat increases, almost intolerable if one has to carry on work throughout the day. In-doors within closed walls there is nothing to complain of until May. Then the air becomes very dry and burning hot winds commence. Ordinarily after May has set in the house should be shut up at 7 A.M. and not opened till 6 P.M., or later. The nights are warm but not troublesome during this month. Both April and May are very healthy months for Europeans. In June the heat increases considerably, and in Lahore civil station the air becomes filled with moisture owing presumably to the extensive canal irrigation now carried on. Neither in May nor June, notwithstanding the hot winds which blow fiercely at times but not steadily, are the watered *tattis*, which are so effectual for cooling houses further down country, of much use in Lahore. The reason for this is partly the heavy moisture pervading the air and partly the unsteadiness of the hot breeze. Even the thermantidote becomes a doubtful pleasure at times on account of the dampness of the air it pumps in. Early in July there should be a burst of monsoon rain ; but owing to its short duration in Lahore its cooling effects last only for a few days, and unless more rain falls the great heat begins again, rendered more intolerable than before by the increased moisture in the air and general closeness of the atmosphere ; all through July and August the days and nights are equally trying unless rain be fairly frequent. In the latter month scorching hot breezes sometimes spring up ; any one wishing to get an easy experience of these should take an evening drive down the Meean Meer road. In September the afternoon sun is very fierce, but the days close in rapidly and the nights begin to be pleasant. From September 15th the mornings begin to get cool and *punkhás* can be left off by the end of the month unless the autumn has been exceptionally dry and hot. Early in October it is quite cool in-doors and by the middle of the month life under canvas out in the district is bearable enough ; the sun is hot between 12 and 4 o'clock till nearly the end of October, but the rest of the day and the night time are delightful. November and early December days are generally bright cloudless and quite still ; the nights become sharp as the end of December approaches, and from the middle of that month clouds come and go, indicating an indefinite prospect of rain which sometimes falls in a few days before December closes and in some years holds up till the end of January. In Lahore these winter rains if not so heavy, yet come more frequently and last longer perhaps than the summer rains. When both are wanted so badly it is hard to say which is the most useful, but the preservation of the spring unirrigated crops and in some measure of the irrigated crops as well depends upon moderate rain at least falling in the latter half of December or in January. No frost to speak of occurs in December, but in January the nights and mornings are extremely keen, and the early morning frosts often last through the first week of February. From that onwards the sun in the day time begins to make itself felt and the nights become very agreeable. March is very variable ; if the spring rains have lasted late it is cool enough; otherwise the day time is unpleasantly warm. In 1892 when no rains hardly had fallen for seven or eight months, the month of March was as hot as May in ordinary years.

The unhealthiest time in Lahore as far as Europeans are concerned is in August and September when their constitutions are exhausted with the great heat they have gone through and the temperature at night and day differs most ; nor can Lahore civil station be said to become thoroughly healthy again until the winter rains have fallen. The following account on the general health and sanitation of the Lahore district has been kindly furnished to me by Dr. Stephen, Sanitary Commissioner.

Health and sanitation.

The most common diseases are those which occur in all malarial countries, *viz.*, malarious fevers, enlargement of the spleen and general anæmia, diarrhœa and dysentery. Bronchitis and pleuro-pneumonia are very common, and the latter is very fatal during the cold season. Ulcers and various forms of skin diseases are also common. In one part of the district, Sharakpur, goitre is very prevalent. From the statistics of deaths published in the tables attached to the Sanitary Commissioner's reports from 1872 to 1891 inclusive, it appears that the registered rate of mortality of the Lahore district is considerably higher than that recorded in the Province as a whole. The average registered death-rate of the Punjab for these 20 years was 29 and in the Lahore district 33 per 1,000.

During 20 years 1872-91 the highest death-rate 50 per 1,000 was recorded in 1890, in which year the provincial death-rate was 47 per 1,000. During this period the lowest death-rate in the district and in the province was recorded in 1874, the rates of mortality having been 23 per 1,000 in the district and 18 per 1,000 in the province.

Fevers.

Statistics show that the mortality from fevers is greater in Lahore district than in the province as a whole. The provincial average fever death-rate for 1872-91 was 19·95 and for Lahore district 21·71 per 1,000.

Cholera.

The average death-rate from cholera during 1872-91 in the Lahore district was 0·55 per 1,000 as against 0·26 per 1,000 in the province as a whole.

During that period there have been four severe outbreaks of the disease in the district in the years 1879, 1881, 1887 and 1891, the number of recorded deaths from this cause having been 1,673, 1,643, 2,035 and 1,548, respectively. Of the 1,643 cholera deaths reported in 1881 as many as 1,101 were recorded in the city and suburbs of Lahore. The Lahore water-works were opened in 1881, and statistics show that the introduction of a pure water-supply has had the effect of diminishing the liability of the inhabitants of the municipality to this disease. During the 10 years, 1872-81 previous to the introduction of the new water-supply, 1,788 cholera deaths were registered in the

Lahore District.]

CHAP. I.—THE DISTRICT.

13

Chapter I, B.
——
Geology, Fauna
and Flora.

Small-pox.

municipality, and during the succeeding ten years 1882-91, 616 deaths from this cause were recorded. The cholera deaths reported in the rest of the district during these two decennia were respectively 3,210 and 3,869.

The average registered death-rate from small-pox during the 20 years 1872-91 was 1·18 per 1,000, the corresponding rate for the province as a whole having been 0·86 per 1,000. Previous to 1881 there was a provincial vaccination staff which visited each district every three or four years. In the cold weather of 1881 a separate vaccination establishment was allotted to each district, so that vaccinators now visit the whole or the greater part of the district annually. That the work of vaccination is more efficiently carried out by the district vaccination staff than it was by provincial vaccinators, is proved by the fact that during the 10 years 1872-81 when provincial vaccinators were at work 13,190 small-pox deaths were reported in the district, and during the following ten years 1882-91 when the work was done by the district vaccinators, only 6,193 deaths from that cause were registered. The attitude of the people of the rural portions of the Lahore district towards vaccination is most favourable, the work is done quietly and efficiently and with little or no friction. It is different in the city of Lahore. The city people to a considerable extent appreciate the benefits of vaccination and most of them have little objection to have their children vaccinated, but what they do object to, Hindús particularly, is the transfer of lymph from their children to others. This objection has recently been obviated by the introduction of animal lymph vaccination. Statistics, however, show that the percentage of children vaccinated continues to be less in the city than it is in the rural tracts of the district, and the Municipal Committee have therefore resolved to apply to Government for the extension of the provisions of the Vaccination Act, XIII of 1880, to the Municipality of Lahore.

The most sickly months of the year in this district are September, October and November : the months in which the largest number of deaths occur on an average are October November and December. The smallest number of deaths are registered in the months of April, March, February and July.

The system of registering births in the district came into force in 1880. There was an average birth-rate of 43 per 1,000 in the district as a whole for the year 1880-91. In the city although bye-laws for the compulsory registration of births are in force, the birth-rate is considerably below that of the district. Means have lately been taken for ensuring more accurate registration of vital statistics in the municipality.

SECTON B—GEOLOGY, FAUNA AND FLORA.

Geology.

Our knowledge of Indian geology is as yet so general in its nature, and so little has been done in the Punjab in the way of detailed geological investigation, that it is impossible to discuss

Chapter I, B.

Geology, Fauna and Flora.

Geology.

the local geology of separate districts. But a sketch of the geology of the Province as a whole has been most kindly furnished by Mr. Medlicott, Superintendent of the Geological Survey of India, and is published *in extenso* in the Provincial volume of the Gazetteer Series, and also as a separate pamphlet.

Mineral products.
Kankar.

The only mineral production that is found in this district of any value is *kankar* (a kind of limestone gravel), which is used for metalling roads, and the smaller particles of which are burnt for lime. This mineral is found in most parts of the district, but principally in the highlands near Lahore. It is dug out at a depth varying from 1 foot to 6 feet, while the smaller particles are found on the surface of the soil in many places, and only require sweeping up for collection before being put into the kilns to be burnt down as lime. The contractors for supplying *kankar* on metalled roads pay the owners of the land so much per ghumao to be allowed to excavate it.

Kallar

The substance known as *kallar* is swept up from old village sites or places of a like nature on the Mánjha uplands, and is much valued by market gardeners and indeed all the more careful agriculturists such as Aráins for its fertilising properties. They throw it over the young cotton and tobacco plants chiefly when they are half a foot or so out of the soil. It is beneficial to other crops also, but is too rare a commodity to use wastefully. There are certain old *Thehs* in the Mánjha where it is found in any abundance, and to these the Aráin agriculturists round Lahore send many miles distance ; the Jat owners, up to this, place no value on the *kallar*, neither using it themselves, nor charging any price to those who obtain their leave to take it. By the time, however, that it has been carried in carts 10 or 15 miles distance to the neighbourhood of Lahore it has become a valuable commodity and fetches a good price among the Aráin agriculturists. On the *Thehs* which have this *kallar* on the surface of their soil, no sooner has the existing supply been taken off than more is formed. The exact nature of its origin has not yet been ascertained. Apparently it is connected more or less with the *kankar* ingredient of the Mánjha soil and with the gradual changes set up by heat and moisture in land which in the past was long the receptacle of men and cattle's evacuations. Lately a sample of *kallar* was sent to the Chemical Examiner of Lahore for examination, and his report thereon was as follows :—

" A detailed analysis has been carried out of the sample of *kallar* received with Lahore Settlement Officer's letter No. 641, dated 10th December 1892, and it is believed that this is the first proportional analysis made of this material, no record being discovered in this laboratory of a previous quantitative estimation. The results are as follows :—

	Per cent.
Total soluble matters (in distilled water)	8·957
Do. do, in slightly acidulated water ...	10·312
½ per cent. nitric acid in 1 per cent. salt solution ...	9·976
Total soluble solids detained by drying the solution in distilled water	8·756

Soluble solids as follows :—

	Per cent.
Sodium chloride	3·859
Do. sulphate	1·061
Potassium nitrate	1·70
(The estimation of all the soluble organic matters is included under the potassium nitrate).	
Calcium carbonate	0·985
Magnasium sulphate	1·352
Iron, only a trace	
	8·957 "

The beneficial properties of *kallar* are attributed to the soluble chlorides and nitrates, and it ·is believed that exposure during a considerable period of time to heat and moisture would set up changes increasing the percentage of these valuable soluble ingredients, some of the insoluble salts undergoing chemical changes by which they are transformed into soluble salts.''

Saltpetre is produced to some extent in this district, chiefly in Sharakpur tahsíl. Licenses for its manufacture are given to any one applying for them, and the licensees make their own terms with the agriculturists for the erection of kilns in suitable places and for fuel. The soil is collected from the sites of old villages (*thehs*), and is boiled in water in large iron pans. After boiling, it is thrown into perforated wooden troughs, placed over earthen vessels imbedded in the ground. The drippings from the troughs congeal in the earthen vessels and become the saltpetre of commerce. In the last three years altogether 150 licenses have been granted, authorising the holders to manufacture saltpetre, each license permitting on the average between four and five hundred maunds to be made. The value of the stuff when made is Re. 1 per maund.

The varieties of trees found in this district are few and unimportant. The commoner kinds are noticed below

The *kikar* (Acacia arabica) grows all over the district wherever the soil has been sufficiently moist to allow of the seed germinating. It is thickest along the banks of rivers or streams, but is now shooting up all over the Mánjha and Hithár where canal irrigation has been extended. Its growth is rapid, but it is not a long-lived tree. The wood which is fit for use after ten years' growth is tough and close grained ; it comes in handy for all the more important agricultural implements, especially for the more prominent portions of the Persian wheel structure.

The *ber* tree grows chiefly near wells and along the edges of lanes or water cuts leading from the well. After six years or so it produces the wild plum which is much valued by natives ; the finest grafted *ber* trees both for their massive shade and for the abundance of their yield are to be found in the more fertile lands near Lahore city ; but every well almost all over the district has one or two *ber* trees. Its wood is fit for use after ten or twelve years' growth. It is put to the same purposes as *kikar* wood when the latter is not to be had.

The *tút* or mulberry tree is found near wells equally
with the *ber* tree : it begins to yield fruit after four or five years
growth, and its wood is available after ten years growth. The
wood of the *tút* tree is somewhat elastic and apt to warp if
not properly seasoned. It is used to make handles for agricultural implements and legs for bedsteads ; also it makes good
fuel. The *phuláhi* (Acacia modesta) is another tree which
like the *kikar* grows all over the district though not so universally ; its wood is strong and durable, and next to the
kikar and *ber* tree is as serviceable as any for making
agricultural implements.

The four classes of trees described above are all of spontaneous growth and are valued greatly by the agriculturists for
their wood. They generally soak the *kikar* log in the village
pounds for several months partly to harden it, partly to keep
off white ants. The smaller branches of the *kikar* and *ber* tree
are used for hedging fields.

Other trees of spontaneous growth in the district are the
farásh or *pharwán* (tamarix orientalis) which grows quickly
in lowlying ground which catches surface drainage, and has
been largely planted along roadsides because the plants require little or no attention ; the *sirin* (Albizzia debbek) which
however is found chiefly along roadsides where it must have
been planted in years past ; and the *reru* (acacia leucophlœa) a
kind of stunted *kikar* which is found chiefly in the *rukh* lands
of Lahore and Sharkpur tahsíls. The *siris* wood is fairly
durable, but is not much used here ; it is most serviceable for
sugar-cane crushers or oil presses, but European demand appears
likely to arise for it for ornamental articles of furniture ; and if
this continues the *siris* will become a most valuable tree. *Farásh*
wood is only useful for burning. The *reru* is good fuel and its
bark is used for tanning.

Of trees that require to be planted and some attention
afterwards for a time, the most universal are the *pipal* (Ficus
religiosa) and *bohar* (Ficus indica). These are planted by the
people for shade at the gates of villages, round the village ponds
and near fakirs' huts and Muhammadan shrines. They take a
long time to grow and being valued chiefly for their shade, stand
till they fall from age. A fine old *pipal* tree is a worthy
object of veneration, and Hindús of all classes hold it in great
reverence. Its leaves and branches unfortunately often fall a
prey to the camels attached to the camps of officers on tour, notwithstanding every effort on the part of the latter to prevent it.

The *bakain* (Melia Azadirachta) or as better known locally
the *dharek* is sometimes planted near wells ; it is a fast growing tree, but not long lived. After 15 years it is apt to rot inside and become hollow. The wood however is free from attacks
by insects and is therefore much used for rafters in the house
roof and for making the sides of bedsteads. It is useless
as fuel.

Other less common trees are the mango, the *jáman*, the *tún*, the *amaltás*, the *burna*, the *ním*, the *lassúrai* and *sohánjna*, which it is not necessary to describe in detail. The *shisham* is recognised as an exceedingly valuable tree, but has not as yet been planted to any material extent by the common agriculturist. It is planted by Government Departments along roadsides and canal banks and there is a very large growth of it in the Chánga Mánga plantation. A large *shisham* tree costs 80 or 90 rupees, while the other trees described above and which are found commonly in the peoples' fields, seldom run to more than 14 or 15 rupees. The only article which the agriculturists always use *shisham* wood for apparently is the triangular platform which makes the body of the village cart. The nave of the wheel also should be of *shisham* wood, while the rest of the cart may be made of *kikar*. The larger beams for the roof of a house should properly be of *shisham*, but the people cannot afford the cost as a rule and *kikar* beams are used instead. Rafters are made of *kikar*, *bakain*, *tút* or *bohur* branches.

The most common shrubs are the *karíl* (Capparis aphylla), the *jand* (Prosopis spicigera), the *wan* (Salvadora oleordes) the *mulla* (Zizyphus nummularia). These are found growing together in all waste land on the Mánjha uplands. The *karíl* is said by the people to be a sign of bad soil, but this means merely that it will grow in poor saline land and highlying ground where other shrubs perhaps won't grow. It flowers twice a year, once in April and again in September. The flower of the *karíl* is an exceedingly brilliant scarlet; the unripe fruit is called *dela* and is used as a pickle. The ripe fruit is called *pinju* and is eaten in its natural state in the month of June. In seasons of scarcity this fruit is a great standby to the poor. The wood of the *karíl* is very hard, and is much used for rafters on account of its supposed immunity from white ants.

The *jand* is chiefly valued for its roots which go very deep into the ground and being tough and strong, make excellent fuel. The weight of the undergrowth is often much more than that of the upper growth Charcoal is prepared from it, but the charcoal is said to emit too many sparks to be much liked. The area under this shrub has been steadily decreasing, owing to the large demand for it from the railway; it is a very slow growing tree and does not repay artificial raising. Natural seedlings of this shrub are said never to be found even in ground strictly closed for grazing, but it is difficult to suppose that the extensive growth of it that still exists in parts of the Mánjha is anything but natural. The seed vessels of this shrub are called *sangra* and are used sometimes as a vegetable. The shrub flowers in April and the seed ripens in June.

The *wan* grows in inferior soil, almost equally with the *karíl*; and saline land appears to suit both. These two are often found also in the lowlands underneath the high Mánjha bank, where the soil has been left untilled for want of fertility. The wood of this is used for roofing to some extent, but is not much good for burning ; it gives out a great deal of smoke and leaves much ash. The shrub flowers in February, and the fruit ripens in June, when it is known as *pilu,* and is greedily eaten by all the poorer classes : Indeed in years of high prices this fruit is one of their chief sources of subsistence.

The *mulla* shrub is found on the uplands only, and is considered an indication of good soil. It is a very prominent feature of all the better *rukh* land in Lahore tahsíl, and is fairly common in other parts of the Mánjha and in the *bár* land of Sharakpur tahsíl. It is also known as the *kokan ber.* Its fruit which ripens in October is much esteemed by the lower grades of the people.

Other shrubs are the *ak* or milk plant, found chiefly in the Sutlej *hithár* lands, on all inferior land left uncultivated for a short time. It grows very rapidly and is easily cut down. It is considered perfectly worthless by the people, and is shunned as fodder by all animals, except perhaps goats.

The *chichra* (butea frondosa) is found to a considerable extent in lowlying land on the north bank of the Rávi and in the Sharakpur tahsíl. It is the same as the Hindustáni *dhak,* but never reaches the dimensions attained lower down country. It is venerated by Hindús and groves of it are occasionally found in tracts otherwise bare. The dye made from the flowers (*kesu*) and the gum exuded by the plant are well known.

Of this class one very common variety is the *pilchi* or *jhao* (tamarix indica), found in flooded lands along the rivers. The twigs are used for making baskets and for lining unbricked wells. It is sold often at the price of a pie a bundle, or at so much per acre. The castor oil plant is also met with occasionally.

Quite as common and more important than the last is the *sarr* which is found for the most part in sandy soil where nothing else will grow, provided soil is fairly near the surface. Thus it is a prominent feature of the Sutlej low lands, where long stretches of *sarr* are met with occasionally, and smaller plots of it are very frequent. Also it may be seen growing thickly along the sandy embankments, which border the distributaries of the inundation canals. The variety which grows white flowers is most common in this district. The reed is exceedingly useful to the agriculturists and is prized accordingly. The lower and thicker portion of the stem is made into chairs, stools, coarse screens and roof thatching. The middle portion is a thinner reed enclosed in a sheath. The reed of this is used for making fine screen or winnowing baskets, the reeds are strung together so as to serve as a covering for carts. The *munj* sheath is burned at one end, then beaten with a mallet into thin fibre which is then twisted into a rope. All the ropes in use in the villages especially the ropework to which the watering pots on a Persian wheel are attached, are made of *múnj.* Also the *sarr* tops are cut for fodder and given to cattle mixed with green food between the months of January and April when all other dry fodder has run out. About the end of February the people often set fire to the *sarr* grass; this makes it grow much better and the fresh green shoots that come out after this operation afford fine grazing for the village cattle. The *sarr* produce brings in considerable profits to the owners, especially in a dry year when better classes of fodder cannot be procured. In the spring of 1892 for instance after several months of drought as much *sarr* as a man could carry was sold for 8 annas. The Rávi villagers however often allow their nearer relations of the Mánjha to come and take what *sarr* they like free of payment. *Káhi* is another river reed, useful for grazing purposes when standing. The growth of this indicates a good quality of soil. It grows very thick and forms an almost impenetrable jungle which is costly to clear.

Lána and láni.

Lána grows plentifully about the waste lands of Sharakpur, except in the Bár uplands. Camels and goats will eat it, and *sajji*, an impure carbonate of soda, is made from it. *Láni* is a different plant from *lána*, being of a blackish purple colour and of no use whatever. The growth of *láni* may be accepted as an indication that the soil is impregnated with saline matter and will not produce anything else.

Harmal is another indication of bad soil, growing about a foot high in thin sandy soil; the people say that no animal will eat this.

Resham is a kind of plant, much found in the sandier soils under cultivation in the Sutlej *hithar*. It grows about two feet high and has a flower of the same shape and colour as that of a thistle.

Grasses.

The following are common grasses in the tracts indicated. *Khabbal* grows everywhere in good soil where the moisture is sufficient, especially along the banks of water cuts. It is too well known to need description. Another grass not unlike *khabbal* in the runners it throws out but somewhat smaller and with a narrower blade of grass is the *chimbar* which grows chiefly in highlying sandyish soil. *Dhaman* is a low vertically growing grass and so distinguishable from *khabbal* which throws out a horizontal stem; also it is much darker in colour. Both *dhaman* and *chimbar* are good fodder grasses, though hardly equal to *khabbal*. *Dabh* is an exceedingly coarse grass which grows principally in old alluvial clay and is not checked by the *kallar* usually so strongly developed in this kind of soil. In such land it spreads rapidly unless kept down by constant cultivation and it is a most difficult grass to eradicate owing to the length of its roots which are said to penetrate down into the soil ever so deep until they reach water. It is worth very little as fodder, though buffaloes may eat it in default of better. *Panni* is a grass found in all lowlying soil which is subject to inundation and is specially noteworthy for its *khas* roots which furnish the material for making *tattis* or grass screens which are fitted into a doorway in the dry part of the hot weather in such a way that whatever breeze there is may pass into the room within through the screen, and this is kept constantly wet so as to cool the breeze as it rushes in. *Dila* is another grass not unlike *panni* and found in the same sort of ground, but not nearly so good for fodder, having little nourishment in it. *Murk* is a small low growing grass with double compound stems and a small red knob at the end of each stem. It is found on the banks of the Deg and is fairly good as fodder.

Núnakh is an inferior grass which grows on the saline lands in Sharakpur; the cattle eat it to some extent when it has come up green after rain. All the four grasses last mentioned are found more in the Sharakpur direction than elsewhere in this district.

Gharm is a tall coarse grass with a strong stem, generally found growing round bushes; cattle do not show much preference for it. *Sawánk* is a good fodder grass, found all over the district, it is said. Other grasses are unimportant.

The *khumb* is a sort of mushroom which grows in soft sandy soil; they are much eaten by the people when fresh and are also made into a sort of pickle. The *túmba* is a ground-creeper, something like a melon that grows in poor saline soil; it is much used as a medicine for horses by native farriers, and is said to be the colocynth of the European pharmacopœia. The *kakeura* is a creeper growing on *jand* and *kikar* trees and bears a bitter fruit which is used sometimes as a vegetable.

Main is a small berry of a dark colour, which falls from the tamarisk tree, and is used to make a brown dye. Gum is got out of the *kikar* and *phuláhi* trees.

Of the weeds that injure the cultivation, the most ubiquitous is that known as *piyazi* or sometimes as *bhukla* or *bughát*. It presents somewhat of the appearance of a young onion plant, but throws out a greater number of green shoots. It is most common in the irrigated lands of the Sutlej *hithár* where the soft sandy soil appears to favour its growth. Sometimes it may be seen growing up as thick as the sown wheat, in which case it absorbs the moisture of the soil and leaves the young crop very little chance. It is easily pulled up, roots and all, when the land is unsown, but when it comes up with the young wheat crop it can only be got rid of by the most careful weeding. Its origin is not quite certain; but the most fruitful cause of its spread is the use of bad seed which has not been carefully cleaned. Another very pernicious weed, but found principally in alluvial lands, is the *leh* or thistle, which when once it has got into the ground can only be extirpated by the most careful ploughing and weeding. Some of the best alluvial wheat land along the Sutlej is overrun with this weed owing to the bad cultivation of the Dogar owners. The best known weed in the Mánjha is the *galvera,* a sort of creeping trefoil which sometimes takes possession of canal-irrigated land, and chokes the growing crops. The *dabh* grass described above is almost worse than the most pernicious weed in the rapidity with which it spreads and the overmastering influence it exercises on the soil.

The capabilities of the district in respect of sport are very poor, except in or round the Chánga Mánga rakh, where good black partridge shooting is to be had in the cotton on the out-skirts of the *rakh* at the latter end of October and early in November, and again in the early spring among the young wheat. Hares too are plentiful about here. In the rakh itself the jungle is usually too thick for small game shooting, though big and successful drives are occasionally organized for Euro-pean visitors of high position. The only large game in the Chánga Mánga rakh are *nilgai* and pig. The latter infest the wood and are destructive enemies to the crops for miles round. Deer are occasionally found and an effort is being made to increase their number, but at present they are very rare. Pea-fowl are at present fairly numerous in the plantation. Grey par-tridges and in canal-irrigated tracts blacks also are fairly plenti-full all over the district, but not sufficiently so to attract sports-men in any special direction, and the Civil Officer even on his cold weather tour will find it hard work making a satisfactory bag. Snipe in any quantity are found only in the lowlands of Bahádarnagar, about 12 miles east of Kasúr, in the marshy land which is flooded now and then by some back water from the Sutlej river, three or four miles away. Even here they only come occasionally and it is wise to make enquiries before going there for the snipe alone. Duck of many varieties are fairly plentiful all along the Sutlej and in its back waters. In the spring wild geese also come to the riverside in great numbers ; these and the sand grouse offer fair shooting near the river at the end of February. Sand grouse abound all over the district from the beginning of November to the end of March. The small bustard and florican are met with occasionally. Wild pigeon are numerous in most parts. Hares are started fre-quently in the *rakh* lands and in the jungle of the Sutlej river tracts. All these varieties make it worth while for the officer on tour to keep his gun with him if his time is fairly free in marching from one stage to another, but the sportsman who goes out intent on nothing else but sport will surely return disappointed, unless he is visiting the Chánga Mánga rakh or the Sutlej riverside. Quail come in here as elsewhere in April and September and are netted in large numbers near the city. Foxes and wild cats may be often seen. Jackals abound everywhere, as anyone who spends a night within the limits of the Lahore district will speedily learn. Wolves are met with occasionally in the lowland wastes of Chúnián tahsíl and in parts of Sharakpur. They sometimes attack children : a boy of 15 or 16 years was lately brought into the hospital badly mauled by a wolf. The villagers sometimes get hold of the wolf cubs and bring them up ; they find a cross between a wolf and a dog a very useful kind of watch dog at their outside wells. It is much more fierce than the ordinary village pariah, and is more feared by thieves.

The number of people returned as killed by wolves during the last ten years in this district is 31, but presumably these were all or nearly all children. In the same period rewards have been paid from the District Office for the destruction of 1,400 wolves. The number brought in as killed shows a great falling off during the last four years, whence it may be presumed that the measures for checking their increase at least have been efficient. There are no other animals that need be mentioned at any length. Otters exist, though not often seen, along the main branches of the canal. Alligators abound in both rivers and may often be seen lying on the sand banks of the Rávi especially. Also enormous water serpents are sometimes observed swimming in the river.

Snakes.

Of venomous snakes the most common are the krait, the viper, and the cobra. The two former are most numerous in the *kallar* tracts of Sharakpur tahsíl. In the last ten years 634 people have been reported as killed by snakes. In the same period rewards have been paid on the destruction of 8,209 kraits, on 3,217 vipers, and on 1,397 cobras, and on more of other kinds.

Fish.

The fish most commonly caught in the Rávi for European consumption are the *rahu* and the *bacchwa,* the former is to be had weighing from five to ten pounds usually, though heavier *rahu* are often caught.. The *bacchwa* is a small fish weighing about half a seer, as usually sold, nine inches long and three or four inches in girth. It is generally to be obtained during the hot weather after rain ; caught in the morning and brought into the Lahore market in the afternoon, the *bacchwa* boiled is delicious eating for dinner. These two fish have one central bone and give no trouble in eating. The *mali* is fair eating but bony.

Chilwa or stickleback are also caught in the Rávi after rain, and make an excellent dish. Other varieties caught from the Rávi are the *tarkanda* weighing between 2½ and 3 lbs., said to be eaten by Europeans ; the *sanghari,* the *pari,* the *saul,* all biggish fish and bony. Also there is the *garúj* or eel, found less in the Rávi than the Deg. In the Sutlej the *rahu, thaila* or *katla,* and *dahi* are common. It is doubtful whether any of the varieties above mentioned would recommend themselves to European taste, except the *bacchwa* which is really excellent, the *rahu* which is fair eating, the *mali, chilwa,* and possibly *tarkanda* and *sanghari.* The rest are too bony and muddy. The *mahásir* is rare in the Rávi and not common in the Sutlej. The fish are generally netted by *máchhis* in the back waters of the two rivers.

CHAPTER II.

HISTORY.

The history of the Lahore district is practically that of the Punjab. Of its condition previous to the Muhammadan invasions we know next to nothing, and such legends or notices in early writers as refer to the ancient city of Lahore will be found in Chapter VI. The following pages furnish a very brief outline of its political fortunes under the various dynasties which succeeded the downfall of the Hindu power in the Punjab. The antiquities of the district are discussed by General Cunningham in his Ancient Geography of India, pages 193 to 203, and in his Archæological Survey Report, II, 202 to 205, and XIV, 47 to 53. A short notice of the history of Kasúr will be found in Chapter VI.

From the numerous ruins of old villages and deserted wells now found in the highlands of the district, there can be no doubt that at one time this portion of the district was more highly cultivated than it is at present. It is difficult to say to what period these prosperous signs may have belonged ; but, considering the wars and dissensions that were constantly taking place in and near the political capital of Lahore, it may be presumed that the depopulation must have taken place during some of the Muhammadan conquests, most probably during that of Nádir Sháh, or of Ahmad Sháh Duráni. But it is probably not alone to these causes that this desertion can be ascribed, for we find that where wells and other signs of former fertility are to be traced, now the water is brackish and the land sterile. The recession of the Beás to the present bed of the Sutlej only occurred about 100 years ago. It has been supposed that this cause alone may have had the effect of turning the springs bitter, and this supposition is supported by the fact that in the neighbourhood of new canals the water of wells which were previously salt has become pure ; it is most difficult otherwise to explain the fact, which is undoubted, that at the present moment the water, in these parts of the highlands where the remains of old wells still exist, is undrinkable by either man or beast.

On the next page is a chronological list of the ruling powers at different periods from A. D. 1001 to A. D. 1754.

Chapter II.

History.

List of rulers and dynasties.

Thus the principal dynasties that have held ascendancy in these parts are :—

I.	Ghazni	from	1001	A. D. to	1188	A. D.,	187	years.
II.	Ghorian	„	1188	„	„	1206	„	18	„
III.	Slave	„	1206	„	„	1288	„	82	„
IV.	Khilji	„	1288	„	„	1321	„	33	„
V.	Tughlak	„	1321	„	„	1398	„	77	„
VI.	Mughals	„	1398	„	„	1412	„	14	„
VII.	Saiyads	„	1413	„	„	1450	„	37	„
VIII.	Pathán	„	1450	„	„	1526	„	76	„
IX.	Mughals	„	1526	„	„	1540	„	14	„
X.	Pathán	„	1540	„	„	1553	„	13	„
XI.	Mughals	„	1553	„	„	1747	„	194	„
XII.	Duráni	„	1747	„	„	1761	„	13	„
XIII.	Sikh	„	1761	„	„	1848	„	86	„
XIV.	British	„	1849	„	„	to date	„	34	„

Year.	Name of Sovereign.	Dynasty.	Parentage.
1001 to 1032	Mahmúd	Ghazni	Son of Sabuktagín.
1032 „ 1040	Masúd	Do.	„ Mahmúd.
1040 „ 1049	Maudúd	Do.	„ Masúd.
1049 „ 1077	Abdul Rashíd	Do.	„ Maudúd
1077 „ 1098	Ibráhím	Do.	„ Masúd.
1098 „ 1114	Masúd	Do.	„ Ibráhím.
1114 „ 1117	Arslán Sháh	Do.	„ Masúd.
1117 „ 1152	Bahrám Sháh	Do.	„ Do.
1152 „ 1159	Khusrau Sháh	Do.	„ Bahrám Sháh.
1159 „ 1188	Khusrau Malik	Do.	„ Khusrau Sháh.
1188 „ 1206	Shahábdín	Gauri	Usurped the throne.
1206 „ 1210	Kutub Aibak	Slave of	
1210 „ 1210	Arám Sháh	......	Adopted son of Aibak, deposed.
1210 „ 1236	Shamsuddín	Balban	Altamash, son-in-law of Aibak succeeded.
1236 „ 1237	Ruknuddín	......	Firoz Sháh, son of Shamsuddín.
1237 „ 1239	Razía Begam	......	Daughter of Altamash.
1239 „ 1241	Bahrám Sháh	......	Son of Shamsuddín.
1241 „ 1246	Alauddín Masúd	......	„ Ruknuddín.
1246 „ 1266	Násiruddín	......	„ Shamsuddín.
1266 „ 1286	Ghiásuddín	Babu	Adopted son of do.
1286 „ 1288	Kaikabád	Do.	Grand son of Ghiásuddín.
1288 „ 1296	Juláluddín Fíroz	Khilji	Usurped the throne.
1296 „ 1316	Aláuddín	Do.	Nephew of Jaláluddín.
1316 „ 1317	Shankatuddín Umar	Do.	Son of Aláuddín.
1317 „ 1321	Mubárik Sháh	Do.	Brother of Shahábuddín
1321 „ 1325	Ghiázuddín or Ghiásuddín Malik	Tughlak	Conquered the throne.
1325 „ 1351	Alaf Khán	Do.	Son of Ghází.
1351 „ 1389	Fíroz Sháh	Do.	Nephew of Ghází.
1389 „ 1389	Tughlak Sháh	Do.	Grandson of Fíroz Sháh.
1389 „ 1392	Abúbakr	Do.	Son of do.
1392 „ 1394	Muhammad Sháh	Do.	„ do.
1394 „ 1394	Sikandar Sháh	Do.	„ Muhammad Sháh.
1394 „ 1398	Mahmúd Sháh	......	„ do.
1398 „ 1398	Timúr or Tamerlane	Mughal	Invaded India.
1398 „ 1421	Ghizin Khán	Saiyad	Made Emperor by Timúr.
1421 „ 1435	Mubárik Sháh	Do.	Son of Ghizin Khán
1435 „ 1445	Muhammad Sháh	Do.	Grandson of do.
1445 „ 1450	Aláuddín Sháh	Do.	Son of Mahmúd Sháh.
1450 „ 1488	Bahlol	Lodi Pathán	Usurped the throne.
1488 „ 1517	Nizám Khán	Do.	Son of Bahlol.
1517 „ 1526	Ibráhím Sháh	Do.	„ Nizám Khán.
1526 „ 1530	Búbar Sháh	Mughal	Descendant of Timúr; conquered Delhi.

Year.	Name of Sovereign.	Dynasty.	Parentage.
1530 to 1540	Humáyún	Mughal ...	Son of Bábar.
1540 „ 1545	Sher Sháh	Pathán ...	Usurped the throne.
1545 „ 1553	Salím Sháh	Do. ...	Son of Sher Sháh.
1553 „ 1553	Muhammad Sháh	Do. ...	Nephew of Sher Sháh.
1553 „ 1556	Humáyún	Mughal ...	Regained his throne.
1556 „ 1605	Akbar Sháh	Do. ...	Son of Humáyún.
1605 „ 1627	Jehángír Sháh	Do. ...	„ Akbar.
1627 „ 1658	Sháh Jahán	Do. ...	„ Jehángír.
1658 „ 1707	Aurangzeb	Do. ...	„ Sháh Jehán.
1707 „ 1712	Sháh Alam	Do. ...	„ Aurangzeb.
1712 „ 1713	Muhaiuddín or Jehándár	Do. ...	„ Sháh Alam.
1713 „ 1719	Farrukhser	Do. ...	Grandson of Azím-ul-shan.
1719 „ 1747	Muhammad Sháh	Do. ...	Son of do.
1747 „ 1754	Ahmad Sháh	Do. ...	„ Jehándár.

At the period of the first Muhammadan invasion in the latter part of the seventh century of our era, we find Lahore in possession of a Chauhán prince, of the family of Ajmer. In A.D. 682, according to Ferishta, the Afgháns of Kermán and Pesháwar, who had, even at that early period, embraced the religion of the Prophet, wrested certain possessions from the Hindu prince. A war ensued, and in the space of five months seventy battles were fought, with varied success, until the Afgháns,- having formed an alliance with the Gakkhars, a wild tribe inhabiting the Salt Range of the Punjab,* compelled the Rája to cede a portion of his territory. The next mention of Lahore is in the Rájputána chronicles, where the Bússas of Lahore, a Rájpút tribe, are mentioned as rallying to the defence of Chittaur, when besieged by Musalmán forces in the beginning of the ninth century. At length, in A.D. 975, Sabuktagín, Governor of Khurásán, and father of the celebrated Mahmúd, advanced beyond the Indus. He was met by Jaipál, Rája of Lahore, whose dominion is said to have extended from Sarhind to Lamghán, and from Kashmír to Mooltan. By the advice of a prince of the Bháti tribe, the Rája formed an alliance with the Afgháns, and, with their aid, was enabled to withstand the first invasion. On his succession to the throne of Ghazni, Sabuktagín repeated his invasion. A battle ensued in the vicinity of Lamghán. The Rája was defeated, and made overtures for peace. His terms were accepted, and persons were sent on the part of Sabuktagín, to take the balance of the stipulated ransom. On reaching Lahore Jaipál proved faithless, and imprisoned those commissioned to receive the treasure. On learning intelligence of his perfidy, Sabuktagín, in the words of Ferishta, "like a foaming torrent, hastened towards Hindustán."

Another battle ensued, in which Jaipál was again vanquished, and he retreated, leaving the territory to the west of the Níláb, or Indus, in the hands of the invader. Chagrined at his double defeat, he performed the Hindu sacrifice of Johár,† or

* Improbably supposed by Abbot to be the descendants of Greek settlers.
† The suicide of Calanus, the Indian, at Pasargadœ, and that of Zarmanochegas at Athens (Strabo, lib. xv., ch. I), are other instances of the performance of this rite. But we need not go back to antiquity for examples. Only a few years

Chapter II.
——
History.
Early struggles
with Muhammadans.

devotion, by burning himself to death outside the walls of his capital. The invader did not retain the conquest he had made, for in A.D. 1008, a confederation, headed by Anangpál, * son of Jaipál, again met the advancing army, now commanded by Mahmúd, son and successor of Sabuktagín, in the vicinity of Pesháwar. In the battle which ensued the naphtha balls of the Afghán army, according to a conjectural reading of Ferishta's text, spread dismay among the Hindu soldiery, who fled, suffering a great slaughter. Lahore was allowed to remain intact for thirteen years longer. Anangpál was succeeded by another Jaipál, called by Al Barúni, Narjanpál, while Mahmúd pushed his conquests into Hindustán. But in A.D. 1022, he suddenly marched down from Kashmír, seized Lahore without opposition, and gave it over to be plundered. Jaipál II fled helpless to Ajmer, and the Hindu principality of Lahore was extinguished for ever. A final effort was made by the Hindús in the reign of Maudúd, A. D. 1045, to recover their lost sovereignty ; but after a fruitless siege of six months they retired without success ; and thus, says Al Barúni, " the sovereignty of India became extinct, and no descendant remained to light a fire on the hearth." Lahore was left in charge of Malik Ayáz, a favourite of Mahmúd of Ghazni, whose name appears in many anecdotes of the sayings and doings of the Emperor. He is said to have built up the walls and fortress of Lahore miraculously, in a single night ; and his tomb, by the *Taksál* or old mint, is still revered by Musalmáns as the burial place of the founder of Lahore.

Social and Political
results attending
the introduction
of Muham-
madanism.

From the above account it will be seen that the princes and people of Lahore played a prominent part in that long continued struggle between Muhammadanism and Hinduism which marks the introduction of the former into India. While Persia was vanquished in three successive battles, and Egypt and the north coast of Africa in less than fifty years, upwards of two centuries elapsed before Muhammadanism had established a footing across the Indus. The strong social action and reaction, which have taken place between the two religions in this part of India, may be traced to the fact that the establishment of Muhammadanism was thus gradual ; and the comparative tolerancy of the earlier Muhammadan dynasties of India is perhaps referable to the same cause,†—the result of those long struggles in which Lahore was so conspicuous ; for history shows that the steady resistance of a people to the religion and customs of their conquerors will, as was the case with the Moors in Spain, teach even bigots the necessity, or policy, of toleration.

---

ago a peasant of the Kángra district, a leper, deliberately burnt himself to death. According to the official report, "one of his brothers handed him a light, and went away; a second brother watched the burning; and a third thought it a matter of such small interest that he went about his usual avocations."

* He is called by Ferishta *Anandpál*, but Anangpál has the authority of the Rájputána chronicles and the Puránas. *Anang* means "incorporeal," or unsubstantial, hence Anangpál is translated by Tod "supporter of a desolate abode "— an ominous name for the monarch of a falling dynasty.

† See the remarks in Elphinstone's " History of India," book V., chapter I.

Even now the Muhammadan of the Punjab is perhaps less bigoted, and the Hindu less grossly superstitious than elsewhere ; and it is remarkable that two of the boldest reformers India has produced, Golakhnáth and Nának, were natives of the Punjab.

Early Muhammadan period.

During the reigns of the first eight princes of the Ghaznivide dynasty, Lahore was governed by viceroys ; but in the reign of Masaúd II (A. D. 1098—1114) the seat of Government was temporarily removed to Lahore, as, the Seljuks having deprived the house of Ghazni of most of its territory in Irán and Turán, the royal family were compelled to take refuge in their Indian possessions. Lahore was again made the seat of empire by Khusrau, the twelfth Ghaznivide Emperor, and would appear to have remained so until the fall of the dynasty, in A. D. 1186, and the establishment of the house of Ghor. The Ghaznivides, especially the later ones, seem to have been a tolerant race, and to have adopted a conciliatory policy towards their Hindu subjects ; we find them employing troops of Hindu cavalry, and some of them even adopted on their coinage the titles and written character of the conquered race. Their popularity may further be inferred from the continual disturbances which arose at Lahore after their expulsion.

Lahore during the Ghorian and Slave dynasties.

During the Ghorian and Slave dynasties, Lahore was the focus of conspiracies against the Government; indeed, it appears throughout the subsequent history of Muhammadan rule to have been the rendezvous of the Tartar, as opposed to the Afghán party. In A. D. 1241, Lahore was taken and plundered by the hordes of Changez Khán ; and in A. D. 1286, Prince Muhammad, the accomplished son of Sultán Ghyás-ud-dín Balban, perished in an encounter with the Mughals on the banks of the Rávi, the poet Amír Khusrau being taken prisoner by his side.

The Khilji and Tughlak dynasties.

During the Khilji and Tughlak dynasties, Lahore is not prominent in the political history of the day. It was once plundered by the Gakkhars, and mention is made of Mughal colonists taking up their abode in the vicinity of the city, the place of their location being still known by the name of Mughalpura.

Invasion of Timúr.

The year 1397 is memorable as the date of the invasion of Timúr, the " firebrand of the universe." Lahore was taken by a detachment of his forces, and from the fact that Timúr did not plunder it in person, it may be inferred that the city was not then particularly rich. On his departure, Lahore was left in possession of Saiyad Khizr Khan, an Afghán noble, native of India, whom he appointed viceroy.

The Lodi dynasty.

From this period, the city was alternately in the hands of the Gakkhars and the ruling dynasty, until, in A. D. 1436, it was seized by Bahlol Khan Lodi, one of the Afghán chiefs, who rose to power on the overthrow of the Tughlak dynasty, and eventually became Emperor. In the reign of his grandson Sultán Ibrahím, Daulat Khán Lodi, the Afghán Governor of Lahore, revolted ; and, Count Julian-like, invited to his aid the great Chagatái prince, Bábar, who had long meditated an invasion of Hindustán, which he claimed as the representative of Timúr.

Lahore taken by Bábar, A. D. 1524.
Bábar came, saw, and conquered. He was met by an Afghán army, composed of the supporters of Sultán Ibrahím, in the vicinity of Lahore ; but it was speedily vanquished, and the victor, enraged at the opposition he had experienced, let loose his soldiery upon the city, which they plundered and partially burnt. Bábar did not remain long at Lahore, but, after a halt of only four days, marched on towards Delhi. He did not, however, get further than Sirhind on this occasion. Daulat Khán Lodi, who had invited him to Hindustán, being dissatisfied with his reward of a *jágír*, had already begun to intrigue against him. He, therefore, returned to Lahore, and having parcelled out the provinces he had conquered among his nobles went back to Kábul. The next year, Lahore was the hot bed of intrigues fomented by Daulat Khán, which it is unnecessary to detail, but the following year Bábar again appeared. An attempt was again made to oppose him at the Rávi, near Lahore ; but the force melted away before it was attacked, and Bábar, without entering Lahore, passed on towards Hindustán. This was his last expedition, and it ended, A. D. 1526, in the decisive victory of Pánipat over the Afghán army, the capture of Delhi, and the foundation of the Moghal Empire.

The Moghal period.
The reigns of Humáyún, Akbar, Jehángir, Sháhjehán, and Aurangzeb, the successors of Bábar, may be considered the golden period of the history of Lahore. The city again became a place of royal residence ; gardens, tombs, mosques, and pavilions sprang up in every direction ; the population increased, suburbs arose until the city became, in the language of Abul-fazl, " the grand resort of people of all nations," and celebrated for its fine buildings and luxuriant gardens. To this day almost all that is architecturally beautiful at Lahore is referable to the period of the early Moghal Emperors.

Humáyún.
On the accession of Humáyún, the Punjab, together with Kábul and Kandahár, became the appanage of Kámrán, Humáyún's younger brother, who seems to have given the first impulse to the architectural adornment of Lahore, by building a palace, with a garden extending from Naulakka to the river Rávi. During the struggle between Humáyún and Sher Khán, the Afghán usurper, Lahore served as the *place d'armes* of the Moghals, and on the temporary expulsion of the former from the throne, narrowly escaped destruction. Sher Khán at one time meditated razing it to the ground, and transferring its inhabitants to Mánkot in the Siálkot range ; and, on his death bed, he lamented his not having done so as one of the errors

of his life. The design was revived in the reign of his successor, but never carried into effect.*

After an exile of fourteen years, Humáyún returned in triumph to Lahore (A. D. 1554) and was received with every demonstration of joy by the inhabitants. After his death, at Delhi, A. D. 1556, and the accession of Akbar, the peace of Lahore was again disturbed by Hákim, the younger brother of Akbar, who descended from Kábul, of which province he was Governor, and seized Lahore in A. D. 1563. He was soon expelled. In 1581 he made another attempt, but the siege was raised by the advance of Akbar in person. From A. D. 1584 to A.D. 1598, Akbar apparently made Lahore his head-quarters, and undertook from thence the conquest of Kashmír and the operations against the Afghán tribes of the frontier. It was during his residence at Lahore that Akbar would appear to have developed to their greatest extent those principles of religious liberality for which he is so conspicuous. His Court was the resort of the learned of every creed, and the arena of religious disputations between conflicting sects.† It is related that the Emperor erected two buildings, outside the city, for the entertainment of devotees of every kind ; one, called Khairpura for Jews, Gabrs (or fire-worshippers) and Muhammadans ; and another called Dharmpura, for Híndus. Weekly meetings were held for discussion, in which Bír Bal, Abul-faizi, Abul-fazl and other independent thinkers, took part. Alchemy, fascination, and magic were also practised, according to one historian,‡ and the Emperor himself is said to have become an adept in the former art. In the same spirit of eclecticism, Akbar revived the old Persian festival in honour of the sun, and appointed Abul-fazl superintendent of fire-temples. A portion of the building, called Khairpura is still said to remain in the vicinity of Dáránagar, on the left of the road to Mian Mír§ and there is a memento of the imperial partiality to sun-worship in an enamelled figure of the sun visible to this day, on the front wall of the palace. Tod notices a similar decoration at Udepur ; "a huge painted sun of gypsum in high relief, with gilded rays adorns the Hall of Audience."

---

* If, as has been suggested, Mánkot was the same Mádhokor, the capital of the Punjab at the period of the Muhammadan invasion, the policy of the transfer is obvious. Sher Khán, though called a usurper, was the representative of the native or anti-foreigner party, and would, therefore, wish to conciliate the Hindús by re-transferring the seat of Government to the ancient capital of their native rulers.

† The *odium theologicum* thus excited led sometimes to fatal disputes. In one of them, Mulla Ahmad a learned Shíab, compiler of the " Táríkh-i-Alfi," was assassinated in the streets of Lahore, by one Mirzá Fúlád. The murderer was sentenced to be bound alive to the leg of an elephant," and thus, adds the Sunni narrator, " attained martyrdom "—See Sir H. Elliot's " Biographical Index of the Muhammadan Historians of India."

‡ Abd-ul-Qádir, author of the " Táríkh-i-Badáuni."

§ It is not improbable that there is an allusion to the practice of alchemy at Khairpura in the following passage in the inscription on the Tomb of Mian Mír which is in the immediate vicinity of Dáránagar :—
The dust of whose portals is envied by stone of the alchemist.

The literary circle which followed the Imperial Court appears to have been peculiarly active during its sojourn at Lahore. It was here the voluminous history of Muhammadanism from the earliest period up to the thousandth year of the Hijri era, compiled by order of the Emperor was finished and revised; and it was here that the translation of the Mahábhárata and the Rája Tarangini into Persian—a work still unaccomplished as regards our own language—was undertaken. The list of poets and the divines who wrote and rhymed and occasionally fought within the walls of Lahore between A. D. 1584 and A. D. 1598, is too long to give here, but there is one among them who deserves special mention in a history of Lahore, namely, the historian Nizám-ud-dín Ahmad, the author of the Tabaqát Akbari—the first historical work of which India forms exclusively the subject-matter. He died in A. D. 1594 and was buried in his garden at Lahore. The tomb of this *celebre*, to whom Ferishta owed so much in the compilation of his history can no longer be traced; even his name and his work are but little known to the modern *literati* of Lahore. It is also worthy of remark that Akbar's able minister, Todar Mal, the best Revenue officer perhaps the Moghal Government ever had, and the ideal of an Oriental financier, expired at Lahore.

It was during this period that some Portuguese missionaries, at the express request of Akbar, proceeded from Goa to the Emperor's Court at Lahore. They arrived with sanguine hopes of Christianizing the country, and, in their journal, they describe Lahore as a "delightful city." On their arrival, they were taken to the imperial residence, situated " on an island in river;" and, being introduced to the Emperor, presented him with a splendid image of the Virgin, which he received with the greatest admiration. But notwithstanding this good beginning their hopes were not realized, and they eventually returned to Goa. Akbar's successor, Jehángír, however, was more liberal than his father. He allowed some Portuguese Jesuits to establish a mission and build a church at Lahore, and even assigned stipends to the priests. But this liberality ceased after his death. Sháh Jehán, a more strict Musalmán, withdrew the pensions and pulled down the church; but some traces of it still remained when Lahore was visited by the French traveller Thevenot, in A. D. 1665. A crucifix and a picture of the Virgin were even then observable on the gateways of the palace.*

It was about this period also (A. D. 1584) that Lahore was visited by four of our countrymen, Messrs. Fitch, Newberry, Leedes, and Storey, members of the Turkey or Levant Company. The former left an account of his travels, but gives no detailed description of Lahore. In A. D. 1594, the Emperor

---

* Among the enamelled fresco designs executed upon the northern front of the palace may still be seen the figures of two cherubs' heads, with wings exactly like the representations of cherubs common in ecclesiastical and scenic decorations in Europe. May not these have been copied from printings belonging to the Jesuit church ?

Akbar quitted for ever the city associated with the brightest period of his reign ; and until his decease was engaged in military operations in the Deccan—latterly, in an unnatural contest with his eldest son, Salím.

The latter succeeded, in A. D. 1606, under the title of Jehángír. His reign commenced, as usual, with a rebellion, and Lahore felt the effects of it. Prince Khusrau, the eldest son of the Emperor, seized the suburbs of Lahore, and laid siege to the citadel. His army was quickly defeated by the imperial troops, and his adherents were punished with fearful severity. Seven hundred prisoners were impaled in two rows leading from the gate of Lahore ; and the prince was marched past them in mock dignity, on an elephant, from Kámran's palace at Naulakka, where he had been temporarily placed, to the fort, where he was kept in close confinement in chains.

The celebrated Sikh Guru, Arjan, the fourth successor of Nának and compiler of the *Adi Granth* was somehow implicated in the rebellion ; he was imprisoned, and his death, which occurred soon after, is attributed to the rigours of his confinement ; though tradition asserts that, having obtained permission from his guards to bathe in the river Rávi, which flowed by his prison he miraculously disappeared beneath the stream. However this may be, he is regarded by the Sikhs as their first martyr, and his death was one of the causes which changed them from a peaceable to a warlike sect, and instilled into their minds that bitter hatred of Muhammadans which stood us in such stead in 1857. His humble shrine* may still be seen between the palace of Moghals and the mausoleum of Ranjít Singh—a fitting locality for the memorial of him who was an unconscious cause of the downfall of the one and the elevation of the other.

Jehángír was fond of Lahore, though to one with any feeling the place would have been fraught with bitter associations. In A. D. 1622, he fixed his court here, and when he died, at Rájauri, in Kashmir† A. D. 1627, it was his express wish that he should be buried at Lahore. He was interred, accordingly, in the garden of Núrjehán, his devoted though imperious wife ; and, through her exertions, the mausoleum at Sháhdára, one of the chief ornaments of Lahore, was erected to his memory. In the immediate vicinity is the tomb of Núrjehán herself, a humble imitation of that of Jehángír, as well as that of Asaf Khan, or Asaf Jáh, her brother, the historian,‡ soldier and *wazir*, and in

---

* A well, said to have been dug by him, may be seen in the vicinity of the golden mosque. Ranjit Singh built a *báolí* on the spot.

†The author of the *Iqbálnámah Jehangíri* states that his death was the result of a shock on the nervous system, brought on by having seen one of his attendants dashed to pieces by falling down a precipice in pursuit of a deer. This is not very credible in one who, in his own Memoirs, gloats over the atrocities committed at the commencement of his reign. Others attribute his death with more probability, to asthma.

‡ He composed a portion of the *Tárikh-i-Alfi.*

the latter capacity, in common with his sister, a great opponent of English interest in the Court of Jehángír* at the period of Sir Thomas Roe's Embassy.

Sháhjehán.

On the death of Jehángír, Lahore was again (A. D. 1628) the scene of a struggle between rival claimants to the throne, which, as usual, terminated in the execution of the vanquished. On the one side was Shahryár, younger son of the late Emperor, supported by the once all-powerful Nurjehán, whose daughter by her former husband he had married ; and on the other, Sháhjehán supported by his father-in-law, Asaf Khan. Shahryár seized the treasury at Lahore, and proclaimed himself Emperor ; but he and his adherents were speedily attacked and defeated by the energetic Asaf Khan, and the prince himself, with the two sons of Jehángír's brother, Daniál, was taken prisoner. The prince and his two cousins were put to death at Lahore, and Sháhjehán and his sons remained the sole direct representatives of the house of Timur. Asaf Khan now enjoyed a position even more elevated than in the preceding reign, and retained it until A. D. 1632, when he failed in the siege of Bíjanpur, from which date he seems to have lost favour. Núrjehán survived until A. D. 1646, but her influence ceased for ever with the death of Shahryár. From that date she lived in seclusion and devoted herself to the memory of her husband. She and a faithful female attendant are buried side by side in the tomb she had constructed during her lifetime.

Dára Shikoh.

Between A. D. 1628 and 1657, Lahore enjoyed an interval of peace and prosperity under the munificent rule of Ali Mardán Khan, and Haki Ali-ud-dín, who is more commonly known by his title of Wazír Khan ; but during the struggles between the sons of Sháhjehán, which cast a cloud over the latter part of the reign of that Emperor, as if in retribution for the atrocities which attended its commencement, Lahore warmly espoused the cause of Dára Shikoh, the eldest son and, according to our notions, the rightful heir to the throne. He had fixed his residence at Lahore, and gained great popularity by his engaging manners and generous disposition, and by the interest he took in the welfare of the city, which he improved by the construction of numerous *chauks* or market places. He collected a history of all the holy men and conventual institutions of the place,† and had, as his spiritual adviser, the eminent Lahore saint, Mian Mír, who, if we may judge of the tenets of the master by those of the disciple, must have been a singularly liberal-minded Musalmán. When pursued by his brother, Aurangzeb, in A. D. 1658, at a time when his cause was almost hopeless, Lahore supplied him with men and money ;‡ and

---

* Until Sir Thomas Roe, bribed him with a valuable pearl, after which "all went on well and smoothly."—*Elphinstone's History of India.*

† The work is still extant, but shows no trace of the alleged heretical opinion of its author.

‡ Among his adherents was Har Rái, the seventh Sikh Guru.

when his wife died, during his hurried retreat to the western frontier, Lahore received her last remains. The disasters of his flight to Gujrát, the scene near Ahmadábád as the city closed its gates against him, his betrayal and cruel death, are matters beyond the scope of the present work, and the reader is referred for an account of them to the graphic pages of Bernier, or the more discriminating narrative of Elphinstone. His name is still held in affectionate remembrance at Lahore, and the costly *Bádsháhi* mosque erected at Lahore by Aurangzeb, a few years after this event, has ever been held in disrepute, because built from the " spoils of blood," that is, from the proceeds of the confiscated estates of Dára.* During the reign of Aurangzeb, Lahore had but little connection with the political events of the time, as the attention of the Emperor was chiefly directed to quelling the rising power of the Mahrattas in the Deccan, and the rebellion of the tribes of Rájputána.

But from the death of Aurangzeb to the accession of Ranjít Singh, the fate of Lahore was singularly unfortunate. As the capital of an outlying province, it was naturally the first to suffer from the weakness of the decaying Moghal Empire. Ruled over by governors inadequately supported, it became the *point d'appui* of Sikh insurrections, and like a second Ariminum, the *iter ad bella* of every invader from the West. Almost immediately after the death of Aurangzeb, the Sikhs, who had been kept under subjection during his energetic rule, broke out into insurrection under a leader named Banda, and at length seriously threatened Lahore. The Emperor Bahádur Sháh, the son and successor of Aurangzeb (A. D. 1712) marched to Lahore, with a view of crushing the rebellion, but died before he could achieve any decisive success. One of the gate-ways of Lahore, the *Sháh Alami* Gateway,† was called after his name, and the fact furnishes some testimony to the popularity of this prince, whose toleration was a great contrast to the bigotry of his predecessor. It has been said, indeed, that "had Bahádur Sháh, and not Aurangzeb, succeeded Sháhjehán, the family of Timúr might have still sat on the throne of Delhi."

His death was followed by the usual contest among the sons; Azím-us-shán, a younger son, but more popular than the others, endeavoured to seize the throne and oust his elder brother, Jehándár. A conflict ensued between the brothers and their respective partizans outside the city walls; Azím-us-shán was driven from the field, and fled precipitately to the Rávi, which he endeavoured to cross upon an elephant. But the river being swollen and rapid, owing to the melting of the snows at its source in the Himálayas, he was swept away and drowned. But his death was not unavenged. Seven months afterwards, Jehándár was prostrate before Farrukhser, the son of Azím-us-shán, who

---

* The mosque was converted into a powder-magazine by Ranjít Singh, and has only lately been restored to the Muhammadans; but the boon is but little appreciated by them.

† It was formerly called the " Bherwála " Gateway.

had marched from Bengal with a large army, and by him was sternly put to death. The struggles between Jehándár and Farrukhser for the imperial throne, and the dissensions and intrigues in the Court of the latter, encouraged the Sikhs to further excesses; they defeated the governor of Lahore in a pitched battle, and it became necessary for even the *fainéant* Farrukhser to take some measures for their repression. He appointed Abdul Samad Khan, a Turáni nobleman, and an officer of known vigour, to the viceroyship of Lahore; the new governor obtained a brilliant success over the rebels, and took Banda himself prisoner, whom he despatched to Delhi. Abdul Samad was succeeded in the viceroyship by his son Zikaríya Khan, under the title of Khan Bahádur, and for twenty-one years (A. D. 1717—1738) the Punjab was peaceful. The weakness of the Court of Delhi raised the viceroy into a satrap, who, safe for a time in his palace at Bagampura, viewed with complacency the failing powers of the house of Timúr and the rise of the Mahrattas.

At length, in 1738, the citizens of Lahore heard with dismay of the approach of a new enemy from the west, led by the Turkománi warrior, Nádir Kúli Khan, who from his humble home by the fountain Margáb, in the vale of Azerbiján, issued forth the conqueror of Khorásán and Meshed, the lord of Persia and vanquisher of the house of Timúr. On the 18th November 1738, he crossed the Indus, passed rapidly without boat or raft, the Jhelum and Chenáb "rivers," writes his Secretary, Mirza Mehdi—"furious as the ocean or as an arm of a destructive sea,"—and pushed on for Lahore. A faint show of resistance was made at Wazírabad, and again in the vicinity of Lahore, but to no purpose, and at length the invading army encamped in the Gardens of Shálamár. Zikaríya Khan, the viceroy, had no particular affection for the Court of Delhi, and was soon convinced that discretion is the better part of valour. He brought twenty *lakhs* of rupees and a vast array of elephants, and presented them before the throne of the invader; the result was that Zikaríya was confirmed in his governorship, and Lahore, this time, escaped pillage. On the 29th December, the troops of Nádir Sháh quitted Lahore for Delhi.

The prostration of the Moghal Emperor by the ensuing victory of Karnál and the sack of Delhi gave fresh courage to the Sikhs, who had been restrained during the vigorous rule of Abdul Samad and Zikaríya Khan; but the latter was now dead, and his son and successor Yahiya Khan was less fortunate. In 1746, a marauding band of Sikhs had collected at Eminábad, a locality associated with sacred recollections to their minds, for here is the shrine of *Rori Sáhib*,* marking the spot where their

---

* *Rori* means "hard ground" and the expression *Rori Sáhib* is an instance of a habit, characteristic of oriental races, of personifying localities. Thus we have Amritsarji, *Darbár Sáhib*, &c.; just as if an Englishman were to speak of "My Lord Parliament House." The Lahore District abounds in localities thus "canonized"; as being associated with some act in the life of Nának,—*e. g. Nankánah Sáhib*, the place of his birth, *Bálkarirá, Sáhib, bál,* a child, *karira,* play, the place where he spent his youth; *Milasthan-ji,* the place of cattle where he tended his herd; *Kyari Sáhib, kyára,* a cultivated bed where Nának cultivated.

Guru Nának, in performance of a vow of penance, knelt down and prayed upon the hard ground. Troops were sent by Yáhiya Khan to disperse the Sikhs, who, inspired by the sanctity of the place, fell upon the detachment with fury and over-powered it. The news of this disaster exasperated the viceroy, who despatched another overwhelming force, under the command of Lakhpat Rái, which succeeded in defeating the insurgents. Those who were taken prisoners were brought into Lahore, and executed on the north-east side of the city, then known as the horse-market, but since the period of Sikh rule by the name of *Shahíd Ganj*, or place of martyrs; and the spot of the execution is indicated by a shrine erected to the memory of Bhái Táru Singh, the chief martyr, who, though offered pardon if he would consent to part with his long hair, the outward badge of his faith, preferred death to apostasy.

Two years from this event, A. D. 1748, a more powerful enemy appeared before the walls of Lahore, in the person of Ahmad Sháh, the successor of Nádir Sháh, who had no sooner established himself on the throne than he marched an army into India. The viceroyship at Lahore was then a bone of contention between the two sons of Zikaríya Khan, Yahiya, and Sháh Nawáz Khan; while the Court of Delhi looked on, too weak or too indolent to interfere. To aid his cause Sháh Nawáz encouraged the advance of Ahmad, recollecting that his father had not fared ill at the hands of the western invader. Ahmad Sháh advanced; but his army was small, and Sháh Nawáz Khan, having prevailed over his brother, thought better of his treachery. He met the invading forces, was disastrously defeated under the walls of the city, and Ahmad took possession of Lahore. * The first invasion of Ahmad, having passed Lahore, met with a check in Sirhind, and the conqueror returned the way he came. Mír Mannu, son of the Delhi Wazír, who had distinguished himself in the battle, was appointed governor of Lahore.

At the close of 1748, Ahmad again crossed the Indus, but the invasion was this time warded off, partly by the bold front assumed by Mír Mannu, at the banks of the Chenáb, and partly by diplomacy. The following year it was renewed with better success. The invader marched without opposition to Lahore, and halted a short distance from the suburb of Shahdára, where Mír Mannu had entrenched himself. He crossed the river, however, at a ford higher up, and proceeded to invest the city, his own camp being fixed in the vicinity of the Shálámár Gardens. For four months Mír Mannu made a good defence. At length, as provision and forage began to fall short, he imprudently risked a general action. On the morning of the 12th April 1752, he marched out of his entrenchment, and took up a position near the village of

Chapter II.

History.

Invasions of Nádir Sháh.

Invasions of Ahmad Sháh.

* At the back of the Jáma Masjid, there is the tomb of one Sábir Sháh who was put to death for advising the people to submit to Ahmad.

Mahmúd Búti. A battle ensued which was sustained for some hours, with doubtful success on both sides, but at length the tide was turned by a charge of the Duráni horse, and Mír Mannu retired into the citadel.* The next morning, however, finding further resistance hopeless, he repaired to the tent of the conqueror to make his submission, when the following dialogue is said to have taken place :—" How is it," said Ahmad Sháh, "that you have not, long ere this, come to do homage to your lord and master ? " " Because," replied Mír Mannu, " I had another master to serve." " And why," rejoined the Sháh ; " did not your master protect you in this hour of need ? " " Because," returned the other, " he knew that Mír Mannu would take care of himself." " and supposing," continued the Sháh, " you had been victorious ? " " I should have put you in an iron cage and sent you prisoner to Delhi," was the reply. " And now that I am victor, what," asked the Sháh, " do you expect at my hands ? " " If you are a tradesman," said Mír Mannu, " sell me ; if an executioner, put me to death ; but if you are a prince, be generous." The conqueror struck with admiration at the dauntless bearing of his youthful adversary, called him the Rustam of India, decorated him with a jewelled sword, and confirmed him in the post of viceroy of the Punjab. †

But Mír Mannu did not long live to enjoy his newly-acquired title ; he died soon afterwards, A. D. 1752, leaving an infant son and a widow. The latter succeeded as guardian of her son, and for a time vainly endeavoured to keep upon good terms with the Courts of both Kábul and Delhi; at length, however, her duplicity was discovered, and the Delhi *Wazir* summarily put an end to her intrigues by having her seized in her own house and carried off a prisoner.‡ This violent act afforded the Duráni a pretext for a fourth invasion A. D. 1755-56). Lahore was occupied without opposition and placed under the conqueror's son Prince Timúr ; but an act of intolerance on his part, in defiling the sacred tank at Amritsar, roused the fury of the Sikhs, now a rapidly rising sect, Sikh horsemen swarmed round the city walls, and assumed so threatening an attitude, that Prince Timúr thought it prudent to retire, and Lahore, for the first time A. D.

---

* The scene of the battle is marked by a large quadrangular tomb of masonry. This, say the neighbouring villagers, was erected by the last surviving son of Aziz Beg; a person of distinction in Mír Mannu's army, who with his five other sons, fell in the battle : the survivor, being unable to recognise the bodies of his father and brothers, to make sure, collected the bones of all those slain in the place where the fight was thickest and buried them in a large vault below the tomb. The plain around is still strewn with human bones.

† His memory is held in great repute by Muhammadans, but detested by the Sikhs, whom he treated with great severity. He was buried near Shahid Ganj, where the remains of his tomb may still be seen. In the reign of Sher Singh, the Sikhs, in a moment of religious frenzy, dismantled the building, dug out the remains of Mír Mannu, and scattered them to the winds.

‡ Bikhári Khán, who built the Soneri *Masjid*, or golden mosque, in the city of Lahore, was a favourite of this lady ; but having, in an unlucky hour, incurred her displeasure, was, by her orders, surrounded and beaten to death with shoes.

1756—58, fell into the hands of the Sikhs. Their leader, Jassa Singh, a kalal, at once assumed the prerogatives of sovereignty, and struck a coin bearing the inscription, "Coined by the grace of the Khálsah." Their occupation, this time, however, was short-lived ; they were expelled by a new enemy in the Mahrattas, under a chief named Rágoba whom Adínah Bég Khan, the deputy of Mír Mannu, had invited to his assistance. With their help, he was installed on the viceregal throne (A. D. 1758) ; but he enjoyed his success only a few months. He died leaving a name still held in some respect as that of the last Moghal governor of Lahore. *

The success of the Mahrattas led to a fifth invasion by Ahmad Sháh (A. D. 1759), which resulted in their disastrous overthrow at Pánipat, A. D. 1761. One Buland Khan was made chief Magistrate at Lahore ; but the Government machinery was powerless, the Sikhs again assumed a formidable appearance, and they beseiged his successor, Obeid Khan, in the fort of Lahore. A sixth descent of the Duráni scattered the Sikh forces, and inflicted on them a terrible slaughter, near Ludhiána. He returned by the way of Lahore, and left one Kábuli Mal, governor, the country being ravaged by the Sikh horsemen. The successes of the Sikhs in Sirhind incited Ahmad Sháh to undertake his seventh invasion ; but he retired, somewhat precipitately, without having effected his object. Kábuli Mal was ejected, and the Sikhs again became masters of Lahore. In 1767, Ahmad Sháh made his eighth and his last invasion, but had to retire without success, harassed by the ever-present Sikh cavalry.

During thirty years following the final departure of Ahmad Sháh (A. D. 1767—97), the Sikhs were left to themselves, and increased in wealth and numbers. They gradually divided themselves into independent *misls,* or bands, under the command of hereditary chieftains, having a common place of meeting at Amritsar, which was to them what Delphi or Dodona was to the Hellenes, or the Farentine fountain to the tribes of Latium. Lahore, meanwhile, was portioned out amongst a triumvirate of Sikh chieftains, named, respectively, Gujar Singh, Lehna Singh, and Sobha Singh who are spoken of to this day as the "Three Hákms." The first had his stronghold in a brick fort between Shálamár and Lahore, which still bears his name ; Lehna Singh in the citadel ; and Sobha Singh in the garden of Zebinda Begam, which he turned into a fort, now known by the name of Nawánkot.

At length, A. D. 1797, the spell was again broken. Sháh Zemán, the successor of Timúr on the throne of Kábul, but known in aftertimes as the blind exile of Ludhiána and the brother of the unfortunate Sháh Shujah, made a new attempt

Invasion of Sháh Zemán.

---

* He was buried at Gujránwála, where his tomb and garden may still be seen.

to establish a Duráni empire from Kábul to the Ganges. His advance created the liveliest sensation not only in the Punjab but even in the Council Chamber at Calcutta. Governors-General wrote long minutes, augmented the Native army, and laid the foundation of that chronic state of apprehension which ended in the expedition to Afghánistán. In the beginning of the cold season, Sháh Zemán appeared before Lahore, and the tall sheep-skin cap of the then youthful warrior is still recollected, as he rode upon a prancing steed on the plain fronting the palace. But his expedition was arrested by bad tidings from home, and he retired, after exacting a subsidy of thirty *lakhs* from the few wealthy merchants who still remained. The next year, it was renewed with no better success; but the event is interesting as being the first occasion on which Ranjít Singh, son of Maha Singh, chief of the Súkhárchakiya *misl*, came prominently into notice, and made the first step towards obtaining the sovereignty of the Punjab by securing from the retiring Duráni Emperor a formal grant of the chiefship of Lahore. The history of Lahore is henceforth merged in the history of its great ruler Mahárája Ranjít Singh, the events of whose life are fully detailed in the now familiar pages of Murray, Cunningham, and the "History of the Punjáb." From this period, therefore, it is not proposed to give more than a brief *résume* of events.

Ranjít Singh.

In 1799 Ranjít Singh became master of Lahore, which was then in possession of Sardár Chet Singh, the son of the triumvir Lehna Singh, after a short contest, in which Ranjít Singh was aided by the treachery of the leading men. In 1801, Ranjít Singh assumed the title of *Sarkár*, established a mint, and commenced his career as a sovereign. In 1802, he obtained the celebrated gun *Zamzamah*, a huge piece which Ahmad Sháh had used in the battle of Pánipat, but had left behind at Lahore, as too unwieldy to take back to Kábul. The gun had hitherto been in possession of the most powerful of the *misls*, the Bhangís of Amritsar, and came to be regarded as the talisman of Sikh empire. Hence its capture by Ranjít Singh added greatly to his prestige. From this period, the tide of success flowed on apace; Jhang, Kasúr, Pathánkot, Siáklot, Gujrát, felt the power of his arms, and the chiefs of Mooltan, Jullundur and Kasauli, were glad to ward off an attack by timely submission, and acknowledgment of Ranjít Singh as lord paramount. In 1812, he became possessed of the person of Sháh Shuja, and of the gem *Koh-i-Núr*; effectually opposed the hitherto irresistible progress of Afghán invaders, and re-occupied the fort of Attock. In 1814 he suffered his first reverse, in an attempt to conquer Kashmír; but he so far succeeded as to obtain from the governor a formal recognition of the paramount authority of the Lahore *Darbár*. In 1818, Mooltan was besieged and taken by his forces, and the province annexed to the Empire of the Mahárája. In 1819, Kashmír was at length conquered. This was followed by the annexation of the Deraját, or tract of country between the Indus and the Sulemán range; and Pesháwar was captured in 1823.

Ranjít Singh died in 1839, lord of the Punjab from the Sulemán range to the Sutlej, and from Kashmír to beyond Mooltan, an Empire little less in extent than that of Jaipál, having a regular army and three hundred pieces of artillery. But the Hindu supremacy, revived by him, was hollow and unsubstantial. It was based, not upon a national movement, but the military ardour of a religious sect whose action he united by the force of his personal character. Hence, like other Empires which have been similarly constructed, it was destined to perish *mole suo*. Its foundation being thus unstable, with no leading principle to give it coherence,—for the consolidating system of its founder had destroyed the bond of union which once existed in the yearly *Gurumata*, or assemblage of Sikh chieftains at the Sacred tank, without even the prestige of antiquity,—the moment the directing power was weakened, the fabric of Government fell to pieces, and the very source of its strength, the large, well-disciplined, army became the immediate cause of its destruction.

As might be expected, it is as difficult, as it is useless, to attempt to analyse the motive which influenced the several actors in political drama which followed the decease of Ranjít Singh ; indeed what is most remarkable in it is the almost total absence of anything like a political faction. There was to a certain extent, what may be called a Dogra party, composed of the Jummoo family who had risen into importance in the latter years of the Mahárája with their adherents ; and the Khálsa party, represented by the Sindhánwáliás, who were related to the family of Ranjít Singh. But neither of these parties dreamt of such a thing as the public good. Personal or family considerations and *zanana* intrigues were the mainspring of their public acts, and their first object was to curry favour with the army.

Successors of Ranjít Singh.

Under Ranjít Singh the principal Sikh feudatories in the Lahore District were Mít Singh of Padhána, Jai Singh of Manihál near Patti, and Gyan Singh of Bahrwál. The history of Kasúr is distinct from that of the remainder of the district, and is related in Chapter VI.

The successors of Ranjít Singh threw themselves alternately into the hands of the one party or the other, as it suited their interest or caprice, and it thereupon became the object of the party out of favour to get rid of their obnoxious rivals. The first act in the drama was the murder of Chet Singh, a minion of the imbecile Kharak Singh, Ranjít Singh's successor.* This was done in pursuance of a concerted design between Nau Nihál Singh, the heir apparent, and the Jummoo party ; but no sooner had the object been attained than Nau Nihál turned against his friends.

---

* He was murdered whilst sleeping in the verandah in front of the Takht or throne in the fort from which the Moghal Emperors administered justice.

Kharak Singh died in 1840. Nau Nihál Singh, who, there is reason to believe, had hastened his father's death by poison, was the same day killed by the fall of a portion of an archway,* as he was proceeding on foot from witnessing the cremation of his father's remains. The ashes of father and son rest side by side beneath two small domes to the left of the Mausoleum of Ranjít Singh.

The death of Nau Nihál Singh, was followed by a struggle between the mother of the deceased prince, in concert with the Sindhánwália party and Sher Singh, a disowned son of Ranjít Singh, aided by Dhyán Singh, the Jummoo prince and favourite of Ranjít Singh. The *soi-disant* queen regent was aided, strange to say, by Guláb Singh,† the brother of Dhyán Singh, who held the fort, and it became necessary for Sher Singh to besiege them. The siege lasted four days, from the 14th to the 18th of January 1841. The main attacks of the besiegers were made from the Hazúri Bágh, where Sher Singh took up his position, in the then unfinished marble pavilion,‡ in front of the massive gateway of Akbar. Twelve cannons were directed against the fort walls, and *zabúráhs*, or light guns used in the mountain warfare of Kashmír, were placed on the tops of the minarets of the Great Mosque of Aurangzeb, which overlook the fort. The bombardment resulted in the submission of the queen and her party, and the coronation of Sher Singh.

Sher Singh in his turn fell a victim to a coalition between the Sindhánwálias and the Dográ chiefs. On the 15th September 1843 he was assassinated by Ajít Singh, the Sindhánwália chief while inspecting levies at a country seat, called Shah Baláwal; and its marble lattice window still bears, it is

---

* The archway was close by the tomb of Ranjít Singh, and led, through another archway, into the Hazúri Bágh; it has since been pulled down. Nau Nihál Singh was a young prince of great vigour and activity, and had been virtually ruler during the last six months of his father's life. He has been called the Hotspur of the Punjab. The fall of the archway was of course attributed by some to design, and Guláb Singh has been denounced as the author. But the proof is confined to the bare assertions of some of the Sikh courtiers and to the fact that some endeavours were made to conceal, at first, the amount of injury sustained by the prince. On the other hand it is not explained by what delicate mechanism the fall of a portion of the archway should be timed to a second, and until this is explained, the assertion must appear incredible, while the accusation of Guláb Singh is inconsistent with the fact that his own son was one of the victims.

† This conduct of Guláb Singh is usually attributed to deep design; he is supposed to have made a show of resistance, in concert with Dhyán Singh, in order to obtain sufficient influence with the queen-mother to induce her to surrender. But Sir George Clerk, whose position and knowledge of the parties give the greatest weight to his opinion considers that Guláb Singh's conduct was not designed, but that being a guest of the queen-mother at the time, he was simply acting in accordance with the Rájput laws of hospitality, in fighting for the protection of his hostess.

‡ The building still bears the marks of bullets and three-pound shot fired from the fort walls on this occasion.

said, the impress of the bullet which passed through his heart.* Having succeeded in their attempt the Sindhánwálias forthwith turned their hands against their late ally, Rája Dhyán Singh, who was shot down and cut to pieces within an hour of the death of Sher Singh, at the summit of the ascent into the fort from the Hazúri Bágh. This led to a second siege of Lahore by Híra Singh, son of Dhyán Singh, aided by the Khálsa army, animated by the prospect of high pay and plunder. The wall was breached ; Ajít Singh, the assassin, sprang over the north-east angle of the fort, and was cut to pieces in the place where he fell ; Lehna Singh, already wounded, fell into the hands of the soldiery, and was shot and hacked to death.

For a little more than a year Híra Singh was virtual ruler, in the name of Dhulíp Singh, the son of the Ráni Chandan (or Jindán), a queen of Ranjít Singh ; he fell owing to a personal quarrel with the Ráni, and his unpopularity with the fickle Khálsa army. He fled, with his adviser Pandit Jallah, pursued by Jawáhir Singh, the Ráni's brother, and troops of Khálsa horse. From Shahdara the pursuit was closely kept up for some twelve miles, until the Pandit fell from his horse, from exhaustion, and was cut to pieces.† Híra Singh conti- nued his flight, and headed his pursuers : but imprudently stopping at a village to get a draught of water, he was sur- rounded and slain, after a desperate resistance. Jawáhir Singh in his turn, became unpopular with the *prœtorians* of Lahore, and was deliberately shot on parade. Lál Singh, the paramour of Ráni Chandán, then became nominally *wazir* ; but the Government was really the will of the army at Lahore. Irrita- tion at the defensive preparations made by the English Govern- ment, restlessness, and desire for plunder prompted the invasion of our territories on the 11th of December 1845. The battles of Mudki, Ferozeshah and Sobráon, and the occupation of Lahore followed ; then, at length, in the words of a local ballad, "sorrow was silenced, and the Sikh empire became a story of the past." ‡

The signature of the treaty of peace at Lahore on March 9th, 1846, was followed by importunate requests on the part of the *Darbár* that the Governor-General would lend a British force for the protection of the young Mahárája and his capital pending the reconstruction of the Government. The request was granted, but with the distinct assurance that the force would not be allowed to remain beyond the end of the year. When, however, the time came for its departure, at the earnest

---

* Sher Singh was far inferior in ability to his predecessor, Nau Nihál Singh. The most remarkable feature in his character was his love of dress ; he is said to have invented a very gaudy silk pattern which still bears his name.

† There are different accounts of this affair, but this is the one commonly received.

‡ Quoted from a spirited ballad current at Lahore, descriptive of the invasion of the British territory by the Sikhs, and the subsequent battles. Specimens will be found translated in Dr. Thornton's Historical Account of Lahore, published in 1860.

request of the most influential chiefs, Lord Hardinge gave a reluctant consent to a more permanent occupation. Then followed the celebrated assembly of the Sikh chiefs in the *Darbár* tent of the Resident and the new Convention signed on December 16th, 1846. A Council of Regency was appointed and the British Resident became the real depositary of authority throughout the province. The British troops had hitherto been quartered in the fort, but it was now determined to build a permanent cantonment; and before the end of 1847 barracks and bungalows had been erected sufficient for the requirements of the garrison. The cantonment occupied a strip of land to the south of the city. A spacious Residency, now occupied by the Secretariat Offices, was constructed, and a Muhammadan tomb was converted into a church. The occupation, however was not intended even then to be final. The arrangement was to last for eight years only, till Mahárája Dhulíp Singh should attain his majority. But circumstances occurred to change the whole policy of the Government towards the Punjab. Múlráj rebelled at Mooltan, and before the middle of 1848, the whole province was in flames. Lahore itself remained unmolested, but even here the position at one time was believed to be critical. All doubts were removed by the fall of Mooltan and the battle of Gujrát (February 22nd, 1849). On March 29th Lahore was once more the scene of a gathering of Sikh nobles. The young Mahárája took his seat for the last time on the throne of Ranjít Singh and in the presence of Sir Henry Lawrence, the Resident, and Mr. Elliot, the Foreign Secretary, and the nobles of his Court, heard Lord Dalhousie's proclamation read, and affixed his initials, in English characters, to the document which transferred the kingdom of the five rivers to the Company, and secured to him an annuity of £50,000 a year. The British colours were then hoisted on the ramparts, and Lahore became the capital of a British province.

The Mutiny.

The following account of the events of 1857 is taken from the Punjáb Mutiny Report :—

The Lahore Division is the chief Division of the Punjab. In it there lie the two largest commercial cities of this province, of which one is also the capital. The country-side is studded with the seats of the native nobility, who under the Sikh rule coveted grants in land in these districts as being near the metropolis and affording conveniences for their constant attendance at Court. The population of the Division amounts to one-third of the population of the whole Punjab. It is watered by four of the five rivers that give their name to the province. Its value as regards the preservation of British rule in India could not be overrated. These several circumstances greatly increased the labours and anxieties of the officers on whom the responsibility of preserving peace in it lay.

The important move which gave us a foothold in North India when the empire seemed well nigh overwhelmed by the flood of mutiny which had burst forth so uncontrollably in the North-Western Provinces, was the disarming of the troops at Mian Mír. The danger on the morning of May 13th was far greater than had been conceived. A plot had been laid for the simultaneous seizure of the fort and the outbreak of the troops in cantonments. To understand the importance of this move it must be borne in mind that the fort commands the city of Lahore ; that it contains the treasury and the arsenal ; that at Ferozepore, 50 miles distant, there is another arsenal, the largest in this part of India ; and had these two fallen, the North-Western Provinces and the Punjab must have been, for the time, irrevocably lost, the lives of all Europeans in these regions sacrificed, Delhi could not have been taken, and India must have been *ab initio* re-conquered. The designs of the conspirators were frustrated. By 5 A.M. of the 13th three companies of Her Majesty's 81st Foot marched into the fort and relieved the Native Infantry guard; while the ringing of the ramrods as the remaining companies of that regiment on the parade-ground at Mian Mír obeyed the order to load sounded the knell of sepoy power in the Punjab. The three regiments of Native Infantry and one of light cavalry were cowed by that stirring sound and by the sight of twelve Horse Artillery guns charged with destruction to them should they resist. The infantry piled arms and marched off with silent and angry astonishment. The cavalry unbuckled their swords and threw them on the ground, and the capital of the Punjab was saved. The next night, May 14th, at 10 P. M., Mr. Roberts, the Commissioner, accompanied by one Military and two Civil officers, brought Mr. Montgomery a paper, in the Persian character, which had just reached him with an injunction of secrecy from the writer. He writes : " It was a report from a Police Officer stationed on the Sutlej, giving a confused account of the attack on the Ferozepore entrenchment that afternoon by the 45th Native Infantry. It gave not any account of the result of the action. We conjectured that my express of the previous day to Brigadier Innes had failed of its design, that the sepoys had gained the arsenal, had crossed the bridge-of-boats, and were in full march on Lahore. In the earnest deliberation which ensued other circumstances occurred to our minds which seemed to make our position in Lahore critical to the last degree. A Punjabi police corps, the only one we had to carry on the civil duties, and which furnished personal guards to all the Civil officers at the station, was reputed to be disaffected. (Happily this turned out to be quite false.) Lieutenant Gulliver, Engineers, volunteered to ride off to cantonments to acquaint the Brigadier with what we had just learnt, and beg him to do what he could to defend himself. Messrs. Egerton, Deputy Commissioner, and Elliott, Assistant Commissioner, went round the station to take note of what might be going on. They returned reporting all quiet. Shortly afterwards, Lieutenant Gulliver also came back, bearing from Brigadier Corbett the joyful news of the repulse of the outbreak and the comparative safety of Ferozepore, the Brigadier having received a despatch direct from Brigadier Innes. There could be no doubt that there had been a plot arranged between the Lahore and Ferozepore brigades ; for on that same forenoon (May 14th) I received two hasty notes from Brigadier Corbett saying that all the troops in Mian Mír were preparing to desert bodily. This caused a panic among the residents of Anarkali, and a rendezvous of all male residents took place at the Central Jail. The guns and Her Majesty's 81st Regiment were, however, so quickly got ready that the natives retired into their lines. Some who did escape were seized by the villagers of the tract called the Majha, and taken to Mr. Thomas, Assistant Commissioner at Kasúr, the chief town of that part of the Majha which lies in the Lahore district, and on the direct route to Ferozepore. Mr. Thomas sent them into Lahore." The stalwart Sikhs who form the population of the Majha were wholly on our side throughout. Many villages have been almost decimated by the number of recruits who have flocked to form our new regiments in memory of the bygone days when they bravely fought against us under the banners of the Khálsa.

Defensive measures were at once adopted in Anárkalli as follows : The fort was provisioned for six months for 4,000 men, and every gate blocked up but one. All the men of the various Punjab regiments who happened to be on leave at their homes in this neighbourhood were called in and collected under the command of Captain Travers. They furnished picquets for guard all round the Central Jail and at other places where danger seemed to threaten. A company of volunteers from the European residents of Anárkalli was raised in 36 hours to the number of 130 men, and for some days Anárkalli was guarded only by them, a half company of Subhan Khan's Police Battalion, and a few ordinary police. A rendezvous was appointed, and danger signals arranged. A chain of mounted police was thrown out along the roads leading to cantonments, which for a length of time were patrolled during the night by the junior Civil and Military officers of the station. The usual precautions in regard to ferries, sepoys' letters, &c., were vigorously observed. On the 26th and 27th the Guide Corps passed through on their famous march to Delhi, and about a week afterwards the movable column under Brigadier Neville Chamberlain arrived. On June 9th two men of the 35th Native Infantry, which was one of the regiments composing the column, were blown from guns on the Anárkalli parade-ground, by sentence of a drum-head court-martial, for sedition and intended mutiny.

Chapter II.

History.

The Mutiny.

Various petty events occurred showing the excited state of men's minds. A trooper of the disarmed 10th Irregulars, on his way down with his regiment, seized a sword, and made a feint of attacking several persons, but gave up his weapon quietly at last. He was punished with five years' imprisonment. A man armed with a sword rushed out from one of the city gates, cut down the sentry, and was eventually shot by a mounted policeman while making for the bridge-of-boats. Many persons fell under suspicion from the discovery of papers which to say the least, were of very questionable loyalty, and several trials of such parties were held. The enigmatical way in which the papers were sometimes worded, or the care with which the real treason had been concealed, had the effect the criminals desired. No proof could be found, and in several cases it was found needful to release on security men whose characters were by no means immaculate. Those who could not give security were detained in jail. On the 23rd May the native newspapers were placed under a strict censorship, which was rigorously enforced, for some time after all disturbance had ceased. On the 23rd and 24th July restrictions were placed on the sale of lead, sulphur, percussion caps, &c. The Hindústáni population, including Civil officials and domestic servants, had been disarmed on the 29th June ; and on the 23rd August a census of all unemployed Hindústánís was taken, with a view to their expulsion The superintendence of this compulsory exodus and the arrest and deportation of numbers of vagrants formed no small part of the Deputy Commissioner's work. Bi-weekly *kafilas* were formed of Hindústánís. They were sent down to Harike ferry under guards of police, with lists signed by a District Officer, and duly checked at certain stations. As many as 2,536 Hindústánís were thus sent home during the siege and in the few weeks immediately succeeding the capture of Delhi.

On the 30th July the 26th Native Infantry mutinied at Mian Mír, and murdering Major Spencer, their commanding officer, one non-commissioned European and two Native officers, fled. They escaped during a heavy dust-storm which concealed them from observation and kept us in ignorance of their route. They were destroyed by Mr. Cooper, Deputy Commissioner of Amritsar, on the banks of the Rávi. This event showed the necessity for some means of tracking any future body of deserters, especially as the loyalty of the remaining regiments was very doubtful. Four strong police posts were established in villages which lie beyond the plain upon which the cantonment is built, and the men were instructed to throw out chains of sentries and to watch narrowly all passers-by. On the 17th September Mr. R. E. Egerton, Officiating Deputy Commissioner, was called suddenly down to the south-west part of his district in order to prevent the taint of the Kharral insurrection from reaching the Musalmán population of that part of the country. Mr. Perkins, Assistant Commissioner, was also for a few days stationed at a remote police post into the boundaries of which emissaries from the insurgents were known to have come. The appearance, with Mr. Egerton, of half a regiment of Wale's Horse, and other demonstrations, deterred the Kharrals of the district from joining their rebellious kinsmen. Mr. Egerton was out on another occasion for three or four weeks in company with the Commissioner, Mr. Roberts, in the Gugera district on similar duty. The civil charge of this important station was confided on these occasions to Mr. R. Berkeley, Extra Assistant Commissioner.

In the two jails at Lahore there were confined on the 11th May, 2,379 prisoners. It was not unreasonable to suppose that, should the native troops mutiny, they would release all these desperadoes, as they did at Agra and elsewhere. It was also likely that the troops themselves would have to be put in jail. Both these considerations pointed to the propriety of emptying the jails as far as possible. With this view, the Commissioner and Deputy Commissioner was authorised to release, on payment of a fine, or even in some cases unconditionally, all such men as were ill, disabled, or had nearly served out their terms. Obedience to this order reduced the numbers considerably. Instructions were also issued to Judicial officers to punish by fine and flogging as far as possible rather than by imprisonment. The jails were fortified, the draw-bridges removed, the guards strengthened, and a supply of blue-lights and rockets sent in to serve as signals in case of attack by night.

Famines.

The Solah famine 1759.

The famine which raged in A. D. 1759 was known by the name of Soláh. For two years previously there had been a dearth of rain. This famine lasted for four years, and was considerably aggravated by the invasion of Ahmad Sháh Abdal,

which happened about this time, and caused agriculture to be
neglected; the inhabitants fled to the Jummoo and Kángra
hills; cattle died, and those that remained were only kept
alive on the bark and leaves of trees; the people ate flour
made from the *jand* berries, called *sangri*; and the flower
of the *karil*, which flourishes best in dry weather, furnished
them with a sort of vegetable of a very poor description;
wheaten flour was four seers per rupee (8 lbs. for 2 shillings),
and then only obtainable with difficulty. The Government
of the day could afford no assistance; and mercifully in
A. D. 1761 a copious fall of rain averted further suffering;
the people returned from the hills, and cultivation was again
undertaken.

The second famine, which is still remembered, happened
about twenty years after this, and was at its worst A. D. 1783.
This was the most grievous of all, and was a very general one.
It is known under several names in different parts of the country,
and was here called Chália or Dahséra. In 1781 and 1782 no
rain fell for two years—the granaries supported the people;
but the Sikhs were plundering the country; and in 1783
wheaten flour was with difficulty obtainable at 2½ seers the
rupee (5 lbs for 2 shillings). The inhabitants, as usual, fled to
Hindústán and the hills; numbers died of starvation. The
seeds of the *kikar* tree and cotton seed are said to have been
greedily devoured. Many of the ruins of old villages are
traceable to this famine. The ravages caused during these
three years were fearful. To add to their misfortune, an insect
made its appearance, called *tittan,* which destroyed all herbage.
The cattle are said to have eaten the insect in their turn, and
the story goes that cow's milk in consequence turned blood-red;
the butter is said to have been eaten, but the butter-milk, of
which the agricultural class are so fond, had to be thrown
away. One blade of *chari* is said to have been sold for the
fabulous sum of Rs. 2; the consequence was that the cattle
nearly all died or were eaten up by the starving Muhammadans.
In 1785, rain again fell, and though the Sikhs were still
plundering, cultivation was resumed.

The next famine of any importance took place thirty years
after, or in A. D. 1813; but it was by no means so severe, and
assistance was at hand. This was called Lakiwála or Sátséra:
for one year previously no rain had fallen, and the price of
grain rose till seven seers only could be obtained for the rupee.
But, providentially a kind of grass sprang up, which was very
much like *khas khas,* or arrowroot, and supported the people
and the cattle were fed on leaves of trees and pounded cotton
stalks; but the country was not depopulated, as Mahárája
Ranjít Singh threw open his stores and granaries. In 1814
rain fell. Ranjít Singh made advances to the people, reduced
the share of grain due to Government, and in other ways
restored confidence.

Chapter II.

History.

Markanwála famine, 1833.

Again in A. D. 1823 the people were reduced almost to starvation. Grain fell to ten seers for the rupee and there was distress ; but rain fell in the following year, and there was plenty again for ten years till A. D. 1833, when the Markanwála famine arose, so called owing to a grass or plant which yielded a seed eaten by the poor people. Grain fell to eight or nine seers per rupee, but the famine was of short duration, and Mahárája Ranjít Singh again threw open his stores and assisted the people, notwithstanding which numbers are said to have died.

Famines of a later period, 1860 and 1867.

In 1860-61, and again in 1867-68, famine visited the land, but the district of Lahore suffered comparatively but little, except from the drain of grain, which was carried away to more distant markets. Grain fell even below seven sérs per rupee. Poor-houses were opened, and famine works commenced ; but the pricipal people who flocked to them were refugees from Málwa, Hissár, and Hindústán, where the famine raged with fearful violence.

Tendency of price in recent years.

The average price of wheat in the district was 16 seers the rupee in 1869 and 18 seers in 1870. In the city it varied between 11 and 15 seers. This was temporary however, being due solely to the scarcity of the two years 1867 to 1869. The price of wheat during the next six years fell, going down as low as 34 seers the rupee in 1877. Then came two bad years, the price of wheat went up to 13 seers the rupee in the Lahore city in 1879 ; largely in consequence of increase of exports during the Afghán war. The next three years' prices fell gradually and for four years wheat was selling cheap. After 1885 prices rose higher and higher, owing to the gradually increasing exportation to England, up to the year 1892, when an exceedingly bad rabi harvest followed on a poor kharíf. From May to July of that year the grain stores were being depleted rapidly all over the province, wheat was given up by the less well-to-do people as a food staple almost from April 1892 and large supplies of jowár were imported and consumed by all the poorer classes. When the monsoon had not reached the hills by the end of June it was confidently anticipated that famine works would have to be started shortly in the Lahore district. The villagers of the Sharakpur tahsíl for the most part moved away with their cattle in search of fodder. The Rávi people were in severe distress ; especially the menial classes. Fodder was very scarce, indeed almost unprocurable in all the well irrigated tracts of the district. Fortunately the monsoon broke about the middle of July and very heavy rain fell between that and the end of August. The next autumn harvest was middling ; the spring crop was very good ; the wheat crop especially was abundant, but the grain was said to be tainted in some way owing to the excessive damp and wet of the spring. Whether from this cause or owing to an immense falling off in the demand from England, much wheat remained on the hands of both growers and dealers at the end of September : From then the price of wheat fell gradually, and at the close of the year 1893 it was selling at 26 and 27 seers the rupee, while the price of gram had fallen to 38 seers the rupee or lower in parts of the district.

As originally constituted the district lay wholly in the Bári Doáb with the exception of 142 estates beyond the Rávi grouped in the Shahdára pergannah. . In 1855 a portion of the Shekhupura pergannah in the Gujránwála district, including 313 estates was added to the Lahore district. The Rávi was no longer retained as a sub-divisional boundary. Of the 455 Trans-Rávi estates, belonging to the district under the new constitution, 75 were attached according to their position to the Lahore or Chúnián tahsíl, and the remaining 380 estates were grouped in a seperate tahsíl with its head-quarters at Sharak-pur. In 1855 on the Rávi twenty-one estates were transferred from Lahore to Gugera, and four estates from Gugera to Lahore. Other changes have taken place since then owing to the action of the rivers.

On the Rávi the custom of *wár pár* or fixed boundary prevails between all villages situate within the Lahore district, but at the last six or eight miles of the river's course on the Lahore side of the Montgomery border the land and villages lying on the left or south side of the river belong to the Lahore district, and those on the right hand or north side to the Montgomery district. As between villages of different districts the boundary is regulated by the deep stream and is liable to change every year. As a matter of fact the river stream at this part is seldom violent, except in years of unusually copious rainfall ; and consequently changes of ownership rarely occur. In 1865 three Rávi estates were transferred from Gugera to Lahore ; otherwise no entire villages have been moved from one side to the other, though as late as 1892 the river made a considerable detour to the right and added a largish slice of land to the left bank. On the Sutlej which flows between the Lahore and Ferozepore districts, changes of land and of whole estates from one side to another have been frequent. In 1864, 13 estates changed sides and 20 in 1874. In 1881, 12 entire estates and parts of five others were transferred from the Lahore to the Ferozepore side. In 1883 ten entire estates and parts of some others came across to the Lahore side ; in other years changes were going on, but not on so large a scale. The boundary along this river is regulated under the same rules as those which prevail between Lahore and Montgomery villages. That is land destroyed by the river and washed up again belongs to the owners of the land on to which it washes. Land transferred by avulsion or change of front (*rugirdáni*) from one side of the deep stream of the river to the other in a recognizable form does not change ownership. The proprietary right only changes in land which has lost its identity. This rule is subject to certain minor provisions of which an important one is that when a village has been totally submerged and all the land destroyed then, on any part of it emerging afterwards, the

Constitution of the District.

Riparian custom.

Chapter II

History.

Constitution of the District.

former owners are entitled to claim and not the people on to whose property the newly emerged land has washed. Formerly land transferred from one side of the river to the other whether by avulsion or by gradual erosion, used to change its district. That is land transferred from the Lahore side to the Ferozepore side, was lost to the Lahore district and became included in the Ferozepore district and *vice versâ*. This led to much administrative inconvenience both for Government and for the people. Now under recent notifications of the Punjab Government each of the river estates has been attached finally to one district or the other, and land only changes its district jurisdiction where it is transferred under river action and the customs observed from the landowners of one district to the landowners of the others.

Development since annexation.

Some conception of the development of the district since it came into our hands may be gathered from Table No. II, which gives some of the leading statistics, so far as they are available; while most of the other tables appended to this work give comparative figures for the last few years.

District Officers.

The following table shows the Officers who have held charge of the district of late years:—

Names of Officers.			From		To.	
C. U. Aitchison, Esq. ...	...	...	1st November	1866	... 15th August	1867.
J. W. Smyth, Esq. ...	...	...	16th August	1867	... 3rd August	1868.
B. H. Baden-Powell, Esq. ...	...	...	4th August	1868	... 2nd October	1868.
J. W. Smyth, Esq. ...	...	...	3rd October	1868	... 19th July	1869.
Lepel H. Griffin, Esq. ...	...	...	20th July	1869	... 7th November	1869.
F. P. Beachcroft, Esq. ...	...	...	8th November	1869	... 17th April	1870.
F. E. Moore, Esq. ...	...	...	18th April	1870	... 1st September	1870.
E. O'Brien, Esq. ...	...	...	2nd September	1870	... 30th October	1870.
F. E. Moore, Esq. ...	...	...	31st October	1870	... 15th May	1871.
D. G. Barkley, Esq. ...	...	...	16th May	1871	... 24th January	1872.
J. W. Smyth, Esq. ...	...	...	25th January	1872	... 9th April	1872.
C. R. Hawkins, Esq. ...	...	...	10th April	1872	... 4th November	1872.
J. W. Smyth, Esq. ...	...	...	5th November	1872	... 31st March	1873.
C. R. Hawkins, Esq. ...	...	...	1st April	1873	... 13th April	1873.
Captain R. P. Nisbet ...	...	...	14th April	1873	... 30th August	1873.
C. R. Hawkins, Esq. ...	...	...	1st September	1873	... 9th November	1873.
Captain R. P. Nisbet ...	...	...	10th November	1873	... 18th November	1873.
J. W. Smyth, Esq. ...	...	...	19th November	1873	... 25th March	1874.
Captain R. P. Nisbet ...	...	...	26th March	1874	... 16th August	1874.
H. W. Steel, Esq. ...	...	...	17th August	1874	... 27th September	1874.
Captain R. P. Nisbet ...	...	...	28th September	1874	... 20th January	1875.
J. W. Smyth, Esq. ...	...	...	21st January	1875	... 2nd February	1875.
Captain R. P. Nisbet ..	...	...	3rd February	1875	... 28th February	1877.
G. Smyth, Esq. ..	...	...	1st March	1877	... 30th August	1877.
F. Bullock, Esq. ...	...	...	31st August	1877	... 19th September	1877.
G. Smyth, Esq. ...	...	...	20th September	1877	... 31st January	1878.
Major A. F. P. Harcourt	...	...	1st February	1878	... 6th July	1878.
F. Bullock, Esq. ...	...	...	6th July	1878	... 30th August	1878.
Baron J. Bentinck ...	...	...	1st September	1878	... 1st September	1878.
Major A. F. P. Harcourt	...	...	2nd September	1878	... 27th May	1879.
Captain J. B. Hutchinson	...	...	28th May	1879	... 18th June	1879.
Major A. F. P. Harcourt	...	...	19th June	1879	... 30th July	1879.
Captain J. B. Hutchinson	...	...	31st July	1879	... 29th September	1879.
Major A. F. P. Harcourt	...	...	30th September	1879	... 10th March	1880.
A. W. Stogdon, Esq. ...	...	...	11th March	1880	... 6th February	1881.
Colonel C. Beadon	...	...	7th February	1881	... 4th January	1882.
R. Clark, Esq. ...	...	...	5th January	1882	... 20th January	1882.
Colonel C. Beadon	...	...	21st January	1882	... 18th August	1883.
C. P. Bird, Esq. ...	...	...	19th August	1883	... 19th September	1883.
Colonel C. Beadon	...	...	20th September	1883	... 1st June	1883.
W. O. Clark, Esq. ...	...	...	2nd June	1883	... 23rd December	1883.

Names of Officers.	From			To	
Colonel C. Beadon	...	...	...	24th December	1883	...	2nd April	1884.
W. O. Clark, Esq.	...	...	...	3rd April	1884	...	15th July	1886.
R. L. Harris, Esq.	...	...	...	16th July	1886	...	23rd October	1886.
W. O. Clark, Esq.	...	...	...	24th October	1886	...	30th July	1888.
Colonel R. Bartholomew	...	...	...	31st July	1888	...	27th September	1888.
W. O. Clark, Esq.	...	...	...	28th September	1888	...	20th March	1889.
Colonel C. Beadon	...	...	...	21st March	1889	...	20th April	1889.
A. Meredeth, Esq.	...	...	...	21st April	1889	...	20th October	1889.
Colonel C. Beadon	...	...	...	21st October	1889	...	6th April	1890.
D. C. J. Ibbetson, Esq.	...	...	...	7th April	1890	...	23rd June	1890.
G. C. Walker, Esq.	...	...	...	24th June	1890	...	27th July	1890.
T. J. Kennedy, Esq.	...	...	...	28th July	1890	...	5th October	1890.
Colonel C. Beadon	...	...	...	6th October	1890	...	12th August	1891.
A. Williams, Esq.	...	...	...	13th August	1891	...	31st October	1891.
Colonel C. Beadon	...	...	...	1st November	1891	...	25th March	1892.
R. M. Dane, Esq.	...	...	...	26th March	1892	...	25th April	1892.
Lieut. C. P. Egerton	...	...	...	26th April	1892	...	5th May	1892.
A. Williams, Esq.	...	...	...	6th May	1892	...	29th July	1892.
H. C. Fanshawe, Esq.	...	...	...	30th July	1892	...	25th February	1893.
A. E. Hurry, Esq.	...	...	...	26th February	1893	...	To date.	

CHAPTER III.

THE PEOPLE.

SECTION A.—STATISTICAL.

Table No. V gives separate statistics for each tahsíl, and for the whole district, of the total area cultivated, culturable and cropped, of the total population, urban and rural, and of its distribution over the area, of the inhabited villages classified according to the population they contain, of the revenue estates uninhabited, and lastly of the number of occupied houses and resident families, these being given separately for towns and villages. Of the uninhabited revenue estates most are those the cultivators of which live within the boundaries of another estate, some few are waste areas which have not been cultivated for some reason, and a few more are very small estates in Sharakpur tahsíl in which no one happened to be residing on the census night.

The town population in each tahsíl is shown below, all places being classed as towns which have been constituted municipalities. There are four other places, two in Kasúr and two in Lahore tahsíl, which have a population of over 5,000 souls, but in para. 15 of Chapter I of the Provincial Census Report of 1891 it is stated that the fact of the population being over 5,000 souls only constituted the place as urban, provided it was also possessed of some real urban characteristics, such as a bázár or the like :—

| Tahsíl. | Name of town. | POPULATION. | | |
		Males.	Females.	Total.
LAHORE ...	Lahore	92,835	66,762	159,597
	Meean Meer Cantonment	11,875	5,382	17,257
CHÚNIÁN ...	Chúnián	5,532	4,807	10,339
	Khudián	1,526	1,395	2,921
KASÚR ...	Kasúr	10,596	9,694	20,290
	Khem Karn	3,215	2,720	5,935
	Patti	3,816	3,679	7,495
SHARAKPUR ...	Sharakpur	2,541	2,383	4,924

The statistics for the district as a whole give the following figures. In all calculations regarding the village unit, the uninhabited estates have been excluded : the word village being used in the popular sense of a collection of inhabited houses. The corresponding figures recorded in the Gazetteer of 1883-84 are shown for purposes of comparison :—

			1881.	1891.
Percentage of total population who live in villages {	Persons	...	77·90	78·73
	Males	...	77·12	77·73
	Females	...	78·79	79·96
Average rural population per village		...	487	559
Average total population per village and town		...	622	706
Number of villages per 100 square miles		...	41	42
Density of population per square mile of { Total area {	Total population	...	253	299
	Rural do.	...	197	235
Cultivated area {	Total do.	...	507	555
	Rural do.	...	395	437
Cultivated and culturable area {	Total do.	...	299	378
	Rural do.	...	233	298
Number of resident families per occupied house. {	Villages	...	1·08	1·49
	Towns	...	1·45	1·37
Number of persons per occupied house ... {	Villages	...	5·75	7·17
	Towns	...	5·83	6·02
Number of persons per resident family ... {	Villages	...	5·31	4·85
	Towns	...	4·01	4·39

The number of inhabited villages in the whole district has increased in the last ten years from 1,486 to 1,515. Most of the new *mauzás* have been created very recently in the Mánjha tract, where the enormous development of cultivation during the last 20 years due to the extension of the Bári Doáb Canal and increased feeling of security have led in many estates to some of the shareholders breaking their connection with the ancestral homestead and setting up separate habitations on the land they hold in cultivation. When the division of interests between the people left in the old homesteads and those established in the new could be shown to be complete, the latter were with the Financial Commissioner's sanction treated at the settlement lately concluded as belonging to a separate *mauza :* otherwise applications for the recognition of such newly separated establishments as distinct land revenue units were discouraged. The total area according to the new measurements of the settlement just finished shows a falling off of 46 square miles on that recorded at last census, which accounts for a large portion of the increase in the density of population per square mile of total area. Notwithstanding the large extension of cultivation of late years, in the period between the two census, it was out-paced by the increase of population, density per square mile of cultivated area being now more than 10 per cent. in excess of what it was in 1881. Little weight can be placed on the relation of the population to the culturable area as recorded ; for much of the land which the official returns show as culturable waste is either very inferior soil which practically would not return the cost of tillage, or would only be culturable under irrigation of which no hope can be entertained. The number of people to each hundred occupied houses in villages is now more by 142 than it was ten years ago. This is of course partly explained by the increase that has taken place in the rural population; but the chief cause is the extraordinary falling off shown by the figures in the number of occupied houses, and this notwithstanding a large increase in the number of resident families. The figures from each census give the following results as to the average size of the rural family and average number of each occupied house for the several tahsils:—

		Lahore.	Chúnián.	Kasúr.	Sharakpur.
Average number of persons in each rural family.	1881	4·2	4·8	9·4	4·9
	1891	4·8	4·9	4·8	4·8
Average number in each occupied house in villages.	1881	6·1	5·2	5·9	5·7
	1891	6·8	7·9	7·9	5·6

The figures for Sharakpur tahsil are consistent: those for Lahore tahsil show that the number of resident families and of occupied houses there have not increased in proportion to the population which is contrary to the general tendency towards severalty observed elsewhere. In Chúnián tahsil the number of occupied houses has been reduced by 9,230, while rural population has increased 14 per cent. In Kasúr tahsil there has been a slight decrease in the number of occupied houses, but in the number of resident families there has been an increase out of all proportion to that in population. The inconsistencies in the two latter tahsils between the various sets of figures can only be due to aberrations in classification at one or the other census; probably the earlier. The average size of the family shown by the later figures is normal. The numbers per occupied house in each tahsil are not inconsistent with the different conditions of each. In Kasúr and Chúnián land is plentiful and only in recent years has a fresh value been added to much of it by extension of canal irrigation. There has therefore not been time for development of mutual distrust which prevents families from living in the same enclosure or *ahata* which is the word used to denote a *house* for census purposes.

Table No. VI shows the districts and principal States with which the district of Lahore has exchanged population and the number of migrants in each direction. Further details will be found at page LXXVI, *et seq.* of the Census Report for 1891, and the subject is discussed at length in Chapter X of that report. The total number of residents born out of the district is 222,309, among whom males slightly predominate in numbers

over females. The percentage of these on the total population of the district is between 20 and 21, as it was in 1881.

Chapter III, A.

Statistical.

Migration a n d
birth-place of popu-
lation.

The total number of residents of other Punjab districts
born in the Lahore district is 87,406, of whom a little more than
half are women.

The figures below show the general distribution of the
population by birth-place :—

| Born in | PROPORTION PER MILLE OF RESIDENT POPULATION. | | | | | | | | |
| | Rural population. | | | Urban population. | | | Total population. | | |
	Males.	Females.	Persons.	Males.	Females.	Persons.	Males.	Females.	Persons.
The District ...	876	817	850	533	660	587	799	786	796
The Province...	996	998	997	899	940	916	974	986	979
India ...	999	1,000	1,000	984	996	989	996	999	997
Asia ...	1,000	1,000	1,000	987	997	991	997	999	998

The attractive influence of a large city and the capital of the
province is at once apparent from the figures : for while nearly
850 per cent. of the rural population is indigenous to the district,
no less than 413 per cent. of the town residents were born outside the limits of the district and about 84 per cent. beyond the
jurisdiction of the province : 11 *per mille* of the urban population
come from outside India, of whom only two belong to Asiatic
countries.

In the rural tracts the indigenous population is swollen
by immigrant cultivators from the more congested districts of
Amritsar, Siálkot, Gujránwála and Gujrát, the attraction being
the excellent canal irrigation and abundant surplus land of the
Mánjha tract where the population is not yet even sufficient to
ensure good and careful cultivation. There are however indications of increasing jealousy on the part of the Mánjha villagers against admitting outsiders, and it is therefore possible
that immigration to the rural tracts of this district will not be
maintained in the future at the same rate as heretofore.

For Gujránwála and Gujrát and Jhang, which also have
hitherto supplied immigrants to this district in considerable
number, fresh fields have been recently opened up by the extension
of the Chenáb Canal in the Bár tract. The only district with
which the exchange of migration is largely against Lahore is
that of Ferozepore, where canal irrigation is abundantly supplied from the Sutlej river to the adjoining lowlands and

Chapter III, A.

Statistical.

Migration and birth-place of population.

population is scanty in proportion to the culturable area. Consequently all the Hithár villages in Lahore district that are overcrowded send men over there.

The following statement shows the proportion of male and female migrants from and to the districts between which and Lahore exchange is most prominent :—

DISTRICT.		MIGRATION TO LAHORE.			MIGRATION FROM LAHORE.		
		Males.	Females.	Total.	Males.	Females.	Total.
Siálkot	... ...	19,258	12,823	32,081	1,178	1,985	3,163
Gujránwála	... ...	14,648	15,301	29,949	3,455	649	4,104
Gujrát	... ...	10,322	1,639	11,961	250	646	896
Gurdáspur	... ...	5,233	6,613	11,846	895	1,137	2,032
Ferozepore	... ...	5,820	8,431	14,251	13,352	11,940	25,292
Amritsar ·	... ...	20,077	32,279	52,356	6,911	14,368	21,279
Montgomery	... ...	8,629	8,271	16,900	8,106	8,452	16,558

From the figures it would appear that the immigration from the first four districts named is of the permanent kind. The exchange made with Ferozepore and Amritsar is partly permanent and partly reciprocal, owing to exchange of women in marriage. The migration between Lahore and Montgomery appears to be reciprocal both in the ordinary and in the technical sense.

The Siálkot, Gujránwála, Gujrát and Gurdáspur districts send immigrants almost entirely to the Lahore tahsíl of this district. Amritsar send them to the Lahore and Kasúr tahsíls, Montgomery to the Chúnián tahsíl and Ferozepore to Kasúr and Chúnián tahsíls.

ncrease and decrease of population.

The figures given below show the population of the district as it stood at the four enumerations of 1855, 1868, 1881 and 1891 :—

Census.			Persons.	Males.	Females.	Density per square mile.
Actuals ...	1855	... ...	700,136	...	...	193
	1868	... ...	788,409	437,626	350,783	218
	1881	... ...	924,106	510,353	413,753	253
	1891	... ...	1,075,379	592,293	483,086	298
Percentages.	1868 on 1855	...	112·63	...	...	113
	1881 on 1868	...	117·21	116·62	117·95	116
	1891 on 1881	...	116·37	116·06	116·76	118

The district had undergone a good many changes of boundary between the first census of 1855 and that of 1868. The figures shown above for 1855 were obtained by adding to the census figures for the district as it then stood the population of the villages which were subsequently attached to the

district, and deducting the population of the villages subsequently transferred to other districts.

It will be seen that the annual increase of population per
10,000 since 1881, has been
161 for males, 167 for females
and 164 for persons. Sup-
posing the same rate of increase to hold good for the
next ten years, the population for each year would be as
shown in the margin. That
is by next census the population will have increased another sixteen per cent. How
far this anticipation may be
realized is difficult to say.
The recent increase has taken
place chiefly in villages and

Chapter III, A.
Statistical.
Increase and de-
crease of population.

	Persons.	Males.	Females.
1892 ...	10,929	6,018	4,911
1893 ...	11,108	6,115	4,933
1894 ...	11,290	6,217	5,077
1895 ...	11,475	6,313	5,162
1896 ...	11,663	6,415	5,248
1897 ...	11,854	6,518	5,336
1898 ...	12,048	6,623	5,425
1899 ...	12,245	6,730	5,515
1900 ...	12,445	6,838	5,607
1901 ...	12,649	6,948	5,701

not in towns : though in parts the land is sufficiently stocked
with people, yet in Chunián tahsil where a considerable extension of irrigation from the Bári Doáb Canal will shortly be
effected, a rapid increase of population is sure to take place
during the next few years. Moreover in the more closely
populated parts of the Mánjha though immigrant strangers are
not regarded with favour, yet the pressure of the present
numbers of owners and cultivators is still much below what the
land could bear, and there is every reason to expect that the
people of the whole Mánjha tract, if their present conditions of
prosperity continue, will go on multiplying in numbers for
some time to come. It is noteworthy that the increase of
population between 1881 and 1891 was more rapid than between 1868 and 1881, notwithstanding predictions to the
contrary at last census.

The distribution of population over tahsils at each census
is shown below :—

Increase of popu-
lation in tahsils.

Tahsil.	Total population.				Percentage of increase.		
	1855.	1868.	1881.	1891.	1868 on 1855.	1881 on 1868.	1891 on 1881.
Lahore ...	292,436	306,832	370,796	430,378	5	21	16
Kasúr ...	156,908	197,667	229,798	280,647	26	16	22
Chúnián ...	138,653	167,465	202,061	230,897	21	21	14
Sharakpur	112,139	117,710	121,451	133,457	5	3	10
Total ...	700,136	789,666	924,106	1,075,379	13	17	16

Chapter III, A.
———
Statistical.
Increase of popu-
lation in tahsíls.

Chúnián and Kasúr tahsíls were greatly reduced immediately after the first summary assessment, partly owing to over-
assessment and partly to bad seasons which occurred just
then. The assessments were largely decreased at the first
regular settlement ; people gradually returned to their villages
and took up the cultivation of the land with increased vigor.
This change in revenue administration between 1855 and 1868
probably accounts partially for the rapid increase of population
in that interval. The extension of the Bári Doáb Canal affected
the entire Mánjha tract lying within all three of the Cis-Rávi
tahsíls more or less from 1868, but Lahore tahsíl was the first
to benefit. At the same time the Hithár tract of Chúnián
tahsíl was having its resources partially developed by improvement of the Sutlej Inundation Canals. The effect of the canal
extension in Kasúr tahsíl was most conspicuous during the last
decade. As already remarked there is plenty of room for
further development during the next ten or twenty years in
Chúnián tahsíl. Sharakpur has hitherto been unfortunate in
its revenue history, and agriculture there has fallen into a
depressed condition : consequently its population has increased
but slowly. Its assessments have lately been revised, and
possibly its cultivation may now improve so as to attract fresh
immigrants from the more congested parts of Siálkot.

Table No. XI shows the births and deaths of males and
females in urban and rural tracts from 1882 to 1891, and the
diseases from which the deaths were caused. Of the total
number born during the ten years in the whole district nearly
54 per cent. were males and slightly over 46 per cent. were
females. In the same interval deaths occurred in the proportion of 53 per cent. for males, to 47 per cent. for females.

It is noteworthy that in towns the number of deaths
during the last ten years has exceeded the number of births by
1,478, while in villages births have exceeded deaths by 98,760.
These figures furnish strong testimony to the general unhealthiness of town life as compared with village. Latterly the
number of deaths recorded in towns has been increasing considerably year by year. Possibly, this is due in part to the
unhealthiness of the years 1889 and 1890, but also no doubt it
arises from the town statistics being recorded more and more
faithfully each year.

The birth and death statements for villages being based
on reports made by the village watchmen to the police, are
hardly reliable except for comparison of the results for different years. The actual number of births and deaths is probably
much understated, but there is no reason for supposing those
of one year more understated than those of another. Births
were fewest in 1881 when the people were slowly recovering
from a long period of agricultural depression; they fell very
low from a similar cause in 1887 and again in 1891. The
death-rate was determined largely by the greater or less

malignity of the autumn fever, as for instance in 1890, when the highest death-rate in all ten years occurred, and 76 per cent. of the total number of deaths were apparently caused by fever.

Statement No. XI A. shows the number of deaths registered from all causes, month by month, during the last ten years, and Statement No. XI B. shows the number registered as due to fever each month. These indicate that for the number of deaths that occur there is little to choose between the three months of October, November and December, while the fewest occur in the month of April.

The figures below show the annual birth and death rates since 1881, calculated per *mille* on the population of that year.

	1882.	1883.	1884.	1885.	1886.	1887.	1888.	1889.	1890.	1891.	Average.
BIRTHS.											
Males ...	37	41	46	43	41	38	42	45	41	40	41
Females ...	40	43	49	45	43	41	45	48	45	42	44
Persons ...	38	42	47	44	42	40	44	46	43	41	43
DEATHS.											
Males ...	27	24	31	25	26	33	30	35	47	33	31
Females ...	29	26	34	26	28	34	34	38	51	33	31
Persons ...	28	25	33	25	27	33	32	37	49	33	32

In the whole ten years the total number of births in the district has exceeded that of deaths by 9 for every hundred of the present population as enumerated at the census of 1891.

Further details as to the number of births and deaths registered in towns will be found in Table No. XLIV.

The figures showing ages of the people of each religion are furnished in Table No. VII of the Census Report of 1891. The data as to age are very uncertain, partly owing to the vague ideas as to their real age, which it is natural an uneducated peasantry would have, and partly to the persistent tendency of the people to prefer certain numbers to others in representing their age. It was not found in 1891 that middle aged females were given to understate their age, but there was a tendency on the part of the old to exaggerate their years, and the ages of marriageable girls are misrepresented. The following figures show the distribution by age of every ten thousand of the population according to the census figures :—

Chapter III. A.

Statistical.

Age, sex and civil condition.

	Under 1 year.	1 year.	2 years.	3 years.	4 years.	5 to 9 years.	10 to 14 years.	15 to 19 years.	20 to 24 years.	25 to 29 years.	30 to 34 years.	35 to 39 years.	40 to 44 years.	45 to 49 years.	50 to 54 years.	55 to 60 years.	Over 60 years.
Persons	446	234	317	303	342	1,426	940	1,111	986	977	507	633	300	577	156	363	300
Males	419	316	209	293	336	1,403	987	1,096	988	968	614	610	313	489	175	373	324
Females	480	339	340	315	348	1,453	882	1,128	991	988	577	661	285	671	133	350	275

Lahore District.]

CHAP. III.—THE PEOPLE. 59

Chapter III, A.

Statistical.

Age, sex and civil
condition.

These figures differ largely from those compiled in the same way from the Census Returns of 1881. The reasons for this difference are given at pages 203 and 204 of the Census Report. A different system of classification was adopted in 1891, in order to bring the results into harmony with those obtained at the time of abstraction in other Provinces. It is always found that the figure 10 and the multiples of 10 are excessively popular with uneducated people when stating their ages, and after them come the uneven multiples of five. Forty, for instance, is more commonly given as an age than either 35 or 45 ; and according as those returning their age as 40 are placed in the column for the age period 35 to 39 or in that for the age period 40 to 44, a difference results. Comparing ages in different religions we find that the Sikhs are much longer lived than either Musalmáns or Hindús. This is due to nearly all the Sikhs being engaged in healthy agricultural pursuits, while a considerable proportion in the two other religions live and work in towns.

The marginal statement shows the number of female children under ten years old to every 1,000 males for each separate religion. The proportion of Sikh female children is lower than that of female children in other religions.

Years of life.	All religions.	Hindús.	Sikhs.	Musalmáns.
Under one year	938	947	745	978
One year	875	871	667	929
Two years	928	915	709	988
Three years	877	852	691	935
Four years	845	848	662	877
Five to nine years ...	845	850	693	881

It is also a noticeable feature that whereas among the Hindús and Muhammadans the girls under ten years of age bear a larger proportion to the total number of females than the boys under ten do to all males, among Sikhs the reverse is the case. Figures are given in the margin. This and the fact that the proportion of females altogether is smaller among the Sikhs than in other religions point to the Sikhs being more careless of their female children than the people of other religions. The matter will be found fully discussed in paras. 163 to 170 of Mr. Maclagan's Census Report, 1891.

Religion.	Sex.	Percentages to totals.	
		0—4	5—9
Hindús ...	Male	16	14
	Female	19	15
Sikhs ...	Male	17	15
	Female	15	13
Muhammadans.	Male	17	14
	Female	19	51

The proportion of women in each religion in this dis-

Chapter III, A.

Statistical.

Age, sex and civil condition.

trict is compared with the corresponding figures showing provincial averages. The falling-off in this district is remarkable under each religion and on the whole number of women; but no reason for it that can command confidence has yet been suggested. Certainly the Lahore district has a higher death-rate than any other in the Province and there is a considerably

Religion.	Provincial average.	Lahore District.
All religions ...	850	816
Hindús	841	763
Sikhs	778	757
Musalmáns	871	851

higher mortality among females than among males, the difference due to which necessarily increases as the death-rate grows larger; no other peculiar causes likely to affect this district more than others are known at present. As regards the general deficiency of females as compared with males the common explanation given is the tendency on the part of the people to omit the women from enumeration either because they look on any enquiry regarding their women as an intrusion on their privacy or because they consider their inclusion or omission a matter of no moment to the authorities. The gradual improvement being made in this respect at each succeeding census is proved from the following statement which shows the number of males among every 10,000 of both sexes :—

	Years.	Villages.	Towns.	Total.
All religions	1855	...	...	5,698
	1868	...	...	5,551
	1881	5,470	5,710	5,523
	1891	5,438	5,767	5,508
Hindús	1891	5,506	5,987	5,641
Sikhs	1891	5,643	6,457	5,691
Musalmáns	1891	5,344	5,578	5,401
Christians	1891	5,778	6,428	6,336

Civil condition.

The civil condition of the people by religion and age is shown in Table No. VIII of the Census Report for the Province and Table No. X appended to this work shows the actual number of single, married, and widowed, for each sex, in each religion, and also the distribution, by civil condition, of, the total number of each sex at their different ages. The figures speak for themselves. All that need be noticed further is that the number of Sikh women married is much larger in proportion than in other religions. For further remarks on the subject of marriage, Chapter VI of Mr. Maclagan's Census Report should be read.

Table No. XII shows the numbers of insane, blind, deaf-mutes, and lepers in the district classified according to age. The proportions per 10,000 of either sex for each of these infirmities are shown in the margin.

Infirmities.	Male.	Females.
Insane	6	3
Blind	39	42
Deaf and dumb ...	10	7
Leprous	1	...

Those were classed at the census as insane, who were stated to be of unsound mind by the head of the family. In this country unsoundness of mind is not a matter of shame among the connections of the person afflicted, but of pity and even respect. Thus there is no reason why this infirmity should be concealed. The rate of insanity for the Province is four to every ten thousand among males and two among females. The rate therefore in this district is exceptionally high.

Only those were to be recorded as blind who were totally blind of both eyes. Probably however some have been included who were partially blind of both eyes. If so, this mistake was apparently made to a smaller extent in 1881 as the rates there shown for every ten thousand males and females were respectively 56 and 59. The large decrease exhibited in the figures of 1891 must no doubt be partly due to more careful enumeration, but it is also capable of explanation in large part at least by reference to the decrease in small-pox under the influence of extended vaccine operations and to the immensely improved facilities that now exist for eye treatment in the numerous dispensaries and hospitals at work in Lahore.

Deaf-mutes include only those who have been deaf and dumb from birth. There is a total increase of 194 or 26 per cent. on the number recorded in 1881. This is singular, but admits of no reliable explanation, save on the score of the greater accuracy of the later returns. It is not easy to ascertain whether children under two years old say are deaf and dumb; also there is a natural reluctance on the parents' part to declare the child deaf and dumb.

For further information on the subject of the above infirmities Chapter VII and Abstracts 42 to 50 of the Census Report for 1891 may be consulted.

The figures given below show the numbers of those who returned their birth-place and their language as European. They are taken from Tables Nos. X and XI of the Census Report for 1891.

Chapter III, B.

Social.

European and
Eurasian popula-
tion.

Details.		Males.	Females.	Total.
Language ... {	English	2,727	1,323	4,050
	Other European languages	39	25	64
	Total European languages ...	2,766	1,348	4,114
Birth-place ... {	British Isles	1,598	293	1,891
	Other European countries	52	11	63
	America	13	8	21
	Total ...	1,663	312	1,975

The foreigners speaking other European languages than
English are naturally comparatively numerous in a large
commercial centre like Lahore. No doubt a number of people
who were really Eurasians returned themselves as Europeans.
The number of European troops stationed in the district is
given in Chapter V.

SECTION B.—SOCIAL.

City life in
Lahore.

To the casual European visitor the city of Lahore is
chiefly interesting for its tombs, mosques and other buildings
which are still left standing as reminiscences of the many
changes of dynasty, in which Lahore has ever played so prominent a part since the extinction of the Hindu principality
in the eleventh century. The history and an account of its
chief buildings, both old and new, are furnished in Chapter VI
of this work. The following is an attempt to give a brief
sketch of inner native life in the city, which must necessarily
be sadly wanting in detail owing to the proverbial ignorance
of Europeans on all such subjects. The streets of Lahore
city are for the most part narrow and winding, the houses
though lofty and to all appearance well built from the outside yet inside are much cramped for space and ill-ventilated.
They generally consist of three or four storeys high, built of
burnt bricks laid in mortar. Very few have even a courtyard in front. On the basement floor is a small dark room,
in which the women of the house spend most of their day,
spinning, cleaning cotton, or working with their needles. Next
this room is a small cell, perhaps 5 or 6 feet square, in which
the grain is ground for cooking, generally by an old woman
who has no other means of earning her livelihood. On the
floor above is a small room used as a kitchen, from which
perhaps a window opens out into the narrow alley outside, or
a skylight lets in light from above. Adjoining it are two
small rooms (*kothris*), of which one is used for a general
store-room and the other as a depository for the family valu-

ables. The third floor generally has three sleeping rooms, all very small, ill-ventilated and hemmed in on three sides by the walls of adjoining houses. In these also property may be stored and, if necessary, food is cooked. The fourth floor contains but one small room at the back, the remainder being an open place in front in a corner of which is a very small latrine. This space and the open roof above are used as a sleeping shed; the latrine is the only convenience of the sort available to all residents of the house, male or female; an open drain (*parnáláh*) leads down the front wall of the house into the alley below, where it is carried off by an open saucer gutter into the main drain in the adjoining street. The filthy indecency and the unwholesomeness of the whole arrangement may be left to the imagination. Night soil and other filths are carried off only once in 24 hours, and before being finally taken to the conservancy carts are stored in one place in the alley exposed to public view. The Municipal Committee has done much to improve the sanitary arrangements of the public thoroughfares, but improvement of the inner alleys and poorer peoples' residences is impossible so long as they are so cramped for space. Even the main streets and bazárs are many of them too narrow to allow of two carts passing, except at certain places purposely widened out. From early morning till 10 or 11 A.M. the conservancy carts are waiting about to be filled up and driven off through the gates. Thus the ordinary citizens' residence in Lahore, as in all other large native towns, is beset with the most unwholesome conditions both inside and outside; any educated member of the native community who can afford it, builds himself a house outside these unhealthy surroundings and pays some attention to ventilation and other sanitary requirements, but so far progress in this respect has been very slight. The furniture in most of the city houses is of the barest description. A piece of carpet or a *munj* mat, a few wooden boards, some reed stools about half a foot high, woven with cotton thread, and a number of ordinary cots complete the furniture of an ordinary trader's house.

The city people are roused from their sleep by the Mulláh's call to morning prayers, by the ringing of bells in the Hindu temples, the grinding of corn for the day's food, and other numerous discordant sounds which render sleep in the city after dawn almost impossible. The Musalmán performs his ablutions and repairs to the mosque for morning prayer, while his women folk pray at home. The Hindu bathes and proceeds to a neighbouring temple for his *puja*; the more devout among the men and many of the Hindu women going to the Rávi for choice, as bathing in a river is considered to be a virtue. Not a few bathe at the tanks and streams running outside the city gates; or at the wells which are found in every alley or street. The house-wife first sweeps the floor and then has her bath in the house; after which she gets ready the morning meal; of this first the males partake and after them the females, who then clean the cooking utensils and tidy up the house. The men having eaten their food go off to their day's work. The women pursue their industries, the most common of which is the spinning wheel (*charkha*). Both cotton and wool are spun, but as the European made cloth can be had more cheaply than home made, the spinning of cotton is on the decline and is being replaced by more profitable occupations, such as silk embroidery or what is generally known as *phulkari* making. Sheets of home made cotton cloth, *khaddar painsi*, &c., dyed with *majith* or *maddera*, are worked in various colours, the embroidery taking the shape of flowers, creepers, &c. The silk work is sometimes studded with small pieces of glass. These *phulkáris* are worn by married girls and a mumber of them form part of the wedding gifts by girls' parents. They also find extensive sale in the hands of Europeans who make curtains and wall hangings of them, but *phulkáris* made in the city of Lahore are principally intended for home use. Some women employ their time in making gloves, collars, socks, or in making dresses for the members of the household, but their number is comparatively small and is perhaps confined to the girls trained in the newly established Girls' Schools.

Young women living in one *mahálla* or alley often form a *tinjan* (party) and work together till very late hours in the night. Over their work they amuse themselves by singing songs in memory of their brothers and sisters whom they left behind under the parental roof when they married.

In the evening the young wife again prepares the second meal for the family, which is eaten at 8 or 9 o'clock in the evening, the males here also eating first and the females after them.

Native games and sports were exceedingly numerous, but now are gradually being superseded by those of European introduction, such as cricket, tennis, football and gymnastic exercises, to all of which the natives of India take readily and show in them remarkable skill. Cricket is the most generally popular; and may now almost be considered as much a national pastime of the present generation in India as it is in England. In the afternoons every playing ground is covered with boys and grown men playing cricket; young boys play at all times in every open space available, sometimes even in the bazárs and roads, with bats and wickets and balls of much the same rough and ready material as village boys are seen using in England.

Of native amusements, the following mention may prove interesting. *Dolls*, or as they call them *gudian patola*, are the amusements of young girls in Lahore as they are in England ; but even here the advanced precocity of the native character breaks out, the doll play generally taking the form of marriages between male and female dolls, *guda* and *gudi*. All the proper ceremonies are gone through by the youthful grown ups even down to exchanging of presents, *kauris* taking the place of rupees with brass and copper ornaments of jewellery. This sort of play is regarded by most people as a fine training for the important realities of life hereafter. Another favorite game with dolls is *dedo*, when a number of girls assemble and pretend a doll has died. They weep aloud, tipping their noses in lieu of the breast beating their elders go through on a death occurring. Young girls also play with *gitas* (small pebbles) this being a game of skill in throwing up a pebble, picking some more from the ground and catching the one thrown up before it falls.

Kili thipa is a game played by the city boys with flat circular disks 2½ inches in diameter and a quarter of an inch thick. These are manufactured in quantities in the bazár. They aim their *thipa* at a brick and have various complicated rules; the last boy who plays out incurs the penalty of carrying the rest on his back turn and turn about.

Karanga is a popular, but somewhat risky game, played by boys up in trees, one boy having to catch one or other of the rest without alighting on the ground.

Thappa, a game somewhat resembling the English game fox and geese, *ghor ghunda* or hide and seek and *ghori tapan* or leap-frog are all frequently played by boys. *Látu* or tops made of clay are spun, and the boy whose top spins the longest carries off the other boy's clay tops, thus developing the gambling instinct early.

Gedian is played with small pieces of wood, the object being to drive these across a line drawn on the ground; whoever succeeds carries off the other boy's pieces of wood.

Kite flying is a very common amusement to the city residents and marvellous skill is displayed in manœuvring the kites. Two boys fly kites against one another. The one whose kite flies highest has first try at the other's string, which he tries to cut by bringing his string against it with a very sudden and rapid swoop of the kite. If he fails his adversary has a shot at him and so on.

Wrestling is practised by illiterate people more as an art than an amusement. Every day, morning and evening, they practice—wrestling in *akharás* (arenas), occasionally wrestling matches are arranged, and notice then is given by beat of drum. A wrestler is considered beaten when both his shoulders are made to touch the ground. Five or six years ago wrestling contests were free to every body in Lahore and were held in open *maidans* outside the city, but of late years wrestlers have taken to demanding money from the spectators, who have to pay two annas for admission to the enclosure where the wrestling match is being held; the management of the show is generally taken by some one who pays the wrestlers to perform and pockets the proceeds. People flock in thousands

Chapter III B.

Social.

Wrestling.

to see these matches. Formerly the Gaikwár of Baroda was the chief patron of the art of wrestling. Now the Mahárájás of Jodhpur and Jeypur take an equal or greater interest in it, supporting a large number of wrestlers. Some of these get handsome pensions, amounting to Rs. 200 a month or more from these princes. The two most renowned wrestlers in India came from Lahore, namely Búta, who has been designated the Rustam of India, and Karim Bux, who won a wrestling match with a celebrated English wrestler two or three years ago in Calcutta.

Bird fighting.

The people of Lahore and the adjacent villages take a great delight in figting matches between birds ; such as cocks, quail, partridge, and *bulbul.*

Animal fighting.

Among animals ram-fighting is the most popular. For months before the fight comes off, they have the combatant rams in training. On the day fixed they colour the animal red and take them along to the fray, to see which a large crowd always assembles. The victorious animal is brought home to the sound of drums and trumpets, while the people in attendance on him cry "shame" on the master of the defeated ram and on his supporters.

Bull and buffalo fights.

Buffalo fights too are arranged in the same way but not so often. Sometimes the people get up a fight between two of the sacred Brahmin bulls, which wander about the city bazárs in some number ; when two of these bulls begin roaring against each other from a distance, as they often do, then some of the idlers in the bazár arrange to drive the two towards each other in the hope that they will meet and fight. This extemporized bull-fighting seldom lasts long and the animals suffer no serious injury.

Among the more refined amusements of the people *bait bázi* or the recitation of Pánjábi verses in public takes a prominent place. Open air meetings between two rivals in this art are largely attended ; and that one wins who endures longest ; that is who has the largest stock of poetry at command and the most staying power.

Indoor amusements.

Cards and chess are both common forms of indoor amusements. Also even among the educated classes parties are made up, in which dancing women and drinking of native spirits play a prominent part. Much money is wasted on these forms of dissipation, though societies have been organized among the people themselves to put a stop to them.

General exercise.

Dumb-bell exercise and putting the weight are both recognized as excellent training for the muscles. For out-door exercise walking is coming into fashion. Boys and young men perform gymnastic exercises on parallel and horizonta bars, which are kept up in all Government Schools and Colleges

The staple food of the city people are wheat, rice and pulses, consumption of other inferior grains being very insignificant. They also use vegetables and green food, chiefly *saron ka ság* or the green leaves of the mustard plant : also such English vegetables as potatoes, cabbage and peas are becoming more and more common. Flesh is eaten daily by the Muhammadan and Sikh residents and to a less extent by Hindus. The Municipal Committee have the city slaughter-houses under their control, those for kine being separate from those for sheep and goats. Round cakes or *chappattis* are made of ground wheat kneaded in water, and are baked on an iron plate placed on the fire hearth. Pulses and vegetables are cooked ; salt, spices and *ghee*, or clarified butter, are mixed with them to give a relish. There are only two principal meals taken in the day, the first at ten or eleven in the morning, and the second at eight or nine o'clock in the evening. But a clerk in a Government Office would have to take his morning meal punctually at nine so as to be at office by ten. Some light refreshments, an ounce of sweets or fruits, roasted maize or gram, is also taken by some in the afternoon. Only Muhammadan families eat together. Among Hindus and Sikhs each member of the family takes his meal separately. A grown up resident of the city eats about three-quarters of a seer of wheat and one chaták of Dál. Children who eat little and often get through about half the quantity of a grown up. The above would represent pretty closely the total consumption of the poorer classes : only those who can afford them, add such things as vegetables, *ghee* or sugar.

The principal cloth worn by the city people is of European import supplemented in part by the country cloth manufactured at Gujrát, Ludhiána and other places in and out of the Province. The locally made cloths known as *khaddar painsi*, *dhotar, &c.*, are not used in men's dress, but form the material which is worked up into embroidered *phulkáris* for married girls' wear. Among the male portion of the city community there are two fashions in dress, one the European style, affected principally by those classed as educated, the other the native style, which is still followed by traders and others of the non-educated classes. The European style consists generally of shirt and collar; trousers below, a long light coat above open on the chest and buttoned below, cut behind like an ordinary frock-coat : the head covering is generally an ordinary *pagri* over a Turkish fez, Bábu cap, or Afghán *kulla* (peaked cap). The native or trading style is a shirt without any collar known as the *kurta*, a waist-coat or *kurti* over that ; on the legs a loin cloth or tight trousers, over the body again is worn a *choga* or long robe by those who can afford it. Rich men use an expensive cloth, poor men a cheap cloth.

The dress of a Hindu or Sikh woman consists of a *kurta* or shirt, a *bhochhan* (sheet), *pajámas* or tight trousers, and

Chapter III, B.

Social.

Food.

Men's dress.

Women's dress.

Chapter III, B.

Social.

Women's dress.

a *ghagra* or petticoat; the last being the most costly article of apparel. A Muhammadan woman would seldom have the *ghagra*, but in addition to the other clothes mentioned above she would wear a tight fitting boddice or *choli* and a *burqá* or veiled *choga* when going in public; a veil is indispensable for Muhammadan women going out into the public streets. A Hindu or Sikh woman would pass through the public streets without a veil, only covering up her face if she happened to meet a known male relative. Hindu women and children in the city are usually profusely decorated with jewellery.

Betrothal and **marriage.**

Marriages in the city are preceded by betrothals, generally contracted during infancy; in well-to-do families a boy is not allowed to remain unbetrothed after four or five years of age. The women of the two families arrange the match, and the men agree to whatever they propose. Often the males of the contracting families never even meet before the wedding takes place. Among Hindús intermarriage is greatly restricted by the caste rules. People of the Bráhman, Khatri, Sudar or Vesh castes never intermarry from one caste into another, and within each caste there is much social grading which must be strictly observed in contracting marriage ties, nor again may people intermarry within their father's or mother's tribal sect. A betrothal, when finally arranged, is announced to the brotherhood and presents of sweets and cash to the value of Rs. 25 to Rs. 200, according to means, pass from the girl's parents to the boy's family. Marriages in Lahore are generally arranged between families living in the city, and foreign blood is seldom introduced.

People in the city are beginning to understand the evils of child marriage and if possible find a boy of maturer years for their daughters; but as all boys marry at four or five years at present, no husband of mature years is available, except a widower. Among these a school boy commands a higher price than an illiterate, a collegiate than a school boy, and a man in Government employ higher than any. For any young man in his teens who has lost his wife there is the keenest competition, the presents or dowry offered rising in value by a process very like that of bidding at an auction. The dowry of course is nominally settled on the girl, but the husband gets it all on her death. Some young men have made large fortunes by the successive deaths of three or four rich young brides one after another. One of the chief reasons why education commands so high a price in the matrimonial market is that educated men when grown up see that their young wives are treated much better than uneducated families are likely to do.

Among Muhammadans the marriage is performed by a Maulvi or Mulláh, who reads the *nikáh* or marriage service. Among Hindús the marriage ceremony is performed as follows— seven bamboo stakes are put up in an open ground fenced by

red strings, to which green leaves of different trees are fastened.
Inside this enclosure two reed seats covered over with a red
cloth are placed for the bride and the bridegroom. In front
sit the family priests of either parties making figures of
Ganesh (a god) and other goddesses, and reciting verses in
their praise. The priest of the bride's family makes the
young couple go through a ceremony of worshipping the
heavenly bodies and then recites from Shástras certain verses
which mean an assertion on the part of the bride's parents
that they give up their daughter; after that he takes the
bride's hand and putting it into the bridegroom's, makes
him repeat a verse signifying his assent to the union. This
is called *háthleva*. A fire is then kindled; round which
the bride and bridegroom have to walk four times; this is called
láwan ; the fire is supposed to be a witness of the ceremony,
as fire is looked upon as a deity. Presents consisting of valuable
jewellery, cash, dresses, almost all kinds of furniture, sweets and
animals (cow, mare, &c.), are then gifted by the bride's parents
to the bridegroom. The marriage is then complete.

Social.

Betrothal and marriage.

Marriages among Bráhmins and the upper classes of
Khatrís of Lahore city are singularly free from the extravagant
feasting and noisy celebration which are so prominent in most
Indian marriages, but their expenditure on presents are very
heavy. A marriage costs the parents, either boy or girl, anything from Rs. 200 to Rs. 4,000. The bridegroom or
his father gets the benefit. Practically among all classes
the expense attendant on betrothals and marriage is very
heavy : so much feeding and entertainment have to be done
for relations by both the boy's and girl's family and for *Fakirs*
and menials. Rájput marriages are especially extravagant.

Expensiveness of marriages.

Widow re-marriages are little known in the city. Hindús
regard them as forbidden by their religion, and Muhammadans
seem to follow suit. Reform in this respect has been much
talked of, but none of the reformers have ventured to set
the example.

Widow remarri-ages.

Woman takes a very low social position in the city compared with man. They are treated more as domestic servants
to their husbands than as their companions. They discharge
all the menial house duties, such as cooking, cleaning, fetching
water and nursing, but do nothing out of doors. On the
death of any distant relative the women must play the part
of professional mourners, beating their breasts and wailing
continually for a certain number of days. She keeps the
family purse, but dare not spend a pice on herself. The
Hindu wife may not eat in her husband's presence; and even
to laugh in public is held to be disrespectful to him. Her husband is her only hope and resource. If he ill-treat her she
cannot get a divorce; if he die she must remain a widow.
Her only chance of happiness is to bear him a son and keep
out other rivals from his affections.

Position of women in the city.

Chapter III, B.

Social.

Village Habitations.

The villages in the district from a little distance outside present the appearance of irregular clusters of mud built cottages exhibiting considerable variety both in height and neatness of appearance : the portion inhabited by the landowners is generally better built and shows higher walls than the rest of the settlement. On another side standing slightly apart from the rest are some low untidy looking huts in which the village scavengers or menials of the lowest class are located. Between these two extremes all sorts and sizes of houses are to be seen. In all the larger villages almost one may expect to find a high building with masonry faced walls, erected in recent years by the village money-lender who has enriched himself at the villagers' expense. In the Mánjha and more rarely in the Hithár large masonry houses in more or less disrepair, built on quite a different pattern from their surroundings, still stand as the chief surviving relic of some Sikh Sardár who attained to power and eminence in the time of Mahárája Ranjít Singh or perhaps before him, but whose family is now probably too scattered or reduced in position to keep up their ancestral homes on the former style.

The village settlements are approached by two or three well worn roads leading from different directions which usually pass by to one or the other side of the village and rarely through it. The edges of these roads and the fields nearest the village are never as clean as one could wish, offering constant evidences of the presence of a people who pay no regard to what Europeans consider the plainest rules of decency and sanitation. On one side or the other of the settlement are lying the manure heaps, composed of litter and house sweepings, each heap being carefully separated off by sufficient space to mark its owner's rights. Another prominent feature is the village pond, full after rainy weather, but dry if there has been no rain for a long time. This was made originally by excavations of earth required for building the village houses and is constantly being drawn upon for fresh earth for repairs. From this pond, when it has water, as is usually the case, men and women take a little for their morning wash if they feel inclined, and have no cleaner water handy. The cattle are bathed and watered in it, clothes are washed ; kikar logs and other wood are sunk to preserve them, and sometimes hemp stalks are left in the water to soak for weeks, in which case the air around is filled with an over-powering smell. As one passes near the village one notices various groups ; men sitting on their rough bedsteads in the open spaces near the entrances to the settlement, or if it is a winter's morning, squatting on the ground in a circle round a smouldering fire with their white cotton wraps gathered over their heads and bodies ; women are spinning and between whiles holding converse, or are engaged in cleaning up their yards and collecting cattle droppings to make fuel cakes. These last adorn the outside walls of most of the outer row of houses, being stuck on to dry in the sun. Most of the cattle droppings within the village itself are appropriated for fuel; only litter and rubbish from the house and cattle pens go to swell the manure heaps near the village; on the other hand the droppings of cattle at the irrigation wells at a distance from the village are usually devoted to manuring the fields. At the main entrance to the village there is usually in the larger villages a pretentious looking gateway with a roof over it, 15 or 16 feet deep, on either side of which is a roofed shed with floors raised slightly higher than the level of the roadway. These sheds are used to lodge travellers for the night, or as meeting places for the villagers in the evening or in wet weather. The only furniture in these sheds is a large wooden bedstead. In the absence of a gateway the main entrance is often merely a wide open space flanked with the walls of houses. The arrangement of the village settlement inside varies greatly according to the class of the landowners. In the Mánjha Jat villages it will be generally found on close inspection that the houses are divided off in some sort of order by narrow lanes according to the *pattis, tarafs* or other internal sub-divisions observed in the village constitution. Some of the lanes are thoroughfares, others mere blind alleys. Whatever purpose they serve, in the Sandhu villages of the uplands they are nearly always flanked by high walls over which one can hardly see even as one rides through on horse back. Behind these high walls are open courtyards which are entered from the lanes by fine large doorways which may be open or shut. Inside the courtyard everything is kept fairly clean; there are separate dwelling-houses, all well built for each family living within the enclosure, only those who are fairly closely connected and generally friendly with another live in one courtyard, and as a rule their land holdings are still joint and not yet partitioned off. The courtyards are large and commodious enough to accommodate all the members of the various Jat families resident and the milk cattle as well which form an important adjunct to every Mánjha Jat's household. Often the better class and wealthier landowners of the Mánjha have separate enclosures for their cattle, and within these houses accommodation for guests or strangers. In the low lands the villages are more cramped for space and less atten- tion is paid to order and method in laying out the settlement. The people, a large proportion of whom are Muhammadans, have evidently never been accustomed to hold the lordly ideas of comfort and spaciousness so prominent in the Mánjha Jats' methods of living. Whatever the reason, whether from a wish to economise space and to save building material, or from an idea that the Hithár riverain soil is not firm enough to bear heavy buildings, the houses of the low lands are much smaller than in the Mánjha and the walls are lower. The people of this low land tract are poor and humble-minded for the most part, and the difference is at once apparent in their habitations. The money-lenders' houses however are as conspicuous here as in the Mánjha. Even here too the Jats' villages can be distinguished

Chapter III, B.

Social.

Village habita-
tions.

easily inside by their greater neatness and firmer structure from
those of Aráins, Dogars and other Muhammadan land owners.
Rájpúts for the sake of their women's privacy have high walls
round their courtyards and houses; otherwise Muhammadan villages exhibit a marked contrast to those of the Jats both in want
of arrangement and orderliness, in absence of regard for cleanliness inside, and in not separating the habitations of the menial
castes from those of the upper class. In respect of conveniences
for ingress and egress villages vary considerably; some have
several thoroughfares, some have only one main entrance.
The latter class are seldom found in the Mánjha, but often in the
river lowlands.

Houses.

The ordinary agriculturist's house is generally built narrow
to save expense in wood, which is the more costly in proportion to the length of beam. The roof is flat, being made
of mud laid over beams and joists of roughly hewn timber;
this is where the jowár stalks are always laid after the autumn
harvest and the amount of stuff visible on the roofs of the
houses affords a very fair indication of the nature of the lately
gathered harvest. Access to the roof is provided by a flight of
mud steps or a wooden ladder; generally the house is single
storeyed, but sometimes a small upper chamber is constructed on
the roof. Inside the house below there are probably two or three
partitions in which different members of the family can sleep;
the furniture consists of a few bedsteads, reed stools, and
spinning-wheels for the women. In the wall there are one or
two cupboards (kotri) for clothes, vessels and other household
stuff, and in one corner stands a large barrel-shaped receptacle
(kotha) made of mud in which the family supplies of grain are
kept. The cleanliness and general tidiness observed in the
rooms depends largely on the class of people living there. Outside the house in front there may be a verandah consisting of a
light mud roof supported on more or less rough standing posts.
In one corner is the family cooking-place (rassoi) partly
sheltered from sun and rain. If not covered in at all it is
called a chauntra. Close by probably is another grain bin. On
one or two sides of the enclosure are the cattle standings, sometimes with mud troughs constructed for them sometimes without. Various agricultural implements also are strewn about the
yard. Here the women spend most of the day spinning or
engaged in other household duties and the children play.
The cattle are tied up here at night, unless a separate cattle
enclosure has been provided near the house. Outside the
family residence there are usually one or more village chauks
in which carts are left standing and the villagers collect
at various times of the day to have a talk and smoke if that way
inclined. All the Hindu villages nearly have a dharmsála where
a copy of the sacred Grunth is kept under the charge of a Sádh;
the villagers attend to hear this read as they feel inclined. The
dharmsála is looked on as the guest house for strangers visiting
the village, and the Sádh, who is responsible for their entertain-

ment, receives a daily allowance of bread from the landowners
and cash payments usually of one rupee on the occasion of
any domestic event. Similarly all Muhammadan villages have
a mosque, at which a Kázi or Mullah is in attendance ; he too
receives certain fixed dues from the villagers ; but often in
Muhammadan villages a *takiyá* or small *Fakir's* hut is kept up
as well as the mosque, and to this a stranger would probably
be sent for bread. These *takiyás* are places of frequent resort
both for the villagers and for passers-by who at least can always
get a smoke there at the small fire which is kept burning for this
purpose. Of all these institutions the Hindu *dharmsála* is far
the best kept up, being usually a clean and well built structure.
In large Sikh villages the landowners sometimes make a grant
of land in favour of the Sádh in charge, or allow him the use
of some common land for the revenue of which they make
themselves responsible. In some villages also *thákur-
dwárás* are kept up, in which little images are placed for the
worshipping by Hindús. But any house can be made temporarily
to look like a *thákurdwárá* if the occupant has any advantage to
gain thereby. Many of these buildings, *dharmsálás*, *thákur-
dwárás*, *takiyás*, mosques and even the tombs of ancient saints
which usually lie at some distance from the village have enjoyed
small endowments from Government for their support ; some
of these bestowed in perpetuity, some for a time only. Most of
the latter have been resumed.

Chapter III, B.

—

Social.

Houses.

The condition of the villagers can generally be fairly well
guessed from the outside appearance of their houses. If the
walls are in good repair and well plastered it may safely be
conjectured that the people stand fairly well with the world
and have both the inclination and the means to follow a
reasonably high standard of comfort in their mode of living.
If the houses look tumble down and uncared for it will generally
be found on further enquiry that the villagers have lost heart
over their struggle to make both ends meet. The Jat houses,
whether in the Mánjha or in the Hithár can be recognised by the
regularity of building observed in their houses and walls,
while Dogars and Aráins villagers exhibit no uniformity either
in height, arrangement or structure. Outside the ring of houses
the environs of all villages, whatever the class of inhabitants,
are much the same. Filth and smells are unpleasantnesses
which must be accepted as part of the village constitution, and
it is to be greatly doubted whether any regard for sanitary
rules could ever be instilled into their minds. The only
indication the best even of the people give of any proper
feeling on the subject, is the rough sort of apology they mutter
as they hurry the European officer along by the least filthy
path they know of. The only safe spot all round the village
is under one of the two or three fine old trees, usually either
Bohur or *Pipal,* which overlook the main entrance to the
homestead or village pond, and then even the ground is often
filthy with cattle droppings.

General appear-
ance.

**Chapter III, B.
Social.**

Food.

The ordinary food of the village people consists of cakes of meals made of wheat, gram or barley in the hot weather, and of maize or *jowár* varied with wheat occasionally in the winter. Maize is the most suitable for the cold weather, but if eaten too continuously it produces indigestion. Their chief meals are two, one at 10 or 11 o'clock in the morning, the other at night before they go to bed. With their morning cakes they take *lassi* or butter milk and *ság* of rape or gram leaves. With their evening meal they eat *dál* of *másh*, *moth* and gram in the summer and *khichri* of rice and *moth* in the cold weather. During the rabi harvesting operations those who can do so give out *ghi* and *gur* mixed to all the workmen to sustain them in their labour ; otherwise these are considered luxuries only to be produced on festal occasions. Those who can afford it eat wheaten cakes summer and winter as well, in preference to maize or gram cakes ; but the staple food of the ordinary cultivator is wheat if possible, otherwise gram in the summer, and maize or *jowár* in the cold weather. *Jowár* is the main food of all the poorer classes. Vegetables are eaten either in the form of green rape or gram tops, or less frequently carrots, onions or turnips grown and sold by Aráin cultivators. If a man wants anything before starting to work in the morning he will probably eat what remains of the evening meal and take a draught of *lassi;* towards evening also at three or four o'clock the people usually have a small meal ; this consists of the remains of the morning meal for those working in the fields ; those at home in the village eat a little roasted wheat or gram in the summer and maize in the winter. *Lassi* or butter milk is as a rule drunk only at the morning meal. Water and salt are mixed with it. At the evening meal salt is eaten with the *dál* or *khichri ;* it is not often mixed with the bread cakes. Most Musalmáns eat meat occasionally, and by the river all the better class of men eat the flesh of goat or sheep. Those who drink native spirits (and these form a large majority in this district) often take a little before their evening meal as an appetiser and then have more at and after the meal. The morning meal is usually taken out to the cultivator by his women or children. Rájpúts and Dogars however whose women are not supposed to go out to the fields by themselves must come back to the village for their morning food. Opium is consumed by a fairly large proportion of men in all classes and *post*, an infusion of poppy-heads, is drunk. Similarly *bhang* an infusion of wild hemp is consumed by some of every class, especially Jats and Khatrís, but not probably to the same extent as opium. The chief *bhang* drinkers are *Fakírs*, who also smoke a great quantity of *charas*, a hemp drug, with their tobacco.

**Village money-
lenders.**

Every village almost has its money-lender or *sáhúkár.* He is usually treated well by the villagers ; even those not dependent on him for loans are civil to him. The money-lenders never bank their money ; they keep it circulating in loans as much as possible, otherwise they bury it in the ground; the general rate of interest is 2 per cent. per month, but Khojás or Muhammadan usurers fix their interest in grain or kind, generally asking a *marla* of wheat as interest for each rupee. Khatris usually allow *chhot* or a deduction of one anna in the rupee of interest charged when accounts are made up. The *sáhukárs* have four sets of books, the *sur* or detail of daily income and expenditure in connection with loans, the *kháta* or daily balance book, the *lekha bahi* or ledger showing each debtor's separate account, the *roznámcha* or general account book for all income and outgoings of the day. If disputes arise between the money-lender and his debtors, *panches* or committees of arbitration are sometimes appointed from among the landowners or others of the debtor's class to settle the dispute; but arbitration is not nearly so freely resorted to, as in the olden days. At present the richer Jat land proprietors of the Manjha who have accumulated wealth from their irrigated land appear likely to supersede the ordinary money-lending classes in their trade, but they are said to be no easier than the latter in the terms on which they loan money.

The material of the common villagers' dress is almost always unbleached cotton, made up by the village weaver from home grown materials spun by the women of the family and supplied to him. The *pag* or *pagri* is universally worn on the head, except perhaps when the man is at work. A *kurta* or loose sleeved jacket covers the body and a *chadar ter* or loincloth is wrapped round the loins. The *kurta* is often discarded during work, sometimes in place of this or in addition to it the *chadar alti* or light wrap of *khaddar* cloth is worn over the shoulders. In cold weather all who can afford it wear a heavy double-folded cotton wrap, *khes* or *dohar*. They never have more than one change of clothes at the most; when one lot gets very dirty they take a change. Sikhs occasionally wear the *kachh* or short drawers, but not always by any means. *Pájámás* are not common, except among the better class who have not to work in the field themselves. Hindu Jats usually wear their clothes white, but they often have a red *khaddar khes*. Musalmáns have black or coloured clothes; Arains especially affect red or green checks. A *sufeid posh* or better class agriculturist who has other occupations than field labour will often get clothes of more expensive material from the city; they wear long white single breasted tunics sometimes, and tight clinging white *pájámás*. The only ornaments worn by men are the *wála* or ear ornament, worn high up on the ear by Hindús or the *durr* worn by Musalmáns. Other ornaments worn by Hindús or Musalmáns occasionally are the *kangan* or *trága*, both being wrist ornaments; but grown men seldom wear these, unless they are the gay young sparks of the village or have lived much away from home in other than agricultural service.

A woman must always wear a *doputta* or *chadar* over her head and shoulders, this may be white or edged with coloured

Chapter III, B.
Social.
Women's clothes.

cloth or it may take the form of a *phulkári*, a cotton cloth of black or red ground with a flowered pattern embroidered in floss silk. They also wear a short skirt (*kurti*) coloured or white with a tight fitting bodice called *choli* over it. Above these again they might have in the winter a *chop* of red *khaddar* or a *sirgah* which is white, and embroidered at the edge. Below they wear coloured *pájámás*, full and broad at the top and tight fitting at the ankles. These are made of a cloth called *súsi*. In the place of the *pájámás* or sometimes over it they may wear a white or coloured petticoat known as *ghagra*. The latter is always worn when they go out. The Hindu women wear their hair gathered in a knot on the top of their head. Musalmán women often wear it hanging down in plaits. The village women usually make a great display of silver ornaments when out for a holiday, though the children are usually more loaded. In the villages one does not notice much wearing of ornaments, except on the small children.

Shoes are worn by all, men and women alike. *Thibbi júti* or shoes with no back at the heel are worn by women in the house; they cost only 8 annas a pair. Women's outdoor shoes cost one rupee. Men's shoes cost slightly more. The ordinary bedding of villagers is the *dotahi*, costing 3 rupees, the *tolái* costing 6 rupees and the *lef* or *liháf* costing 2 rupees, all these are varieties of quilts.

Sports and games.

Village boys have not so much variety in games as the boys of the city, whose amusements have already been described. *Gedian*, the game of shooting sticks over a line. *Billi baccha* a kind of prisoner's base played in a ground marked out with squares, and other games somewhat too intricate for brief description may be seen being played every evening round a village. Cricket and other European games have hardly taken hold of the rustic community yet though the former is played to some extent in village schools; bar exercises also are taught at all schools. Among the grown up agriculturist folk amusements are hardly looked for, except on special festival days or occasions on which domestic occurrences are celebrated. For ordinary every day solace or diversion after his day's work the Jat resorts to opium or native drink or *bhang*, chiefly the two former.

The richer men among them have now adopted a habit of getting out dancing girls from the city on any festal occasion, and at the Holi festival the village community often subscribes two or three hundred rupees for a dancing girl. Now too a band to play so-called English music (*viláyati bája*) is a common accompaniment to most village entertainments.

Most days of course the working men come home tired out with their field labour and fit for nothing but gossiping with each other about their land and harvest prospects, the doings of the various bad characters of the neighbourhood, the latest eccentricities of the Sirkár, or the bribes they have just been made to give to some of its officials. Sometimes however a break is made by a marriage or betrothal either in the village or at a distance, to which, on the score of blood connection or friendship, they are bound to attend at the risk of creating a life feud. Other ceremonies connected with births and deaths give them a chance of marking the day by an extra good feed. Then there are the periodical fairs and festivals in various parts of the country, to which large parties of the villagers, men and women together, travel in bullock carts, sometimes a distance of 50 or 60 miles; provided the fairs or festivals come at a time of the year when the land is more or less at rest and the villagers have leisure to think of other matters than cultivation. The best time is the month of June when the spring crop has been harvested. Then may be seen carts dragging slowly along the village tracks crammed with gaily dressed women and children, the men of the family running or walking along side, behind and in front, the younger members singing aloud snatches of country songs; as they approach the fair one party enters into a singing competition with another, and if the rivalry become very keen the two parties collect and sing against each other for a time, until the applause of the spectators decides which party should be considered the victor.

The chief fairs or festivals in this district are as follows :—

Káli Devi fair held at Niazbeg, situate on the left bank of the Rávi, about seven miles from Lahore, in honour of the Hindu goddess *Káli Devi*. Formerly her temple was at Khudpur, a large village about 16 miles further down the Rávi; the Brahmins moved her away from there because they were constantly being plundered. *Kali Devi* is supposed to be potent for good and evil. Votive offerings are constantly being placed on her shrine, especially by women who pray to her for the fulfilment of their wishes. The offerings usually take the form of cocoanut, flowers, coloured thread, sweatmeats, cash and sometimes even a goat. All such offerings are appropriated of course by the *pujári* in charge. At different times various buildings have been constructed in *Káli Devi's* honour near her temple, including a fine masonry tank surrounded by a red brick colonnade. A revenue free grant of Rs. 500 per annum has been conferred by Government for the support of the temple, and a smaller grant is enjoyed by the Brahmins in charge of the temple. One Brahmin only remains in charge ordinarily; the temple has been supplied with a nice set of small bells by the munificence of some of *Káli Devi's* Hindu devotees of Lahore. These bells are rung always every morning and evening at prayer time. The fair to *Káli Devi* is held at sometime between the 15th of May and the 15th of June, lasting three days. People of all classes frequent it from Lahore city, but the villagers who come are principally Sikhs from the Lahore and Amritsar Districts.   The number of visitors varies between 30,000 and 60,000.   Sweatmeat and *sharbat* booths are opened there during the fair and a brisk business done.   The income arising out of the offerings on the fair day is reckoned at about Rs. 600.

Basant ka Mela, held in this district in January at the tomb of Hakikat Rai near the village of Kot Khwaja Said, three miles out of Lahore.   The same fair is held in other parts of the Punjab.

Basant means " yellow," and the fair is held about the time that the yellow leaves of the mustard plant are in bloom. Some four or five thousand people assemble, mostly Hindús from the city.   Many of them wear mustard seed in their turbans in token of the day.

Chirághon ka Mela or fair of the lamp held at the Shálimár gardens, five miles from Lahore, on the last Saturday and Sunday in March.   The latter is the principal day.   Originally it was a religious pilgrimage (*ziyarat*) to the tomb of Mádho Lál Husein in Bághbánpura.   Gradually as the fair became more frequented it was transferred to the Shálimár gardens which are near the shrine.   Some illuminations take place in the evening, but the garden is thronged with people all day. All classes of people of the male sex attend it from Lahore, not the better class of women.   Of late years the occasion has been used to hold a horse fair at Shálimar during the three days preceding the great fair day.

The *Rám Thamman* fair, held in the village of Thamman, the centre home and depôt of the Bairági *faqírs.*   Thamman is situated about three miles south-west from the Railway Station of Rukhanwala on the Ráiwind extension to Kasúr.   The fair is held in April on the Hindú festival of *Baisákhi*; about 60,000 people collect; it lasts for two days.   The fair has lost some of its importance since the Railway has been opened, people now preferring to visit the more important *Baisákhi* fair at Amritsar which takes place about the same time.   Formerly it was the most important fair in the district; it is principally resorted to by the young agricultural sparks of the district, who collect here in their holiday costume; there is considerable license allowed, and the morality of the majority of the women attending the fair is doubtful.   There is a prettily situated tank with shady trees and buildings around it, which is the centre of the fair.   The Bairági *faqírs,* who have been wandering all over India, time their tours so as to return to their home for this important meeting, and receive a share in the large collections made from their devotees. *Rám Thamman* was a cousin of Bába Nának, but not his follower, being a true Bairagi.

Id-ul-zúha and *Id-ul-fitar.*—Of these two Muhammadan festivals, the first is celebrated on the tenth of the Arabic month *Zi'lhijjá,* when an animal is sacrificed in commemoration of

Abraham's sacrifice of his son Ismail according to the Muhammadans. It is also known as *Id-ul-kurbán* or feast of sacrifice.
A cow, sheep, goat or camel is sacrificed by all good Muhammadans, who eat some and give some away in alms; in
Lahore sheep or goats are mostly killed. Before the slaugh-
tering a largely attended service is held at 9 A. M., in the *Sháhi*
and other mosques. The *Id-ul-fitr* is the festival of breaking
the fast that has been observed all through the month of Ram-
zán. This day precedes the *Id-ul-zuha* by six weeks or so.
The Musalmáns of the city on this day assemble at the *Sháhi*
mosque between the hours of 8 and 9 A. M., and offer prayers;
their number is usually between four and five thousand: services
are held also in other mosques. About 4 P. M. a fair is held
near the tomb of Sháh Abdul Muali outside the Mochi gate
of the city. Orthodox Muhammadans however do not attend
this fair.

Kadamon ka Mela is a fair held in the month of February at
the mosque of Sakhi Sarwar in the Anarkali Bazar. An account
of this Musálman saint and his followers is given at pages
132 to 137 of the Census Report for 1891; he lived about the
12th century, his priests are all Musalmáns, but his followers
are drawn from all religions and castes, the Sultani cult being
hampered by no religious creed. The saint is believed to be a
patron of young children; and many of these on the occasion of
his fair are presented at the tomb and danced about in front
of it. The fair lasts about three days and the visitors to it
number five or six thousand.

Nankána Fair, held at Nankána, situate in the north-west
corner of Sharakpur tahsíl in the Bár, about 45 miles from
Lahore. Nankana is the birth-place of Bába Nának, the founder
of the Sikh religion. The principal attendants at this fair
therefore are Sikhs and Hindús. They do not generally exceed
five or six thousand in number, the fair lasts for one day and is
held on a Hindu festival called *Nirjala Ikádshi*. Nankána
repays a visit to any one who happens to be in the neighbourhood. There are some fine buildings belonging to the Sádh
settlement, the Guru of which holds a *jagir* of Rs. 1,040 in the
Nankána estate.

Guru Arjan's Fair is a religious fair of the Sikhs of recent
institution 'held in the month of May at what is said to be the
tomb of Guru Arjan near the Fort of Lahore. It is alleged
that large numbers of Sikhs attend this fair to commemorate
the anniversary of Guru Arjan's death.

The *Dasehra* festival is a Hindu celebration held generally
in October and lasting about ten days, it commemorates the
conquest gained by Rám Chander, a distinguished and well-be-
loved Rája of Oudh over his adversary and rival Ráwan who
had run away with his wife. The first nine days are
devoted to general holiday making by the people taking part
in it, and they are kept amused by illustrations showing the

history of the valiant Rám Chander's life, the hardships he endured, and his earlier skirmishes with Ráwan. On the tenth or last day of all, the people collect on the parade ground in front of the Lahore fort, fifty or sixty thousand in number, to witness a representation of the last grand battle of all. Effigies of Rám Chander and Ráwan are carried about, made up with bamboo frames and paper. The fight having ended with Ráwan's defeat his effigy is burnt amid a grand display of fireworks and illuminations, after which the people disperse.

The *Mohurram* festival begins on the first of the month of Mohurram. It commemorates the massacre of Imams Hussan and Husain, the sons of Ali, who was the son-in-law of the prophet Muhammad and the fourth Khalifa of Islám. An account of this ceremony as celebated in Lahore city is given on pages 270 to 271 of Khan Bahádar Syad Muhammad Latif's History of Lahore. On the 7th of the month, the Mahndis, which commemorate the marriage of Husain, start about eleven in number, and go all round the city. On the 10th the Taziás, some two-hundred in number, make the rounds of the principal streets. The Taziás of Lahore are noted for their splendour. The *Karbala* to which the Taziás are taken for burial is outside the city on the bank of the old Rávi. It is a purely Muhammadan festival, though a large concourse of Hindu people collect also to see the Taziás. If there is any ill feeling existent between the Hindús and Muhammadans, this meeting offers plenty of opportunity for a row. Also it has sometimes been the occasion of a free fight between the two Muhammadan factions, the Sunnis and the Shiáhs, who are divided principally on the question of the rightful successor to Muhammad, the Shiáhs upholding Ali and his sons, and the Sunnis favouring the three Imáms Abu Bakr, Asman and Umar, who usurped the caliphate from Ali's family. The Sunnis detest the Taziás that commemorate Husain's martyrdom and would gladly see them stopped.

Marriage in villages.

The betrothals which always precede marriages are usually effected in villages at any age between 9 and 12 years old. The girl should not be older than nine. Girls must be married, if possible, in villages as in the city; with the boys of agriculturists it is merely a question of preference or of means to support a wife. Thus the first proposals come from the girl's parents through a go-between, usually a Brahman or the village barber. If the parents of the boy selected send a favourable reply, then the girl's people in a few days send tokens to the boy's house, a few dates usually or other trash of the sort; these are offered to the boy's parents in the presence of relatives and if accepted they form an outward and visible sign of the conclusion of the betrothal. In villages the dowry given to a girl by her parents is very insignificant as a rule, except when the boy is of a higher social status than the girl, when the latter's parents have to make presents accordingly. Otherwise among the Jats so far from the girl's parents giving anything there is a custom, partly clandestine, partly recognized, under which money varying in amount from Rs. 50 to Rs. 200 is paid for the girl to her parents. The wedding may take place any time after the betrothal, but often does not for several years. The time of marriage rests with the girl's father or guardian, who of course is guided by his own and the girl's convenience. Eventually after consulting the Brahmans, he fixes on a day and sends intimation to the boy's parents who are bound in honour to accept it. Very soon after they send the girl presents of clothes and jewellery. A day or so before the wedding day the relatives on the boy's side assemble and proceed in procession to the girl's house where the marriage ceremony is peformed in the manner described earlier in this chapter for city marriages.

When the ceremony is complete then alms are distributed to *fakirs* and other beggars ; all present, including village menials are fed, and the bride is put into a *doli* or hand car and carried off to the boy's house. She stays there a couple of days and then returns to her father's house. How long she is detained there is a matter of arrangement between the pair themselves ; the bride's father probably wishes to keep his daughter as she is useful about the house, but she may not stay away over the year without her husband's leave. The final bringing home of the bride is called *mukláwa*.

These are the same in this district as elsewhere. Inter-marriage between people of different tribes is unlawful : on the other hand marriage between two of the same section of Jats is not countenanced. The Jat must select a woman of a different section from those to which his father or mother belonged and one too who lives at some distance from his village. Muhammadans other than Jats do not appear to observe this rule, nor indeed do the *Virk* Jats of Sharakpur tahsíl observe it strictly.

Marriage within the 6th degree of blood relationship is unlawful ; or between members of different religions, but for this purpose no difference is made between a Hindu woman or one of a Sikh family.

Re-marriage of widows is common among the Jats and is recognized in villages among all tribes, except perhaps some Muhammadans of high social standing. Among Jats a widow is bound to marry one of her deceased husband's collaterals who will succeed to the property on her death. Such a marriage would be made by the simple form of *chadar-dali* or sheet throwing. If for any reason she cannot or will not marry one of the collaterals, and wants to marry elsewhere, she is generally at liberty to do so, provided she abandons her claim on her deceased husband's property and lives far away from his relations. A marriage of a widow with a man outside the circle of her husband's relations is performed by the ceremony known as *Karewa*, which is little more than the fact of the man and woman living together.

Immorality is discountenanced to some extent by the elders of the villages, and the strong feeling which exists

Chapter III, B.
———
Social.
Village morality.

against intermarriage within the same section of a Jat tribe, no doubt, discourages illicit intercourse also. However undoubtedly there is a good deal of free intercourse in Jat villages between married women and their brothers-in-law; sometimes even between them and their fathers-in-law. The Mánjha Jat has small regard for the sanctity of family honour. In the larger Jat villages prostitutes are often obtained by the richer landowners from the city, or the village menials are willing to lend out their women for a consideration.

The position of women in villages.

The village women for the most part stay at home discharging domestic duties, which include cleaning up the house and outer courtyard, spinning, boiling the milk to be made into *ghi* and cooking the food. Some of them also have to carry the morning meal to the male relations working in the field. Rájpút women get off this duty as they are not allowed out. Aráin women are the most useful of all out-of-doors, helping their husbands to dig vegetables and thresh the grain and collect manure; at home, however, they are very bad managers and have little idea of household economy. Jat and Dogar women pick cotton, but do no other field work. All round the women's life is far more monotonous even than that of the men; and they must look forward to an occasional visit to their people in a distant village or to a coming fair with great anticipations of temporary relief from home drudgery.

Hospitality.

In every village almost there is some guest house or enclosure in which benighted travellers are accommodated and fed at the village expense. Many villages have covered sheds at the main entrance to the settlement intended expressly for village guests or strangers. Some of the better class landowners have separate enclosures of their own where they keep their cattle; generally at the entrance to these there are rooms which can be adapted for a night's lodging. Besides these there is the *dharmsála* in a Hindu village and the mosque or less pretentious *takiya* in Muhammadan villages, where strangers can always be sent in default of better accommodation. Food and beds are provided for such guests by the village headmen who are supposed to refund themselves at the expense of the remaining shareholders of the village. A public fund is generally maintained for charges of this nature either by fixed annual collections in the form of a small percentage on the land revenue known as *malba deh* or by contributions from what they call the *Dhart* Fund. This is the contract price paid by the village weighman for the monopoly of weighing all grain sold or bought in the village during the year. The income the weighman derives from fees in his business is considerable, and in large villages the price received by the Lambardárs each year in return for granting the monopoly may often exceed Rs. 200. Of late years however the villagers have rather taken to asserting the right of each man to appoint his own weighman. Simultaneously a strong dislike has arisen of the custom of imposing the additional tax alluded to above under the name of village *malba*. There is also an increasing tendency to question the headmen's right to spend the public funds at his own discretion, not from any public spirited wish on the villager's part to control the expenditure within proper limits, but solely from a petty feeling of jealousy against the appropriation of such funds for any but each man's own individual interests. The headmen in this district have often complained in previous years of the insufficiency of the funds at their disposal for entertaining purposes and of the losses constantly entailed on them by their position of responsibility for the rest of the villagers. At the recent settlement a greatly increased number of villagers declared against the surrender of any contribution into the headmen's hands, so that now the latter will find matters more difficult than ever and there is a danger of the former fashion hospitality to all wayfarers gradually dying out.

The prevailing language of the district is Panjábi. That of the Mánjha is remarkably pure, that of the Hithár or trans-Rávi tracts is mixed with Persian or Hindústáni phrases. Table No. VIII shows the numbers who speak each of the principal languages current in the district, separately for each tahsíl and for the whole district, More detailed information will be found in Table No. X of the Census Report for 1891.

The figures in the margin show the distribution of every

Hindustáni	...	...	...	225
Pahári	...	...	...	5
Kashmíri	...	...	...	25
Panjábi	...	...	...	9,653
Pashtu	...	...	...	10
Other Indian languages		...		38
Non-Indian languages		...		44

10,000 of the population by language, omitting small figures. Pashtu is spoken to some extent by Afghán traders who come down bringing horses and ponies for sale, dried fruits and other commodities from Afghánistan.

Table No. XIII gives statistics for education as ascertained at the census of 1891, for each religon and for the total population of each tahsíl. The figures for female education are probably less reliable than those for males. From the mention made of female education in Chapter V, it would appear that the total number of native girls receiving education in schools under Government inspection in the Lahore district is 1,381, and that though there are a few schools established by private enterprise in Lahore city, outside little is done by private education. Even so, however, the census figures would appear to be understated.

			Rural population.	Total population.
Males ...	Learning	...	56	169
	Literate	...	293	646
Females	Learning	...	2·6	16·6
	Literate	...	4·4	43·7

The figures in the margin show the number educated among every 10,000 of each sex according to the Census Return.

Comparing the figures in the margin with those furnished in 1881 we find a large falling-off in the number of the rural population under instruction and a less falling-off in the number of total population who are learning. Of *literates* the male rural population show a falling off of 34 per ten thousand and the total males show an increase of 97. Female *literates* have increased in number both in villages and towns.

Education in each religion.

The following statement compares the condition of education in each of the three main religions as existing in 1891 with that shown in the previous census of 1881 :—

RELIGION.	YEAR.	MALES.			FEMALES.		
		Total.	PER TEN THOUSAND.		Total.	PER TEN THOUSAND.	
			Learning.	Literate.		Learning.	Literate.
Hindús ...	1891	153,317	301	1,348	118,432	9·8	36·5
	1881	110,298	380	1,391	83,021	10·7	19·2
Sikhs ...	1891	86,530	109	533	65,493	2·1	18·9
	1881	71,533	99	406	54,058	3·7	5·0
Muhammadans ...	1891	348,400	116	290	296.683	8·7	17·1
	1881	324,672	138	214	274,805	10·5	7·3

Among Hindús and Muhammadans the number of those under instruction shows a comparative decrease, very large in the case of the former. Both religions show a considerable increase of female literates, but this is probably due in great measure to improved accuracy of enumeration. In the Census Report for 1881, it was noted that wrong returns had probably been made intentionally as to female education, owing to the disinclination on the part of the people to admit that their wives and daughters were able to read and write. The Sikhs show considerable progress in the education of males. The leading place taken by Hindús in education among the three religions is remarkable. It is not understood why the proportion of Sikh literates should be so much higher than that of Muhammadan literates, while the proportion of Sikhs learning is lower. Probably this peculiarity is due to some confusion of enumeration between *literates* and those learning.

English education.

Table XIII shows the number in each religion who know English. Here the Sikhs are markedly backward compared with other religions. Excluding Native Christians the Khatri class which supplies so many clerks to Government service is foremost in this district in knowledge of English among natives of the country. Their superiority in this respect to Arorás is most conspicuous. Each caste numbers slightly over 40,000 souls. Among Khatrís 1,293 know English, including 23 females, while only 336 Arorás know it.

For further information on the subject of education, Chapter VIII of Mr. Maclagan's Provincial Census Report should be studied.

A district which includes on the north-west the Kharrals who may almost be said to make cattle stealing their profession, the Dogars on the south who certainly are not the men to lose chances at their neighbours' cattle, and in the centre of the district a large number of Jat villages, some of the residents of which are known to the police as burglars and highway robbers; such a district can hardly be classed among the law-abiding parts of the Province, and yet none of the tribes mentioned deserve to be stamped as criminal. Cattle stealing has always been regarded as a venial offence if not as an amusing pastime by all classes of the people including even Jat agriculturists who might be expected to have a fellow feeling for any one deprived of the means of working his plough. To Kharrals and Dogars of course it comes as a sort of second nature, and they even are showing gradual indications of regeneration. A far more serious aspect of the district crime than cattle stealing is the more vicious propensity observed among so many of the Mánjha Jats to planned attacks on both house property and on the person, and the indomitable persistence certain villages display in breeding, maintaining and harbouring such men. If any men deserved to be classed as criminal in the district, some might say that it should not be the cattle stealing Kharral or Dogar, nor even the less ambitious Mahtam who seldom organizes crime on his own account more than petty theft, but is a willing instrument in others hands, but rather the Mánjha Jats who supply so many house breakers and road dacoits. These again, namely, the Jats of the uplands, and among them the Sandhús most prominently, are the class among which murder and homicide most frequently occur and at present appear to be increasing in frequency. The chief causes of such violent crime have always been quarrels about land, building sites, or cattle trespass on crops, and naturally as the land and crops increase in value, as they have been doing of late years, the oftener disputes regarding them occur, and the more keenly are they fought out. Putting aside, however, the tribes indicated, the rest of the people comprising Sidhu Jats, Aráins, Rájpúts, Khatrís and numerous other classes of lower status are undoubtedly peaceably inclined and law-abiding : nor can it be said that such crime as exists is beyond control. The Dogars are showing distinct improvement and taking much more than formerly to cultivation of the land. The Kharrals are an unimportant and not numerous class who could, if necessary, be easily dealt with by means of one punitive post in their midst. The more criminal villages of the Jat community in the Mánjha are the only serious difficulty to the Police administration, and they need only firm and persevering treatment to make them gradually abandon de-

Chapter III, B.
——
Social.

Crime.

liberate and preconcerted crime. For several years of late, that is, since the Excise Administration became more vigilant, the Mánjha Jats have also had a bad name for illicit distillation of liquor ; but this habit was formed when facilities for purchase of licensed liquor were much fewer and less convenient than now, and it was impossible to expect the people to forego their former methods immediately to order. There is no ground for thinking that illicit distillation is carried on to any great extent now. Drinking of spirituous liquors is no doubt on the increase, especially among the Mánjha Jats and Sikhs. They also drink *post* and *bhang* and consume a considerable quantity of opium. Muhammadans drink *post* and smoke to excess.

Litigiousness.

In the Civil Courts litigation seems to be on the increase. Jats are by nature a persistent race and never drop a claim, however trivial, which they believe to be based on equity. Law is a matter for which the Jat has no regard and of which he knows nothing, except that it will get him all he wants if he can get it on his side, and that can only be secured by his swearing everything to be false which his opponent swears is true. The Jat peasant, who is reasonably frank and truthful in his village and fields, sees matters from an entirely different aspect when he comes into the Civil Courts at Lahore.

Condition of the people.

In the Mánjha tract the Jat villages are for the most part in good condition. Many of the people can afford to live even luxurious lives, and there are few who deprive themselves of what people in this part of the country regard as ordinary comforts. Even the village menials of the Mánjha share in the general abundance of good things and easy style of living arising out of the enormously increased productive powers of the land under irrigation from the Bári Doáb Canal. There are of course exceptions to this favourable aspect. A few of the central Mánjha villages to which canal irrigation has not been extended are much depressed in condition. In the Hithár tract there is very little of luxurious living to be found ; with a few exceptions perhaps the larger number of villages barely manage to maintain a reasonable standard of comfort, and some there are which have fallen into impoverished and depressed circumstances. This however can only be expected in a tract of precarious rainfall in which the cultivation is dependent upon an expensive system of irrigation on a not more than moderately fertile soil. Along the Rávi many of the villages are short of land, and moreover all are constantly subject to severe losses, both of land and houses from the river action ; on the whole the landowners here are in middling condition and the village menials are badly off. On the right bank of the Rávi, especially at the upper portion of the river's course in this district, the pressure of the population on the land is very severe and many of the villagers are greatly impoverished, partly from this and partly from other causes. In the rest of the Trans-Rávi tract north of the sandy zone that fringes the Sharakpur tahsil on its south, agriculture is for the most part in a

Chapter III, C.

Religion.

Condition of the people.

depressed state, partly owing to the uncertain rainfall and intractable nature of the soil, and partly owing to the apathetic disposition of the Muhammadan cultivators who own or till most of the land in this direction. Consequently most of the people here are poor and have no stores of any sort in provision against adverse seasons; the larger number of them desert their homes temporarily if the seasonal rainfall fail, taking themselves, their families and their cattle to the Rávi lowlands, perhaps, or other regions, wherever they think they are likely to get food and employment for themselves and fodder for their herds.

The moneyed classes of the district.

Outside the city of Lahore most of the money is with the money-lenders and tradesmen of the larger villages—Khatrís, Arorás and Khojahs; and among these there are very few making what can be called large incomes. There are probably not above a hundred traders, not resident in Lahore city, who make an income over Rs. 2,000 a year. The total number of assessees to income tax in the whole district including the city are 2,569 and the amount of tax realised from them is Rs. 68,584. Of this far the larger portion comes from traders in the Lahore city. Of the agriculturists the richest are to be found in the Mánjha of the Kasúr tahsíl and in the adjoining large estates of Chúnián tahsíl. A fair number of these have acquired considerable wealth since the extension of the Bári Doáb Canal irrigation to their land, and some of them have taken to money-lending as an additional means of accumulating wealth. In the next few years the Mánjha Jats, who have much land of their own and do not waste their easily acquired wealth in dissipation and riotous living, will almost certainly accumulate large fortunes and are likely to increase their present holdings rapidly at the expense of their poorer neighbours, to whom they are now beginning to advance money on loan. At present it looks as if in the Mánjha the large Jat landholder would eventually take the money-lending business out of the Khatrís' hands.

SECTION C.—RELIGION.

Religion.

Table No. VII shows the number in each tahsíl and the whole district who follow each religion as ascertained at the census of 1891, and Table No. XLIII gives similar figures for towns. Further details will be found in Tables Nos. V, VI, VII and VIII and supplementary Tables A, B and F of the Census Report of 1891. The distribution of every ten thousand of the population by religions is shown in the margin. Comparing these with corresponding figures of 1881, we find a large increase in the number of Hindús and Sikhs and a corresponding falling off under Musalmáns. This is contrary to the natural tendency; Hindús expel those who have broken

RELIGION.	POPULATION.		
	Rural.	Urban.	Total.
Hindús	2,305	3,349	2,527
Sikhs	1,688	399	1,414
Jains	1	35	8
Musalmáns ...	6,009	6,003	5,999
Christians ...	9	206	51

Chapter III. C.

Religion.

Religion.

their caste and they become Musalmáns. Also conversion to Islám still continues. The alteration in the former population of the two religions is largely accounted for by the figures of each census for Chúhrás. In 1881 the number of Hindu Chúhrás was 27,891 and of Musalmán 24,277. In 1891 the corresponding figures were 58,615 and 4,600. This discrepancy cannot be explained ; Chúhrás generally adopt the religious tenets of the owners of the village in which they are settled, and Hindu landowners would not admit Musalmán Chúhrás. Nothing is to be gained by comparing figures of the two census showing distribution of other than Musalmáns between Sikhs and Hindús. In 1881 all were recorded as Sikhs who declared themselves such. The instructions to the supervising staff in 1891 defined the true Sikh as one who wore long hair and abstained from tobacco, thereby restricting the term to followers of Guru Gobind one would think. Others were to be classed as Hindu by religion, and Sikh or Nánakpanthi or whatever they liked to return by sect. The rule, however, does not appear to have been clearly understood or carefully followed in this district, for we find that of the 86,630 males recorded as Sikhs by religion, 37,244 were classed as Nánakpanthís or "worshippers of Nának" by sect and only 36,458 as Guru Gobindís. In the adjoining district of Amritsar nearly all the Sikh religionists were classed as Guru Gobindi by sect. The distinction between the two is worthy of a brief notice here. Nának was the first of the Sikh Gurus, who was born in 1469 A. D. and died in 1538 A. D. The doctrines he inculcated were chiefly the unity of God, the uselessness of ceremonial and the vanity of earthly wishes. He was of the Punjab and had his following among the Punjabi Khatrís and Jats. It never seems to have been large during his lifetime and was hardly distinguishable to outsiders from other quietest sects of Hinduism. It was under his successors that Sikhism rose to importance as a military, political and religious organization. Guru Arjan, the compiler of the Adi-Granth now in use, was the first of the Gurus to get into trouble with the Government. With his son Guru Hargobind, A. D. 1606—1638, the long struggle between the Sikhs and Muhammadans commenced and he it was who first taught the Sikhs to fight and plunder. Guru Gobind Singh, the tenth and last Guru, headed the Sikhs from 1675 A. D. to 1708 A. D., when Aurangzeb's persecution was at its height. To bind his followers together he grafted strange ceremonial observances on to the more vague doctrines of Gurus Nának and Arjan, and the new faith strengthened by increased numbers of adherents and by occasional successes in fights with the Musalmáns rose in public recognition to the dignity and importance of a distinct religion. Briefly speaking, Guru Gobind added five points to the religion of Nának. The first was the *pahul* or solemn initiation into Sikhism which consists of drinking a mixture of sugar and water, stirred up with a dagger (*khanda*) of steel. The initiation cannot be performed until the subject has reached years of discretion, and once initiated he becomes a Sikh and adds Singh to his name. Secondly, the Singh has to carry about his person five marks beginning with the letter K, which are known as the five Kakkás; namely, the *kes* or uncut hair; the *kachh* or short drawers; the *kara* or iron bangle; the *khanda* or steel dagger; and the *kanga* or comb. Thirdly, the followers of Gobind must abstain from smoking tobacco. Fourthly, they must not eat any flesh except of animals which have been decapitated by a blow on the back of the neck (*jhatka*). And fifthly they are not to observe the distinctions of caste or to pay special reverence to the Brahmans. There are other ordinances laid down by the Guru, but even these are not rigidly observed except by the strictest Sikhs. In this district few Sikhs will be found ordinarily bearing about their persons more than three of the five marks, namely the *kes*, the *kanga* and the *kachh*, and the latter is often not worn. They are generally strict in abstaining from tobacco and in the matter of *jhatka* meat; the last having by this time acquired the binding force of custom. They observe distinctions of caste to some extent and undoubtedly revere Brahmans. In his religious observances the Gobindi Sikh hardly differs from the Nánakpanthi, they both go to the *dharmsála* at least twice a month and hear the Granth read, but do nothing more. Practically therefore the only noticeable distinctions between the two are that the true Gobindi Sikh wears long hair, avoids tobacco, and bears the title of Singh; on the other hand all Sikhs are followers of Nának, and hence in a sense Nanakpanthi, thus many of the true Gobindi Sikhs in the district may from want of understanding have styled themselves Nánakpanthis. Then again we find that at the recent enumeration as many as 14,051 males recorded themselves Hindús by religion and Nánakpanthís by sect. Similarly 1,438 Guru Gobindís by sect said they were Hindús by religion, which only indicates that in this district as elsewhere Hindús have been very much influenced by the teachings of Guru Nának and his followers; their doctrines allowing for much greater laxity of opinion and of ceremonial observances than Hinduism does. It would be fruitless to discuss further the classification of Sikhs as we have it. The only conclusion one arrives at is that the enumeration as actually made in this district did not succeed in drawing any reliable distinction between the strict Guru Gobindi Sikhs and the laxer followers of Guru Nának; and that possibly many Nánakpanthís were recorded as Hindús who were as much Sikhs in religion as those actually written so.

Similarly with regard to the Hindu sects it is admitted that the figures recorded at the recent census were, as a rule, no sort of guide to the strength of the sect, and the notice of the various sects was mainly directed to putting on record the names which the people returned as their sects. This branch

90   CHAP. III.—THE PEOPLE.

Chapter III, C.

Religion.

Religion.

of the enquiry has been discussed fully in Chapter IV of the Provincial Census Report, and it would require a very prolonged and careful investigation into the inner life of the people before any information, reliable or worth having, could be added to that furnished on the subject by Mr. Maclagan. Generally speaking it may be said that the ordinary villagers of the Hindu persuasion in this district pay very little attention to religion. The Hindu Jats and all Sikhs go to the *dharmsálás* and hear the Granth read at least twice a month, on the first and the fifteenth, unless any special business stands in their way ; the Arorás and Khatrís, who are not Sikhs, worship images of some of their numerous deities in *thakurdwárás*, Krishna being regarded as the chief impersonation of the one God. The Granth is read by a Sádh who may be a Brahmin, a Khatri, a Jat, or of any other class apparently. Most villages have their *Prohat*, a Brahmin priest, who performs religious ceremonies and receives a daily feed of bread and an indefinite portion of grain at each harvest. The *Pándah*, also a Brahmin, is a more learned priest than the *Prohat*, and is shared between six or seven villages perhaps ; he is usually called in to assist the *Prohat* at wedding ceremonies. The *Acháraj* performs the funeral ceremonies : when a Hindu dies his body is burnt, his *kirya* performed, and the ashes are conveyed to the Ganges by the nearest relation who can make it convenient to go. As to what will happen after his death the ordinary Hindu rustic neither knows nor cares, but if they think about it they conclude that the question of their having to enter on another life depends greatly on how they behave in this.

Religion in Lahore city.

The urban population situate within Lahore municipal limits which takes in the city and its suburbs, the civil station and Meean Meer cantonments, is distributed according to religion as below—

Hindús	...	...	...	62,077
Sikhs	...	...	...	7,306
Jains	...	...	...	339
Musalmáns	...	...	...	102,280
Christians	...	...	...	4,697
Others	...	...	...	155
		Total	...	176,854

The bulk of the Hindús in the city perform their religious observances with some strictness, influenced no doubt by their women folk, who cling to religion and the various superstitious practices associated with it as the chief source of diversion and recreation in their otherwise monotonous existence. Strict Hindús, Sikhs and Jains hold many beliefs in common and have no scruple against worshipping in each other's temples.

Sanátan Dharm Sabha.

The most prominent of the formal associations of orthodox Hindús established for the conservation of the ancient Hindu religion as taught by the Vedas, Puránas and other Shástrás is the *Sanátan Dharm Sabha*, which was started in Lahore in 1889 and subsequently registered under Act XXI of 1861, on the 25th February 1890. The number of its enrolled members is said to be 300 only, but at the recent census 4,898 Sanátan Dharmís were recorded in this district, of whom 2,799 were males. The number of its sympathisers probably is much larger. The business of the *Sabha* is conducted by an executive committee, elected annually at a general meeting of the society. The committee which is provided with a President and Secretary follows rules framed and altered from time to time at general meetings of all the members. The objects of the *Sabha* as noted in the memorandum of constitution are—

Chapter III, C.
——
Religion.

Sanátan Dharm Sabha.

1. To preserve the old orthodox Hinduism in the country and to promote it.

2. To establish a college for imparting modern education together with religious instruction.

3. To establish a library in which all works treating of the Sanátan Dharm may be kept.

The work at present undertaken by the *Sabha* for attaining these objects consists of—

1. Weekly lectures and sermons delivered and preached on Sunday evenings at the *Sabha* premises, where admission is open to followers of all creeds and beliefs.

2. Occasional special lectures which are open to orthodox Hindús only.

3. Annual lectures delivered on the occasion of fixed anniversaries.

4. Instruction in an Anglo-Vernacular School, containing 240 boys, and teaching up to the Entrance Standard.

5. Instruction in a purely Sanskrit *Patshála* (School) to a number of nearly 40 students.

6. Feeding of poor homeless students from outstations, conducted not directly by the *Sabha* but by a body of orthodox Hindús which is affiliated to the *Sabha.*

7. Maintenance of the temple attached to the premises of the *Sabha.*

8. Consideration of questions of a religious or socio-religious character by Pandits.

9. Maintenance of a library of Sanskrit works which is as yet only of limited pretensions.

Of modern developments of deistical unorthodoxy, the most prominent instances in Lahore are the Brahmo Samáj and the Arya Samáj ; the origin, history, religious and social aims of these two have been fully described by Mr. Maclagan on pages 172 to 179 of his Provincial Census Report. The

Modern developments.

Chapter III, C.

Religion.

Brahmo Samáj.

Brahmo Samáj was introduced into the Punjab from Bengal, but has not met with much success having extended nowhere but to Lahore and Simla, and there it is very weak in numbers ; at present on the Lahore register there are not more than 70 registered members. The doctrines of the Brahmos are opposed to Vedas and to all scriptures which can be interpreted to support polytheism ; they reject caste restrictions and seek to establish a theistic faith which shall take the place of all other beliefs. The Samáj was established in Lahore in 1864, and eight years afterwards, in April 1872, the Brahmos built a *mandir* (church building) of their own in the Anárkalli bázár. Here they hold their weekly prayer service every Sunday morning and evening, and a religious debate in which men of other religions also take part is held every Friday. Their prayers are somewhat after the style of the English church service and are addressed to Brahma (the one God), the chief purport being that all men including Hindús, Christians and Muhammadans may be converted to Him and become Brahmos. The congregation which seldom exceeds 50 or 60 is drawn from the ranks of the well-to-do middle class of the native society of Lahore. The Samáj has no educational institutions of its own but is said to have helped in founding a Middle School for girls in the city, of which it has the management. The Samáj maintains a charity fund from which allowances are made to widows and orphans. They have recently sent two men to Calcutta to be trained as missionaries.

The Arya Samáj.

The basis of the *Aryan* faith is the revelation of God in the Vedas and the revelation of God in nature. The Puránas and other Shastras are rejected as their teaching is inconsistent with the proved results of Natural Science. The Vedas, no doubt as translated by the European Sanscritists, appear entirely inconsistent with scientific accuracy, but this the *Aryas* explain away by ascribing metaphorical significations to the Vedic texts. Their interpretations of the scriptures on which they rely are directed towards defending them from all imputations of pantheism and polytheism, and discovering in them indications of an accurate acquaintance with the latest inventions of modern science. In common parlance the *Arya* is a Hindu by religion, but the stricter members of the Samáj have a prejudice against being classed as Hindús. They say " their fundamental principles are founded on solid reason and science." Idolatry and all its attendant ceremonies have according to them no basis in the Vedas and no place in true religion.

The Samáj finds an efficacy in prayer and worship, but discourages the formal rites and ceremonies which play so prominent a part in popular Hinduism. They find that cremation is inculcated by the Vedas on sanitary grounds and therefore burn their dead, but omit the ceremonies of the *kirya karam* and do not think it necessary to take the *phul* or ashes to the Ganges, any other stream serving equally well. As regards the

soul and future life the Arya's faith is described by Mr. Maclagan as follows :—

" The three entities of Dayanand's philosophy are God, the soul and *pra-
krite* or matter. Soul he regards as physically distinct from God, but
related to Him as the contained to the container, the contemplated to the
contemplator, the son to the father. Soul enters into all animals, and
there are indications of soul in the vegetable kingdom also. In most
of its details the Aryan system retains the terminology of the traditional
philosophy of Hinduism. It maintains above all things the law of metempsy-
chosis and places the aim of virtue in escape from the law, but the *mokhsh* or
beatitude is for an era (*kalp*) only, after the termination of which the soul
resumes its wanderings. The localisation of the Hindu paradises, *Parlok* and
Swarg, is rejected ; heaven and hell lie in the pleasures and sorrows of the soul
whether these be in this life or in the life to come.

The Arya Samáj recruits almost entirely from the educated
class, their tenets and theories being unfitted to the understanding of the unlearned. Any person, however, professing be-
lief in the fundamental principles of the Samáj, is eligible for
membership, and may after probation be admitted as a full
member, and obtain a vote in the affairs of its society. There
are at the present time on the Lahore register about 600 members, among whom pleaders, Government servants, and others,
who have the greatest pretension to mental enlightenment, take
a leading place. As regards caste the main bulk of the society
are Khatrís, Súds, Baniás, and others found in the clerical and
commerical classes.

It is said that though Lahore is the centre of "Aryanism"
in the Punjab, yet even here their religious zeal has cooled
down a great deal since the death, a few years ago, of their
leader Sawami Dayanand, who founded the sect twenty years ago.
However they still hold weekly meetings, generally on Sundays,
so as to admit of the presence of Government servants and
pleaders. At these meetings prayers, lectures on the Vedas and on
other subjects are read, hymns are sung on the Sama Veda system,
and there are other miscellaneous proceedings. At an annual
meeting, a report is read and an executive committee with
office bearers appointed. A good deal of influence is undoubtedly exercised by the Dayanand Anglo-Vedic College, which was
founded in Lahore some time ago, and has been conducted
entirely on Aryan lines. The college, while preparing students
in the ordinary subjects with considerable success for the
University Examinations, pays special attention to instruction in
Sanskrit and Hindi, and imparts a certain amount of religious
training by the institution of morning and evening prayer in
the boarding-houses, and by the reading of extracts from the
Satyarth Parkásh of Dayanand.

There are no statistics available from which the increase
or decrease of the *Arya* Society in Lahore can be ascertained, and
it is not easy to see what progress it is making in general
influence on social and religious opinions. Quite recently the
Arya Samáj in Lahore has received a severe check, for the time
at least, from a split in its ranks which threatens at present to

Chapter III, C.
Religion.

The Arya Samáj.

develope into permanent separation. The dispute arose on the question of eating flesh. Vegetarianism has always been regarded as one of their tenets inculcated by the Vedas ; but several of the leading members have not abstained from eating flesh. Some of the strictly vegetarian members lately charged these with hypocrisy, and so the quarrel originated. Those of the Society who eat flesh deny that the Vedas as properly interpreted prohibit it. A hot controversy on the subject continued for some time and eventually the two parties found they could not agree on any matters that might be put forward for discussion. The vegetarians, who appear to be the younger party, in November 1893, when the election of office bearers took place, succeeded in ousting some representatives of the other party from the ranks of the governing body and bringing in some of the most junior members. Thereupon the advanced party left the meeting in disgust, and hired a separate building in Anárkalli for their meetings. At present therefore there are two parties ; the younger party has possession of the Samáj building, and the advanced party is said to have retained the management of the Anglo-Vedic College. Efforts are now being made to effect a reconciliation and these may succeed, but the incident is instructive as showing how easily schisms in the ranks of a society so constituted may occur.

The Deo Dharmís.

The Deo Dharm was founded on the Jubilee day, February 16th, 1887, in Lahore, by a Brahman Pandit Satya Nand Agnihotri, who was formerly a master in the Government School at Lahore : while there, he came under the influence of the Brahmo School, and in 1879, became a missionary of the Sadháran Brahmo Samáj. Subsequently finding himself unable to continue with the Brahmos he started a religion of his own, the leading principles of which are the absolute omnipotence of God and the eventual absorption of human soul into God. Lahore is the head-quarters of the society at present, but its numbers are few at present. The Deo Dharmís are at bitter feud with the Arya Samajís and have lately been indulging in an acrimonious pamphlet warfare.

Musalmáns.

The distribution of every 1,000 of the Musalmán population is shown in the margin ; the *Shiás* are found almost entirely in the Lahore city. The *Wahábís* are returned very short of their real number ; p r o b a b l y many Muhammadans, who were true *Wahábís*

Sect.	Total population.	Rural population.
Sunnís	989·1	986·3
Shiás	6·0	8·3
Wahábis	0·3	0·3
Others	4·6	5·1

thought it safer not to record themselves as such. The Musalmán sects are discussed in Part IV of Chapter IV of the Census Report for 1891, and further notice of the matter here is not required. The general distribution of native religions by castes in each tahsil can be gathered from the figures of Table No. VII.

The distribution of Christian religionists by race is shown below—

Details.				Males.	Females.	Total.
Europeans	...	...	...	2,306	905	3,211
Eurasians	...	...	...	434	411	845
Armenians	...	...	...	16	17	33
Natives	...	...	...	721	676	1,397
Total	...	...		3,477	2,009	5,486

The races and sects of the Christians are shown in Table A of the Census Report for 1891. The figures, however, are not reliable as regards Native Christians. To quote from Mr. Maclagan's Report: "It is a notoriously difficult thing to "ascertain the sect to which some Native Christians belong as " they often do not know themselves, or if they do, can only " give its name in some unrecognizable form." It is noteworthy that there has been a large increase in the number of Native Christians since 1881, when the number recorded was 760. Many of the converts are of the Chúhra caste. The Eurasian Christians number 844, of whom 536 belong to the Church of England, 189 to the Roman Catholic Church and 57 to the Presbyterian Church. Of Christians other than Natives and Eurasians 1,614 males and 629 females belong to the Church of England, 359 males and 193 females to the Roman Catholic Church, 170 to Presbyterian Church; and 147 are Wesleyans.

The following brief notices are given of some of the principal missions at present in the district :—

An account of the American Presbyterian Mission has been kindly furnished by the Revd. C. W. Forman as follows :— This Mission in connection with the Board of Foreign Missions of the Presbyterian Church in the United States of America, was established in the year 1849 by Messrs. Newton and Forman, who arrived in Lahore in November of that year. The staff of missionaries now consists of the Revd. Messrs. Forman, J. C. R. Ewing, D. D., H. C. Velte, J. H. Orbison, M. D., J. M. McComb, U. S. G. Jones, J. G. Gilbertson, their wives and Miss Thiede.

The work of the mission is carried on by means of teaching in schools for boys and girls and in a College, by treating the sick in two dispensaries, by preaching in four places in and near the city and in villages in the district, by the distribution of religious tracts, and by the supervision and instruction of

Chapter III. C.

Religion.

American Presbyterian Mission.

two churches. The schools for boys consist of a main school, six branch schools and one night school for adults.

There were in attendance last year in the main school 393 pupils, in the branch schools 395, and in the adult night school 58, making a total of 848. The fees realized amounted to Rs. 4,808. The Assistant Inspector after examining the school at the end of the year wrote in the log book as follows :— "I know of no other school in the circle where the teaching and discipline exert a better influence on the manners and character of the scholars than the Lahore Mission School." The total number of pupils in the Girls' Schools is 328. These schools are regularly inspected by the Government Inspectress. Four of the missionaries give a large part of their time to the college and are assisted by a Professor of Physical Science, an Assistant Professor of Mathematics, and Professors of Sanskrit, Arabic and Persian, respectively. There were enrolled in November 1892, 185 students, of whom 38 passed the Intermediate and 13 the B. A. Examination. The income from fees during the year amounted to Rs. 9,029.

There is one *general* dispensary, and one for women and children, under the management of Dr. Isa Dás and Dr. Phœbe Isa Dás, both of whom hold Government certificates. The number of visits to the former in 11 months of the year amounted to 22,250 and in the latter to 19,209. In the general dispensary there were 680 minor operations and in the female 537, and 864 special female cases. Preaching is kept up at the four places mentioned, and there are usually fairly large, attentive, and well-behaved audiences. In the district work is carried on in four out-stations, in three of which considerable numbers have been baptized. This work is done by the Revd. and Mrs. U. S. Grant Jones, Miss Thiede the Revd. Dharm Dás and three assistants.

At the end of the year the number of church members was 213. The whole Christian community numbered about 450. Sixty-four adults were admitted during the past year by baptism, chiefly from the Chúhra caste. There exist now small but growing Christian communities in the villages of Wágah, Munnihála and Sugga, in the Lahore district. These communities are as yet connected with the Lahore Church.

Methodist Episcopal Mission.

The following account of this Mission has been kindly supplied by the Revd. A. T. Leonard :—

The Methodist Episcopal Mission is the youngest of the Evangelical Missions in Lahore, having occupied the field in February 1881. It is connected with what is now officially designated the "North-West India Conference" of the Methodist Episcopal Church of the United States of America. The Mission is supported by the Missionary Board of the above Church, and by funds raised in India. It owns a neatly built red-brick church, costing Rs. 10,000, and having a seating capacity for nearly three hundred persons. It is situated near the Railway Station, and was built for and is used chiefly by the Railway community. From 1885 to 1891 there were two missionaries resident in Lahore, having charge of the Native and European congregations. At present there is but one missionary, the Revd. A. T. Leonard, who is assisted by his wife and a staff of European (unpaid) Local Preachers and Exhorters, and paid native workers. The official statistics for the year 1892 show a Native Christian community of two hundred and thirty (230) adults and ninety-seven (97) children baptized from heathenism, one hundred and sixty-six (166) adults and eighty-eight (88) children, living chiefly in Shahdara and adjacent villages ; and of the lower castes.

Chapter III, C.

Religion.

Methodist Episcopal Mission.

There are three primary schools, not under Government supervision. These schools are established chiefly for the benefit of the children of the recently baptized converts.

This institution was founded in 1870 by the Revd. T. V. French, then a missionary of the Church Missionary Society and now Bishop of Lahore, for the purpose of training Christian natives of this and the neighbouring provinces as clergy and catechists. At first the Divinity School was conducted in a hired bungalow in Anárkalli, but in 1871 it was located in a set of buildings specially purchased and adapted for the purpose, known as Maha Singh's garden, near the Mayo Hospital. These consist of the Principal's house, chapel, library and class room, Native clerical teacher's house, and quarters for some 25 students, married and unmarried, grouped round three courts.

St. John's (Missionary) Divinity School.

The course of instruction in the Divinity School is almost entirely theological, and the students do not, therefore, appear in any of the Government examinations, nor does the college receive any grant from Government. Students who have not passed the Middle School Examination are expected to pass a similar examination on entering the Divinity School. The course of study lasts three years, and the following subjects are taught : Elements of Hebrew and Greek ; Exegesis of Holy Scripture ; Church History ; Christian Doctrine and Morals ; the Evidences of Christianity ; the Hindu and Muhammadan controversies ; Pastoral Theology and Homiletics (including criticism of sermons to Christians and others) ; the Book of Common Prayer ; the rudiments of Physical and Mental Science ; and Singing. The teaching staff consists at present of two European missionaries, who fill the office of Principal and Vice-Principal respectively, and a native teacher who has been trained in the college itself. Both Principal and Vice-Principal have, however, other duties also to perform, connected with the missionary work of the station. All the teaching, except in special cases, is given through the medium of Urdu, and various theological text-books in that language have been produced from time to time by the teaching staff. The number of students, who have attended the Divinity School since its establishment in 1870 up to 1894 is somewhat over 100. The students are drawn

Chapter III. C.
—
Religion.
St. John's (Missionary) Divinity School.

from all classes of the Native Christian community. It will be seen from the above that the accommodation of the Divinity School has not been entirely exhausted by the requirements of its theological pupils. Advantage has been taken of this circumstance to form a hostel for Christian students attending the various educational institutions in Lahore, and at present there are some twelve secular students living in the Divinity School under rules specially framed for them.

The funds for purchase and adaptation of the premises and for stocking the library (which contains several thousand volumes) were raised mainly by the founder the late Bishop French. The Church Missionary Society gave a large grant, and the property belongs to that body. A few scholarships have been endowed or are annually contributed by friends. The late Revd. G. M. Gordon (who was at one time on the teaching staff) left a legacy towards building a college chapel; and this, with a testimonial fund raised to Mr. Gordon's memory, has almost sufficed to cover the cost of erecting the Gordon Memorial Chapel. This is the most conspicuous and ornamental object among the college buildings. It is built of red brick in a Saracenic modification of the Northern Italian style.

Church Missionary Society settlement at Clarkabad.

Under the authority of the Punjab Government in 1868 a lease of land in Chúnián tahsíl of this district, estimated to measure 1,935 acres, was granted for ten years from the 1st April 1869 to certain leading members of the Church Missionary Society in Lahore district. The estate was called Clarkabad after the Revd. Mr. Clark, a leading missionary of the Society. In 1882 the lease was renewed for a further term of five years from 1879 in the name of the Revd. Mr. Bateman, who had been acting as agent for the lessees. This was renewed again on the old terms from the year 1884 for the remaining term of settlement. Since 1881 the estate has been paying to Government Rs. 500 a year under the lease. Now the question is under the consideration of Government whether ownership of any of the land, and if so, of how much, should be conceded for the benefit of the Christian settlement at Clarkabad, and under what terms and in whose favour such a grant should be made. At present out of the total area attached to the estate 740 acres are cultivated by Christians and 870 acres by non-Christians; the latter class of tenants are made to pay double as high rents as the former. The Christian tenants are mostly converted Chúhrás from the Amritsar district. The land is all very good and receives excellent irrigation from the Bári Doáb Canal. The Church Missionary settlement have gradually built up a model village provided with good roads and well-built cottages.

The principal buildings and institutions there are as follows :—

A masonry built church consisting of a nave, chancel, one aisle and a vestry surmounted with a spire. The church has recently been enlarged and now has accommodation for 300. Prayers are read daily, morning and evening, and full services are held on Sundays : the services are read in Punjabi.

A Girls' Orphanage and Agricultural School constructed of burnt brick, and including dormitories and a school-room for the children. There are now 54 boarders, and 91 names are on the school register.

A Boy's Orphanage and Industrial School, at present built of unburnt brick.

There are 91 names on the school books, and 25 orphans in the Orphanage. Some of them are taught trades and all work for a time every day in the fields. Both girls and boys read up to 5th Class Upper Primary.

There is a good dwelling house, with a dining room, sitting room and four bed-rooms for the use of the C. M. S. Missionary, and another for the Superintendent of the settlement in secular matters. A substantial building is in course of erection for a hospital, consisting of two wards, which will hold four or five beds each, and four other rooms for dispensary, operating room, consulting room, and store room. A native apothecary is in charge. The secular affairs of the village are managed by a village committee, and the religious affairs by a Church Committee. Two ladies of the Church Missionary Society have recently come to live in Clarkabad and work among the women.

The present pastor of the village is the Revd. Thomas Howell; and the Revd. T. R. Wade, Chairman of the Church Missionary Punjab District Church Council, visits the settlement from Amritsar once a month. The estate lies about four miles east of the Kot Rádha Kishen station on the Mooltan Railway, and is approached by a fairly good unmetalled road.

The Punjab Religious Book Society was established in 1863, and has its central depository in the Anarkalli bázár; it is in connection with the London Religious Tract Society, and has for its object to supply the public with religious tracts and books in English and the Vernacular languages. The steady increase of the sales of this Society has been remarkable. Thirty colporters are engaged in Lahore and other stations in the Punjab in the sale of tracts, books and copies of the Bible, for which there is a steadily increasing demand. The receipts from the sales of books are large. A considerable number of books are published by the Society each year. Subscriptions are apparently not very liberal. Funds for the publication of Vernacular Scriptures are provided by the British and Foreign Bible Society at Home. The central depository for the whole Province at Lahore contains a large supply of books which have been received from many Societies and Publishers, both in England and India.

SECTION D.—TRIBES, CASTES AND LEADING FAMILIES.

Table No. IX gives the figures for the principal castes and tribes of the district, with details of sex, but not religion, while Table No. IX A. shows the numbers of the less important castes. It would be out of place to attempt a minute historical description of each. Many of them are found all over the Punjab, and most of them in many other districts, and their representatives in Lahore are distinguished by no local peculiarities, while each caste will be found described in Chapter VI of the Census Report for 1881, and Chapter XI of that for 1891. The tables appended to this edition do not include any statement which shows the local distribution, by tahsíls, of any of the tribes and castes, but Abstract Statement No. 35 appended to the Census Report for 1891 gives these details for a few selected castes and may be referred to.

The Jat tribe.

The most important tribe numerically and otherwise is the Jat, which covers over 16 per cent. of the total population of the district. The Jats show an increase of 10 per cent. on their numbers as recorded in 1881. The distribution of these by religions is 4 per cent. Sikhs, 53 per cent. Hindús, 43 per cent. Musalmáns. Their distribution by locality is shown in the marginal statement. Out of the total number of Jat vil-

Lahore city	...	...	...	11,099
Lahore tahsíl	...	...	...	68,109
Chunian tahsíl	...	...	...	35,150
Kasúr tahsíl	...	...	...	39,129
Shárakpur tahsil	...	...	...	20,075

lages in the district, amounting to 728, if 139 villages partially Jat be included, 268 are in the Mánjha tract, 100 along the Rávi on either side of the river, 208 in the Sharakpur tahsil, and 152 in the Sutlej Hithár. The Sikh Jats are a far more important section of the tribe than their mere numbers would lead one to think. Though the rules of conduct as laid down by Gúru Gobind Singh for the guidance of his followers are not observed so strictly as formerly and disregard for them is undoubtedly on the increase, yet still Sikhism retains in part the prestige of the military organization, which made it the splendid power it was in the Punjáb in the time of Ranjít Singh and might very easily sometime in the future be utilized by malcontents to form the nucleus of a dangerous combination against British rule ; and if any such occasion did arise in the future, undoubtedly the Jat Sikhs of the central districts of the Province, and among them not least of this and the Amritsar district, would constitute the important element in the situation. The marauding instincts instilled into the minds of his followers by Har Govind, the first warrior of the Gúrús, though fifth in order of descent from the original Gúru Bába Nának ; the fighting habits fostered in the race by the sword rule of Ranjít Singh and by the constant faction broils that prevailed between the separate units of the Mahárája's military following when not engaged against a common foe reveal themselves continually in the every day life of the Sikh Jat of the present day, in his grasping rapacity and in his readiness to take up arms in defence of what he considers his rights. From an agricultural point of view the distinction of religion is important, because the rules of conduct at present observed by the Sikhs are much better adapted to the necessities of a cultivating life than the habits of Muhammadans at least, if not Hindus. Chief among these is the rule prohibiting smoking ; the Muhammadan and to a less extent the Hindu wastes his time, dulls his faculties, and to some extent predisposes himself to luxuriousness and indolence by excessive smoking. The immunity of the true Singh Sikh from this habit undoubtedly makes him a more efficient agriculturist as a rule than his brother Jat of any other religion. Similarly being somewhat lax in his religious observance he has much more liberty as regards his times for going to and stopping at his work in the fields than the Muhammadan Jat, who though he may not carry out strictly the prescribed ritual of prayers five times a day must conform more or less to the custom of his coreligionists. On the other hand the Muhammadan and Hindu Jats are much less addicted, openly at least, to the vice of drinking, which is sanctioned by the Sikh religion, and which incapacitates many a Sikh cultivator for steady perseverance in cultivation and quiet domesticity of life to which the ordinary Jat in the absence of disquieting circumstances appears to be naturally inclined. This is sufficient mention of the distinctions in Jat character that appear to be based on differences in religion. Next come those found to accompany difference in locality of habitation. In physique, intelligence, and general strength of character without doubt far the finest specimens of the Jat tribe are to be found in the Mánjha, and among the Mánjha Jats the Sandhus, occupying 159 estates in all respects rank first. It was from these that most of Maháraja Ránjit Singh's military leaders were drawn; and indications of the wealth and power to which they then rose are to be found in the large masonry houses belonging to ancient Sikh Sardár families, which still stand in many of the Mánjha villages ; though for the most part in bad repair. Before and during the Sikh rule all the Jats of the Lahore Mánjha formed an important contribution to the Imperial army, but after the general disbandment that followed the extension of British rule over the Punjab, they appear to have returned to their villages and taken kindly to an independent rustic life, supporting themselves partly by means of a carrying trade which brought in considerable profits before the expansion of our railway system ; and partly by the precarious fruits of a cultivation which was then almost entirely dependent on an uncertain rainfall, canal irrigation not yet having been extended to the Bári Doáb tract. Of late years the attractions of farming rendered easy by the new resource of canal water and general abundance of land have proved superior to the prospects held forth in Government service, whether military or police, so far as the Mánjha Jats generally are concerned. This is the more remarkable as in the adjoining district of Amritsar, the Sandhus have taken largerly to service in the army and in the military police. In the Lahore district the sons seeing their fathers for the most part preferring an agricultural life have followed suit and stayed at home. It is merely a question of custom or example. One small village of Sandhus in Chúnián tahsíl with a population of hardly more than three hundred souls now contains twelve army pensioners and more than that number serving in the army, and yet in the whole Mánjha the total number of pensioners at present is 524 and of soldiers only 1,663.

As an agriculturist the Mánjha Jat is only moderately good. Hitherto their farming has been conducted on broad and rough principles; they have had large areas to deal with, which until within the last few years were dependent mainly on dry cultivation, and this was dependent for its success far more on the season than on any special efforts on the cultivator's part. The canal extension even has hitherto made little difference in the character of the farming; the Mánjha Jats still have plenty of land, which under irrigation gives excellent produce in return for very little trouble on the cultivator's part. In the more congested parts however of this canal irrigated tract, on the north for instance, towards the Amritsar border, where population is beginning to press on the soil and the land in places shows signs of exhaustion, the people are coming to understand that to make their land yield continuously something more is required than a sowing preceded by two or three ploughings and followed by copious canal irrigation.

Socially the Mánjha Jat's character is often open to reproach. The majority of them drink, and many of them drink to great excess: a considerable number of Mánjha Jat villages have obtained an unenviable notoriety for the numerous bad characters, thieves and highway robbers they shelter. Murders and murderous assaults in the Mánjha occupy far too prominent a place in the criminal records and appear to be increasing steadily as the Jats grow rich and riotous on the proceeds of their newly irrigated lands. They are generally reputed to be deficient in chastity. This might be more truly said of the women than of the men. It is not often that the village life is disturbed by any serious scandal of immorality. The fact that a Jat who has a woman of his own section outside his family to live with him incurs the general opprobrium of the brotherhood, and, also the custom whereby a Jat usually takes to wife the widow of his deceased brother by the simple ceremony of *chadár dáli* or throwing of the sheet, no doubt both act as a check on immoral tendencies. In their dealings with one another the Mánjha Jats often exhibit excessive greed and intemperate cruelty. In their villages they are democratic by inclination and impatient of control by those they do not fear, but to the Government officer paying them a friendly visit, especially to the Englishman, they are frank and concilia-

tory without losing their outspokenness and customary in-
dependence of manner. Taken all round, notwithstanding his
numerous faults, the Mánjha Jat is a fine fellow with great
capacities for good under careful guidance : Though naturally
restive and resentful as individuals under injury done and
always extraordinarily tenacious of their purpose, yet as a
body they are quietly disposed in the absence of disturbing
elements and easily led. Whether as peasants or soldiers
they yield readily to firm discipline, provided it is accompanied with justice and fair dealing. Both in their faults
and in their virtues, Sandhús are the most prominent
among the Mánjha Jats ; as they are the most striking
in their external appearance, the features becoming hand-
somer and more decidedly marked, the older the Sandhu
grows.

In the Hithár of the Sutlej Beás nearly all the Jats are
Sidhu, who have here 60 villages. Sandhús here are only located in 24 estates. The Sidhu Jats occupy principally the western
half of the Hithár, which forms the southern portion of the
Chúnián tahsíl. They came here probably from the Ferozepore
district, on the opposite side of the river. An account of the
Sidhú's migration in this direction is furnished on page 59 of
the Ferozepore Gazetteer for 1888-89. The Sidhu is a far more
peaceable, well behaved, and industrious member of society
than his Sandhu brother. Having lived for many generations
on the meagre profits derived from cultivation dependent on a
precarious rainfall and a slow and expensive process of well
irrigation by the Persian wheel, the Sidhu Jat has gradually
become accustomed to regard the cultivation of his land and
constant attendance at his well as the chief, if not the sole
reason for his existence ; he has little money and little
time to spend on luxuries or on amusements. He is a
thrifty hard-working peasant cultivator, who prefers to
regard farming as a pleasure as well as a means of subsistence, and will not therefore bother himself with the
more ignoble and laborious market-garden style in which
the Aráin delights. In enterprise, pluck and perseverance
under adversity, the Sidhu Jat is immeasurably the superior of the Aráin. He is the true "zamíndár" or "hus-
bandman" of the Province, and his women and children
assist him all they can. Curiously enough a reduction in the
number of Sidhús on the figures of 1881 census is shown in the
1891 figures. This must be due to wrong enumeration at one
census or the other.

The Jats along the Rávi are principally Sandhús who have
some large settlements along the lower course of the river
through this district, mostly in the Chúnián tahsíl ; on its
left bank near the Montgomery border there are six or
seven settlements of *Manhes* Jats ; these are a somewhat
idle, disorderly lot, who appear to find difficulty in paying

Chapter III, D.

Tribes, Castes
and Leading
Families.

Hithár Jats.

Jats of the Rávi
villages.

any revenue demand however light and to have a great faculty for getting into debt.

The Jats in the Sharakpur tahsil are for the most part of the Virk section, of whom slightly more than half are Musalmáns. Of the Hindús, the larger number are recorded as Sikhs, but they observe the rules of their sect much more loosely here than in the Cis-Rávi portion of the district. The Hindu Virks are fairly good cultivators and in the main industrious. Some of the Musalmáns are not inferior to the Hindús, but the large majority have given way to the idleness and general depression that appears to have seized on most of the Musalmán peasantry in that tahsíl. In Gujránwála district, where the Virk Jats own 132 villages, a number of them return themselves as Rájpúts, but they marry freely with the Jat tribes of the neighbourhood. They say their founder was descended from the founder of the *Manhás* tribe of Rájpúts. The tribe were formerly of considerable political importance until they were subdued by Ranjít Singh.

The above account indicates sufficiently the locality and features of such sections of the Jats as are most prominent in different parts of the district. Other principal sections are described below.

Bhullar Jats.

The *Bhullar* Jats occupy a few large estates in the centre of the Kusúr Mánjha. They in common with the *Her* and *Mán* Jat sections, who also are found in a very few scattered villages of Lahore district, call themselves the *asl* or original Jats and are said to have sprung from the Jat or matted hair of Mahádeo, whose title is Bhúla Mahádeo. In character the *Bhullars* resemble the Sandhús, but are inferior in physique.

Gil Jats.

There are several *Gil* Jat settlements near the Sutlej in Kasúr tahsíl, one in the Mánjha of Lahore tahsíl, and three or four on the Rávi in the Chúnian tahsil. They are principally Sikhs, but they have not a good reputation in this district as cultivators, and are said to be ill-suited for the toil and risks of cultivation by well irrigation, on which they are largely dependent in the tracts where they happen to be settled. This is possibly owing to their having long been used to the luxuries of river inundation, which now neither on the Rávi nor Sutlej is as good as it used to be. They give one the impression of being both querulous and quarrelsome. In physique they are inferior to the ordinary Mánjha Jat.

Dhillons.

The *Dhillon* settlements are few and scattered over the whole district, chiefly in the Mánjha. Their largest village is that of *Bhasin* on the Amritsar border near the Rávi. The leading man Gurmukh Singh was lately deposed from the zaildárship for incapacity and failure to support the police properly, or control the evil propensities of his sons. The *Dhillon* section at present bears a bad character with the police, and many of them have been placed on security for good conduct. They are however pleasant men to meet. There are many other miscellaneous sections of Jats scattered about the district, but further detailed mention of them does not seem required.

The next most numerous tribe to the Jats are Aráins, who are settled mostly along either bank of the Rávi at the upper half of its course through the district ; as usual they lie thickest near the towns of Lahore and Sharakpur. Like the Aráin elsewhere, so here he is a humble minded peaceable creature, without a thought almost except for his land ; this he works up to a high pitch of cultivation by tillage and manuring. The Aráins land holdings in this district generally originated in individual occupation of as much land as was then needed to support the squatter and his family ; thus no surplus waste land would be included ; now their families have increased, sub-division has continued generation after generation, and the average property of most households has been reduced until it is quite insufficient to support the family, notwithstanding the proverbial capacity of the Aráin to make soil yield double as much as it will under another's management. Partly owing to the pressure of population on the land and partly in consequence of extravagant habits induced either by the example of others or by exaggerated ideas of the value of his land, the Aráin near Lahore has become deeply involved in debt and has had either to sell much of his land outright or to mortgage it for a price he can never make good or on terms he can never fulfil. A similar condi-tion of indebtedness, though on a less scale, and of conse-quent depression of agriculture is found in some of the smaller Aráin villages in the Sutlej Hithár, notably in the Kasúr tahsíl ; there however the Aráin labours under difficulties, as manure, the one thing absolutely necessary to enable Aráins to carry on with any success their niggling market garden style of farming, is not procurable in sufficient quantity. On the other hand in two or three large Aráin villages of the Kasúr Hithár, the very best cultiva-tion of the ordinary crops such as wheat and maize is to be seen, and the people themselves are thriving and not much in debt. Generally speaking however the Aráin is inferior to the Jat as a peasant cultivator and as a revenue-payer. Though exceedingly industrious and painstaking he lacks perseverence ; he succumbs to adverse conditions easily ; debt especially appears to cripple him more than it does the Jat. He has no notion of keeping his home neat, clean or comfortable, Aráin villages are proverbially filthy and untidy, his women folk are not to be compared with the Jat housewives for attention to domestic details or for economical management of their resources. There are very few Hindu and Sikh Aráin villages scat-

Chapter III, D.

Tribes, Castes
and Leading
Families.

Rájpúts.

tered about, the people of which claim to be called and regarded as Játs.

The Rájpúts are the third most numerous tribe of importance in the district. They are practically all Musalmáns ; no village is owned by any people who call themselves Rájpúts, and at the same time profess the Hindu religion. The predominant section in this district is that of Bhatti Rájpúts, who number nearly 20,000 souls or about two-fifths of the total Rájpút recorded population. Next to Bhattís are the Chauhans, who number 2,870 according to the recent census ; Joya 1,710, Naru 1,655. Other clans of Rájpúts in this district are very insignificant in numbers. Accounts of these clans and other Rájpúts will be found in Chapter VI of the Provincial Census Report for 1881. The figures for Rájpúts however must be received with caution, as it is well known that many Muhammadans of lower caste call themselves Rájpúts, who by birth have no claim to the name. This is probably the case with those classed as Rájpúts in the Lahore city, enumerated as 14,647 persons; many of these probably are men engaged in daily labour or other menial occupations, who thought fit to class themselves as Rájpúts. The uncertainty of the enumeration of this class is indicated by the fact that contrary to the result for every other tribe the recorded numbers have fallen off since the census of 1881 by 11 per cent. The true Rájpút agriculturists are notorious for extravagance, idleness, and slack cultivation. In almost every Rájpút village the mass of the people are impoverished and encumbered with debt though on the other hand there are generally one or two leading men in prosperous circumstances. The worst specimens of the Rájpút clan are in the Sharakpur tahsil. In the north-west corner of the Kasúr tahsil there are a few settlements of so-called Rájpúts, who are as competent agriculturists as any Jats to be found in the Mánjha.

Khokhars.

At the census of 1881 the Khokhars apparently were counted as Rájpúts ; at the recent census of 1891 they were enumerated separately. Their number is recorded to be 12,835 distributed as shown in the margin ; the most

Lahore city ... 2,014
Lahore tahsil 4,124
Chúnian do. 2,978
Kasúr do. 1,172
Sharakpur do. 2,517

important colony of them is along the bank of the Rávi, a little outside the Lahore city comprsing 16 estates, of which Niyázbeg is the largest. These all call themselves Rájpúts, ranking their section as fifth in order, and marrying women only of their own section or of the four above them. They are all luxuriously disposed and very extravagant, spending money wastefully on clothes, horses and marriages. They take no payment for their daughters nor do the parents of the girl have much expense, but the boy's parents spend anything from Rs. 500 to Rs. 2,000 on feasting the relations of either side, distribution of alms and dancing women. Also the *Tambol* or marriage gifts to the boy's father are very extravagant among this class, and the jewellery given to the girl from the boy's people comes to a good round sum. Similarly at funerals this section is

reckless in their expenditure. Thus it comes about that the
Khokhar Rájpúts are generally overwhelmed with debt. They
are also very inferior agriculturists, being too proud or indolent
to do heavy manual work themselves. The Khokhars in
the Chúnián tahsíl however are rather Jats than Rájpúts and do
not appear to have the idle expensive habits of the Khokhars
in Lahore and Sharakpur.

The Dogars are of importance only in the lowlands near the
Sutlej, where they own 68 estates in entirety and 11 others in
part. They are said to have come there from the neighbourhood of Pákpattan about 160 years ago. They are all Muhammadan by religion and call themselves converted descendants
of the Chauháns of Delhi. They were always a wild and law-
less race in the past having no settled habitations, and this to
some extent is their character still. Their houses by the riverside are for the most part wattled structures which can be put
together or taken to pieces with very little expenditure of time
or trouble. The Dogar generally establishes himself near
rivers partly from preference for the easy and inexpensive
form of cultivation which natural river inundation enables him
to carry on, partly also no doubt to have greater facilities for
indulging himself in his favourite pastime of cattle stealing.
Once the stolen animal can be brought across the river all trace of
it from the other side is lost. The Dogars in this district keep
up their name for indolence and bad cultivation almost better
than they do for cattle thieving. In this latter respect they
are exhibiting a slight improvement. Whether from their
habitual laziness and inclination for opiates or from their extravagance and carelessness in which they strongly resemble the
Rájpút, the majority of the Dogars villagers are very poor, but
the community usually includes at least one highly respectable
member who comes out to meet the Government official well
mounted and expensively dressed.

The Kambohs in this district are comparatively few having only 22 entire villages, and 22 which they own in part.
Of the former 13 are Hindu Kambohs and 9 Musalmán. Of
those they own in part, eleven are Hindu and eleven Musalmán. The large majority of these are situate in the Sutlej
Hithár, principally in the Chúnián tahsil. In 1881 the Kambohs
numbered 17,694 : the enumeration of the late census showed
20,448, of whom 63 per cent. are Hindús. 11 per cent. Sikhs, and
26 per cent. Musalmáns. The Musalmán Kambohs are hardly distinguishable from Aráins and very probably are of the same
stock ; the Sikh Kamboh is better than either, being equal to the
Aráin in industry, but more enterprising and more provident.
He matches the Aráin in market gardening when necessary
and is not inferior to the Sidhu Jat in general farming.
He is however of smaller physique than the Jat and of
much less intelligence. The Hindu Kambohs are seldom
found in the depressed and debt crippled condition into which
so many Arián villages have sunk.

Chapter III. D.

Tribes, Castes
and Leading
Families.

Khokhars.

Dogars.

Kambohs.

The Kharrals are an important section in the north-west portion of the Sharakpur tahsil, especially in the Bár uplands, where they lead a life partly pastoral, partly agricultural, mainly the former ; Musalmáns by religion. They pretend to a descent from the Rájpúts and look down with contempt on men whose main business it is to handle the plough. Some cultivation they do themselves or make a pretence of doing so; but probably most of the real work is done by the menial castes working under the owners or by tenants who give them a share of the produce. Their importance is derived chiefly from their propensity for cattle stealing, and indeed thieving of all sorts. It is not said that they aspire to higher forms of crime in this district. They are often spoken of as turbulent, quarrelsome and impatient of control, and no doubt their wild life in the Bár at a distance from the usual centres of administration partly encourages this condition of things, but they do not appear to have been implicated in much violent crime for a long time now. The worst that one can say of them on the experience of late years is that they are idle bad cultivators and practised thieves. In their persons they are striking, being both tall and handsome.

Gujars.

There are 19 Gujar villages in the district: that is, 10 are wholly Gujar, 9 are owned by Gujars in part. They have settled to a considerable extent near the rivers. Four of the 19 villages are on the Rávi, three on the Sutlej, seven are situate in the Mánjha and five in the Sharakpur tahsil. They are all Musalmán Gujars: their villages are for the most part in fair order, and the people are moderately industrious. They do not bear out the bad reputation that generally attaches to their class further down country ; but they combine pasturing of cattle with agriculture to some extent.

Mahtams.

The Mahtams have decreased, for some reason unknown, from 9,551 in the 1831 census to 8,438 in 1891. Of these slightly less than half are Musalmáns. The rest are equally divided between Hindús and Sikhs. The Musalmán Mahtams seldom own any land, but make their living by catching wild game, chiefly pig, which they eat ; by odd jobs in the fields ; by making ropes out of *sarr* grass, cutting down jungle and clearing land for cultivation in inundated tracts. However they own three estates on the north bank of the Rávi ; one of these villages, that namely near Sharakpur, is proclaimed under the Criminal Tribes Act. The Hindu and Sikh Mahtams own seven villages entirely and parts of four others ; their cultivation appears to be fairly good, but all Mahtams are looked on as a wild unreliable lot ; they are quarrelsome and addicted to thieving when they get the chance.

Labanás.

Formerly this was the class from which the carriers of Upper India were drawn, and they plied their trade in former days on bullocks of which they kept large herds. Then they took to agriculture, not instead of trade, but as an additional means of livelihood. Now, however, their carrying trade

has been superseded by the railway, and they have settled
down more or less to agriculture for which their hardy spirit,
power of endurance, and industry well suit them. In this
district they own 35 estates in entirety and considerable shares
in nine others, all of which lie north of the Rávi, ten in the Lahore
tahsíl and the rest in Sharakpur. In all these estates the
pressure of population is more than the land can bear, and
many of them go out to seek a living elsewhere. This perhaps
accounts for the small increase in their numbers since 1881
when their figures were recorded as 10,116. The Sikh Labanás,
found principally along the Rávi bank, are far the best cultivators.

The Sheikhs were recorded at the late census as 16,579 in
number and in the previous census of 1881 as 17,853. The
title is a very vague one, adopted generally by those Musalmáns who wish to assume a higher status than they really
possess, and dare not make claim to a higher or more precise
term than Sheikh. But of the number returned in 1891 considerably more than half were enumerated in Lahore city. The rest

Lahore tahsíl ...	1,178
Chúnián do. ...	2,392
Kasúr do. ...	1,835
Sharakpur do. ...	1,199

were distributed as shown in the margin :
most of these must no doubt be professedly
Koreshís, the Arab tribe to which the
Prophet belonged. In Sharakpur there
are seven or eight estates owned by true
Koreshís, and there they are notoriously bad cultivators :
in fact they do not do anything with their own hands : they live
principally on alms received from their followers and leave their
land to tenants who give them a share of the produce ; or more
rarely, and if they cannot get tenants as often happens owing to
the Koreshi's well known avarice and extortion, they make it
over to village menials to cultivate in their name. In the other
tahsíls it is believed that there is no village owned by Koreshís,
and in them probably a large number of the recorded Sheikhs
are wrongly returned as such.

Of the Moghals far the larger number belong to the urban
population : and the same may be said probably of the Sayads,
though some of these also are found about the Sharakpur tahsíl.
As cultivators, they are no better than Koreshís, being lazy,
thriftless and very hard on their tenants.

The word Khojah is the same as the Arabic word Khwájah,
meaning a man of wealth and respectability. In this district it
is used to denote a Muhammadan trader as opposed to Khatris
and Arorás who are Hindu traders. They are not landowners
in the proper sense, but in the course of their money lending
transactions they have acquired a good many wells and odd
plots of land, mostly on mortgage, but some in absolute transfer.
They are most numerous in some of the larger villages along the
Rávi, especially Manga Faizpur and Sharakpur. They are
chiefly noted for the severity of their money-lending terms.

Chapter III, D.

Tribes, Castes and Leading Families.

Trading classes. Khojahs.

When making advances of grain for food and seed they value such advances in cash at the dearest rates prevalent in the market during the year, and record the amount so estimated in their books : they claim as interest a marla (the twentieth part of a kanal) of produce to be delivered each harvest or twice a year. If produce is actually offered in discharge of interest or principal its value is reckoned not at the high prices at which the advances were valued, but at the lower rates prevailing after harvest. By such devices as these the Khojah on each advance he makes adds interest cent. for cent. on each year's out-standings : and practically the original loan may be quadrupled in a couple of years if no payment or delivery of grain has been made in the meantime. The people fully recognize the iniquity of this class' transactions and constantly make a complaint on the subject, apparently regarding themselves as helpless victims : the Khojah is established in the village and manages to keep out other village traders : the villagers must have advances occasionally, and there is no one else to go to but the Khojah. A large increase of population, amounting to 26 per cent. in ten years, is shown for this class.

Khatris and Aroras.

The Khatris and Aroras live chiefly in towns, but also are found in most villages as petty traders or money-lenders. Their terms of interest are more lenient than the Khojáhs and they are much more ready to take up a mortgage in security for a debt, and this is to the interest of agriculturists inasmuch as a debt secured by a land mortgage ceases to have interest added to it.

Also if there is anything over in favour of the mortgagee after making full allowance for the interest due, he will probably allow the mortgagor some reduction on the principal. Of the two classes, Khatris and Arorás, the former has much the best position as a village trader and gets on better with the people. They each have a population slightly over 40,000, and each show an increase of 22 per cent. since the census of 1881. The Arorás have a slightly larger proportion of Sikhs than the other, but in neither class are Sikhs numerous. The Khatri is far the more enterprising of the two and is much readier to take up land in permanent transfer by sale. Many Khatrís indeed in this district cultivate themselves. They have 35 estates entire and are shareholders in 55 others, besides owning wells and detached plots in many others. Of the estates they own in whole or in part, 22 are situate in the Mánjha, 19 in the Hithár, 14 along the Rávi ; in the Sharakpur tahsíl they own 12 whole estates and are shareholders in 22. These last they have acquired gradually from the Sharákpur landowners, for the most part in satisfaction of loan debts.

* Menial classes and village artisans. Chuhrás.

Numerically the *chuhrás* or scavengers are important, being in this respect second only to Jats. They fill also a prominent and necessary position in each village. In this district of the *chuhrás* enumerated 90 per cent. are Hindús, 7 per cent. are

Musalmáns and 3 per cent. are Sikhs. There is one village, if not more, of Mazbih Sikhs, who do good cultivation, but probably these were not included as *chuhrás*. Some of the village *chuhrás* perform their hereditary duties of sweeping and scavenging for certain families, to whom they also render occasional assistance in field work by working at the manure folding and feeding the cattle, or in busy seasons helping to drive the plough. This class also would carry messages from village to village, do all sorts of odd jobs which crop up on occasion, make the *chhaj* or winnowing pan and the *sirki* or grass thatch used to cover carts. For all these services he receives a share of all grain harvested by the houses which get his attentions; the share varies from 3 to 5 per cent. Besides this class, however, there are other *chuhrás* distinguished as *athri*, who confine themselves entirely to field labour and are the regular farm sweaters of the cultivators, their principal duties being to attend to cattle, collect the manure and scatter it over the land, drive the plough and the Persian wheel, and do all sorts of hard farm work which their employers would sooner be excused. For these services the *athri chuhra* is fed every day, provided with clothes and shoes, and gets a considerable quantity of grain each harvest.

The Musalmán *mochi* is of the same caste as the Hindu *chamár*. Their proper occupation is with leather, with which they make and mend shoes, whip thongs, and blinkers for the oxen; in return they receive small payments in grain from their patron cultivators. They also do field labour sometimes, cultivating land on their own account, if they can get it. Like the *chuhrás* they are put to odd jobs in the village, but they are above them considerably in social position and would never be expected to touch night soil as the *chuhrás* do. On the whole the *mochi* in this district has a status considerably superior to that of the ordinary Hindu *chamár* and is looked upon more as a village artificer. They are found in every village.

The *juláha* confines himself in this district wholly to weaving as a trade, though ready to take up cultivation when he can get the land. A number of *juláhas* are found among the district patwárís. He is paid for his weaving work by the piece and not by customary dues.

These two names embrace a class of men whose occupations are concerned mostly with water, and there is no known distinction between the two, except that *máchhis* are all Muhammadans and *jhinwárs* only mostly so. They carry water to the cultivators in the field, to the houses, and to all places where villagers meet and require water. They net fish and work at the cultivation of water nuts. They carry *palanquins* and all such burdens as are borne by a yoke on the shoulders. Like the *bihishti* among domestic servants, so these men out in their villages are the most willing and good tempered lot. Their womenfolk furnish midwives and

Chapter III, D.

Tribes, Castes and Leading Families.

Menial classes and village artisans.

Chuhrás.

Mochi.

Juláha.

Machhi and *Jhinwár.*

Chapter III, D.

Tribes, Castes
and Leading
Families.

*Máchhi and Jin-
wár.*

wet nurses; and also the *bhattyáris*, who cook maize and wheat grains in the *karáhi* or iron-plate for afternoon consumption of the village, or bake the bread at the common oven. Both the *karáhi* and the common oven are very common features of village life in the district, and a *machhán* or *jhinwari* invariably presides at them in villages, though in towns males of the Khatri class sometimes take up this business if they are in poor circumstances. For their water-carrying services, the Jhinwars and máchhis often recieve customary payments in grain.

Lohár.

The *lohár* or blacksmith is a necessary feature of every village ; he being the only man who can fit iron on to the plough and other agricultural implements. He is quite separate from the *tarkhán*, or carpenter, in this district. The iron is supplied to him, and he makes or repairs as required, receiving in return customary fixed payments of grain ; amounting to half what the carpenter and potter receive. The *lohár* also cultivates land. In the Sharakpur tahsíl, there is a whole estate owned by *lohárs*.

Tarkhán.

The carpenter (*tarkhán*) is also a necessary institution to every village ; all repairs of wood-work are made over to him, the wood being supplied ; for these services he receives on each irrigation well 2 or 2½ maunds of wheat in the spring from each cultivatior whom he serves, and the same amount of maize or rice in the autumn. Some *tarkháns* set up on their own account and get a name for good carpentering, so that people send long distances to them for carts and big wheels of the Persian wheel apparatus. Not a few *tarkháns* turn cultivators, and very good farmers they make, especially the Sikh *tarkháns*.

Kumhár.

The *kumhár* is the potter and brick-burner of the country, who is responsible for providing all the earthenware in use, especially the water-pots for the Persian wheel. For these services he receives the same grain payments each harvest as the carpenter gets. He also keeps donkeys, and it is part of his business to carry grain within the village area; outside that area he will only carry for extra payment. He is the general carrier for all small articles such as manure, fuel, bricks, and the like. This fact and his connection with manure, which is much used for brick burning, puts him on a lower social status than either the *tarkhán* or *lohár*.

Other classes.

Of other classes the *teli* is the oil-presser who also keeps large herds of sheep and goats, for their milk, wool, and flesh, all of which he sells. The *teli* is of very low social standing. The *nái* is the village barber who also carries messages, especially those relating to betrothals, the *chhimba* combines the trades of washing, dyeing and tailoring : in this district *darzi* or tailor is often spoken of as a *chhimba*. *Changárs* are menials of low caste, generally called in to plant, reap, or thresh rice. *Mirásis* are the village minstrels who recite on festal occasions, and also act as go-betweens in domestic matters.

The following is a list of the Ráises of the district who have a place assigned to them in the Divisional Darbár List. /Those who have the letter P prefixed to their names are Provincial Darbárís :—

1	Rája Harbans Singh P	25	Kanwar Bhup Singh ... ...
2	Nawáb Nasir Ali Khan P ...	26	Sheikh Muhammad Hussain ...
3	Diwán Rám Náth P ...	27	Uttam Singh .. ..
4	Sardár Narindar Singh, Sardár Bahádur P.	28	Fatteh Jang Khan ... ...
		29	Sodhi Hukam Singh P ... ...
5	Sheikh Ghulám Mahbúb Subhání P	30	Rái Bahádur Seth Ram Rattan P
6	Bhái Nand Gopál P	31	Sardár Baghel Singh ... ...
7	Rái Bahádur Bhai Mián Singh P	32	Colonel Sikandar Khan ... ...
8	Bhái Gurdit Singh P	33	Sheoram Dás ... ...
9	Diwán Narindar Náth P ...	34	Sardár Buláqa Singh ... ...
10	Sardár Udham Singh P	35	Mian Karím Bakhsh ... ...
11	Sardár Sarup Singh P	36	Lála Kaka Mal ... ...
12	Sardár Sher Singh	37	Sheikh Nának Bakhsh, Khán Bahádur.
13	Diwán Bhagwán Dás P ...		
14	Fakír Sayad Jamál-ud-dín. Khan Bahádur P.	38	Harkishen Dás ... ...
		39	Mian Jamál-ud-dín ... ...
15	Pandit Bansi Lál P	40	Indar Singh ... ...
16	Lála Rám Dás P	41	Sardár Chanda Singh ... ...
17	Raza Ali Khan	42	Sardár Bahádur Sayad Amír Ali Shah.
18	Pandit Jowáladat Parsháá ...		
19	Ahmad Yár Khan	43	Sardar Tará Singh ... ...
20	Missar Sundar Dás	44	Pandit Janárdhan ... ...
21	Khan Bahádur Fakír Kamar-ud-dín P.	45	Lála Madan Gopál, M. A., Barrister-at-Law.
22	Fakír Mehráj-ud-din	46	Zulfikár Khan ... ...
23	Kanwar Bakhshísh Singh	47	Sáhib Khan ... ...
24	Kanwar Thákar Singh	48	Rasaldár Sáwan Mal ... ...

The following is a list of official Darbárís in the Lahore District, who are entitled to a seat in the Lieutenant-Governor's Darbár by virtue of their office, vide para. 13, Punjab Government Circular No. 19-262, dated 4th March 1872, as modified by Punjab Government No. 563, dated 29th August 1889 :—

Number.	Name.	Official rank.
1	Khán Bahádur Fakír Kamar-ud-dín, ..	Honorary Magistrate.
2	Diwán Bhagwán Dás	Ditto.
3	Bahádur Bhái Mían Singh, Rái	Ditto.
4	Sardár Chanda Singh	Ditto.
5	Sayad Alim Sháh	Ditto.
6	Sardár Narindar Singh Sardár Bahádur ...	Ditto.
7	Fakír Sayad Jamál-ud-dín, Khán Bahádur	Ditto.
8	Sardár Buláqa Singh	Ditto.
9	Sardár Atma Singh	Ditto.
10	Dr. Muhammad Hussain Khán, Khán Bahádur.	Ditto.
11		
12	Shekh Ghulám Mahbúb Súbhání	Ditto.
13	Khán Bahádur Muhammad Barkat Ali Khán.	Vice-President, Municipal Committee, Lahore.
14	Badan Singh	Do. of Khem Karm.
15	Lála Tulsi Rám	Do. of Patti.
16	Lála Guránditta Mal	Do. of Khudián.
17	Lála Kirpa Rám	Do. of Sharakpur.
18	Lála Gopi Lál	Do. of Chúnián.

The following remarks on the leading families of the district are confined to those families of which mention is made in the volume known as Griffin's *Punjab Chiefs*, recently brought up to date by Major Massy, and of these only such have been here noticed, as still contain gentlemen of prominent position in this district. Other gentlemen equally prominent perhaps to those mentioned under the above category, but not mentioned in the *Punjab Chiefs* have been designedly omitted from this brief notice.

Rája Harbans Singh—Sardár Bahádur Narindar Singh.— Rája Harbans Singh was the younger brother of Rája Teja Singh, described on pages 4 to 18 of the *Punjab Chiefs*. Harbans Singh was born in 1846 by a different mother from Teja Singh's; soon after his birth he was adopted by Teja Singh, who at that time had no son. Teja Singh died in September 1862, and Rája Harbans Singh was made a ward of the District Court at Lahore. The Rája came into a very large and unembarrassed property in 1867 at the age of eighteen years. Now the estate is considerably involved. Rája Harbans Singh's *jagírs* were fixed in 1870 at Rs. 58,192 per annum of which he surrenders a small portion to others of his family. The *jagir* lands lie almost entirely in Gujránwála, but he receives Rs. 4,460 of his *jágir* from 16 villages in this district. The Rája lives generally at Shekhúpura, a large town of Gujránwála district, close to the Lahore border, and there exercises the judicial powers of a 2nd class Magistrate and Assistant Commissioner with special powers in the villages of his *jagir*. Sardár Narindar Singh was born to Rája Teja Singh in 1859 subsequent to the adoption of Harbans Singh by his elder brother Teja Singh. By an agreement effected in 1886, Rája Harbans Singh made over to him a considerable portion of his property. Sardár Narindar Singh was appointed a member of the District Board of Lahore in 1884, and now holds by election the position of Vice-President of the Municipal Committee of the Lahore city. In 1890 he was invested with judicial powers as a Magistrate of the 1st class and as a Munsiff of the 2nd class in the district of Lahore.' In 1892 he was created Sardár Bahádur.

Nawáb Nasir Ali Khán is the head of the well-known family of Kazilbásh, of which a full account will be found at pages 22 to 28 of the present edition of the *Punjab Chiefs*. The first Nawáb, Ali Raza Khán, rendered valuable service to the British Government at Kabul in the first Afghán campaign of 1839. These services were performed by him at the greatest personal risk and to the loss of his wealth and hereditary estates. Finding his life in danger in Kabul he accompanied the British forces to India. From then onwards the family has resided in Lahore. When the mutiny broke out the family came greatly to the front and did valuable service, in recognition of which Ali Raza Khán, the head of his family was granted a *talukdári* of 147 villages in Bahraich, Oudh, worth Rs. 15,000 per annum. He also received the title of Khán Bahádur and was created a Nawáb in 1864, two years before his death. Ali Raza Khán left three sons, the eldest of whom Nawázish Ali Khan was appointed Nawáb on his father's death. This gentleman proved himself a worthy successor to his father and earned for himself a name much revered by Europeans and natives alike. In 1835 the Companionship of the Indian Empire was conferred upon him and three years later he was created a Knight of the same Order. He held the difficult position of President to the Lahore Municipal Committee for several years, and in the discharge of his arduous duties in that appointment gave much satisfaction to the Government and to the public. In 1886 he received as a grant from Government the proprietary rights free of revenue in Rakh Juliána of Lahore tahsíl, a most valuable estate under excellent canal irrigation and well provided with tenants and tenants settlements under the careful and judicious management of the landlord. In 1887 Nawáb Nawázish Ali Khan was appointed an Additional Member of the Supreme Legislative Council of India. In August 1889 he started on a tour through Europe, his ultimate destination being the pilgrimage to Mecca. He arrived in Karbala and there contracted an illness, of which he shortly died in October 1890. His younger brother, Nasir Ali Khán, succeeded to all Nawázish Ali's estates in Oudh and in the Lahore District; he was also confirmed in the title of Nawáb in 1892.

Diwán Rám Náth is the grandson of Rája Dina Náth whose history and services are given at pages 29 to 35 of the *Punjab Chiefs*. After the annexation of the Punjab Rája Dina Náth was confirmed in all his *jágirs* worth Rs. 46,460 annually, which he held till his death in 1857. Buildings left by him in the Lahore city are a *shiwála* near the Police Court, for the support of which he alienated a *jagir* of Rs. 500 still maintained in perpetuity, and another *shiwála* near the Wazír Khán mosque. Amar Náth, the eldest son of Rája Dína Náth was a man of considerable ability and was the author of some very beautiful sonnets, also of a valuable and interesting history of Ranjít Singh. He enjoyed from Government a cash pension of Rs. 4,000 per annum, which on his death was converted into a *jágir* of the same amount to descend in perpetuity according to the rules of primogeniture. Diwán Amar Náth died in 1867, leaving two sons, Diwan Rám Náth and Pandit Mán Náth. The former has been serving under the Punjab Government since 1863. He was appointed an Extra Assistant Commissioner in 1869 and a District Judge in 1884. The latter office he now holds in Hoshiárpur. He is a Fellow of the Punjab University.

Sheikh Ghulám Mahbúb Subháni.—The founder of the fortunes of this family was Sheikh Ghulám Mohiy-ud-dín, who born in Hoshiárpur, when very young attracted the attention of Diwán Moti Rám and so came to the notice of Mahárája Ranjít Singh. His history is given at pages 39 to 44 of the present edition of the *Punjab Chiefs*. His son, Imám-ud-dín Khán was Governor of Kashmir, when that province was made over to Mahárája Guláb Singh by the Treaty of the 16th March

Chapter III. D.

Tribes, Castes and Leading Families.

Leading families.

1846. In 1848 when almost all were traitors to their Government in the Mooltan rebellion Sheikh Imám-ud-dín remained faithful, and both he and the troops he raised, to the number of 2,000, behaved well before Mooltan and distinguished themselves in several actions with the rebels. For these services he subsequently received a life cash pension of Rs. 11,600 and his *jagir* of Rs. 8,400 was confirmed to him. In 1857 he raised under the orders of Government two troops of cavalry for service at Delhi. He died in March 1859, aged 40, leaving one son Sheikh Ghulám Mahbúb Subhani, who was born in 1842. In 1862 at the recommendation of the Punjab Government the Supreme Government sanctioned *jágirs* of Rs. 5,600 being upheld in perpetuity, while the remaining *jágirs* with Ghulám Mahbúb Subhani are to lapse at his death. He had two sons, who died in their infancy. He lives at Lahore, but takes no part in public affairs. His uncle Sheikh Feroz Dín performed eminent services in the Baháwalpur State, where he was appointed Wazír in 1878, but died soon after, leaving a son Sheikh Nasír-ud-dín, who is now an Extra Assistant Commissioner in the Punjab.

Bhái family.

The history of this family will be found at pages 48 to 55 of the present edition of the *Punjab Chiefs*. Basti Ram was the first prominent member of the family; he and his son Harbhaj Rái were both in high favour with Mahárája Ranjít Singh. When the Punjab was annexed in 1849, the family held *jágirs* amounting to Rs. 49,000, of which Rs. 22,447 were maintained; some permanently and the rest temporarily. The present head of the family Bhái Nand Gopál, son of Bhái Gobind Rám, lives at Lahore. Bhái Mián Singh has been granted the title of Rái Bahádur, and is an Honorary Magistrate of the Lahore city.

The *jagirs* held by the various existing members of the family are as follows in value:—

						In perpetuity.	For life.
						Rs.	Rs.
Bhái Mián Singh	...	...	...	...	...	1,463	...
Bhái Nand Gopál	...	...	...	...	...	2,523	1,559
Bhái Tára Singh	...	...	...	...	...	433	...
Bhái Partáb Singh	...	...	...	...	...	433	...
Bhái Gurdit Singh	...	...	...	...	...	1,935	...
				Total	...	6,787	1,559

Diwán Narindar Náth is son of Diwán Baij Náth and grandson of Diwán Ajudhya Pershád, whose family history is given at length in pages 122 to 131 of the *Punjab Chiefs*. The grandfather gained a high character with all English officers after the annexation of the Punjab, for his upright and honourable dealings, and a good name with the public for justice and impartiality. The *jágirs* of the Diwán had lapsed to Government at annexation, but he was granted a pension of Rs. 7,500, and of this Rs. 1,000 was sanctioned to be upheld to him and his heirs in perpetuity. Also in 1864 an area of 1,200 acres was granted to him from Hinjarwál Rakh, which is now known as Ajudhiápur. Diwán Ajudhia Pershád died in 1870 and his son Baij Náth in 1875. Diwán Narindar Náth was 11 years old when his father died, his estate, which was saddled with a heavy debt of Rs. 40,000, came under management of the District Court of Wards at Lahore. A life pension of Rs. 1,625 was sanctioned to the young Diwán. The latter obtained the degree of Máster of Arts in 1886 and in 1888 was selected for an Assistant Commissionership in the Punjab under the Statutory Civil Service Rules. He owns two estates in the Lahore tahsíl, Ajudhiápur and Amírpura. The thousand rupee *jágír* has now increased to Rs. 3,926 as the assessments of the eight villages assigned to his family in 1864 to make up the grant of Rs. 1,000 have since then been twice revised; and the Punjab Government in their letter No. 209 of 12th March 1863, ruled that the *jagirdar* should get the benefit of all increases on account of extension of dry cultivation.

Sardár Udham Singh of Behrwál is the present head of the family of Sardár Kahn Singh, Nakkai, described at pages 68 to 72 of the present edition of the *Punjab Chiefs.* The family gained a large amount of territory in Chúnián, Kasúr and Gogera parganahs, but was deprived of it by Maharája Ranjit Singh and Sardár Kahn Singh, who then represented the family, was left with only a few estates round Behrwál village near the Rávi in the Chúnián tahsil. After annexation Sardár Kahn Singh was left in possession of a life pension of Rs. 3,840 in addition to a *jágír* revenue of Rs. 11,980. The family is now represented by Udham Singh, who holds a *jágír* of Rs. 2,000 per annum granted in 1862 to Chattar Singh, son of Sardár Kahn Singh and his heirs male in perpetuity according to the rules of primogeniture. Other members of the family at present living are Ishar Singh, who lives in Jajja village and is known better as Abdul Azíz, having been converted to Muhammadanism many years ago; Lábh Singh, Zaildár of Behrwál circle; and Narayán Singh younger brother of Udham Singh. The family owns a considerable amount of land in the Chúnián tahsil.

Sardár Sarúp Singh comes of a Jat family, the history of which is given at pages 91 to 95 of the latest edition of the *Punjab Chiefs.* The grandfather of the present Sardár held *jágírs* amounting to Rs. 75,000 per annum. Soon after his death, which he met at the battle of Sobráon in February 1846, these *jágírs* were reduced by Rája Lál Singh to Rs. 25,000, and continued to the son Sardár Kirpál Singh. When Rája Sher Singh's force rebelled Kirpál Singh separated himself from it, and with a few sowars came into the camp of Major Edwardes with whom he had previously served in Bannu. On annexation his personal *jágír* of Rs. 4,000 per annum was confirmed to him for life, and a new *jágír* of Rs. 5,000 for loyalty at Mooltan was granted him in perpetuity. Sardár Kirpál Singh performed

good service for Government in 1857 and received a *khilat* of
Rs. 500 and a sanad of approbation. He died in 1859; his
widow receives an allowance of Rs. 1,200 per annum, and his
son Sirdár Sarúp Singh holds the *jágir* which, owing to
increase of assessment now amounts to Rs. 7,703. On his death,
under existing terms of the grant, this will be reduced to
Rs. 5,000. The *jagir* is at present distributed over 12 estates,
4 in Lahore tahsíl, 6 in Chúnián tahsíl and 2 in Sharakpur.

  Diwán Bhagwán Dás is the son of Diwán Rattan Chand,
whose history is given at pages 113 to 116 of the latest edition
of the *Punjab Chiefs*. Rattan Chand had done good service
in the Postal Department, and on the annexation of the Punjab
certain of his *jágirs* amounting to Rs. 6,800 were released to him
for life free of all service and a garden worth Rs. 200 near the
Shahálami Gate of Lahore was released to him and his male heirs
in perpetuity. He was appointed an Honorary Magistrate of
Lahore city in 1862; in this capacity he showed much activity
and intelligence. He was always liberal when money was
required for any work of public utility, he built a fine sarai
and tank near the Shahálami Gate and had a large share in
the formation of the public gardens round the city. He
was created a Diwán by the Supreme Government in 1865.
He died in 1872. His eldest son, Diwán Bhagwán Dás, received
a *jágir* grant under sanad, dated 7th January 1874 valued
at Rs. 2,585. He too is an Honorary Magistrate of Lahore,
takes a keen interest in city matters, has erected several buildings and all together is a gentleman of public and enlightened
spirit. His *jágirs*, granted in perpetuity to him and his male
heirs subject to the continued loyalty and good conduct of the
recipient, amount to Rs. 2,617 under recent re-assessments.
He also holds a village, Ratanpura, of Sharakpur tahsíl in fee,
simple, the latest assessment on which is Rs. 396.

  The *Fakir* family is described at pages 96 to 112 of the
latest edition of the *Punjab Chiefs*. Aziz-ud-dín, famous chiefly
as having been the best and truest adviser of Mahárája Ranjit
Singh, also had a great reputation for his courtier-like manners, his eloquence, poetry and elegant writing. The best
known of the present members of the family is Fakir Kamar-
ud-dín, nephew of Azíz-ud-dín, who has considerable influence
in native society and is best known perhaps to European officials. He enjoys a political pension of Rs. 700 per annum
and a *jágir* in 700 acres of land in mauza Jalálábad of Lahore
tahsíl. Zahúr-ud-dín, also a nephew, and equally well-known,
died very recently. Fakir Jamál-ud-dín, Khán Bahádur, son of
Azíz-ud-dín, is an Honorary Magistrate of Lahore with first
class powers, he has a political pension of Rs. 1,000 per
annum. Iftikhár-ud-dín, grandson of Zahúr-ud-dín, is a
young and promising member of the family.

  Pandit Bansi Lal—Pandit Jowala Dat Pershad—The
history of this family is given at pages 117 to 121 of the
latest edition of the *Punjab Chiefs*. All the family ahve been

great Sanskrit scholars, but Pandit Rádha Kishan did an immense deal by his personal exertions in the cause to promote Oriental learning. He had a splendid Sanskrit library of his own. Sir Donald McLeod recorded in a certificate that Pandit Rádha Kishen was one of the worthiest, most respected and most valuable of the citizens of Lahore ; he had been a hearty promoter of the Punjab University College movement and had creditably assisted Government officers in all educational matters. A grant of 2,000 acres in the Chúnián tahsíl was made to him in proprietary right, afterwards known as Kot Rádha Kishen. This came to his son, Rikhi Kesh, to whom was also confirmed a *jagir* income of Rs. 1,200 out of the larger *jágír* enjoyed by his father. Rikhi Kesh died in 1888. To his son, Pandit Bansi Lal, a *jagir* of Rs. 500 from the revenue assessable on Kot Radha Kishen was continued and he also holds two small muáfis that were, granted in perpetuity to Pandit Rádha Kishen and his male heirs. Pandit Bansi Lal in 1891 was appointed Honorary Magistrate, with 2nd class powers, and a Munsiff of the 3rd class in 55 villages of the Chúnián tahsíl.

The history of this family is given at pages 122 to 126 of the present edition of the *Punjab Chiefs*. The family is of Brahman origin and came originally from Jhelum. Two of them occupied the post of Treasurer to Ranjit Singh, one in Lahore the the other in Amritsar, but Rúp Lál was the most famous member of the family, having gained a tremendous name for justice and equity as Governor of the Jullundur Doáb under the Mahárája Ranjít Singh : he subsequently joined in the Mooltan rebellion and his estates were confiscated. Two of Rúp Lál's sons are still living, of whom the eldest Sawan Mal, Ressaldár, has served in the army with great distinction, and in recognition of his services obtained from Government a *jágír* in four villages, which now yields him Rs. 961 a year.

This family rose during the reign of Mahárája Ranjít Singh by their own strength and prowess in battle. The history of their family is given on pages 130 to 132 of the latest edition of the *Punjab Chiefs*. The best known member under British rule has been Ressaldár Maná Singh, who served for three years with distinction in the Bandá Military Police ; in 1861, when that force was reduced, he was made zaildár of Mokul and received a grant of 720 acres of waste land in Rakh Mudki of the Chúnián tahsíl. He died in 1884. Another well-known and highly respected man of the family was Ressaldár Gudar Singh, who died in Mokul in 1890. Maná Singh was succeeded as zaildár by his son Naráin Singh, who was lately murdered over some land dispute. Shamír Singh, zaildár of Sultánke belongs to the same family. Some of Maná Singh's and Gudar Singh's sons became converts to Islam, much to their father's distress. Two of these, Bashír Ahmed, son of Maná Singh, and Abdul Rahmán son of Gudar Singh, are Deputy Collectors in the Canal Department.

Sardár Indar Singh is a Viceregal Darbári of the Lahore District, who has been granted land in rakh Lidhar, some of it free of revenue in return for the excellent service he has rendered from 1857 onwards to 1892 as orderly officer to the Lieutenant-Governors for the time being of the Punjab. He holds the highest testimonials from Lord Lawrence, Sir Robert Montgomery, Sir Henry Davies, Sir Robert Egerton, Sir Charles Aitchison, and Sir James Lyall. When the last named retired from office Indar Singh also retired to enjoy a well-earned repose in his native village Thithar, where he now is. His grandfather Sahib Singh and his father Sher Singh were noted swordsmen and held in high respect in the Court of Mahárája Ranjít Singh. His two sons Tej Singh and Talmeja Singh are in Government service, the former as a Deputy Inspector of Police, the latter as a Jamadár in the 1st Punjab Cavalry. Rájendra Singh, brother of Indar Singh, took part in many campaigns and rendered valuable service to Government; he died after his return from the Kábul war of 1881. Other members of the family are serving in the army and are keeping up the old name for good and faithful service. The whole family may be described as in flourishing circumstances. A more detailed account of them will be found on pages 181 to 184 of the latest edition of the *Punjab Chiefs.*

Sardár Atma Singh is the chief representative of the family of Sukha Singh, the first Sikh convert of the descendants of Changa who was thirteenth in descent from Sandhu the founder of the Sandhu Jat colony in the Mánjha after their emigration from Gházni in Afghánistán. Changa was an influential chaudhari and founded the village of Padhána, 16 miles south of Lahore where the family still resides. The history is given on pages 137 to 141 of the latest edition of the *Punjab Chiefs.* Sardár Jowála Singh, son of Sardár Mit Singh, who was the son of Sukha Singh was very eminent at the beginning of the present century both for his bravery and his munificent generosity. He held very large *jágírs* from Mahárája Ranjít Singh, but on his death in 1835 most of these were resumed. No direct descendant of his now lives, but there are several of Ganda Singh, the younger brother of Sardár Mit Singh; and among these Atmá Singh is the leading representative. He has been created a Sardár and given a sanad under the hand of the Viceroy. He lives at Padhána, where he is Honorary Magistrate, having jurisdiction in 51 villages of the Kasúr tahsíl. The *jágír* allowances have ceased, but the Sardár has proprietary rights in four villages and is in flourishing circumstances. The family is connected by marriage with some of the best houses in the Mánjha.

Sardár Bhola Singh of Jodhpur is a man who comes little before the public at present, but deserves mention as the son of Káhn Singh, whose history is given on pages 166 to 169 of the latest edition of the *Punjab Chiefs.* Káhn Singh was the bravest and the keenest of the Sikh chiefs who fought against

Lahore District]

CHAP. III.—THE PEOPLE.

121

Chapter III, E.

Village communities and tenures.

Leading families.

the English during the campaign of 1848-49 : after annexation he lost the *jágirs* which he had received for excellent services rendered at the head of his Dragoon regiment under the Sikh Government, but received a cash pension of Rs. 600 per annum. When the mutiny of 1857 broke out Kahn Singh was one of the first chiefs selected by the Chief Commissioner for service before Delhi. He was in bad health, but nevertheless went and rendered noble service to the English, fighting for them until he was badly wounded and then engaged in procuring information and winning over his countrymen to the side of the English. In return for these services the Government gave him considerable *jágir* grants. He died in June 1864 under suspicious circumstances, and Bhola Singh was selected by the Government to succeed him in his *jágirs*. Bhola Singh was Jamadár in the 11th Bengal Lancers, but now lives in his village of Jodhpur.

SECTION E.—VILLAGE COMMUNITIES AND TENURES.

The varieties of tenures existing in this district are shown in Table No. XV. The upper portion of the statement is taken from Table No. XI of the Revenue Report for 1892-93. The lower part is a classification of estates in each tahsíl, based mainly on the system according to which the village community is responsible for payment of the revenue recently assessed. Also estates still retaining common land (outside the village homestead) undivided are separated from those having no common land left. As the number of proprietors increase and subdivision of land becomes more minute, the tendency is for those who are suffering most from insufficiency of land to insist on all the common land being partitioned.

The classification of estates according to their form of tenure in each tahsíl has been made very carefully, after consideration of the conditions found to exist in each estate, but it is impossible to distribute them under any one of the ordinarily recognized tenures with satisfactory preciseness and the entries in the lower portion of Table No. XV represent merely the nearst approach to distinct grouping that has been found practicable. A good description of the various forms of tenure and of the way in which one form is developed out of another is contained in the following paragraphs quoted from a Report by Mr. E. A. Prinsep, Settlement Commissioner, from 1862 to 1867. The remarks were made more especially with reference to the Amritsar District, but they apply almost equally well to this district.

" Generally speaking, the Theory of Tenure may be described as at one time or other coming under one of the following stages ":—

" I.—The Partriarchal or Landlord."
" II.—The Communal or Joint stock."
" III.—The Divided, regulated by ancestral shares."
" IV.—The Divided, regulated by customary shares."
" V.—The Accidental regulated by possession."

"I know of no better way of shewing the transition from one stage to another, and the causes which produce it, than by giving the following illustration."

"The founder of a village secures a property by purchase, grant, appropriation or conquest. He has a family of six sons, he holds it all himself. This represents the first period, and corresponds with the pure Landlord system."

"At his death the six sons being connected by a strong tie, hold the property in common; those sons too prefer to maintain the joint interest in this form, land is abundant, revenue is taken in kind, they have no differences to occasion any necessity for resort to division, so the "communal" system is maintained intact, the interest of each brother or shareholder being regulated by the *laws* of *inheritance*."

"In course of time population increases, and with it the demand for land; dissensions begin. The descendants of one son have been cultivating less—those of another more, than the shares which regulate the division of profits. To prevent future disputes, the estate is divided according to the *laws* of *inheritance* and here we come to the third type."

"As generation succeeds generation, and the country is subject to change of rule, stress of seasons, and accidents occur, leading to hardship to individual co-partners; or some die off, others leave the village; some get involved in difficulties, others mortgage their properties; it can be conceived that mutations would follow, which would increase the holdings of some, while others being unable or unwilling to succeed to lapsed shares additional reason would appear for not disturbing possession and resorting to the law in times when little attention was paid to rights and the influential could generally do as they pleased. In such a state of things it is easy to see how ancestral shares would die out, and customary shares take their place which would agree with the land actually held by each co-partner. Villages of this class would represent the fourth type."

"Ultimately all resort to shares dies out; there may have been many settlements in former days; poverty may have driven out the old proprietors, who may have been succeeded by cultivators, located by the Kárdárs; the land may lie near a large town and have become so valuable as to have utterly changed hands; or, if still belonging to the old brotherhood, owing to distress, misrule and a hundred causes they found it their best interest to make each man's occupancy the rule of his interest in the estate; or men of different castes may have become owners by original or subsequent appropriation; whatever was the cause, there is no trace of any kind of shares, the village custom is to throw the liabilities on the total area cultivated by each person. This takes us into the last stage. Generally it is to some accident or defect in succession that this tenure may be attributed, so I have termed it the "Accidental stage.""

Of the estates shown in Table No. XV as held by single owners, the greater number are new, having been recently formed out of grants from Government rakhs to deserving native gentlemen. Estates held jointly by groups of owners belong mostly to Dogars along the Sutlej bank, or to Khatrís and Aroras, who have at no distant date acquired the estates by purchase from the original owners. It is noteworthy that there are still as many as 219 estates, in which the revenue is paid according to the original ancestral shares. A careful examination of these would probably bring to light considerable deviation in the areas of actual holdings from what each man was entitled to have according to his ancestral share: in many such, however, there would be some common land still left, from which some adjustments will be made perhaps hereafter in favour of those who hold less than their proper share. The majority of estates now make liability for the land revenue follow possession; some observe this rule throughout for the whole estate: others, after the sum total of assessment has been distributed by *Taraf* according to ancestral or customary shares, then distribute responsibility within the *Taraf* by actual

possession of the land. Not a few estates have different
systems followed by their several component subdivisions; in
which case distinct classification becomes impossible. Undoubtedly a strong tendency was exhibited at the recent reassessment
to elect for the *bhaiáchára* system or distribution of revenue
according to the area of assessed land in each shareholder's
possession. The rule observed in cases of dispute was to
maintain the system hitherto followed in paying previous
assessments unless a clear majority could be shown in favour of
a change. The fairest way of course is to make each man pay the
exact amount of land révenue assessed on the land he actually
holds, and until this becomes general, more or less inequality
of assessment must exist: on the other hand it is not advisable
to weaken the theory of joint responsibility according to
ancestral shares, where the people are willing to maintain it.

Along the Rávi river the large majority of estates are
under the *bhaiáchára* tenure, and divide rights and responsibilities according to possession: on the Sutlej many of the
Lahore estates are held either jointly or according to ancestral
shares: but some here too follow possession. Those on either
river who are under the *bhaiáchára* tenure profess to follow one
or other of two principles as to land newly emerging from the
river. Some villages allege a custom of treating such land as
the common property of all the shareholders of the estate,
subject to partition when it has become valuable, the men who
bring it under cultivation being meanwhile regarded as mere
tenants-of-will of the community. Other villages say that land
submerged or destroyed by the action of the river, and afterwards becoming culturable again may be claimed by its former
owners and by no one else. As a matter of fact the latter rule
is declared for in nearly all river villages having fixed
boundaries, and the former rule is confined mainly to cases of
entirely new land accreting on to estates whose riverside boundary is liable to shift as the bed of the deep stream changes.
But it is only possible for the original owners to claim land
re-emerging on the site of their former land, when dialluvial
records are prepared carefully year by year, and when all new
land as it emerges is mapped out afresh according to the survey
numbers that existed before they were submerged. Unfortunately this work has not in past years received as much
attention in this district as it should have done; and on the Rávi
where constant changes are occurring yearly in the river alluvial
area, much of the new land has been taken possession of by
men who had no rights in it before it was submerged. Having
been in occupation a long time they refuse to make way for the
proper owners, who on the other hand are often too poor to
resort to legal process in pursuit of their rights.

Table No. XVI shows the distribution of the land between
owners and tenants. More than one-half the area under cultivation is farmed by the owners themselves who in this district are
early all peasant proprietors, the number of estates owned by

single landlords being very few. Taking large and small holdings together the average area for the district of each owner's
holding is bewtcen six and seven acres of cultivated land. It is
smallest in Lahore tahsíl and largest in Chúnián tahsíl. But
this calculation includes all sorts of petty holdings in the hands
of faqírs and village servants, granted to them by the landowners, and often less than one acre in area. Such landholders as
these cannot be included among the proprietors proper. On the
other hand it is exceedingly difficult when one comes to examine
each holding to know which to exclude from calculation and
which to leave in for the purpose of ascertaining the true average
holding. Different methods were followed in preparing statements to accompany the assessment reports of the several tahsíls
at the recent settlement. In Kasúr tahsíl, taking all holdings and
all cultivated land, the average area per holding was found to
be 33 acres, and the average area for each separate *málguzár*, or
co-sharer responsible for the revenue, was found to be 18 acres ;
according to which land must be very plentiful there: on the
other hand, even excluding all petty holdings in the hands
of faqírs and village servants, there were still found to be a
large number of small holdings, less than 10 acres in area,
which covered between one-fourth and one-fifth of the total
cultivated area : the average of such holdings hardly exceeded
five acres. In Chúnián tahsíl, as noticed elsewhere, population is
hardly yet developed in proportion to the land and there are a
considerable number of large holdings over sixty acres in area.
These were excluded and also all miscellaneous holdings
including Government land and fragmentary plots belonging
to faqírs, máfidárs, and favoured village servants. The average
cultivated area to the owner on the balance was found to be
ten acres. This calculation did not include land mortgaged with
possession either, as such land cannot be of any benefit to the
nominal owner. Here again the calculation was partly vitiated
by the fact that many of the proprietors own land in more than
one estate, and were therefore apt to be counted more than
once. However the conclusion arrived at from the figures was
that not a few villages in the Hithár tract of this tahsíl and
a considerable proportion of the Rávi villages had insufficient
land compared to the number of the proprietors. In Lahore
tahsíl there is severe pressure of population on the land near
Lahore itself. The original proprietors as recorded at the first
regular settlement were Aráins for the most part. These from
the very first had no more land than was sufficient to support
their numbers as then existing. Since then their families have
increased greatly and continued subdivision of the land has
left many houses practically destitute. In many of the estates
round Lahore, if a few exceptionally large holdings be excluded,
the average area with each owner hardly exceeds half an acre.
The result has been that much of the land has been sold and
mortgaged to rich city people, who are willing to pay large prices
to gratify the pride and pleasure every one takes in having a
piece of land he can call his own. The former Aráin proprietors

on the other hand are often glad to get rid of land which is insufficient to maintain one man even, let alone a crowd of hungry relatives. In other Rávi villages of the Lahore tahsíl at a greater distance from the city pressure of population diminishes slightly, but still continues somewhat more than the land can bear ; and excluding all larger holdings the area to each individual owner is only four acres or thereabouts. Some of the Rávi people such as Aráins and Labanás can get along with this much land. The Jats however who own about a fourth of the Rávi land in this tahsíl find considerable difficulty, and the Rájpút villagers who own about one-sixth of the area along the river are absolutely impoverished. In the Mánjha tract of Lahore tahsíl land though not abundant yet so far is sufficient. In the eastern portion where irrigation from wells and canals covers much of the land, each owner averages eight acres which under the circumstances is ample. In the Western Mánjha, where irrigation is not so universal as in the eastern portion, the average area per owner is 11 acres ; and this too may be accounted sufficient. In Sharakpur tahsíl the land is not distributed at all evenly ; there are far too many holdings comprising more land than their owners can cultivate, and on the other hand there are a very large number with insufficient property ; the latter cultivate the surplus land of the former, partly but not to the extent one would expect, and the owners with superabundant land often find great difficulty in finding tenants ; this being due chiefly to the reluctance with which cultivators take tenancies in land dependent entirely on well irrigation, unless they can induce the owner to agree to find them in food, seed-grain, and bullocks till such time as a successful harvest brings in some return for their labour.

Table No. XVI shows the number and area of holdings cultivated by the various classes of tenants with some detailed figures as to rents paid in cash and kind. This again is supplemented by Table No. XXI which gives the average rent paid in each tahsíl per acre for each class of soil by tenants-at-will. According to the most recently obtained figures 52 per cent. of the cultivated area is in the hands of the owners themselves, and of this a small proportion amounting to two out of the fifty-two is cultivated by owners working as mortgagor tenants to the mortgagees to whom the former have temporarily hypothecated the land. The remaining 48 per cent. is distributed as shown in the margin.

Chapter III, E.

Village communities and tenures.

Size of proprietary holdings.

Tenancies.

The tenants cultivating free of rent are favoured artisans, village menials, Faqírs, Kázis, Mullahs, Sádhs or

Tahsíl.	In hands of owners.	CULTIVATED BY TENANTS.		Tenants-at-will.	
		Tenants free of rent.	Mau-rusi tenants.	Paying cash rents.	Paying kind rents.
Lahore ...	52	2	6	12	28
Kasúr ...	53	2	10	12	23
Chúnián ...	52	1	5	7	35
Sharakpur...	52	1	3	2r	23
Total percentage	52	2	7	12	27

Chapter III. E.

Village communities and tenures.

Occupancy tenancies.

Brahmans to whom the landowners have presented small plots of land. The general name for all tenants having rights superior to those of tenants-at-will is *maurúsi* or " hereditary." This also includes in this district upwards of three thousand tenants distinguished as *panáhi* (protected) or as *pattehdárs* (lease-holders). Some of these appeared to have been granted protection for ever, being called *Dawami Panahi*, some for a term, distinguished as *miyádi*—some under certain conditions; and they were distinguished as *kamil* or *shartiya*. The conditions and modifications recorded for each variety in the settlement of 1868 are somewhat numerous, but in the earlier settlement of 1856 most of them were recorded as *maurúsi*, and in practice they are all treated much as if they were occupancy tenants or tenants with hereditary rights. The rents payable by *maurúsi* tenants or those holding the same status are generally made up of the revenue and cesses payable on the land occupied by them with a small *málikána* or landlord's due added.

Classes of tenants-at-will.

It is not unusual to find that a large proportion of the tenants-at-will belong to the class from which the landowners mostly come. For instance, in the Mánjha between seventy and eighty per cent. of the land is owned by Jats and over one-third of the land held by tenants-at-will is found to be cultivated by Jat tenants. In the Hithár tract Aráins who own more than one-fifth of the land and generally cultivate themselves all they own, also hold one-third of the area cultivated by tenants-at-will. In the Rávi villages Jats own over one-third and Aráins one-sixth perhaps ; they cultivate in addition one-sixth and one-quarter respectively of the land held by tenants-at-will. When this is the case to any great extent it is reasonable to suppose that many of the tenants-at-will are themselves landowners who are endeavouring to supplement the profits they are able to make on their own diminished holdings by cultivating at fixed rent rates land belonging to others of their brotherhood. Next to the landowning class, or perhaps now-a-days taking priority of them in the number of tenants-at-will they supply, are the classes from which village menials or village artisans come, such as the carpenters (*tarkhán*), potters (*kumhár*), blacksmiths (*lohár*), weavers (*julláha*), leather-workers (*mochi*), oilmen (*teli*), barbers (*nái*), watermen (*máchhi* or *Jhinwár*), sweeper, and scavengers (*chúhra*), and others. The majority of these however, are Musalmáns : and Hindu landowners prefer to get Hindu tenants if they can. Some of the *tarkháns* are Sikhs and some of the *nái* class are Hindús, and nearly all the *chuhrás* are Hindús. The rest are Musalmáns. No Hindu tenants will work in a Musalmán village, but Musalmán tenants are often found in Hindu villages. One way or another of late years the menial classes have been contributing more and more to the cultivation of the land, generally of unirrigated land, the owners preferring to reserve the irrigated in their own hands : in a way too this suits the cultivating menials who still go on discharging the customary duties for which they receive customary payments in kind from the village proprietors. Unirrigated land makes no call upon their time except at ploughing and sowing time ; with irrigated land on their hand they would have no time for any thing else. Thus many of these village menials regard the small tenancies they get hold of as a mere additional resource not as their sole means of livelihood. They can therefore afford to pay higher rents than those who are prevented by custom, habit or prejudice from following any other trade but agriculture. The above facts, especially the increasing competition for land on the part of a large and competent class of men, largely account for the comparatively high rents paid in parts of this district on unirrigated land. As cultivators the menial classes give moderate satisfaction. The *tarkháns*, especially the Sikhs among them, furnish some of the best agriculturists : next to them perhaps come the *lohárs*. The others though not deficient in industry are hardly up to the mark in capacity and natural aptitude for farming.

Chapter III, E.

Village communities and tenures.

Classes of tenants-at-will.

Tenancies-at-will are arranged by the year. Terms are settled in the month of *Cheyt* (March—April) when there is a temporary rest from work as the crop is ripening, but the tenant does not take complete possession of his holding until June when the spring harvest is finished ; though no doubt the retiring tenant would make no objection if the incoming tenant wanted to plough earlier for cotton. With yearly tenants rent is paid half-yearly in arrear, as a rule, at the same time as the revenue. In tracts where tenants are difficult to procure, such as the Chúnián Hithár or the central parts of Sharakpur tahsíl, the landowners often have to make advances to their new tenants of seed, of food grain, and of money to purchase plough cattle. More often no cash is actually advanced, but the village *bunya* or the cattle trader is authorised to supply the tenant on the owner's responsibility for payment. Not unfrequently the tenant foreseeing an indifferent harvest and despairing of making enough on it to balance the advances he has obtained from his landlord makes a bolt for it and leaves his cattle, cultivating material, and ungathered crop to the latter, who is of course wholly unprepared to take up this additional charge. Landowners in well-irrigated tracts are sometimes put to serious loss and inconvenience by their tenants in this and other ways, but nevertheless are driven by force of circumstances to accept whatever tenants they can get. Resident cultivators prefer to take land of any sort near their homes rather than change their place of residence. When however there are not enough of these in the village, the landowners who have more land than they can arrange for have to fall back upon migratory tenants who make their temporary abode just wherever they can get land to cultivate ; and these are the class from which stray tenants for well-irrigated land are often picked up. Canal irrigation being comparatively easy and certain to yield fair returns attracts the better and more reliable classes of tenants.

Rents may be paid in cash or in kind, or partly in one form and partly in the other. Cash rents are paid by tenants-at-will on 10 per cent. of the cultivated area. There are three different systems of cash rent followed in this district usually. One is to fix rent at so much the *ghumhao* or *bigha* or even *kanal*: the *ghumhao* is the more common measure taken. The *bigha* or half *ghumhao* is adopted as the unit in the Mánjha lands near the Amritsar border. The *kanál* which is one-eighth part of the *ghumhao* is only rated to rent in the more valuable lands near Lahore where tenants or dealers in special produce are glad to get hold of even the smallest plots, and the rent often runs as high as ten or twelve rupees the *kanil*. The second system is one applied most frequently to well-irrigated lands. A lump sum is fixed on the well: for instance in the Sutlej Hithár where wells irrigate thirty acres or so, but have attached to them often much larger areas, the lump cash rent on a well varies from Rs. 40 to Rs. 90. The same system, however, is sometimes applied to a holding of land of any class, though much more rarely. The third system is to arrange for the tenant to pay the land revenue assessed on the land with an added percentage thereon as *málikána* rent. This form in most parts of the district is in vogue only for tenants with rights of occupancy, but it is fairly common also in the case of tenants-at-will in Sharakpur tahsíl and in the less fertile tracts of Chúnián tahsíl. Generally speaking it may be held to indicate that competition for tenancies is very slack and that the landowners are glad to get the land and its responsibilities off their hands on any terms short of actual loss. So far there has been no clear indication of cash rents becoming more popular. Near Lahore where cultivation and the rents paid for their land have reached a very high pitch, the landowners prefer cash as a rule; and it is unlikely that the cultivators would care to expend so much money and labour as they do on the best land, if they had to give up a large portion of the produce in kind rent: but even there the landlords are much more ready to let their worse and less productive land for cash rent, than they are land which by the manuring and cultivation of former years has been put into a position to yield with fair certainty each year, such for instance as the better class of garden land. Elsewhere in the district kind rents are much preferred by the landlords for irrigated lands, and cash rents for unirrigated lands, the yield from which is usually very precarious owing to the feebleness and uncertainty of the local rainfall. The interests of the tenants of course lie in the opposite direction. Which is able to get his own way depends entirely upon whether the land available is short of tenants or the tenants available are short of land. At present in the Mánjha tract the proportion of irrigated land under cultivation of tenants-at-will to unirrigated is about eight to eleven: on the West Mánjha where the wells are very deep a special system prevails under which

CHAP. III.—THE PEOPLE.

cash rents for well lands are calculated at two or three rupees for every yoke of oxen working at the well paid each harvest. True competition rents are paid more in the Lahore tahsíl than elsewhere; especially along the Rávi, where the struggle for existence has raised them unusually high. Very often the landlords are unable to realize their cash rents in full, and this may go on for several years, but they prefer to maintain them at as high a nominal a rate as they can get the tenant to agree to, and take their chance of realizing it; fearing that if they once lower the scale they will never be able to raise it again.

The rates of kind rents vary in different parts of the district, in some measure according to the variations in fertility of the soil, in rainfall and in depth of the water bearing stratum; but more still according to the custom prevalent from former times; and also they are influenced to some extent by the pitch of the land revenue. In Chúnián tahsíl where competition among tenants for land is very weak, the custom is to take one-fourth or one-fifth on well-irrigated lands, one-fourth and to a much less extent one-third on unirrigated land, and one-fifth or one-fourth on canal-irrigated lands. Latterly the canal dues for irrigation have been raised materially; if the owner consents to pay any share of these dues in Chúnián tahsíl he may perhaps establish a claim raise his rent rates, otherwise the tenants will for a long time in this tahsíl be strong enough to resist any attempt at increase on the owner's part. In Kasúr tahsíl one-fourth produce is almost the universal rent-rate for well-irrigated land, and one-third or one-fourth for unirrigated; while in Lahore tahsíl one-third is the more common rate on the former soil and one-half or one-third on the latter. The higher pitch of rents in Lahore tahsíl is due largely to more intense competition, partly to custom arising from the higher pitch of Government revenue that has always been taken in the Lahore tahsíl and from the greater proximity of the latter to Amritsar district where the rent rates are universally higher than in Lahore, and partly perhaps to the fact that the rainfall is less precarious in Lahore tahsíl than in Kasúr. The same difference is seen in the rent-rates prevailing for canal-irrigated land in the two tahsíls, that is, in Kasúr one-third or one-fourth *batai* is as common as one-half or one-third in Lahore, but a custom is now growing up whereby the owner pays a portion of the canal charges corresponding to the portion of produce he receives: Thus if he takes one-third of the produce he pays one-third the canal charges; if he takes one-half the produce he pays one-half the water charges and also one-half the cost of seed: the latter system is very common now in Lahore tahsíl and is very likely to spread both there and in Kasúr to the exclusion of other rent rates, as being the one most calculated to identify the owner's and tenant's interests. In Sharakpur tahsíl the produce rent rates are lower than in any other part of the district owing partly to the poverty of the soil and partly to the difficulty of procuring tenants; two disqualifications which are very closely connected together.

Chapter III, E.

Village communities and tenures.

Kind rents.

One more system of kind rents is for the owner to stipulate for a fixed quantity of special produce each year whatever crops are grown or harvested : for instance the tenant is to pay him two maunds of wheat on each acre for the spring harvest and a certain amount of maize or cotton for the autumn crop. This is less common here than in the adjoining district of Amritsar, and while prices are as unstable as they are at present is not likely to spread.

It should have been added above that before the landlord and tenant divide the common heap of produce between them, deductions are first made in the case of certain crops, usually wheat in the spring harvest and maize in the autumn, for the village artisans, namely the *tarkhán* or carpenter, the *kumhár* or potter, the *lohár* or blacksmith, the *mochi* or leather-worker, and some also for the village *chuhra* from each crop harvested. Fuller mention will be made of these menials and their deductions further on ; but it must be understood that as a rule their deductions are made from the whole heap and not from the owner's or tenant's separate share. Another matter worth noticing is that of the straw. On well-irrigated lands all produce grown for purposes of cattle fodder is assumed to be necessary to keep the cultivation going. The landowner therefore can claim no share of such crops, though the tenant is bound to let him have one entire *kanal* of fodder from each well for his home cattle. Similarly the owner can claim no share of the straw of produce grown on well-irrigated land. He does, however, take a share of the straw cut from land cropped otherwise than by well irrigation, namely, the same share as he is entitled to take of the grain.

Mixed cash and kind rents are rare, but sometimes the tenant agrees to pay a fixed amount of produce and some small cash rent as well ; or he may take upon himself the responsibility for the fixed land revenue and a small share of the produce.

In all the systems of produce rent described above, except that last mentioned, the owner is invariably responsible for the fixed land revenue. Water advantage rate, or as it is sometimes called owner's rate on canal-irrigated lands, when taken, is, as a rule, treated as part of the canal water charges and follows the agreement made with respect to them.

Cultivating partnership.

True agricultural partnerships are seldom met with in the Lahore district. Full brothers sometimes cultivate land together, but even this is uncommon. Several members of a family down to second or third cousins continue to be recorded as joint proprietors of land and have no wish to be recorded otherwise, but on enquiry it will generally be found that each shareholder cultivates his separate land. On the other hand it is not uncommon for joint shareholders while cultivating separately to share all profits and expenses. The most frequent instance of a true cultivating partnership is where the land owner associates with him a working partner, probably one of the village menials, who brings no agricultural material, but only his labour, which is counted equal to that of one bullock. This man is called an *adhjoghia*, and receives at the end of the harvest a half share of the produce corresponding to a single plough of oxen. Thus if his proprietor partner had contributed three plough of oxen the *adhjoghia* would get one-sixth share of the produce ; if six plough of oxen, the *adhjoghia* would get one-twelfth and so on, but before the division between the two takes place, one-fourth or sometimes one-fifth is set apart from the common heap as an equivalent to the land revenue and something is deducted for seed. Then from the *adhjoghia's* share when separated, the landowner appropriates the equivalent of the advances made in his name by the village weighman to the *adhjoghia* for food while the crop under division was being cultivated and grown ; so that the produce which ultimately comes to the *adhjoghia* is probably exceedingly reduced in amount, and practically he is little better than a labourer kept in food and other necessaries by his master while at work, and yet the *adhjoghia* system is common in Chúnián tahsíl.

The most common farm labourer is that known as *athri chuhra* who is always taken on when there is much work, as, for instance, on land irrigated from wells or from canal water lifts. He is the regular ploughboy, who always attends at ploughing and other field work, folds the cattle and spreads the manure. In return for these services his master gives him bread twice a day, a blanket and a pair of shoes, and every six months grain varying in amount with the extent of service he has rendered ; sometimes fixed weights of 10 or 15 maunds in the autumn and 40 or 50 maunds in the spring ; sometimes a varying percentage of five or ten per cent. of the produce that comes to his employer. Besides the *athri chuhra*, the ordinary village scavenger, also called *chuhra*, renders assistance on the land to three or four different people as they require his services. Thus he might come to each of the three or four cultivators who patronise him once or twice a week ; any day he came he would assist in the ploughing or other farm duties for most of the day ; and would get his food from his employer. At harvest time he is allowed to take from the entire produce from three to five per cent. and this deduction is made before any division is made between the owner and tenant, in case the land is under cultivation by a tenant ; this being a form of payment not only for farm services from which the owner and the tenant, where there is one, have benefitted in proportion, but also for general menial services performed in the village. Another kind of farm labourer is the *káma* who is paid in cash one rupee or two rupees a month, and also receives his bread every day ; and a pair of shoes and suit of clothes every year. This is the least common form of labourer in this district.

The village artisans who are also recognized as belonging to the menial class are the carpenter, potter, blacksmith and

Chapter III, E.

Village communities and tenures.

Cultivating partnership.

Farm labourers.

Village artisans.

leather-worker as noted above. The carpenter's business is to make and repair ploughs and other agricultural implements, any articles of furniture used in the house, to repair the wood-work on the Persian wheel of irrigation wells and carts or cart wheels. For all these purposes he must be supplied with wood, it is only his skill and service that he is supposed to give, and even for these he may ask for special payment in return for constructing large and important articles anew, such as carts or the two big wheels on which the well-working principally depends. In return for his services the carpenter receives fixed amounts of grain each harvest, wheat usually in the spring and maize or rice in the autumn. The exact amount varies somewhat in different parts of the district and is much more for well-irrigated land than for other soils. In the calculations on which the recent assessments were based it was estimated that the carpenter's customary payments were $2\frac{1}{2}$ maunds of wheat for each irrigation well in the spring harvest, and $2\frac{1}{2}$ maunds of maize in the autumn and on other than well-irrigated land 10 sérs to each plough of land.

The potter's duties are to supply pots for the Persian wheel of the irrigation well or of a canal water lift and earthen vessels for domestic use. Thus if any Civil Officer comes on tour and wants the temporary loan of water-pots for culinary or bath-room use the potter would be expected to produce them, and if money was offered to him the landowners would with justice point out that this was part of his customary services for which they paid him at certain seasons of the year and that he was being paid twice over for the same service. His payments in kind are the same as those made to the carpenter.

The iron smith's duty is to fix all the iron work on agricultural implements and to keep it in repair, but the iron must be supplied to him or he will charge for it ; he would also shoe the cart bullocks when necessary ; his payments in kind are half those of the carpenter and potter.

The *mochi* or leather-worker has little to do, but make blinkers (kopi) for the well and plough cattle ; the *chhát* or thong tied on a stick as a whip ; also he has to make a pair of shoes once a year for each of his patrons. The *mochi's* payments are half those of the ironsmith ; in the assessment calculations he was not treated as a farm *sepi* whose kind payments could fairly be deducted from the assessable produce. For the other three artisans it was estimated in para. 64 of the Settlement Report that the total grain payments on well-irrigated lands averaged six maunds of wheat and six maunds of maize or of rice per well. This was reckoned to be equivalent to one-twentieth of the well-irrigated wheat and one-sixth of the well-irrigated maize. On other soils the artisans receive 25 sérs per plough which amounts to about 2 per cent. on canal-irrigated land and 5 or 6 per cent. on other soils. It must not be supposed that all the men present in the village, belonging to the classes named, confine themselves to doing *Sep* as their customary duties are called. Many take up quite different occupations such as land-cultivation, carrying for hire, &c., and some combine their *Sep* work with other methods of making a livelihood.

Other village menials are paid in kind for services rendered, such as the water-carrier (*máchhi* or *jhinwar*), the village minstrel (*mirási*) and the barber (*nái*). Also *faqírs* and Brahmans are not forgotten. The separate amount each class receives is small, but taken all together these payments mount up and form a heavy charge on the cultivation. Sometimes they are paid from the common heap of produce before division is effected between owner and tenant; sometimes from each one's separate share. But a self-cultivating owner has to give away probably not less than 20 per cent. of the total produce on his well-irrigated land; on other classes of land the proportion is much smaller. All this is over and above payments made to regular farm labourers, such as the *athri chuhra* described above, to *láwis* or hired reapers who must be employed in the spring harvest when there is much land under wheat, to the men who plant out the rice, an operation known as *Láb* or to hired threshers. How much these operations add to the expenses would be hard to say; the practice of employing hired labour varies so much among different classes. Rájpúts and Dogars would not stoop to any such severe work as reaping or threshing if they could hire others to do it for them. Jats have no objection to threshing or reaping ordinary crops, but would not plant or reap rice and would much prefer having some one to do the dirty and more irksome work of cleaning up his cattle stands and manuring the fields. Aráins and Kambohs on the other hand would do all and anything they could find time to do.

Small grants of land, sometimes subject to revenue, sometimes revenue free, are given by the village proprietors to deserving village servants. If they are given revenue free the landowners must make good the revenue to the Government. The most frequent recipients are attendants at mosques, shrines and temples, water-carriers or village watchmen. Many máfis of this description found in existence at the first regular settlement were confirmed by Government and were recorded in the máfi registers. At the recent settlement all such máfis relating to land less than three acres in area were, if thought worth maintaining, handed over to the control of the village landowners for the term of the new settlement. That is they were allowed to count for the purpose of reducing the khálisa revenue payable by the landowners of the estate, but the latter were at liberty to confer the máfi on any one they pleased; or if they preferred, not to grant it out as a máfi at all: as a matter of fact however the landowners would always grant such máfis to some or other of their village servants provided it cost them nothing.

The proprietors in this district are in the habit of collecting various feudal taxes from non-proprietors living on their

Chapter III, E.

**Village communi-
ties and tenures.**

Village dues.

estates and in their villages. They are as follows :—(1) *Hakk
Thána-Patti,* a tax on marriages varying from Re. 1 to Rs. 5
for each marriage ; (2) *Hakk dhart,* a commission on all sales
varying from 1 to 2 pice in the rupee of the price. This is very
common and exists in most villages; (3) *Hakk atráfi,* a charge
on village shopkeepers varying from 4 annas to one rupee a
shop ; (4) *Hakk charai,* a grazing tax paid by non-proprietors
on all cattle grazed on the common land. This is rarely de-
manded. Also in some villages the landowners have a right of
pre-emption in all houses built by non-proprietors and claim
even to take one-fourth the price realized by the sale of the
buildings. The latter claim would hardly be admitted now by
money-lenders who have built themselves large masonry houses.

**Village officers,
lambardárs or head-
men.**

Tahsíl					Number of headmen.
Lahore	...	...	..	...	... 808
Kasúr	...	...	...	...	... 868
Chúnián	...	...	...	...	... 722
Sharakpur	...	...	...	...	... 579
Total	...		...	2,977

The figures in the mar-
gin show the number of
headmen in the several tahsíls of the district. The
average to each village is
1·9.

The number appointed to each estate is, as a rule, the same as
was fixed at the first regular settlement of 1856 ; and is need-
lessly large in many cases. The Lambardár's duty is to collect
the land revenue and account for it to the Tahsíldár or chief
revenue authority of the tahsíl, to render assistance and furnish
information in respect of all police revenue and administrative
matters affecting his village, and to perform various duties which
are set forth in Section 181 of the Rules under the Land Revenue
and Tenancy Acts. Two headmen are ordinarily sufficient to discharge these duties in any estate however large, except where the
village is constituted in subdivisions or *pattis* of different clans or
tribes, when it is often advisable to have a separate headman
representing each separate clan or tribe. In small estates one
headman is ample. An excessive number of headmen in a village
causes a division of responsibility which cannot but be prejudicial
to the administration. The desirability of reducing the numbers has been kept in view now for some years, but under
existing rules the claim of a son to succeed his father as
village headman cannot be ignored save for special cause, and
few opportunities of reducing occur. A five per cent. additional
cess on the land-revenue collections is levied from the landowners
of each estate to pay their lambardárs ; each of whom gets less
or more of this according to the number of headmen in the
estate. In addition to the duties imposed by law or rule on
the lambardár, he is also responsible to the rest of the village
community for entertaining and providing a night's board and
lodging for all strangers coming to the village. In connection
with his administrative duties he is liable to be summoned at
any moment on due cause to wait on the Tahsíldár, Deputy
Inspector of Police, Canal Zilladárs or other officers of higher
rank than these, and may occasionally be detained from his
home sometime. All round the office of village headman is

by no means a complete sinecure, and the remuneration he gets is small. Moreover, as the people, who in this district are by nature democratically inclined, learn better and better that so long as they keep within the strict letter of the law, no harm will come to them, they heed administrative control less and less and, if it suits their interests, have little scruple in setting their headman's authority at naught. It is not therefore to be wondered at that village landowners are growing less keen to be appointed headmen, and exhibit more indifference about losing the position, after enjoying it for a time, than used to be the case.

The office of chief headman was instituted at the revision of settlement in 1868. One man was selected from among the village headmen to take the lead and represent them if neces-sary in all administrative and social functions. In addition to the remuneration he received as headman of the village, the Ala-Lambardár was allowed an additional one per cent. cess on the land revenue and the temporary occupation of a small plot out of the village waste the revenue on which Government under-took to remit when any was assessed ; which as a matter of fact was very seldom the case. Of late years the large body of Revenue Officers in the Province pronounced in favour of the abolition of this office of chief headman, which by general consent is regarded as a useless addition to the administrative wheel ; as the outcome of a lengthy correspondence on the subject the Government decided in favour of its *partial* abolition. By subsequent sanction to the proposals made in pursuance of those orders, chief headmen will eventually be retained in this dis-trict in 78 villages only, which have been selected as offering conditions which from certain points of view render retention of the office possibly beneficial. The appointment in all other villages is to be abolished as existing incumbents die, and the ála-lambardári cess will simultaneously cease to be levied. The grants of waste made to chief headmen on their appoint-ment in 1868 were resumed at the recent settlement and cash *inams* of small value allowed in their place. As existing chief headmen die and their appointments are abolished these cash *inams* will be resumed and credited to Government, but when a sufficient sum has been credited on this account, then two or three *inams* in each *zail*, varying in amount from Rs. 40 to Rs. 60, will be created and *inam-khors* appointed to enjoy them as remuneration for rendering assistance as required under the rules regarding such appointments.

A *zail* is a circle of villages, the size of which may vary ac-cording to circumstances and the limits of which are fixed as far as possible with reference to the principles laid down in Revenue Circular No. 27. The zaildár or representative of the *zail* is to be appointed from among the village headmen of the *zail* in accor-dance with the rules on the subject framed under the Land Reve-nue Act. His duties are to make reports and render assistance in all subjects connected with the police revenue and adminis-trative business of his *zail*. The office was first instituted in this

Chapter III, E.

**Village communi-
ties and tenures.**

Village Officers.

Zaildárs.

district at the revised settlement of 1868 when 49 zaildárs
were appointed, but the limits of the *zails* then fixed conform-
ed to none of the principles laid down now as guides for
arranging *zails;* that is to say, their boundaries did not correspond with those of police stations, patwári's circles or tribal
location. It was therefore found advisable to reconstitute them
at the recent settlement. They could not be fitted in with the
boundaries of the several police station divisions, as these last
in this district often take in parts of two different tahsíls. The
new proposals were based principally on tribal subdivisions,
each *zail* being constituted so as to include villages of one tribe
as far as possible, and also care was taken that patwári's circles
should not come into more than one *zail.* The new arrangement
was accepted by the Government. In the place of 49 *zails*
there are now 50. Formerly zaildár's emoluments were collected
in the form of a one per cent. additional cess on the land
revenue of the *zail.* Now the cess has been abolished and
the zaildárs are paid by Government out of revenue collections, the rate being still maintained at one per cent. on the
zail revenue. A table is appended showing by tahsíls the
head-quarters and name of each *zail,* the number of estates
in each and the amount of land revenue they pay, as well as
the prevailing tribes in each.

Tahsil.	Zail.	Number of villages.	Annual land revenue.	Prevailing caste or tribe.
			Rs.	
LAHORE.	Awán Dhaiwála	25	14,299	Labánas, Jats, Rájpúts & Dogars.
	Shahdara	25	14,277	Aráins and Rajpúts.
	Lahore and Dholanwál,	38	43,207	Do. do.
	Bághbánpura	27	19,329	Do. do.
	Bhasín	39	23,601	Jats and Rájpúts.
	Bhangali	45	23,269	Do. do.
	Ichhra	28	15,614	Jats and others.
	Niázbeg	44	29,504	Rájpúts, Aráins and Labánas.
	Khudpur	23	27,348	Jats and Aráins.
	Halloke	30	21,608	Jats.
	Kahna	31	22,774	Do.
	Ghawind	14	23,922	Do.
	Manihála and Padhána ...	25	24,104	Do.
KASUR.	Sur Singh	28	24,253	Jats.
	Patti	35	26,141	Do.
	Dasuwál and Gharyála ...	20	24,440	Do.
	Algun	20	20,598	Do.
	Wan	22	20,884	Do.
	Kasúr	25	20,925	Jats, Kambohs, Rájpúts & Aráins.
	Luliáni	16	20,727	Jats.
	Hardo Sahari	12	13,103	Do.
	Sattoke	20	21,123	Jats and Rájpúts.
	Jaura	27	22,979	Jats, Aráins, Rájpúts & others.
	Burj Kalán	38	25,251	Aráins.
	Sultán Shah Wála ...	31	9,869	Dogars.
	Sabjra	29	44,495	Jats and Dogars.
	Sitto	43	23,802	Do.

Tahsíl.	Zail.	Number of villages.	Annual land revenue.	Prevailing caste or tribe.
			Rs.	
CHUNIAN.	Killa Dharam Singh ...	34	10,829	Jats.
	Beharwál	34	12,273	Do.
	Gagga Sarai	18	9,802	Do.
	Bughiána Kaláu	20	14,054	Do.
	Hundal	33	24,832	Do.
	Khudián	31	19,034	Jats, Kambohs and Rájpúts.
	Mojoke	29	20,864	Jats.
	Chúnián	16	15,704	Do.
	Ghelan	30	14,432	Rájpúts and Aráins.
	Kanganpur	43	17,474	Jats.
	Kul	30	16,882	Do.
	Ganja Kalán	55	23,234	Dogars, Aráins and Kambohs.
	Mokal	41	14,643	Dogars, Jats, Mahtams, and Khatrís.
SHARAKPUR.	Tapiála and Labanwála ...	36	19,005	Labánás, Jats and Rájpúts.
	Muridke	44	17,623	Rájpúts, Jats and Labánás.
	Kot Pindidás	28	13,716	Jats, Rájpúts and Khattrís.
	Sahuke Mallián	47	17,311	Jats.
	Moranwála	46	14,119	Jats, Labánás, Aráins & Rájpúts.
	Sharakpur	67	19,393	Jats, Aráins, Rájpúts and Dogars,
	Mangtánwála	45	12,949	Jats and Aráins.
	Natha	31	12,322	Jats.
	Khairpur	23	6,429	Rájpúts, Jats, and Kureshís.
	Fattah Thatta	34	6,387	Jats and Kureshís.

The patwári is a revenue official who is responsible for the maintenance and preservation of all village records affect-ing the land revenue estates in his circle; he also has other duties to perform, which are ordered in accordance with instructions issued from time to time by the Controlling Revenue authority of the Province. His circle comprises a fixed number of villages which varies according to the size of the several estates. The standard average number of fields in a patwári's circle is 5,000. In this district there are 1,576 revenue estates, and 1,526,129 survey numbers or fields. The number of pat-wáris in the entire district has recently been raised from 293 to 316 under due sanction; the average number of estates and of survey fields to each patwári therefore in this district is now 5 and 4,830 respectively. A five per cent. cess on the land revenue is levied from the landowners for payment of the patwári. *Patwáris or village accountants.*

Statistics of sales and mortgages are furnished in Table No. XXXII. Since the year 1868, eight per cent. of the land under cultivation has been sold and at present fourteen per cent. of such land is mortgaged with possession. *Transfers of land.*

The sales have been most frequent and have covered a proportionately larger area in the estates along the Rávi and in Sharakpur tahsíl. In the Mánjha and Hithár tracts they have covered respectively 6 and 7 per cent. of the cultivated *Sales.*

Chapter III, E.

Village communities and tenures.

Sales.

land. Sales are generally resorted to either when the agriculturist is no longer able to obtain relief by mortgage, or with some ulterior motive apart from the money to be realized, as for instance when childless proprietors negociate fictitious sales to the favouring of certain relatives and the prejudice of others. Of those who have been driven of necessity to sell, it will generally be found that many are men who have wasted their substance, having been guilty of extravagant expenditure on matters wholly unconnected with land agriculture, as for instance on drinking, gambling, building costly houses or buying expensive horses. This is particularly the case in the Mánjha and only somewhat less so in the Hithár tract of this district. There land is fertile and always repays careful cultivation ; any man who pays ordinary attention to his agriculture, and is not throwing away his money on unnecessary articles of luxury, can always keep his head above water more or less, and if he gets into temporary difficulties, all he has to do is to borrow on his land by a mortgage and continue cultivating it under the mortgagee, paying him a small share of the produce, until he has paid off the debt. A good agriculturist should never have reason to nor feel inclined to sell his land where the cultivating conditions are ordinarily good. In the Rávi estates and the Sharakpur tahsíl on the other hand the landowner may often be forced to sell land outright by conditions for which he is hardly altogether responsible. In the former land is very insufficient for the number of owners living on it, and often some of the members of a family, in which subdivision of land has reached an excessive pitch, give up the struggle, sell the diminutive share they have left, and go out to work elsewhere, either as tenants-at-will or daily labourers. In Sharakpur tahsíl agriculture is in a very depressed condition and people do not seem able to make headway against the physical difficulties of soil and climate or their own want of energy, when once they have begun to go down hill. The mortgage debts increase gradually out of all proportion to the land mortgaged, until there is no power of redemption, and the mortgagee has no choice left but to take over all the land he can get in permanent transfer.

Mortgages.

Existing mortgages of the usufructuary kind cover 14 per cent. of the cultivated area in the whole district. They are heaviest proportionately in the Rávi estates and least in the Mánjha tract. Most mortgage transactions are *bonâ fide* alienations for necessity. Some, however, are due to an owner having more land than he can manage or having property in more than one estate ; in such cases the most convenient course often is to alienate some of his land temporarily by mortgage. Far the greater part of the land mortgaged is cultivated by the mortgagee himself or by some tenant other than the mortgagor under him. A small proportion, however, about one-seventh of the whole, is cultivated by the mortgagors who give the mortgagees a share of the produce in lieu of interest. This is far the most desirable form of mortgage for the owner in every way. His debt is not being increased by interest : he is constantly reminded of his

obligation to rid himself of the debt incumbrance ; and it is his
interest to husband the resources of his own land where the
mortgagee or another tenant might by bad agriculture spoil the
fertility of the soil.

All land transfers, except those made fictitiously or for the
convenience of the owners, originate in a book debt to a money-
lender. It does not follow that the latter always gets possession
of the land transferred. Sometimes the borrower mortgages his
land to a fellow zamíndár, either of his own or of another village,
for a sum of money which enables him to clear himself of his debt
to the money-lender. In this district not more than half the
alienations have been made to professional money-lenders. The
latter have the upper hand in all the well-irrigated tracts almost ;
and there unfortunately land is accumulating rapidly in the
hands of a few well-to-do men of the trading class who know
little of agriculture and take small interest in the improvement
of the soil.

The present recorded mortgage debt is equivalent to between
five and six times the newly assessed revenue. There is in
addition an enormous amount of unsecured and therefore unre-
corded indebtedness. The causes of so much debt differ in different parts of the district. In the Mánjha where both land and
money are fairly plentiful, extravagance is the main cause ; but
in some villages debt can be traced to heavy cash payments for
the use of canal water, especially in those villages which lie at the
tail end of a canal distributary and get an inadequate supply of
water. Undoubtedly these large cash payments come very
heavy on the people to meet, unless the irrigation is exceptionally good and the resulting crop abundant. Until lately
estates at the end of a distributary fared badly ; now-a-days
the general distribution is being put on a much more even
footing. Outside the Mánjha indebtedness is generally brought
about by causes beyond the debtor's own control, chiefly by
losses incidental to agriculture, such as the falling in of wells,
disease among the cattle, a run of bad seasons, destruction of
land by the river or of crops by hail. Practically all small
agriculturists are in debt more or less : providence and economy
are not strongly developed traits in the ordinary cultivator,
and it is very seldom one can find that the plenty of one year
is stored up as provision against the deficiency of another.
Sooner or later the grain stores are certain to run out, plough
cattle die, seed grain is wanted for sowings ; and recourse to
the village money-lender becomes inevitable : once in the
latter's books the ignorant cultivator is at his mercy almost,
and though he may keep the debt down he will hardly free
himself altogether, except by borrowing a lump sum elsewhere
under conditions probably no better than the ordinary Khatrí
money-lender is ready to grant him.

CHAPTER IV.

PRODUCTION AND DISTRIBUTION.

SECTION A.—AGRICULTURE, ARBORICULTURE AND LIVE-STOCK.

Chapter IV, A.

Agriculture, Arboriculture and Live-stock.

Table No. XIV gives the general figures for cultivation and irrigation in this district; the rainfall and the manner in which it is distributed throughout the year is shown in Tables Nos. III, III A and III B.

Cultivation.

Of the total area of the district, amounting to 3,602 square miles, more than half is under cultivation either with or without the aid of artificial irrigation. The remaining area consists of waste land fit for cultivation but not yet broken up for some reason, and land not available for tillage either because it is under buildings, roads, canals, railways, &c., or because its soil is unproductive. Forty years ago before the extension of the Bári Doáb Canal the district contained more waste than tilled land. During the currency of the first regular settlement cultivation increased 24 per cent. Between the second regular settlement (1868) and 1892, the increase was 33 per cent. The area at present recorded as culturable waste in the whole district is 579,064 acres, of which 33 per cent. and 43 per cent. are in the Chúnián and Sharakpur tahsíls respectively, about 440,000 acres lying in the river lowlands and the remainder in the Mánjha. Much of the former is too sandy to be productive even under well irrigation : the Mánjha waste lies almost entirely in tracts to which the Bári Doáb Canal has not yet been extended. In the Western Mánjha at any rate in the absence of irrigation the rainfall is ordinarily too feeble and precarious to ripen crops by itself, and it is a general rule there to leave all land under dry cultivation surrounded by a considerably larger area of waste, which serves as a catchment basin off which the surface drainage during rain can be conducted by means of low temporary ridges of earth on to the land which is to be sown. The extent to which the Mánjha waste is likely to be broken up during the currency of the present settlement depends entirely on the amount of Bári Doáb Canal water supply available for further extension in the western portion of the Mánjha tract.

The principal soils under cultivation are as follows :—

Principal kinds of soil.

Rohi.—This is lowlying land which collects surface drainage water. In the Cis-Rávi part of the district the drainage channels of the Mánjha are known locally as *Rohi.* For instance the Hudiára Rohi is the largest drainage channel of the district. The soil in these channels is stiff, containing little sand. It is fertile under irrigation and in a year of good rainfall produces good crops without artificial irrigation

Otherwise the soil remains very dry and hard. Generally it is considered a great advantage to have some of this Rohi land within the estate, but unless the slope of the channel is very gradual an untimely flood after the crops are sown causes the cultivators considerable loss. In the Trans-Rávi portion of the district the term Rohi appears to denote a crisp loam which has become hardened under the action of occasional flood water. All the more fertile land in the Sharakpur tahsíl lying on the north-east between the sandy ridge that borders the district on the north and the Deg stream is spoken of locally as Rohi.

Kállaráthi—This is land impregnated with kállar or saline matter, but not sufficiently so to be completely unfertile. The most intractable specimen of this is to be found in the low-lying stiff clay lands south of the Deg on the east border of the Sharakpur tahsíl. These yield fine rice crops, but very little else.

Maira.—A loam of varying density and colour according to the proportion of sand mixed with it : found principally in the Mánjha, where it is in parts inclined to be gritty, but as a rule is a clean dry soil.

Tibba.—A weak soil in which sand and grit predominate enough to prevent clods forming under the action of moisture. This is only fit for growing the inferior pulses.

Dosháhi.—An intermediate soil between Maira and Tibba, often consisting of good fertile land covered by a slight coating of sand. This, though never bearing abundantly, is regarded as a very safe soil for dry cultivation. It bears best under regular and moderate rain. When the people wish to be-little such land with an eye to the coming assessment they will speak of it as Tibba, to which the upper surface of Dosháhi has a close resemblance. This soil is hardly found, except in the eastern portion of the Kasúr Mánjha.

Gasra.—A soft grey alluvial loam found in the river tracts. Sometimes also the term is used of a sandy Maira. Gasra is easy to work and fairly fertile.

Sukkund.—A hard alluvial soil just the opposite of Gasra : The term is used to denote land of a darkish colour, which splits into fissures when drying after irrigation. It usually has a sub-stratum of pure sand not far below : provided the sand is not too near, Sukkund land bears well if properly cultivated, but it requires plenty of irrigation and heavy plough cattle : on this account it is not so well liked by the people as Gasra.

Sterile soils.—The two best known terms for wholly unfertile land are Rukkur and Kallar. The former is a bad sandy land in river tracts fit for growing nothing but Sirkána or thatch reed : but sometimes th people, when they wish to disparage their cultivated land, even talk of it as Rukkur.

The worst kind of Kallar is found along the river bank, where the only indication of its presence is the absence of all

Chapter IV, A.

Agriculture, Arboriculture and Live-stock.

Sterile soils.

vegetation : there is not much of this. A milder form of *kállar* is seen in the west Mánjha along the Rávi bank where in places a thick crust of *reh* forms ; or again in Sharakpur, which is remarkable for its long stretches of saline land growing nothing but most inferior classes of salinaceous vegetation.

Name of tahsíl.	Area irrigated.	Area unirrigated.
Lahore	51	49
Kasúr	50	50
Chúnián	69	31
Sharakpur	82	18
Total District ...	60	40

The distribution of the cultivated land under the heads irrigated and unirrigated is shown for each tahsíl in the margin, the figures denoting percentage fractions of the total area under tillage.

Well irrigation.

The form of well always used in this district is that known as the Persian wheel : but near the river the *dhingli,* consisting of a long pole swinging on a fulcrum and with a bucket attached at the end, is sometimes found : these however only irrigate an acre or so of land. Usually wells are lined with brickwork in which case they are called *pukka :* without brickwork they are called *kucha,* being lined with nothing more than grass. *Kucha* wells seldom last more than two or three years and then fall in : and while standing they cannot irrigate as much as a masonry well. On the other hand a *kucha* well costs Rs. 30 or Rs. 40 to build, while a masonry well costs from Rs. 200 to Rs. 600 according to the depth of the water. At present in this district there are 12,996 masonry wells, of which 608 have two wheels ; and 4,879 unlined wells. The area a well can irrigate depends so much on the nature of the soil, the character of the season, the state of repair in which the well is, the quality of the cattle employed, and the industry of the cultivators, that it is not possible to say the area irrigated is so much and no more.

The statement in the margin shows the depth of water and average cropped area of wells

Name of tract.	AVERAGE DEPTH OF WELL.			Average area cropped.
	To water.			
	Maximum.	Minimum.	In water.	
Mánjha	52	20	16	22
Hithár	25	65	6	28
Rávi villages ...	28	12	8	20
Trans-Rávi	54	16	7	24

in different parts of the district as they appear to be according to the information collected at settlement. But no wells would crop as much as is here shown unless they were provided with at least six yoke of oxen in the Mánjha and five yoke in the lowland tracts.

The construction of a well is a great event in the lives of the brotherhood : and operations are inaugurated with various formal ceremonies. The expenditure incurred is somewhat as follows :—

	Lowlands.	Mánjha.
	Rs.	Rs.
For digging the hole (pár khodna)	7	14
Wooden frame on which the brickwork is constructed (chak).	25	30
Distribution of gur when putting in the chak ...	4	10
Bricks for lining the well	100	220
Carriage of bricks to well	20	40
Two bricklayers at Re. 1 a háth of work done ...	21	50
Food for bricklayers	9	20
Mortar for laying bricks	10	65
Other labourers' wages	12	25
Pay of three divers at Rs. 2 a háth	8	25
Food for divers	12	30
Miscellaneous alms	12	21
Total	240	550

The calculation does not pretend to be exact, or quite exhaustive : on the other hand considerable economy can be effected if the brotherhood choose to dig the ground and do other common labourers' work themselves. The alms are distributed at different stages of the operations. The divers have terribly hard work going down below the water and fixing the excavating shovel called the *chamb* into the ground before it is pulled up by a rope from above. They are fed very sumptuously on bread, *ghi, gur* and tobacco. Four divers is the usual allowance for excavating at an ordinary well. In case of difficulty they get more assistance. When the proper water bearing stratum is reached, they say *tung ágaya*. If they cannot reach this stratum, they say there is no *tung*. Some times they come on a hard sticky clay which the divers cannot get through : in this case they must either give up the site, or sometimes they evade the difficulty by sinking a smaller cylinder inside the original one. These smaller cylinders are known by the name of *bacchha*. Similarly when the water level in an old well has sunk below the brickwork or when sand comes into the well along with the spring water (*Kú pungaya*) a *bacchha* is sunk. When the well is once built, assuming that it remains in good order the only expenditure required on the well itself is for cleaning, which must be done every three or four years. The wood-work, however, by means of which the well is worked costs a considerable amount and requires to be constantly repaired or replaced as it wears out under continual use. Its first cost ranges from Rs. 40 to Rs. 60 and the annual cost of repairs varies from Rs. 12 to Rs. 20. The cost of the wood-work falls on the owner of the well and not on the tenant. The *chakl jora*, or two main cog wheels, are usually bought from the village carpenter and cost from Rs. 26 to Rs. 34 according to their make. If, however, the owner has the *kikar* wood available, he makes it over to the carpenter who would charge Rs. 14 or so for the job of making up the wheels. Most of the other pieces of wood-work can be

made up by the owners themselves if they have the wood
which need not necessarily be of *kikar*. Generally for such
purposes the trees growing round the village wells supply
material. Wells are for the most part owned and also cultivated in shares ; the shareholders have their turns, usually lasting
three hours each, fixed by lot, but the shareholder who takes
the trouble to put on the rope ladder and water pots is allowed
to take first turn. When once the order is fixed it is strictly
adhered to. It is very seldom that any dispute arises among
the shareholders on this account.

The course of cropping on wells varies in different parts of
the district. In the sweet water wells of the Mánjha, out of a
total well area of 28 acres, between 4 and 5 acres would be
sown for the kharíf harvest and about 22 acres for the rabi.
The reason for less land being sown in the former than the
latter is that there is much less time for preparing the land in
the summer than in the winter months. The kharíf area would
be distributed roughly as follows : 2 acres maize, $\frac{3}{4}$ acre
cotton, a little sugarcane or rice and the balance would be
fodder. In the rabi 17 acres would be sown with wheat
and the balance would be devoted to fodder or perhaps a few miscellaneous crops. In the Western Mánjha where the wells are
bitter the autumn cropping is very limited and the spring cropping is almost all wheat with a little barley. In the Hithár tract
where well areas are large and there is little pressure on the land
the rabi cropping covers a much more extensive area than the
autumn cropping ; the latter occupies 10 acres about, of which
3 are under maize, $1\frac{1}{2}$ acres under cotton, half an acre
under pepper and the rest is left for fodder and other miscellaneous crops. In the spring 16 acres are sown with
wheat, 2 with barley and 4 with fodder crops. In the
Hithár wells fallowing is relied on as much as manuring to improve the land. In the Rávi estates where well areas are much
smaller and land is not plentiful, more proportionately is kept for
the valuable autumn crops which ripen quicker and occupy the
land a shorter time than the spring crops. This involves heavy
expenditure on manure, otherwise the land lying fallow so seldom
as it does would decrease in fertility. On the whole well cultivation in this district is carried on with sufficient care and economy.
The landowners in well-irrigated tracts are for the most part
very industrious both by inclination and habit. They understand the requirements of their land and carry these out as far
as circumstances permit. The difficulties they have to contend
with are never ending. Cattle disease, short fodder supplies,
constantly recurring defects in their wells are calamities which
the cultivator of well lands is always having to face. Of the
total number of wells now in existence 31 per cent. have been
constructed since last settlement and 69 are old, but the fact
of a well being new by no means insures its being in good
repair. It often happens that owing to hurry and scamping of
their duties on the part of the divers or of the bricklayers, the

well settles immediately after it has been completed and the brickwork cracks from the very foundations, in which case the well must take in a quantity of sand with the water and soon gets choked up. Many wells are now working notwithstanding defects which interfere sadly with their working and diminish greatly the water-supply.

The *Jhallár* or waterlift is merely the Persian wheel of a well transferred to the bank of a canal or a pond or river stream : they are found most in Sharakpur where some work all the year round at the upper part of the D̓eg, and others for a short time only, until the water-supply being drawn upon is exhausted. As long as there is sufficient water their irrigating power is as good as or better than that of a well of the same depth.

This is regulated by the officers of the Irrigation Department. In the Mánjha the Bári Doáb Canal is perennial, but in most years has to be closed for repairs for six or seven weeks in the cold weather months, generally from the first week in January to the second week in February. No doubt, this closure is inevitable, but its duration should be made as short as possible ; otherwise the crops are certain to suffer more or less. The people differ in their views as to which is the best time, some say January when all the rabi land dependent on canal-irrigation has been sown after one watering : others say February when most of the land will have had two waterings. The best time is probably from January 10th to February 10th, but the closure should not begin earlier or end later. Even then it may do much harm unless there are fair winter rains, but as a rule rain falls within the period named.

The general principle followed by the Canal Department in distributing water is to supply enough to irrigate one-fourth of each estate to which the canal is extended. The standard of measurement for distribution of the water is the *nál*, which is supposed to supply enough water to irrigate from 25 to 50 ghumáos.

The *nál* represents a round opening about four inches in diameter. A *nál* of water again is distributed on the basis of ten shares. Sometimes one *nál* of water issues from the distributary by a piping of baked mud ; this can be closed with grass or straw consolidated with earth. More often, however, the water is let out from the distributary to the amount of several *náls*, by means of a masonry head. If the water let out is equivalent to two *náls* then the masonry head is called a *mogha* ; if to more than two *náls* then it is called a *dihána*. Of late the number of *moghás* has been greatly reduced, the water suppliers being concentrated at large *dihánás*. These are closed by boards secured by locks, which are opened when it is the turn of the shareholders in that head to receive water. Below the *nál* or masonry head is a water-cut or *khál* for the digging and clearance of which the shareholders in the water are responsible according to the extent of their share. Further distribution is made by smaller

Chapter IV, A.

Agriculture, Arboriculture and Live-stock.

Well irrigation.

Jhallárs.

Canal irrigation.

water-cuts opening out of the main *khál*, the water being diverted into each of such small cuts for a fixed time according to the share of its proprietors in the main *khál*. Only one of these is kept open at a time, all the rest being closed by mud embankments. The shareholders usually settle for themselves in what order each shall have his turn (*wári*) at the water, but if they have any dispute over the matter, it is referred to the Canal Officer. If any shareholder takes water out of his turn by any unfair or illegitimate means, on detection he is liable to fine and has to pay double water charges on the land irrigated.

The large *kháls* are bridged over where necessary at the expense of the villagers sharing in the water. Irrigation may be by lift or flow. The former is only adopted when the land is too high for the water to flow on to it. The people all say they prefer to get their water by flow : they think they get more of it, and *jhallárs* require four or five yoke of oxen and four or five men to work them. Also owing to the large supply of water raised by these canal *jhallárs*, heavy and expensive oxen are required. On the other hand it can hardly be doubted that the *jhallár* which leaves the water under the control of the irrigator is much more suited to sensitive crops like cotton or red pepper or even maize. Hitherto the people have not learnt the value of economy in utilising canal irrigation. They irrigate recklessly and profusely with as much water as they can get. If the supply is short they sow more land than they can get sufficient water for and then cry out at the Canal Department when the short-irrigated canal crops fail. If they have a copious supply they deluge their land to its detriment.

The Canal Department always does its best to distribute water fairly, but often owing to the nature of the season or other unforeseen causes circumstances are too strong for them and some people must suffer.

The principal crops grown on canal-irrigated land in the Mánjha are wheat, gram, cotton, maize, rice and fodder. The first named crop occupies about half the total irrigable area : maize, cotton and rice between one-fourth and one-fifth. Maize cannot be grown to any large extent in tracts where there are many rakhs, as for instance in Chúnián tahsíl, for wherever rakhs are, there are sure to be pigs and jackals, which go miles to get at a field of either maize or sugarcane. In such a neighbourhood cotton is generally sown in preference to maize. Somewhat less than one-fifth of the canal area is sown with fodder crops. The plough cattle used on canal-irrigated land are usually strong and highly priced animals, partly because it has always been the custom of the Mánjha people to keep strong cattle, and partly because heavy animals are required to plough both deep and firmly in the water-soaked Mánjha soil. One pair of good oxen can work about 15 acres of land, of which perhaps 5 acres will be sown for the autumn harvest and 10 acres for the rabi ; they usually sow a larger rabi area than kharíf if they háve plenty of land, but if the holding is small they sow an equal area in both. Of the kharif area about 3 acres on the average are sown with maize, cotton and rice, the exact area reserved for each of these depending on the special circumstances of the tract ; one and a quarter acres with fodder crops, and the remaining three-quarters of an acre with miscellaneous crops of which sugar-cane is usually one. In the spring out of 10 acres at least 7 are sown with wheat, 1½ with fodder and the rest with gram or barley. On all irrigated land, whether from canal or well, some of the wheat grown is cut green for fodder. Rough-ly speaking the amount so utilised varies from one to two acres for every well, and somewhat less proportionately in the case of canal-irrigated wheat.

The Sutlej inundation canals flow generally from May or June to September or October, this being the period at which the river floods are at their height. The water remains long enough generally to ripen the autumn crop and to flush con-veniently situated land preparatory to rabi sowings ; but the supply is much more precarious than that of perennial canals and the crop areas irrigated from these canals in different years exhibit considerable fluctuations. Somewhat less than half the irrigable area is sown for the kharíf harvest and about one-third for the rabi ; the remaining one-sixth is made up of land here and there which for various reasons remains unsown. In the autumn rice is the principal crop sown, the unrestricted flow of water from these canals and the Hithár soil where the land lies low being well adapted to the requirements of this crop. For sensitive crops like maize, cotton and red pepper, the canal water is not sufficiently under control, con-sequently their united area is hardly half that irrigated for rice. For the spring crop the land is flushed early in Sep-tember as a rule. A mixed crop of gram and wheat is commonly sown, because after the September flushing the land will get no moisture but that of rain. If the winter rains are favour-able the wheat will yield well. If the season turn out dry something at least will be saved out of the gram. Some-times barley is mixed with one or the other of those two crops. A considerable area also is sown with gram only.

On well-irrigated lands rotation of crops and fallowing are attended to more or less. If there is a large enough area attached to the well as in the Sutlej Hithár the people like to leave one-third or one-fourth of the land vacant, so that all the land gets a rest once every three or four years. In the Rávi estates the well areas are small, consequently fallowing is seldom practised and more reliance is placed on manuring. Maize is the chief crop to be considered on well lands, first because it is the staple on which the people depend for their winter food, secondly because it requires more careful cultivation than any other. If land be plentiful the maize area is changed nearly every year, otherwise it will remain the same for many

System of culti-vation on irrigated land.

Chapter IV, A.

Agriculture, Arboriculture and Live-stock.

System of cultivation on irrigated land.

consecutive years. Whether changed or not the maize land is always manured more or less; consequently it is followed by a spring crop, usually some kind of fodder. Occasionally wheat follows maize, but if so the wheat crop is certain to be poor. Generally speaking wheat is sown in land cropped once only in the year. Rice is nearly always sown in the same land year after year because the soil selected for rice cropping is usually low and clayey, and in the Hithár the rice land is often so saline as to be fit for no other crop but rice. Cotton is generally sown in fallow land from which *jowár* or *chari* has been cut six months before: sometimes it is sown in wheat land after a slight manuring. Cotton like maize is usually followed by some inferior fodder grass which is sown in the standing crop. The extent of double-cropping on well lands depends entirely on the amount of land in the holding and on the manure available. In the Hithár for instance, double-cropping is almost limited to fodder crops following cotton or maize. In the Rávi villages where land is very limited, three or four crops are taken off the land sometimes in the year. Cultivation on canal-irrigated land in this district is at present on a broad and lavish scale. Rice is generally sown in the same land year after year: maize may be sown in land last cropped with wheat, but must be manured first. With this exception wheat land as a rule is kept free of other crops. Cotton is sown either on fallow land, or in land from which a gram crop has just been cut as the gram leaves are supposed to manure and strengthen the soil. In many parts of the Mánjha where maize and sugarcane can be grown, cotton is not sown except by cultivators who have plenty of surplus land.

The double-cropping on canal lands is   rice followed by gram which is generally sown immediately after the rice is cut, while the land is still moist from the rice irrigation: maize followed by fodder crops for which often a second manuring is done: and cotton followed by inferior fodder grasses.

Cultivation on unirrigated land.

With artificial irrigation cultivating operations can be carried on more or less briskly all the year: unirrigated land in this district can only be cultivated after a fall of rain: without that the soil is too hard to plough. Generally a few thundershowers fall in March or April and advantage is taken of these to plough land and sow cotton dry. Whenever rain falls in April, May or June, ploughing is done on unirrigated land as far as leisure can be found from the other very urgent operations of harvesting the rabi crop and sowing and irrigating the late spring crops. The great object is to have enough land ploughed at least once before the July rains burst. Then a second ploughing is done and *jowar*, *chari* or *moth* is sown according to the nature of the soil. When all the land required for autumn crops has been sown or when the sowing time is past, any other rainfall that occurs in July or August is utilised to complete rabi ploughings, and industrious cultivators roll the land after ploughing it and press it down so as to retain as much moisture as possible for the rabi sowings : these are usually done in September. Gram and rapeseed are sown first, wheat and barley a little later; for wheat all the lower lands in which most moisture has remained are generally reserved. The term *dofasla-dosála* so well known in other districts more fortunate in their rainfall is not in common use here ; but in practice the two years' system is followed as far as possible. That is starting from the month of June with which the agricultural year commences the cultivator sows such sufficient area as he can make ready for the kharíf, reserving of course some of the land in his holding for rabi sowings. The former is reaped in November and then the land is probably left fallow until the following summer when if the rains are favourable it is prepared for a rabi crop. Land sown dry for the rabi in September is harvested in April and, if possible, is sown again for the following kharíf harvest. In this way assuming the rainfall to be propitious, from June in one year to June two years after one kharif crop and one rabi crop are sown. During the time between the harvesting of the one and the sowing of the other the land lies fallow the first seven months, and is in course of preparation for the rabi for four months. The period ends with the rabi crop, which again, if the rotation can be strictly preserved, should be followed immediately by a kharíf crop. The chief points of importance, however, to be noticed in respect to the unirrigated cultivation of this district are the immense fluctuations each year in the cropping and the enormous area which is sown and fails from drought. Generally speaking if the summer rains are favourable for autumn sowings they close early and a very large proportion of the sown crops fail. Again if the autumn rains are favourable for spring sowings then the winter rains often fail.

The crops grown by river inundation are on the Sutlej principally wheat in the spring and *másh* in the autumn : they each occupy about a third of the *sailáb* area : the wheat is not very first class at present, as of late years the Sutlej has been working generally towards the Lahore bank : and consequently the good alluvial soil has been forming on the opposite side : This, however, is a state of things that may change any year. The *másh* cultivation is of the roughest kind : the ground sown with this crop barely gives the appearance of having been ploughed even once : but the produce is good in a favourable year : sometimes much loss is caused to the villagers by the submersion of the *másh* crops just when they are getting ripe. Gram and *massar* are grown on a considerable area : other crops are comparatively very unimportant and give an indifferent yield. In the Rávi Bet land, half the *sailáb* area is given up to wheat. The better class of Rávi wheat is famous for its excellent yield and quality, this being grown in low alluvial depressions where the thick deposit soil receives regular inundation. New land however is often sown with wheat, this being looked on as the test crop to show the quality of the soil : it gives a

Chapter IV, A.
—
Agriculture, Ar-boriculture and Live-stock.

River inundated land.

very poor outturn for the first year or two. A fair amount of maize is grown on the Rávi flood lands, but the yield is only middling. Other crops occupying any area of importance are barley, gram, *másh* and fodder crops. *Sailáb* land is not manured ever ; but it requires frequent ploughing to keep down the weeds. For wheat the land should be ploughed eight times, three times before the floods come and five times afterwards in September. For other crops three or four ploughings are required. Sowings in *sailáb* land are done after the summer floods have subsided. Rice (*dhán chatta*) however is sown in new land during April or May before the floods have risen.

Sowing.

The grain used for seeding generally comes from the previous year's crop, or if that is exhausted then it is taken on loan from the money-lenders. Generally speaking on well-irrigated lands the stock of the seed is seldom changed; but under the influence of canal irrigation old seed is said to change colour and a fresh stock must be brought in from time to time. Those cultivators who are well off and have the leisure, sometimes pick out from the standing crop the ears of corn which appear in best condition, and these are kept for seed. Sowing in this district is generally done broadcast (*chattah*) except when the land is dry when gram and wheat are sown by drill (*puri*). Indeed gram is nearly always sown by drill. When the seed is very small it is sometimes mixed with earth before being sown, as otherwise it would be difficult to distribute it equally; cotton seeds are smeared together to pre-vent them from sticking together. Some crops are grown from seedlings (*paneri*) raised in nurseries, such as tobacco, chillies, onions, and rice generally.

Ploughing.

The general name for plough in this district is , *hal,* but the people recognise the distinction between the *hal* plough and the *munna* plough here as in other districts. The latter is the heavier kind of the two and is used chiefly in the Mánjha tract, the *hal* being reserved for the lowlands. They are both made almost entirely of wood, the ploughshare being the only solid iron ; but the joints of wood are strengthened with iron fastenings. Altogether the *hal* has about three sérs of iron in it and the *munna* somewhat more. The *munna* makes a deeper and broader furrow than the *hal* and requires heavier oxen. This perhaps is the chief reason why it is con-fined chiefly to the Mánjha, where alone in this district heavy oxen are to be found. The *hal* goes into the soil about 3 inches the first time of ploughing, 5 inches the second, and 7 or 8 inches the third. A *munna* plough may go deeper. The people recognise the value of deep ploughing, but say they cannot afford the cattle. A plough can do two-and-a-half kanáls a day, on the first ploughing and three kanáls on the second. When the land has been ploughed once, the second time it is ploughed cross ways.

The field may be ploughed in sections up and down, or in narrowing circles, beginning round the edge of the field.

If the cultivators can manage it and are in a hurry to finish, three or four ploughs work at a time, each following the other, but in a different furrow. They recognise the value of frequent ploughing and of having all the soil exposed to the air turn and turn about, but they do not often find leisure either to plough the land as often as they should or to begin ploughing early enough in the season to give the soil a fair chance. No ploughing is done unless the ground has been first moistened by rain or by artificial irrigation. The former does not always come, and the cultivators cannot find leisure for the latter. At the end just before sowings they are rushed for time and scamp the ploughing to the future detriment of the crop.

Ploughing.

After ploughing the land is usually smoothed down with a heavy squared beam called *schága*, dragged by one or two pairs of bullocks, the drivers of which stand on the beam. This is partly to break clods and pulverise the soil and partly to con-solidate the surface with a view to the retention of the moisture in the soil. Generally in irrigated land for all crops but gram, each ploughing is followed by a rolling with the *sohága*. Un-irrigated land should always be rolled as soon as it is ploughed, otherwise the moisture (*watar*), on the strength of which the ploughing was done, will be lost to the soil; and the seed when sown will not germinate. Neglect to carry out this precaution results in much of the field sown lying completely bare for the rest of the season. As a matter of practice rolling is, as a rule, done once or twice in land under preparation for rabi sowings except river flooded land which is seldom rolled for any crop but wheat. But unirrigated land intended for autumn sowings other than cotton is seldom rolled for want of leisure: the ploughing even on such land is very restricted. The summer rains on which such dry cultivation depends last a short time only, and the chief object is to get in the seed as early as possible after the rainy season has begun. For dry cotton sowings the land is often ploughed first as early as February or even January, and consequently a rolling to follow is indispensable if the soil is to be kept moist. After the sowings are done, the land may be ploughed and rolled once more to cover over and press down the seed.

Rolling.

The last operation of all while the seed is still under the ground is to divide the land into compartments for greater convenience of irrigation. This, however, is confined in most part to well lands which are always partitioned off into small *kiyárís*, by, means of ridges of earth raised by two men working at the instrument known as the *jandra*, which is a large wooden rake: one man holds the handle and the other pulls a string attached to the handle at its lower end where it joins the rake. These *kiyárís* on well lands are never more than one-eighth or one-tenth of an acre, and often are much less.

Forming *kiyárís*.

This duty, known as *godi-choki*, is carried out more or less carefully on well lands for the autumn crops, especially when the cultivators are Aráíns, Kambohs or Labánás. Wheat is never

Weeding.

weeded notwithstanding the rapid growth of the onion weed known as *bhugát* or *piyázi.* The weeding instrument in use is the *ramla* or trowel : near Lahore under special conditions weeding is sometimes done by running a light plough between the rows of sugarcane or maize or cotton. The crops which are most weeded in this district are chillies and maize. Wheat is never weeded. It is exceptional for weeding to be done on any soil but that under well irrigation. It is of course equally necessary and sometimes more so on canal-irrigated land, but the cultivators do not seem able to find the time or energy. River flooded land requires more weeding than any other, to get rid of the thistles that spring up after ploughings and choke the rising crop : there however weeding is seldom or never done.

It is curious to find that not even yet has the absolute necessity of re-invigorating their irrigated land every now and then with manure come home to the Mánjha cultivators. Of late they have been taking to it more, but even now large heaps of unused manure are seen lying outside the village settlements ; no custom exists in the Mánjha of selling manure, though all the villages which have no irrigation could make a considerable profit thereby ; and the Mánjha people actually give away the valuable substance described on page 14 under the name of *kallar,* asking no price for it. All this, however, will soon change. In well-irrigated tracts the addition of fertilisers to land, to improve its productive powers, is well understood and is practised by the people as far as their means permit. The principal manure is that of the farm yard, but as the droppings of cattle are largely needed for fuel, the fields do not get all these : also in well-irrigated tracts the cattle are very poorly fed for most of the year, so that the supply at the best would be small compared with the amount of live-stock. The manure available for cultivation is collected in heaps outside the village settlement. Each shareholder knows his own heap. Every morning the cattle droppings, not appropriated to make fuel cakes, are carried out with the other house sweepings and refuse litter, and thrown on to the house heap. The refuse of non-proprietors' houses is either collected in a common heap which is divided among the shareholders at intervals, or if the non-proprietors have been divided off among different proprietors, they put their refuse on the heaps of their respective patrons. Little care, however, is exercised in collecting manure and much more might be accumulated if the people would pay a little more attention to the cleanliness of their homes, of the village street-ways, and the vicinity of their homesteads. Leaves are not swept up and rags of all sorts disfigure the ground. Bones which were formerly looked on as useless are allowed to be taken off by sweepers for the mere trouble of collecting them: the sweepers make a fair profit by selling them for export to bone-dealers at Lahore. Large cart loads of these may often be seen making their way to the city.

From the manure heaps round the village, manure is carted to the land as it is required. Also there are contributions usually collected at the wells where the working cattle stand for a good part of the year. The crop which is always heavily manured is maize, and on the manure laid down for it a second crop, usually fodder but sometimes wheat, follows the maize. Cane, chillies, tobacco and all sorts of vegetables other than melons only do well in manured land. Rice sometimes requires manure if the soil is hard and stiff. Wheat is never manured in this district and cotton seldom. The early *haru chari* should have some manure : other *jowár* wants none. The fields close to the homestead are fertilised naturally by the visits of the population, and if the land so benefitted is under cultivation, it is known as *niain* or *gora* land. Sometimes, however, the breezy expanse of the village common is preferred for operations of nature, and that is nearly always waste land. The manure described above is thrown down on the land in amounts varying from forty to one hundred maunds an acre as far as one can judge from the different accounts given, and it is then ploughed into the soil. Another method of manuring is by throwing topdressing over the crops when they are about a foot high. The dressing consists either of pulverised manure or of the *kállar* described on page 14. Tobacco and sugarcane, and if the cultivation is very good such as is found in Aráin villages near Lahore, cotton and wheat are treated in this way. It is not easy to say what proportion of the land in this district is manured. In 1868 it was reckoned that 8 per cent. was so treated ; but that calculation must have been based largely upon the individual opinions of the subordinate officials engaged in surveying the land and cannot have been very reliable. It may be assumed without fear of much error that all the irrigated maize area, all land cropped with tobacco, sugarcane, chillies, poppies, which are grown only under irrigation, one-half the irrigated vegetable area, and one-quarter of the irrigated rice and autumn fodder crops should be classed as manured ; this assumption points to about 6 per cent. of the total area under cultivation as being under manure, but it is quite possible that this calculation is short of the mark : certainly it is not over it.

Manure is carried from the village to the fields or from one village to another in carts (*gadhi*). They are also used for transport of fodder, wood, or *kunkur* on hire. Grain however is usually carried on donkeys or camels, the former carrying from $1\frac{1}{2}$ to 2 maunds and the latter from 6 to 8 maunds. The village cart consists of a triangular framework on wheels, the framework being about twelve feet long and four feet broad behind, but tapering to a point in front. This is the important part of the cart, and there lie any points of superiority one cart may have over another. The platform is known as the *gadh* and is made of the strongest wood, shisham ; its strength varies with the quantity and quality of ironworking about it. The

carts used in the Mánjha are much stronger than those made for
the Hithár; the difference probably dating back from old days
before the extension of the Bári Doáb Canal and railway when
many of the Mánjha villages kept large numbers of carts for
hire and subsisted chiefly on the earnings. Even as lately as
1880 during the Kábul War not a few of the Mánjha villagers
amassed considerable sums by letting out their carts for Government transport. Now improvement of agriculture and extension of railways have largely superseded cart hire as a means
of livelihood, but still there are villages near Lahore from which
carts are constantly let out on hire to kunkur contractors.
Apart from this, however, the Mánjha carts have to carry fodder
and manure greater distances than the Hithár carts and should
be stronger for this reason alone. A Mánjha cart of ordinary
make costs Rs. 60 and a Hithár cart costs Rs. 40. The wheels
of the one cost Rs. 20 and of the other Rs. 14 or 15. A cart
intended for two pairs of oxen is of course larger than one
intended for one pair, and requires to be made much stronger.
If a *dobaldi* costs Rs. 60, a *chaubaldi* of the same make would
cost Rs. 80. One pair of bullocks is the usual number, but for
a load over 20 maunds over an unmetalled road, two pairs
would be necessary. The framework of the cart is fitted at its
edge all round with a number of uprights, which are laced
together with ropes: sometimes these are fitted with cross bars
over which a blanket, coarse sacking, or a movable thatch
made of light *sirki* can be stretched if necessary. Covered carts,
however, of this kind are not easy to procure from the villages
when required in wet weather. The animals accustomed to
draw these carts are inferior, the best bullocks in the Mánjha
being kept at work in the fields.

Fencing.

Some sort of fencing is generally put up to protect fields
which adjoin a frequented road or open space near the village.
Similarly the chief paths near the well, leading to and from the
well are fenced on either side. The fences are made of boughs of
trees, bushes or anything that comes handy. Important crops like
sugarcane are surrounded with hemp plants planted in a single
row for the protection of the cane. Reed screens are erected
to shelter crops from wind and sand.

Watching.

Maize and *jowár* always require to be watched during
the day while the grain is ripening, otherwise crowds of birds
would collect and spoil the crop. The watchman sits on a
high platform called the *manna* which is raised on four
stakes some ten or twelve feet from the ground: he is armed
with a *ghubáni* with which he slings mud pellets, made by
himself, at the birds. Near rakhs a watch over many crops,
particularly sugarcane and maize, has to be maintained at
night against pig and jackal. The watchman here walks about
all night armed with a spear, and cracking a long whip or making
discordant yells. Sometimes owners of adjoining lands club
together to pay one or more common watchman, and it is not
unusual for them to agree together as to what lands shall be

CHAP. IV.—PRODUCTION AND DISTRIBUTION.

sown with what crops, so as to facilitate arrangements for sharing the expense of such watchmen as may be found necessary, but as a rule for maize or sugarcane, to which very close attention must be given, each house provides its own watchman. Scare-crows are sometimes used to frighten away birds and are put up in various shapes.

Except cotton, pepper and poppy which are picked by hand, all other crops are reaped with the *dátri* or sickle. It is no easy work as the stooping or squatting position combined with an advancing motion becomes very laborious after a little time and both hands are employed, one holding the sickle and the other the stuff to be cut. The work therefore is only fit for able-bodied men : women and children, however, can help in tying up the sheaves in villages where custom permits women to work in the field. Ordinarily the autumn harvesting is done by the cultivators themselves assisted by village menials. The rabi crop, however, in tracts extensively irrigated from well or canal is more than the villagers can manage by themselves if the harvest is to be finished within a reasonable time. Much of the wheat reaping therefore is made over to hired reapers or *láwas,* who are paid in kind, being allowed to carry off a shock of wheat each evening. The *láwa* can cut on the average about two kanáls in a day and the shock weighs about one maund zielding 10 or 12 sérs of grain when threshed, so that this charge comes to about one maund of grain for each acre cut.

When the reaping is done the stuff is collected near the threshing floor, which is a circular piece of ground pressed down hard and firm, and carefully cleaned : the site of the threshing floor is selected to suit the holding : generally each well has its separate floor and the cultivating shareholders thresh in turn : a stake is driven into the ground in the centre of the floor ; the crop to be threshed is placed around the stake, to which one or more yoke of cattle are fastened by a rope : sometimes three or four bullocks or buffaloes are driven in a row. To them is yoked a rectangular handle made of pieces of wood tied together which is covered with straw and weighted with clods of earth or other heavy substance that comes in handy. The cattle are muzzled as a rule : each row requires a driver, and another man is needed to put back the straw which gets out of the track of the cattle. The handle is called a *phala.* It is always used for threshing wheat or wheat and gram mixed. Other crops are often threshed without the *phala,* the trampling of the oxen being sufficient to separate the grain from the sheath. Maize and *jowár* heads are usually beaten out with sticks, the maize cobs having been first picked out of the sheath by hand. Rice is generally beaten against the edge of a circular hole in the ground. *Moth* and some few other grains are beaten out with a pitchfork.

When the grain has been separated and the straw thoroughly broken, the stuff is tossed up into the air with a pitchfork and then further cleaning is done by shaking the grain and chaff still left mixed in a winnowing basket (*chaji*) held

Chapter IV, A.

Agriculture, Arboriculture and Live-stock.

Watching.

Reaping.

Threshing.

Winnowing.

up aloft in a man's hands above his head to catch the breeze. In the month of May when the spring crops are being harvested there is generally a hot wind blowing at some part of the day which helps the process, and the hotter and fiercer the wind the sooner the harvesting is over.

The following statement shows for each month the different stages of field work connected with the various principal crops, and the kinds of weather which are desirable or the reverse. Each native month occupies approximately the latter half of the English month first mentioned and the first half of the second.

Cheyt (March—April).—Sugarcane, cotton, tobacco, melons and onions are sown. Rapeseed and some of the grain are reaped. Ploughings should be done for kharíf sowings. The less rain this month the better, provided there has been moderate rain in the earlier spring months. Atmospheric disturbances are frequent and the people live in dread of hail storms which if they come destroy any crops they pass over.

Bisákh (April—May).—Melons, cotton and vegetable sowings continue. Early autumn fodder crops are also sown. All crops recently sown are watered. Rabi reapings generally completed except wheat in canal-irrigated tracts. Autumn ploughings still in progress. Sudden showers occasionally come, but it is best to have no rain, otherwise the crops lying out in the field may suffer.

Jeth (May—June).—Rabi harvesting completed. Autumn ploughings and sowings continue on irrigated land. Cane, cotton, tobacco and vegetables are weeded and watered. Tobacco, vegetables and melons begin to be gathered. Moderate rain is necessary for the unirrigated cotton and is beneficial to other crops that have been sown, but if too early in the month is apt to injure the cut crops. Sutlej Inundation Canals should begin to flow and Bári Doáb Canal should be in good working order. A strong hot sun and wind are desirable.

Hár (June—July).—Ploughings for kharíf in progress on irrigated soils and on unirrigated land if any rain falls. Rice planted out. The late spring crops are gathered. Maize sowings commence. Waterings in progress on cane, cotton and early fodder crops. These last may now be cut as required. Fine weather is desirable in the beginning of the month, but the summer rains should break before the end, otherwise the heat becomes intolerable and kharíf ploughings and sowings on unirrigated land are in danger of being postponed too late : also grass is very necessary by this time to supplement the existing fodder stores. Canals should all be in good working order and the Deg stream should begin to fill.

Sáwan (July—August).—Maize sowings completed. Late fodder crops sown on irrigated land. Weeding and watering done in sugarcane, chillies, cotton and maize. Other operations on unirrigated land depend on the rainfall. Kharíf *bárání*

sowings should be completed by the end of the month and
rabi ploughings should be in progress. Rain is required at
intervals. Much strong sunshine is injurious. Wind should be
moderate and from the east. Canals and Deg stream should
all be running.

Chapter IV, A.
—
Agriculture, Ar-
boriculture and
Live-stock.
Agricultural ca-
lendar.

Bhádron (August—September).—Waterings done on all
irrigated autumn crops. Ploughings in progress as far as possible for all rabi crops. Some weeding should be done on maize,
chillies, sugarcane and vegetables. Gram and rape sowings
commence. Rainfall occasionally is necessary, otherwise the
unirrigated crops begin to dry up; the well cattle fail under
the pressure put on them to irrigate the whole area sown. Also
in the absence of rain the heat becomes excessive; the season
becomes unhealthy; and the cultivators begin to go down
with fever.

Assu (September—October).—Other unirrigated rabi crops
are sown and all early rabi fodders at wells. Ploughings continue for irrigated rabi sowings. Kharíf unirrigated crops
are partly harvested. Sutlej Inundation Canals begin to slacken
off. Cattle disease is usually prevalent and fever is general.
Slight rain is beneficial early in the month but injurious later.

Katak (October—November).—Kharíf harvesting continues.
All maize and most of the rice are cut and threshed. Cotton
picking commences. Irrigated wheat ploughings and sowings are carried on busily; and rabi fodder crops are sown.
Sunshine and moderate wind are required. Rain is injurious
as it beats down the young rabi crops as they emerge from the
ground. Sutlej Inundation Canals cease to flow: and probably the Deg stream. The Bári Doáb Canal is usually working
well. The season becomes healthy and sickness generally ceases.

Maghar (November—December).—Wheat sowings continue
in canal-irrigated land. Rice reaping and threshing is completed. Cotton and chillies picking goes on. Watering is done
for rabi fodder crops. The weather should be the same as in the
previous month. Fodder supplies begin to run short.

Poh (December—January).—Wheat sowings on canal-
irrigated land must be completed in the first half of the month.
Barley sowing may continue a little later. Sugarcane is cut
and ploughings for the next cane crop are begun. Well-irri-
gation goes on busily for all crops. Wheat straw and other
dry fodder has probably run out, but the early rabi fodder crops
are probably ready for cutting as required. People begin to
look anxiously for the winter rains to bring on the young wheat
and fodder crops and save the well cattle. Rain should certainly fall before the end of the month. Bári Doáb Canal is usually
closed for repairs towards the close of the month.

Mágh (January—February).—Sugarcane is cut and early
fodder crops. Well irrigation is carried on day and night.
Ploughings begin for early rabi crops. Dry fodder is difficult
to procure. Occasional rain is desirable, followed by bright

Chapter IV, A.

Agriculture, Arboriculture and Live-stock.

Agricultural calendar.

sunshine to avert rust. Moderate wind generally blows and the cattle suffer greatly from cold. Unless there has been rain the night frosts injure the crops, especially gram. Bári Doáb Canal may continue closed without much harm, but should certainly be opened at the end of the month or before if possible.

Phágan (February—March).—Ploughings done for cane, cotton and tobacco. Some cane, tobacco and vegetables are sown. Irrigation absolutely necessary for all canal and well crops. Moderate rain desirable so that the grain may swell. Bright sunshine also is necessary. Late frosts and strong wind in day time very hurtful.

Cropping.

Name of crop.	Percentage of area under crops in acres.
Rice ...	3·4
Wheat ...	39·8
Jowar ...	11·0
Bajra ...	·3
Maize ...	4·9
Barley ...	3·7
Gram ...	15·4
Moth ...	2·2
Poppy ...	·1
Tobacco ...	·3
Cotton ...	4·9
Sugarcane ...	·5
Vegetables ...	·9

The areas under each of the principal crops grown in this district during the last six years and the tahsíl averages of the last five years 1888 to 1893 are stated in Table No. XX. An abstract of these in percentage fractions is shown in the margin. Below an account is given of the method of cultivation followed in the case of all the more important staples.

Rice.

Rice is grown chiefly by aid of canal irrigation in the Mánjha and Hithár tracts and very little by well irrigation. In Sharakpur tahsíl rice is a speciality, being excellently adapted to the clay and *kallar*-ridden soils there found; it is grown by well irrigation assisted by flood inundations from the Deg. The outturn per acre in the Mánjha averages about sixteen maunds, somewhat more in the Hithár, and about fifteen maunds in Sharakpur tahsíl taking good and bad together. The methods of cultivation vary in different parts of the district, but generally the land to be sown is ploughed three or four times and rolled after each ploughing; the last two ploughings the land should have water standing on it a foot deep. The cattle of course should be both heavy and powerful; they are not always so except in the Mánjha. The land must always be manured if it is inclined to be hard or poor in soil, as in Sharakpur tahsíl or the Chúnián Hithár. In the Mánjha, where the soil is soft and good, manure is not always used. When the ground is ready the rice plants are put in or the seed is sown broadcast after being soaked in water. The former method is the safest and produces better results but cannot always be followed for want of time. The young rice plants are grown at the irrigation wells in small plots which are sown in the month of May in land that has been first carefully cleaned, ploughed and manured. The young plants are ready for transplanting about a month after sowing, being then about one foot high. The planting out is generally done by hired labourers. In the Cis-Rávi portion of the district *Changars* and *Púrbias* are employed; in Sharakpur menials from the villages. They are usually paid in kind; but sometimes in cash at 4 or 5 annas a day. The kind payments are made in wheat, this being the only crop available at the time. After being planted or sown the rice must be irrigated sufficiently to keep the soil in a constant state of saturation, and weeding must be done now and then. Rice is the most sensitive crop to drought and is brought to maturity with diffi-culty both in Sharakpur, where the Deg inundations cease at the latest by October in most years, and in the Hithár, where the inundation canals may cease running as early as September. In those two tracts no rice is really safe unless it is covered by an irrigation well. The area of matured rice is very apt to be over-estimated, because the Patwári makes his record in October and the rice crop is not harvested much before Novem-ber : in the intervening days much of the area recorded as matured may have dried up unless a full supply of water was available. When ripe also the grain is very loose, and in estimating the yield allowance must be made for the grain dropped during harvesting. After being cut the rice is usually threshed out by hand, the labourer bringing the sheaf down on the edge of a small clay trough. For this hired menials receive 4 or 5 annas a day or sometimes payment in kind, amounting to about one-sixteenth of the crop sown. It is husked by being pounded either by hand or by lever in a large hole in the ground paved with stone. The rice husks are burnt or thrown away as refuse. The straw of rice is used principally as litter for horses and cattle : but in the Trans-Rávi part of the district it is given to the cattle as fodder ; it is however not good feeding, being very soft and devoid of strengthening properties. The names for rice in this district are *munji* and *jhona*, the latter being more common Cis-Indus. The two best known varieties are the "white" (*sufeida*) and the "*mushkin*" or scented. The former is the most generally consumed. The latter weighs heavier and fetches a higher price in the market but requires more labour and manure in its cultivation. There are also coarser kinds, namely *dháin* and *kharsu*, the former of which is grown in the beds of drainage channels and the latter in the moist alluvial lands along the river.

Of maize there are two recognised kinds : one a small kind known as *Lahori*, which has white cobs and the grain is white : the plants of this stand about five feet high ; the other *desi*, a much larger plant with yellow coloured cobs and grain. This requires more ploughing and irrigation to mature and its outturn is much heavier. Either kind is grown according to the cultivator's capacities or inclinations. Maize is grown to a slight extent in river flooded lands ; otherwise it is never grown in this district without irrigation, and it does better on well than canal irrigation, the crop being very sensitive to over watering.

160 CHAP. IV.—PRODUCTION AND DISTRIBUTION.

Maize is sown early in August. A month or more before sowing
time, or earlier, if possible, ploughings commence, the land being
first irrigated unless there has been a timely fall of rain.
Manuring is done either before ploughing or immediately after ;
the amount of manure varies greatly. In highly farmed land
not less than one hundred maunds the acre are put down ; and
all the people if asked profess to use as much, but as a matter
of fact they cannot spare this amount in rural tracts. Forty or
fifty maunds would be nearer the mark. The land is ploughed
in all five or six times before sowing and oftener if possible :
after every other ploughing at the least the ground should be
carefully rolled (*sohága*). Then the seed is sown broadcast
or more rarely by dribbling from the hand, about eighteen
sérs to the acre. After sowings they plough and level the
land once or twice again. When the crop is about half a foot
out of the ground, they weed it and then give it the first
watering. After that the crop should be irrigated every
seventh or eighth day unless good rain falls. A second weeding
is done when the crop is a foot and a half high. The cultivators
either weed their own fields or employ hired labour at three
annas a day. While the crop is ripening all the plants that
do not promise well are plucked out and given to the cattle.
Maize has a good many enemies to contend with before it comes
to maturity. When the stalk is a foot or a foot and a half
high the top is often attacked by a sort of blight (*khiri*), which
either produces complete failure of the crop or reduces the
yield greatly. In the autumn of 1892 the maize crop all over
the district was rendered almost worthless from this blight.
Also while the crop is still quite young its roots are sometimes
eaten by white ants in which case all the plants affected are
certain to dry up ; no remedy has been found for this. A little
before the grain ripens a caterpillar (*sundhi*) sometimes forms
in it and totally destroys the plant. This pest does not necessarily attack all the crop but parts only here and there. The
worst enemies, however, of maize in this district, next perhaps
to blight (*khiri*), are pig and jackal, which abound in the
Government rakhs. The former will travel several miles at
night after a maize crop. They tear up the roots and eat off
the heads. Jackals and village dogs as well eat the grain
without injuring the stalks or roots. In the day time the crop
is very subject to depredations by birds of various kinds. For
the first ten or twelve days after sowing a strict watch has to
be maintained in the day time to keep the birds from grubbing
up the seed, and when the crop is ripening it is patrolled
by night and day. Sometimes the zamíndárs perform this duty
themselves, sometimes they retain paid watchmen at various
wages varying from 2 to 5 rupees a month. When the grain is
ripe it is reaped with the cobs still on and left to dry on the
ground for three or four days, after which it is piled together in
a stack in the field : it stands like this for a week or so, after
which the cobs are picked off by hand : This is called *chillái*
and is generally done by women sitting down who get two

sérs in the maund for their trouble. The maize stalks are left in a heap to be tied up later if worth while and the cobs are spread out to dry ; in the field if there is much of a crop: otherwise on the roofs of their houses. Threshing of maize is done with sticks either by members of the family or by labourers who get as pay two sérs per maund of grain cleaned. The average outturn of maize cobs when first plucked may be taken to be eighteen maunds in weight per acre. From this eleven or twelve maunds of dry grain should be obtained. Maize is the food of the people in the winter months. It is therefore seldom sold.

Cotton is grown under dry and irrigated cultivation. The extent sown on irrigated land depends largely on the space available after other possible crops have been provided for, such as maize, chari, rice and cane. Dry cotton sowings are done in March after as many ploughings and rollings as there has been leisure for, generally, however, not more than six or less than three. On irrigated land cotton sowings are done any time between the middle of April and the middle of May, the ground being cultivated more carefully for these than for dry sowings : manure is not usually put down for this crop. About ten sérs of seed are required for each acre. The seed is carefully smeared with cowdung to prevent it sticking together. All cotton must be weeded at least once and should be weeded twice. Sometimes in the place of weeding the land is worked over with a plough when the plant is two feet or so high ; sometimes melons are sown in the rising cotton crop, in which case a third weeding is required for the sake of the melons. Unless the rainfall is favourable the crop should be irrigated five or six times, on each occasion very cautiously as too much water injures it. Cotton picking begins as early as September and goes on at intervals till December, the most productive pickings being in November. The pickers are invariably women from the village, some from the cultivator's family, others of the menial class : these last get as pay a small share of the cotton they have picked each day. There are usually as many as twelve or fifteen pickings and the final picking of all is left for the village menials and their women. The outturn of cotton is exceedingly difficult to estimate : every one gives a different account. Reliable experiments can hardly be made on a crop which is picked at various intervals over a period of three months. A fair average yield per acre is probably about six maunds, but some allowance out of this must be made for the wages in kind taken by the hired pickers and for the last picking or two which is left by custom to the menials of the village. The irrigated cotton area in this district is fairly constant and averages 33,500 acres. Unirrigated cotton in this district is very uncertain and yields indifferently. The early spring rains are favourable for dry cotton sowing more often than not, but the late autumn rains never hardly last long enough to bring the crop to full maturity. The average dry yield per acre certainly cannot exceed two mounds especially as in a favourable year much of the dry cotton is grown on the previous year's roots. Of the unirrigated cotton about three parts are seed and one part fibre. A considerable quantity of the cotton grown on well lands is retained for domestic use ; only a small surplus is sold ; but a large business is done in canal-irrigated cotton, which is disposed of at 10 sérs the rupee in its unginned state to large contractors, who have it cleaned at local steam gins of which there are three or four in the district, and then send it to Karáchi or Bombay, some for consumption in India, but chiefly for export to England. The cotton seed used is generally taken from the previous year's crop. Cotton sticks are used chiefly as fire wood. The only enemy of cotton beside drought and over-watering is an insect known as the *tela* which gets into the pod and causes it to wither without coming to maturity.

Sugarcane.

The average area under sugarcane in the whole district is 5,100 acres : but it is chiefly of the *kátha* kind, which is a thin red hardy cane used partly for extraction of *gur* and partly for cattle fodder. *Kátha* is now sold at prices varying from Rs. 40 to Rs. 70 the acre. *Pona* cane is the kind eaten in its natural state. The cultivation of this is generally confined to localities where manure is easily procurable. This kind is very valuable, fetching from Rs. 200 to Rs. 300 an acre, but the cost of cultivation is enormous. At present it is grown in 94 villages of the district, most of which lie in the Mánjha and get canal irrigation from the Bári Doáb Canal. Another rare kind is the *kao*, which has a very thick cane and a broad leaf ; this requires even more water than *pona*, but not as careful cultivation in other respects. This kind is grown only in 25 estates. *Kátha* is grown in 545 villages of which 130 are in Sharakpur tahsíl. Here, however, at least half the *kátha* grown is used for cattle fodder. There are 256 sugar mills of which 136 are in the Lahore tahsíl, mostly of the iron Behea pattern.

The method of cultivation for sugarcane is as follows. In February or March after repeated ploughings and heavy manuring of the land prepared for them the seed canes forming about one-twentieth part of last year's crop are unearthed from the pit in which they have lain buried for three or four months, cut into lengths of about nine inches, and placed lengthways in the highly pulverised soil into which they are pressed down with the foot. From that time the crop requires constant irrigation and weeding : it is usually carefully fenced sometimes by a line of hemp planted for this purpose, sometimes by made hedges. Also the cane must be carefully watched and saved from depredations by pig, jackals and village dogs.

Cutting is carried on during December, but the *kátha* cane which is required for fodder is left standing to be cut as it may be required. The process of extracting the *gur* is well known and need not be described here. The *pona* and *kao* cane are usually sold to dealers, often before they are cut. They fetch very large prices no doubt, but the cane occupies the ground for at least a year, and the labour and cost of cultivating it are immense.

Jowár is grown on irrigated and unirrigated soils; on the former it is more generally intended for cattle fodder (*chari*) though not always : in the Hithár one or two acres of *jowár* to each well are sown exclusively for the grain, though the stalks of course come in useful for the cattle. At the sowings 3 or 4 sérs a kanál will be thrown down if the crop is meant to be used as fodder and one and a half or two sérs if it is to be ripened as a grain crop. But if in the latter case the crop turn out badly then the best heads are picked out, and the rest left standing for the cattle. The fodder *jowár* crops are cut green as required, and if any of it is still standing when the grain is ripe the cattle are turned in to feed on it. A fair amount of irrigated *chari jowár* is sown in May under the name of *háru ;* for this the land is manured as heavily as for maize, and water is given every fourth or fifth day. This is ready for use in June and July ; also *babul moth,* which is sown at the same time as the *háru,* sometimes with it, sometimes separate : more *babul moth* than *háru* is grown in the Mánjha and *vice versâ* in the Hithár. In July again both *chari* and grain *jowár* are sown. The *chari* then sown is ready for use in September and October; and the grain ripens in the latter month. Manure is not used for this second crop, nor does it require so much irrigation as the *háru ;* it is often sown on the higher lands under irrigation. As an unirrigated crop *jowár* is generally sown as a food grain, but may come in useful for either purpose : any crop that is not a success is left to serve as fodder. After a favourable autumn harvest, large areas of *jowár* may be seen standing, the cultivators having been too busy over other matters to cut it down. *Jowár* is sown dry either by itself or mixed with *moth,* more often the former in this district. Sowings usually take place in July and reapings in October. When the crop is ripe it is cut down and stacked ; after a time the heads are cut off and beaten or trodden to separate the grain. The stalks are left in the field for a time to dry and then piled on the roofs of houses and other dry places to be used as fodder during the early winter months. *Jowár* stalks are known as *tánda ;* they are looked on as excellent fodder. If fodder is plentiful, the stalks are thrown down whole and the cattle eat half, leaving the harder ends. If fodder is scarce, the stalks are chopped up small and given to the cattle mixed with other kinds of fodder. This makes the *jowár* stalks go further than when they are given whole. The *jowár* heads are attacked sometimes by " smut," known as *kungiari,* especially if the summer rainfall has been excessive : other diseases detrimental to this crop are *tela* and *khiri* which exhaust all the juice of the plant and dry it up. Birds devastate the *jowár* crops which are usually

Chapter IV, A.
—
Agriculture, Arboriculture and Live-stock.

Jowár.

Chapter IV, A.

**Agriculture, Ar-
boriculture and
Live-stock.**

Jowár.

watched by a birdscarer from a platform known as the *manna*
erected in a central position among the *jowár* crops.

Jowár grain is eaten in the form of bread to the same
extent as maize, generally at the morning meal with the *ság* of
the rapeseed as a condiment. It is of course a much more
reliable food resource than either wheat or maize, being so much
more plentiful. In the winter of 1891-92 when wheat was
exceedingly dear and the maize grain had been exhausted
jowár was the main staple food of all the poorer classes in the
district.

Kharíf pulses.

Moth and *másh* are the principal pulses grown in the kharíf
harvest. *Mung* is not much cultivated in this district. The
only form of irrigated *moth* in this district is that termed
babul moth, sown in May along with the early *háru chari*.
Unirrigated *moth* is raised chiefly in light sandy soils and only
requires very moderate rain ; consequently the *moth* cropping
may be fairly successful though the *jowár* crop fail through
want of sufficient moisture. The grain enters largely into the
food of the people, being usually eaten with the evening meal
in the form of *dál*. The straw is known as *missa bhusa*, and is
much valued for cattle fodder. The times of sowing and reaping *moth* are the same as for unirrigated *jowár ;* and the same
degree of cultivation is required, namely two or three ploughings at the most.

Másh is far the more valuable of the two pulses, being
much prized for the excellent *dál* it makes ; it comes in very
palatable at the summer evening meal. It requires a fairly
stiff soil with a good deal of moisture ; it is grown largely in
the alluvial lands of the Sutlej, where its cultivation is exceedingly rough and sketchy. So careless and perfunctory is the
ploughing that when once the crop is removed it would be hard
to say whether the land be fallow or old waste. The straw of
this crop also is useful as fodder. If *másh* matures well and is
successfully harvested, it gives as good a return on as little
expenditure of time or trouble as any crop. It is, however, very
sensitive both to drought and over-flooding ; there is on this
account much loss and waste of *másh* seed each year.

Chillies.

Chillies or, in the vernacular, *mirch* is a crop confined
principally in this district to well lands under the cultivation of
Aráins, Kambohs and other equally painstaking farmers drawn
from the village menial classes. It is a crop that requires
immense care and trouble throughout all its stages ; the young
plants are grown in nursery grounds on which an immense
amount of manuring and cautious irrigation is done. The plants
are put out in June in land which has been ploughed six times
and manured as heavily as, or more heavily than, for maize.
One kanál of nursery should supply sufficient plants for four
ghumáos. At first the plants are watered every third day until
they become strong, when water need not be given oftener than
every fifth or sixth day, and not so often if there is rain. The irri-

gation requires to be very cautiously done as too much water spoils the crop. The land is weeded usually four or five times at the least. The crop begins to ripen towards the end of October, and the berries are picked as they get red in the course of the next two and a half months. The pickers are usually women who receive as wages 4 sérs a maund of what they pick. Thirty maunds an acre wet or 8 maunds dry is a fair outturn ; the cultivators usually sell it wet to dealers at thirty séts or one maund the rupee. Chillies like cotton contribute largely towards payment of the revenue ; and if a large surplus of the latter is grown then all the less of the former will be required.

Til or sesamum is usually grown as an unirrigated crop on high sandy lands ; its yield is very uncertain, but in a favourable year it brings in considerable profits to the cultivators.

There are four varieties of wheat in this district, the *pumman* or *wadhának* wheat distinguished by its height, by the large ear and by the bluish green tinge of the plant before it turns colour. This requires much more care and cultivation than any other variety and fetches a higher price, being sold chiefly in the city for pastry purposes. It is grown principally on well lands in the Mánjha and Rávi villages. The *daudkháni* or white bearded wheat is found generally in the Hithár. *Ghuni* or beardless wheat is also grown there, but is not so common. In the Rávi estates the small red wheat predominates, this being the most popular for consumption on that side of the district. This too is the one most usually grown under dry cultivation. The Hithár *gasra* soil under irrigation is perhaps better suited to wheat than any other in the district but the soil there being very soft gives much encouragement to the onion weed known as *bhukla* or *bhughát* which comes up with the wheat and often chokes it. This weed is very easily pulled up by the roots, but where it appears it always seems to get the better of the cultivators. Land intended for irrigated wheat ought to be ploughed six or seven times, but the cultivators seldom find leisure to plough more than three, four or, at the most, five times. It is only when rain has been falling occasionally throughout the summer that the full complement of ploughings is attained. Not seldom on canal land and sometimes even in the case of well lands the first irrigation for commencing ploughing is put off and off in the hope that rain will fall, until the people have no leisure but to irrigate, plough once, sow the seed and then plough over the land once more. This is called "*uppar karna*," and the wheat yield produced by so sketchy a process is usually poor. As a rule one may say that in this district far too little ploughing is done for wheat. Irrigated wheat is seldom sown in land that has just borne another crop, except that well land copiously manured for maize is again sown with wheat immediately following the maize on the strength of the manuring ; and sometimes on canal land cotton and wheat follow one another. Ordinarily wheat sowings on irrigated land continue through November and

Chapter IV, A.
—
Agriculture, Ar-
boriculture and
Live-stock.

Chillies.

Til.

Wheat.

December ; then they must stop. If intended for fodder the wheat is sown earlier mixed with some fodder crop. Nearly a maund of wheat seed goes to the acre, sown sometimes broadcast and sometimes by drill ; usually the former unless the land is dry. The yield is, roughly speaking, ten maunds or more per acre on canal-irrigated land and twelve maunds on well lands. The *wadhának* wheat would weigh heavier. On unirrigated land in this district contrary to the usual custom wheat is sown by itself except in nallahs or depressions of the surface, such as occur frequently in the Hithár, where wheat is sown often mixed with gram or barley. The time for sowing this crop dry is in the months of September and October while the soil is still moist after the late autumn rains. The yield of wheat without irrigation depends of course on the rainfall, and so to a large extent does the yield on well-irrigated soils. It is important to remember that in the Hithár and Rávi soils, however good the well irrigation may be, the yield is sure to be much below the mark and the straw very stunted, unless there has been some rain during the winter months. On the other hand a shower of rain soon after sowings is apt to do much harm, beating down the surface so that the seed cannot emerge. This incrustation is called *karand*. Under dry cultivation the amount of seed sown is much less than for irrigated, and the sowing is usually done by drill. Some excellent wheat is grown in the river inundated lowlands of the Rávi Bet. As the wheat is cut it is put up in small sheaves ; before threshing operations commence the sheaves are heaped up close to the threshing floor ; the threshing is done in the manner already described.

When the grain is cleaned it is taken off on donkeys to the village, where it is stored for household use or for sale. The people usually keep what they require for themselves and make over the rest either to money-lenders of the village in satisfaction for their debts or to traders who have come to buy for export. Of late years in the chief wheat tracts a custom has sprung up of selling the wheat while still standing to agents of the large exporting firms. In the three years 1890 to 1892 much wheat was sold in this way at prices varying from 15 to 18 sérs the rupee. The broken straw or *bhusa* of wheat is gener-ally stacked under a neatly plastered thatching which pre-serves it against the wind and rain. This is the main dry fodder for the plough and well cattle during the year. The *bhusa* is raked out as required through a small hole made at the foot of the stack. It is usually given to the cattle mixed with green fodder crops, if any of the latter are available. If not, as often happens in well-irrigated tracts during a dry season, then the cattle have to put up with wheat straw mixed with nothing better than green loppings from *kikar* trees. Wheat suffers chiefly from rust (*kungiári*) brought on by excessive rain followed by many days of cloudy weather.

Barley is a much hardier crop than wheat ; can grow in worse land ; requires less irrigation ; and ripens earlier. Every cultivator who is not well off is certain to grow a little barley in his holding as well as wheat, because the ripe barley enables him to provide food for himself, and something wherewith to meet the pressing demands of his money-lenders, just at a time when all other supplies have run out, before the wheat is ripe. Usually on wells barley is sown at the furthest part available to which the irrigation can be expected to reach, all the nearer land being kept for wheat. Also barley can be sown much later than wheat, with a fair prospect for maturing ; thus much land which might have been sown with wheat had the cultivator had leisure, or if the rain had fallen more opportunely, is sown ultimately with barley in preference to being left fallow. The outturn of barley weighs somewhat lighter than that of wheat. Irrigated barley is cut green for fodder, if necessary, indifferent-ly with wheat. Unirrigated barley is generally sown with gram or wheat in lowlying depressions of land. Especially in alluvial tracts, if the soil is not good, gram and barley are usually mixed under the name of *gcja*.

This is as a rule grown under dry cultivation, being sown on the moisture left by the summer rains which has been retained in the ground by careful ploughing and rolling. Two or three ploughings are usually done. It is one of the crops that is always sown by drill. When the seed has once germinat-ed gram is a hardy crop, and stands a prolonged drought fairly well, but is subject to injury from frost at the end of January or beginning of February and from the strong March wind known as *bulla*, unless there has been some winter rain. If the weather continue cloudy and unsettled at the end of March when the gram should be forming there is a risk of total failure. The people too assert that lightning injures the crop at this stage. Gram is usually sown by itself in the Mánjha except in the sandier soils in the Kasúr tahsíl where it is sown with wheat or with barley. In the Hithár nallahs it is sown mixed with either crop, because if the winter rains are heavy, the gram will be spoilt in depressions which col-lect the water. For the same reason it is sown mixed in the alluvial lands. In the Hithár large areas are flushed from the inundation canals about September for gram sowing or for gram and wheat mixed. These are recorded as canal-irrigated and have to pay canal water-rates though they get no more water after the preliminary flushing on which they are sown. Similarly a considerable area of gram is grown by aid of canal irrigation in the Mánjha, but this may be given more than once if required. Gram is often sown in the rice stubbles, in which case the yield is usually poor. If any of this crop is grown on well lands it is usually intended for fodder. Gram is eaten by men at all times of the year, either dry and whole, or in the form of *dál* ; if it has been sown mixed with wheat they do not trouble to separate the two but eat them together. When the crop is quite young, the people pull the top leaves and after soaking them in water, eat them with bread as herbs. Also

Chapter IV, A.

Agriculture, Ar-
boriculture and
Live-stock.

Barley.

Gram.

Rape.

Masar.

Tárámíra.

Tobacco.

they graze their cattle on the crop up to December with the object of preventing it from coming on too soon. Well-to-do men turn in their horses to graze even after the pulse has formed, or sometimes the gram is cut green for horses in March. The crop is harvested generally about the middle of April.

This crop is grown principally in the Mánjha either under canal irrigation or under dry cultivation. In the former case it is usually sown by itself; in the latter it is more commonly sown among the gram in rows eight or ten feet apart at right angles to the gram lines. Much of it is plucked up unripe for fodder or for use as *sáq* or greens when the crop is about a foot high. From the tendency of its plants to spread and from the brave show which it makes with its yellow blossoms it is apt to look a much better crop from a distance than it really is. A close inspection shows the plants to be somewhat thin and straggling. Rape is usually sown with a drill in furrows specially made for it after the field has been ploughed. The crop is harvested early. Of late it has been a source of considerable profit to the Mánjha villagers, being sold at 8 or 10 sérs the rupee. On well lands rape is seldom sown except with wheat when the two are intended to be cut together for fodder.

This pulse is grown on the river side in the cold season. It comes up and ripens very quickly and requires very little tillage. Thus it can be grown on land from which the annual inundations do not subside early enough for the cultivation of cereals. In fact it takes the same place in the spring sowings as *másh* does in the autumn. It is often sown with gram or barley on river lands. The pulse is used for making *dál*.

This is a crop which is sown dry in the autumn along with another crop such as *moth* or *chari* and is harvested in the spring. It can be sown late in the autumn; thus large areas of it are sure to be sown when the winter rains commence early. It does fairly well in an inferior soil, and as the *til* crop may be accepted as an indication of loose sandy ground, so *tárámíra* may generally be found where the soil is too thin to do justice to other crops. On the ground its plants appear to be very scattered and far apart, which fact gives the impression that much of the crop has failed. As a matter of fact the bare places are those from which the autumn crop has been harvested. *Tárámíra* is valuable for its oil and sells well. Also it is often cut early for fodder. On well lands *tárámíra* is sometimes found growing up with the fodder wheat.

The varieties of this, as found in this district, are four: (1) *Sámri*, (2) *Kanketi*, (3) *Kakkar*, (4) *Desi*. The last appears to be best liked by most classes of the people. The first three kinds are planted out in January or early in February and are ready for cutting in May. Their outturn wet is from three to five maunds a kanál which can be sold at something over one rupee per maund. The cultivators, however usually sell these three kinds while they are still in the ground. The *Desi* kind is sown a month later and is ready for cutting a month later than the other three kinds. It yields from two to three maunds a kanál wet, and sells at between two and four rupees a maund. Tobacco requires extremely careful and laborious cultivation. An immense amount of manuring is done before sowings and topdressing after the crop has come up. Irrigation should be given every third day. Out in the villages the custom is to cut off the *Desi* tobacco level with the ground, leave it so in the sun for a day, then shove it into a hole in the ground which they close up with branches and leaves covered with earth so as to exclude the air. There they leave it for six or seven days after which they take the tobacco plants out cut off the leaves from the wood and tie them up in a bundle. They keep them like this till they are sold. Some tobacco is grown on most of the wells in the district where the cultivators are Muhammadans. The Sikhs in this district do not actually grow tobacco themselves, whether because it is contrary to their religion or because the cultivation is too laborious, is not quite clear : but they allow their tenants to grow it and take from them the full owner's share, selling it generally to the village traders at two rupees or more a maund when it is nearly dry.

Some small area is usually reserved for poppy at every well. This requires as careful and laborious cultivation as tobacco. Sikhs on the Rávi and in the Hithár both grow it and consume the opium, or sometimes they drink a preparation from the pods (*post*). The usual custom is to tap the plant for opium three different nights, and then cut off the poppy heads, storing them for use as required. These are put in water and soaked for a time ; the preparation is then drunk. Of course this is all the stronger if no opium has been extracted from the plant.

This is a shrub grown only in a very few villages of the Sutlej Hithár. There is some of it in *Sádh* village of Kasúr tahsíl and in three or four villages of Chúnián tahsíl. It takes a long time to grow, but in the course of time becomes very profitable ; it flowers twice a year, and the juice is sold well in the bazaars for colouring purposes. The following note on it is taken from Punjab Products, Vol. I. : "Used to dye the hands red by rubbing the powdered leaf between them, also as a medicine to purify the blood."

The commoner varieties of vegetables, such as onions, radishes, turnips and *kadús* are grown more or less on every well under cultivation by an Aráín, or indeed by the more industrious workers of other classes. The growers hawk them about in other villages where they are not grown and obtain a very fair price for them. Vegetables take a prominent place in the summer evening meal. But vegetable growing is carried to its highest pitch of excellence in the more fertile lands around Lahore where manure is easily procurable. There several crops in the year are taken off the land. The soil

Chapter IV, A.
—
Agriculture, Arboriculture and Live-stock.

Tobacco.

Poppy.

Mendi (*Lawson Alba*).

Vegetables.

Chapter IV, A.

Agriculture, Ar-boriculture and Live-stock.

Vegetables.

undergoes a thorough preparation of ploughing, levelling and manuring before the principal crop is planted, and after that any cultivation required before the land becomes free again has to be done by hoeing and weeding. The best land near Lahore is usually taken by traders on a sub-lease for which they pay from a hundred to two hundred rupees the acre. It may therefore be imagined that they would not let any of the land lie idle ever. Sometimes the land is kept free for vegetables, sugarcane and cereal crops, sometimes it is planted out with garden and fruit trees. The most profitable vegetables are potatoes, chillies and onions. Of potatoes, two crops are grown in the year, the kharíf or country potatoes, which are planted in November and ripen in February yielding from three to seven maunds a kanál, and the rabi or hill potatoes, which are planted at the end of February and ripen in May yielding from four to ten maunds an acre. The price of potatoes varies according to the season and quality of the root from 20 to 50 sérs a rupee. Chillies have already been noticed in detail. Onions are planted out from the nurseries in February and are ready in June ; their yield is from ten to fourteen maunds a kanál and they sell at about four maunds a rupee. Another vegetable closely resembling potatoes and grown largely near Lahore is that known as *Arbi ;* its larger roots are called *Kacchálu.* This is sown in March and ripens in August and September, its yield is from six to twelve maunds ; it sells very cheap, namely at 1½ maunds the rupee at the beginning of the season and one maund only later on. Garlic is grown in some quantity and water-melons ; but these last never do very well, the soil not being adapted to them. Altogether upwards of two thousand acres in the neighbourhood of Lahore are reserved for vegetable growing, and of this nearly half is under potatoes.

Fruit trees and flowering shrubs.

Fruit trees and flowering shrubs bring in as large profits as vegetables, and the initial expenditure on the former is heavier ; also land once taken up for these cannot be utilized for anything else. For three or four years the land under fruit trees yields no return except on the fodder crops grown by aid of the irrigation and manuring given to the young fruit trees. Every kind of fruit is grown near Lahore. Oranges are the most profitable of any, and on this account are more common than any other kind of fruit. Mangoes sell well, but they are a more precarious crop than any other, being very liable to be destroyed by storms in March and April, or by insects of various kinds which settle on the trees and destroy the young fruits when first in blossom. The flowering shrubs are *Bed Mushk* and *Gulzár.* From the former an essence is extracted, which is used by the natives as a cooling medicine. *Gulzár* includes species of roses and other flowers ; the roses are valuable principally for the essene extracted from them, which is used either as medicine or to make attar of roses. The other flowers are used more by native ladies for adornment, but preparations of scented oils also are made from them. These fruit and flower trees are sometimes looked after by the owner himself and sometimes by a tenant who, as consideration for his trouble and expenditure in connection therewith, either takes not more than one-third of the produce or holds some other land rent free. The fruit or flowers are nearly always sold to a dealer, sometimes before they are ready to gather. From the time the dealer comes to terms he is responsible for the protection of the produce from thieves, but not for irrigation or weeding of the land. The price paid by the dealer varies greatly according to the outturn, and this again differs according to the soil and the amount of cultivation bestowed on it. The expenditure on these trees and shrubs is very heavy, and the return, though excellent in some years, is often inadequate.

The crops supplying fodder for cattle are *chari, jowár,* maize, *moth, mash, kangni, kátha,* sugarcane, *china,* wheat, barley gram, *masar,* rapeseed, *táramira, sinjhi* and *metha,* turnips (*shalgham*). Of these only *chari, sinjhi, metha,* and turnips are grown exclusively for fodder. The other crops are at sowing time intended to be matured for other purposes, but are often eventually diverted to use as cattle fodder. *Chari* of course, whether sown early or late, goes to the cattle. *Jowár* is utilised for the same purpose if it is a poor crop or if the *chari* runs out; also *jowár* stalks are invaluable as fodder in the early winter months. Maize is even sown expressly for fodder sometimes on the Rávi, about the same time as the *háru chari* described above under *jowár*. Otherwise maize may ultimately be used as fodder for the same reasons as *jowár* often is. Maize stalks are used like *jowár* stalks, being sometimes cut up for the cattle and sometimes given to them whole. *Jowár* straw is more strengthening than maize. *Moth* and *mash* can both come in useful as fodder though it is waste to give it until the grain has matured and been threshed out. *Moth* straw is much better than *mash* straw. *Kangni* is grown in the late spring and autumn alike, sometimes for fodder, sometimes for grain. It affords a strengthening food for cattle. It has already been noticed how the *kátha* sugarcane is often reserved for the cattle. *China* is sown twice a year, first in August so as to ripen in November; secondly in February or March so as to ripen in May. It requires soft land and is only grown here and there; it is however a very useful crop to the people, both for grain and fodder, because it ripens so quickly. Wheat and barley are often cut green for the cattle and their straw is of course invaluable, especially of the former. Gram is more useful for fodder as a standing crop than after it has been cut. The same may be said of *masar*. Rapeseed is often sown for fodder on well lands either in the standing maize crop when the rape should be ready for use in December, or it is sown together with wheat or turnips when the mixed produce will be taken for fodder in February. Also rape sown

Chapter IV, A.

Agriculture, Arboriculture and Live-stock.

Fruit trees and flowering shrubs.

Fodder crops.

originally for ripening is often cut for fodder. The same is the case with *táramíra* which however is always given to the cattle mixed with some other crop, as by itself it is too bitter and the cattle do not like it. Turnips are largely grown for fodder in well lands at a distance from the river; alluvial or sandy soils do not appear to suit them. In the Hithár near the river pure wheat fodder or wheat and rape mixed are grown in the place of turnips. These last are never considered good food for cattle, being very filling but not strengthening: they are sown on well lands after two or three ploughings in August or September and require watering about once every ten days. The crop comes into use as fodder from the beginning of December. They are chopped up and given to the cattle mixed with other stuff generally. The roots grow to a great size and are all ready for use by the end of January, but as fodder is always scarce in December and January in well-irrigated tracts, the turnips are usually consumed as they become ready for use. The plough cattle in this district are all stall-fed, except when they are turned into the wheat fields after the crop has been harvested or into the standing *chari* and *jowár* crops when these are plentiful. The common and regular course of feeding is, in the summer months, wheat straw alone or mixed with green *chari* or *babul moth*; in the autumn dry *chari*, maize and *jowár* stalks, *moth* and *mash* straw; in the early winter months wheat straw mixed with turnips or other early spring fodder crops. In well-irrigated tracts the wheat straw is generally finished by January and then the green fodder crops whether turnips, *sinjhi*, *metha*, rape, *táramíra* or early green wheat are mixed with *dubh* grass or the tops of the river thatch reed or sometimes in seasons of drought with the twigs of *kikar* trees. This is their food during the first four months of the calendar year after which the straw of spring crops becomes available.

Some of these have already been mentioned in the accounts of the crops principally affected by them. *Tela* attacks cane, cotton, *jowár*, gram, barley, rape and other minor crops. It takes shape in an oily liquid exuding on to the crops affected. Good rain alone stops it. *Sundi* is a small caterpillar which attacks maize, tobacco and gram, especially the latter. There is no remedy for this. *Toka* appears to be a sort of insect which injures cotton, tobacco and fruit trees. *Kungiári* is a blackening blight which comes on wheat and barley and turns the grain black. The cause is not known but it cannot be averted. *Kungi* is rust which injures wheat principally and is caused by cloudy weather following on a long course of rain. The leaves of the plant turn yellow and the grain either fails to form or is stunted. *Bulla* is a strong west wind which blows sometimes at the end of February or beginning of March and causes gram to dry up and the grain to shrivel in the pods, specially if the dews are heavy at night. Lightning also is said to injure gram and *masar*. White ants (*sewank*) attack most crops in dry sandy soils in case of a prolonged drought. Rats and mice also do immense mischief at times, especially in the sandier tracts of the river lands. In March and April heavy hail-storms pass across the southern part of the district in a narrow belt totally destroying all the crops they pass over. Further north such storms are rarer but occur sometimes. Plagues of locusts afflict the district at intervals. In the spring of 1891 they came too late to injure the wheat, but destroyed all the later rabi crops and some of the young autumn crops.

Chapter IV, A.

Agriculturre, Arboriculture and Live-stock.

Crop diseases.

Consumption and food supply.

The statement in the margin is the estimate of food grains consumed by an average family of five, which was prepared for the purposes of the Famine Commission of 1879.

Grain.	Agriculturists.	Non-agriculturists.
	Mds.	Mds.
Wheat	720	880
Barley	160	...
Jowar and maize ...	240	...
Rice	...	10
Grain	200	} 120
Other pulses	120	}
Total ...	1,440	1,040

This is a larger allowance than was made in Amritsar district and smaller than that framed for Ferozepore. On the whole the figures can hardly be taken seriously, though very possibly they are as likely to be right as any others that can be framed. For a population of 789,666 souls as estimated at that time the total consumption of food grains within the district was reckoned to be as shown in the margin in maunds.

	Agriculturists.	Non-agriculturists.	Total.
Wheat	1,143,471	2,061,849	3,205,320
Inferior grains ...	640,344	98,183	738,527
Pulses	503,128	294,550	797,678
Total ...	2,286,943	2,454,582	4,741,525

A rough estimate was framed at the same time of the total production, exports and imports of food grains; and it was stated page 152, (Famine Report) that some nine lakhs of maunds of wheat, gram and pulses were annually exported from Kasúr to Amritsar and Sindh and a similar quantity of the same grains imported from Ferozepore, Montgomery and Farídkot. The rates of yield from each crop on which the above calculations were based were adopted in a large measure from the data furnished in previous Settlement Reports. Since then the subject of produce yield has received increased attention, and at the recent settlement special rates of yield were framed for each crop in each assessment circle according to the system of irrigation by which the crop was grown and according to the nature of the soil, the class of people, and other agricultural conditions peculiar to the assessment circle. The resulting average rates of yield of the different crops for each entire tahsíl are furnished in Table No. XXI as well as the average rates for the whole district. Taking these last and applying

Chapter IV, A.

Agriculture, Arboriculture and Live-stock.

Consumption and food supply.

	Produce in Maunds.
Wheat	3,177,807
Barley	273,844
Gram	938,111
Rice	475,163
Maize	577,538
Jowár	207,635
Inferior grains and pulses.	52,464

them to the average area under each crop, irrigated and unirrigated crops being kept distinct in the working, we find the *total* production in grain and pulses to be as shown in the marginal statement. Assuming the estimate of total consumption that was made in 1879 to have been correct for a population a little short of eight lakhs, then the present population amounting in round figures to 10¾ lakhs would consume about 44½ lakhs of maunds of wheat and 20½ lakhs of maunds of other grains. If these calculations were correct then there would be no grain left for export and inferior grain would have to take the place of wheat to some extent in the people's consumption. But it cannot be doubted that the consumption per head (0·79 sér for agriculturists and 0·57 for non-agriculturists) was over-estimated. In the Amritsàr district, for instance, the average consumption per head for non-agriculturists was held to be 0·71 sér and that even was afterwards believed to be an over estimate. There is no doubt any how that quantities of wheat are exported from the district. From Kasúr station alone by rail over two lakhs of maunds of wheat were exported on the annual average of the three years 1887 to 1889 according to the railway export returns ; and in the next two years many lakhs of maunds of wheat were purchased from the Mánjha villagers by the firm of Ralli brothers for export to England. How far this export is compensated by import of inferior grains such as *jowár* is hard to say. Undoubtedly large quantities of such grain are imported as the above calculations include no allowance for the consumption of animals, which in this district must be very large.

Rakhs.

Table No. XVIII shows the whole area of land under the management of the Forest Department. The following is an account of all the Lahore rakhs, both those under the Forest Department and others. The statistical figures have been kindly furnished by Bábu Fazal Díu, Deputy Conservator, Lahore district. There are 94 rakhs in the Lahore district with an aggregate area of 250,146 acres (390·85 square miles) or nearly 11 per cent. of the entire district area. Most of these were transferred from the Civil Department to the control of the Forest Department between 1869 and 1873. The present distribution of these as regards control is as follows :—

Description of control.						Number of rakhs.	Area in acres.
Military Department	...	...	...	...	...	5	13,624
Forest do.	...	...	...	...	...	60	185,755
District	...	...	...	...	...	20	15,443
Partly district } District ...	...	...	...	...	} 9	{ 7,131
and							
Partly Forest } Forest	...	...	...	...	...		{ 28,193
			Total	...	...	94	250,146

The five rakhs under the Military Department are rakhs Terah, Padri, Dahuri, Bhangali and Backuntha, all situate in the Lahore tahsíl, the first four being within six or eight miles of Mián Mír and the last named nearly 12 miles away. These are all gazetted as military reserves under Section 17 of the Forest Act. Of the rakhs under the Forest Department ten with a total area of 24,917 acres (38·93 square miles) are gazetted as reserved forest under Section 34 of the Forest Act, and the rest are unclassed forests. The rakhs under District management are for the most part only rakhs in name, most of the land having been brought under cultivation by the grantees and lessees to whom Government has alienated its rights either permanently or temporarily on favourable terms as to revenue. Of the ten rakhs reserved under Section 34 to the Forest Department six are grouped together and known generally as the Chánga Mánga reserve : the six rakhs so grouped are Jalleke, Monjoke, Chánga Mánga, Bhoa Asal, Gandian and Shahpur. This large reserve of Chánga Mánga is divided into two circles :—

Chapter IV, A.
—
Agriculture, Arboriculture and Live-stock.
Rakhs.

		Acres.
Plantation circle	... ...	10,132
Rakh circle	... ...	10,041
	Total	20,173

The Plantation circle contains all the planted portions of the rakh and is divided into four blocks, each block comprising a certain number of compartments of different areas. The compartments are 125 in number. Of the Plantation circle 8,399 acres are irrigated from the Mooltan Branch of the Bári Doáb Canal.

Plantation circle.

One hundred Beldárs are maintained to look after the canal water-courses in this rakh and to keep them clean. They also have other duties in connection with the roads through the rakhs.

The plantation consists chiefly of young *Shisham* trees. There are also other varieties such as *Tun*, tallow, Eucalyptus and mulberry trees. The forest is being exploited by the method of coppice with standard on a rotation of 16 years as provided for in the Working Plan sanctioned by the Government.

The transport of wood is generally affected by a small portable Decanville's tramway of 16″ gauge and four miles in length.

Most of the wood produced has hitherto been consumed by the railway. The main grass of the plantation is " *Garm* " (*Panicum Antidotale*) : this is consumed by cows and buffaloes while still green. When there is scarcity of grass elsewhere this rakh grass is sold to any villagers who like to take it. A monthly permit for which they pay one rupee entitles them to take away every day as much as a man can carry. Besides *Garm* there are the following grasses : *Chhimbar, Palwan,*

Chapter IV, A.

Agriculture, Arboriculture and Live-stock.

Plantation circle.

Dhaman, Panni and *Dabh*. The undergrowth in this rakh is generally *Báthu* (*Chenopodium Sp.*) and is of no use. Besides this mulberry seedlings form a dense undergrowth in places. The strength of establishment kept in the reserve is—

One Officer in charge, who also holds charge of the unclassed forests in the Chúnián tahsíl.

Two Foresters and 18 Guards.

In the planted portion of the reserve the following wild animals are found :—

1. Pigs.
2. Nilgais.
3. Jackals.
4. Deer (in small number).

Besides the above animals there are pea-fowls and black partridges found in the plantation.

In 1886-87 and 1887-88 efforts were made by the Forest Department to reduce the number of pigs and jackals through netters and snarers to whom certain rewards were offered for each animal thus killed, but these measures did little to reduce the number, and of late years they have been discontinued. The pigs are partly kept down by shooting parties visiting the rakh and by the zamíndárs who kill any they can catch in their fields outside the rakh.

No cattle are allowed to graze in the Plantation circle with the exception of those belonging to the local establishment, which only graze in certain compartments where there is no fear of damage being done to the young coppice or trees.

Rakh circle.

The Rakh circle of the reserve is composed of the following rakhs :—

	Acres.
Part of Rakh Jalleke	3,047
Gandián East	2,283
Gandián West	2,479
Part of Rakh Shahpur	1,009
Do. do. named Shahpur-Jand extension	1,223
Total	10,041

Gandián East and Rakh Shahpur are open for grazing all the year round ; the others are open for part of the year only.

Unclassed forests.

Of the 62 unclassed forests (including 53 wholly under the Forest Department and 9 partially so) 40 rakhs with a total area of 116,199 acres are situated in the Lahore and Chúnián tahsíls between the rivers Rávi and Beás and on either side of the North-Western Railway line to Mooltan. The remainder are on the north side of the Rávi, four lying within the Trans-Rávi limits of the Lahore tahsíl and 18 rakhs with an area of 72,832 acres within the Sharakpur tahsíl.

The statement below shows the distribution by tahsíls of unclassified rakhs under the control of the Forest Department and the District.

1	2	3	4	5	6	7
Name of Tahsíl.	Under Forest Department.		Of the divided rakhs under Forest Department.		Total.	
	No.	Area in acres.	No.	Area in acres.	No.	Area in acres.
Lahore	10	5,906	4	6,812	14	12,718
Chúnián	26	92,465	4	11,016	30	103,481
Sharakpur	17	62,467	1	10,365	18	72,832
Total	53	160,838	9	28,193	62	189,031

The rakhs in Chunian tahsíl lie in a few compact blocks ; in other tahsíls they are much scattered ; about three per cent. of the total forest area is within the influence of the river floods. The rakh land in the Mánjha shows traces of kallar in parts but would all yield readily under canal irrigation ; the Sharakpur land is, much of it, unfertile by reason of kallar and the wood growth is generally poor, but fair grass is obtained during the rains. With the exception of Rakh Mudki in the Chúnián tahsíl in which Mahant Hari Dás, the successor of Mahant Dhián Dás has the right to graze cattle and cut wood for the boná fide use of his lungar at Bhaipheru, the other forests are unencumbered by any rights save those of Government.

With the exception of 2,561 acres closed with a view to preserving the young coppice all the unclassed forests under the control of the Forest Department are thrown open to grazing under different systems as shown below—

Tahsíl.	Number of forests unclassed.	Area entirely closed to all classes of animals.	Area closed for part of the year to all classes of animals and open for the rest of the year to kine.	OPEN ALL THE YEAR ROUND.	
				To all classes of animals.	For cattle only.
Lahore	14	1,133	3,843	3,468	4,476
Chúnián	30	1,128	10,688	57,418	34,442
Sharanpur	18	300	23,618	29,523	19,588
Total	62	2,561	38,149	90,409	58,506

The present system is to retain under direct management of the Forest Department the grazing in those Rakhs over which effective supervision is possible : and to sell the others by auction, giving a preference to the villagers who live near the Rakhs.

In the case of the grazing leases sold by auction an upset price is fixed for each Rakh, and if no one bids up to it, the Rakh grazing is kept under direct management. Consequently most of the grazing remains each year under the Forest Department. Many complaints are constantly made by the people living near the Government Rakhs of Sharakpur, and to an outside observer their complaints appear reasonable. Probably however the rules are being made easier for them as years go on.

The following are the annual grazing rates per head realized from the cattle owners :—

	Rs.	a.	p.
Camels	1	0	0
Female camels	1	8	0
Buffaloes	1	9	6
Cows	0	12	9
Horses and mares	0	12	0
Donkeys	0	6	0
Sheep and goats	0	1	6

The young ones (khirás) of all classes of animals are allowed to graze free, till they have got out their two teeth when the usual fee is charged on them. These fees are taken from cultivators and non-cultivators alike. The cattle brought in from other districts (which generally remain for two or three months only) are charged the following monthly rates per head :—

	Rs.	a.	p.
Cows	0	2	0
Buffaloes	0	4	0

The khirás are free.

The following statement shows the yearly income derived by the Forest Department from the Lahore Rakhs during the last three years :—

Name of forest unit.	Wood.	Grass and grazing.	Munj, kána and others.	Total.
	Rs.	Rs.	Rs.	Rs.
Changa Manga Plantation ...	37,433	1,129	105	38,667
Sháhdara Plantation	10,245	609	384	11,238
Other Reserved Rakh lands ...	1,286	5.814	901	8,001
Unclassed Rakhs, Lahore Tahsíl	133	5,432	51	5,616
Ditto Chúnián Tahsíl	699	17,882	93	18,674
Dttio Sharakpur Tahsíl	1,629	8,983	1,342	11,954
Total ...	51,425	39,849	2,876	94,159

The grasses that grow in the Rakh lands are as follows :—

1 Dabh.	5 Khabal.	9 Panni.
2 Chhimbar.	6 Márak.	10 Sawánk.
3 Lunakh.	7 Khavi.	11 Kahi.
4 Dal.	8 Sirkána.	12 Dhaman.
		13 Palwan.

Of these the best fodder grasses are *Dabh, Chhimbár, Khabal,
Sawánk, Dháman* and *Palwan. Sawank* is found chiefly in the
Sharakpur tahsil in the land inundated by the Deg stream, or
where water accumulates during the rainy season; the *Sawánk*
seed is eaten sometimes and the grass when green is greedily
devoured by cattle. *Káhi* is found mainly in the river alluvial
lands, *Sirkána* in all lowlying sandy tracts subject to inundation.
The others grow indifferently in all sorts of lands.

The *Sirkána* plant provides reeds which are used for making chicks, chairs and thatching houses : from its husk is made
the *Munj* grass for making ropes or for lining kacha wells.
The tops are grazed on by cattle and the leaves of the plant
afford a very good substitute for dry fodder during the winter
months when all straw and *Bhusa* is exhausted. The *Sir* (leaves
of kána) is chopped up and given to cattle mixed with green
food. The *Panni, Sir* and *Káhi* are used for thatching houses
and other purposes.

The principal trees in the Rakhs are the *Jand, Karíl, Farásh,
Ber* (small kind) and *Wán.* The most common perhaps are the
Jand and *Wán* which grow all over the Rakhs. The *Karíl,* usually
is found on high and dry land where other bushes will not grow.
The *Farash* is found principally along lines of road and has
probably been cultivated there : also in low land where water
occasionally comes. The *Reru* and *Jandi,* other varieties of the
Jand, are found in the better kind of soil. The shrub known
as the *Mulla* grows extensively in all the lowlying fertile portions of Rakh land, especially in the Lahore tahsil. Near the
Sailába land and in good *Maira* or *Rohi* lands are also found
the *Sissu, Mulberry, Kikar, Bakáin, Dhák* and one or two others.

The Rakhs on the Manjha land on an average contain
from 100 to 200 cubic feet of fuel per acre, while the Changa
Manga and the *Sailaba* artificial plantations give an average of
1,000 to 2,500 cubic feet per acre. The selling rates of the fuel
range from 3 rupees to 7 rupees 8 annas per hundred of cubic
feet stocked ; it is used by the North-Western Railway, and is
also taken into the market at Lahore, Amritsar and Ferozpore.

The roads in this district are fairly well stocked with trees :
of those under the Local Boards 185 miles of road are provided
with avenues good or bad, and young trees are now being
nurtured along many miles of road. There are eight nurseries
for young plants covering more than seven acres. In the same
way under the Public Works Department out of 135 miles
suitable for avenues, 102 miles are fully stocked with trees
according to the returns of last year ; of which 13 miles failed

lately. There are also 23½ acres of old groves under this Department, and nine nurseries of small areas, out of which six are along the Lahore and Ferozpore road. The expenditure on trees under Local Boards was a little short of Rs. 4,000 and nearly Rs. 6,000 under the Public Works Department. Against this a small income is obtained by sale of trees, wood and tree loppings.

Table No. XXII shows the live stock of the district as ascertained at the latest enumeration. The people do not, as a rule, rear their plough cattle for themselves, but purchase from itinerant dealers who travel up from Hissár, Mooltan, Montgomery or Baháwalpur with picked animals suitable for well and plough work. The north of the district is supplied chiefly from Amritsar, Gujránwála and Jhang. The price agreed upon is generally paid in two instalments, half at the autumn harvest and half at the spring. If the cultivator fail to pay up at the stipulated time, several of those interested go to his house and quarter themselves on him until he satisfies their claim. The imported cattle are generally four years old or so : they do fairly well, but do not stand heavy work as well as the locally bred cattle. Probably the reason that cattle breeding receives so little attention is that in the well-irrigated tracts where cattle are most needed the cultivators have quite enough to do to keep their working animals properly fed. The super-fluous animals, such as milch cows and young bullocks have to take their chance on such grazing as can be got off the village lands. Only the working cattle are regularly stall-fed. Some of the richer men in the Mánjha do a little in the breeding line. At Algon in Kasúr tahsíl there is said to be a particularly fine breed of cattle and the milch cows bred there are in some request even in other districts. Whether bought or bred the Mánjha plough cattle in strength and condition present the greatest contrast to the weakly starved creatures usually found in the well-irrigated tracts of the Sutlej and Rávi valleys, the reason being partly that the Manjha people can much better afford the luxury of good cattle ; and partly that the heavy draught work required of the cattle both at the deep Mánjha wells and in ploughing canal-irrigated land or in drawing heavy transport carts for long distances could not be done unless the animals had strength and weight above the average. Indeed at the Mánjha wells it is not unusual to employ bull buffaloes from choice, these being much heavier than bullocks and less expensive. Their weak point is that they easily succumb to the fiercer heat of the sun. In Sharakpur tahsíl also more bull buffaloes than bullocks are worked at the ploughs and wells. There fodder is often very scarce, both in the autumn and winter and buffaloes are much easier to feed than bullocks. Cow buffaloes are often found working at the wells in this district, and if this is for want of means to buy better animals, it is an unmistake-able sign of poverty. Sometimes, however, cow buffaloes are put in to help the other cattle because they are past calving.

In Sharakpur tahsíl, which, taken all round, is the most depressed tract in the district, 35 per cent. of the well cattle are bullocks, 53 per cent. bull buffaloes and 12 per cent. cow buffaloes. The price of a Mánjha bullock varies from Rs. 40 to Rs. 80 and of a Hithar or Rávi bullock from Rs. 20 to Rs. 40. A male buffalo varies in price between Rs. 20 and Rs. 50, a cow buffalo if in milk is worth Rs. 50 or more : but if dried up for good she fetches very little money. As a rule a landholder does not stall-feed more cattle than are necessary to work his well and plough and to keep him and his family in butter milk. For the latter purpose one or two buffaloes are sufficient: but in parts of the district especially in Sharakpur and Chunián tahsíls, there are large numbers of superfluous animals belonging to non-proprietors. These are more loss than profit; they consume all the field and waste-land grazing, and being very prone to disease owing to their poor feeding and low condition are apt to spread sickness among the working cattle. A large trade in *ghi* and milk is done in some of the villages within easy reach of Lahore cantonments and civil stations : from eight or ten of these milk *eckas* run once or twice a day. Also in the Bár lands which form the north-west portion of Sharakpur tahsíl, the people subsist almost more on the profits derived from their herds than on agriculture, selling their *ghi* to traders and their young cattle to dealers. Elsewhere in this district little actual profit is made on the cattle : it must be remembered that the greater proportion of the cattle stock shown as existent in the district, other than well or plough cattle, belong not to the men who are responsible for the land revenue but to village retainers who generally get their grazing free. Similarly the sheep and goats of which there are such large numbers belong to menials of the village, chiefly of the *Teli* or oilman caste : the sheep are kept for their wool and the goats for their milk or for slaughter ; they vary in price from one to five rupees. Horses and ponies are most numerous in the Mánjha where many of the landowners are in a position to indulge in this luxury : also most traders keep a pony of sorts. Good horses are occasionally found, especially in villages of Rájpúts who are reckless in their expenditure on horse flesh as on everything else. Mules are comparatively few. Donkeys are largely used in the carrying trade as pack animals; especially for grain. They belong mostly to *kumhars*. Camels are not in much use locally, but some men keep them for riding purposes. Most however of those in the district belong to contractors who hire them out by the month. Chunián tahsíl has the largest number of camels, grazing waste being much more common there than in either of the two other cis-Rávi tahsíls. At present the common rate of hire for a camel is six or seven rupees a month. They sell on the average for eighty or a hundred rupees.

Hissar bulls have been provided by Government for breeding purposes to the number of five each in three tahsíls, but one only in Sharakpur. In the three tahsíls two each have died and

Government Bulls.

there are now ten Hissar bulls in the district : they are not held in much esteem here.

Large numbers of cattle die in this district every year from disease, especially in Sharakpur tahsil and in the lowlands of Chunián tahsíl. The most common forms of disease are, rinderpest, called by the natives *máta* or *pir* : *Mukhor* or foot and mouth disease, which of late years has been very prevalent in the Chunián Hithár : *Gal ghotú* or anthrax : *Sokar* a disease brought on by eating *jowár* stalks that have dried up for want of rain : *Aphára* or swelling of the stomach, which according to the natives is caused by the cattle eating a worm which sometimes breeds in the grass known as *Senji*. Cattle are con-stantly dying in Sharakpur from inflammation of the bowels, which the natives generally say is brought on by the cattle taking to the hard *jowar* stalks after they have got used to the soft rice straw of which the cattle there eat a great deal in the autumn. Others say the complaint is induced by drinking water from the Deg.

There are two Salútrís maintained from District Funds, one for the two tahsíls of Lahore and Sharakpur and the other for Chunián and Kasúr. Their chief duty is to attend wherever cattle disease prevails.

Horse-breeding operations were first started in Lahore at the end of 1881 when the branding of mares fit for breeding purposes was introduced and stud horses were distributed by the Department of Horse-Breeding Operations. At present there are nine horses and six donkey stallions located in the district. Particulars are given below :—

Name of Tahsíl.	Name of station.	Number of horses.	Breed of horses.	Number of donkeys.	Breed of donkey.
Lahore	Lahore ...	2	1 T. B. E. ... / 1 Norfolk Trotter	1	Italian.
	Ráewind ...	2	1 Norfolk Trotter / 1 Arab	1	French.
	Kána Kácha	1	Norfolk Trotter ...	1	Do.
Kasúr ...	Kasúr ...	2	1 Norfolk Trotter / 1 Studbred ..	1	Italian.
Chúnián ...	Chúnián ...	2	1 T. B. E. ... / 1 Norfolk Trotter	1	Do.
Sharakpur ...	Sharakpur ...	1	Norfolk Trotter ...	1	Punjabi.

The Norfolk Trotter breed appears to be generally preferred in this district.

The young stock got by Government stallions out of mares is shown in a table below. Mares suitable for breeding purposes are now branded with the letters V. I.

Year.	HORSES.			DONKEYS.		
	Horses.	Mares.	Total.	Stallions.	Mares.	Total.
1888-89	104	113	217	126	132	258
1889-90	75	151	226	75	115	190
1890-91	79	94	173	68	85	153
1891-92	95	91	186	58	114	172
1892-93	81	88	169	57	88	145

The number of mares served by horse stallions in 1892
was 419 and the number served by donkey stallions was 488.

The District Committee has recently invested in four Arab
ponies with a view to improving the breed of district ponies.

An annual horse show was established for Lahore in
1879; the first show being held on the 11th March 1879
on the parade-ground overlooked by the fort. A sum of
Rs. 500 was granted for distribution in prizes. In 1881 the
show was held on a plain near the Shálámár gardens : and next
year it was moved to the *Ináyat-a-Bágh*, a garden opposite the
main entrance to the Shálámár gardens, where it is still held a
day or two before the *Chiràghán-ka-Mela* mentioned at page 78.
This fixes it to the last Friday and Saturday in the month of
March. The locality is well suited for holding the horseshow,
but there is a doubt whether it gives enough now for the annually
increasing number of horses brought. The grant for prizes was
increased to Rs. 750 in 1883 and again to Rs. 1,000 in 1884.
The latter sum is still awarded in priyes each year and small
sums are distributed at the cost of the District Board to the
poorer dealers who fail to secure prizes, as a consolation in case
of disappointment. The amount so distributed averages about
Rs. 100. The following statement shows the results of the
fairs held during the last five years :—

Year.	Number of animals attending the fair.	Number of horses competing for prizes.	Number of mules competing for prizes.	NUMBER OF ANIMALS SOLD.			Average price.
				Cavalry Remounts.			
				British.	Native.	Others.	
							Rs.
1889	459	223	29	9	9	51	244
1890	571	356	16	20	3	16	186
1891	641	301	25	11	...	41	200
1892	675	297	24	16	...	59	222
1893	693	201	21	9	3	21	267

Horse fair.

This statement shows a steady increase in the number attending the fair. The quality of the animals exhibited is said to be good on the whole. Unfortunately many of the prizes are carried off not by local breeders but by dealers who take their animals from fair to fair in the hope of securing prizes and purchasers. Another feature of the show for which some remedy perhaps is required is the large number of very young stock that are bought up by the dealers—consequently both the native of the district and the Government lose much of the benefit aimed at by the Horse-breeding Department.

Horse diseases.

The ailments most commonly treated in the Veterinary Hospital are bowel complaints and lameness. But the 1881 edition of the District Gazetteer furnished the following note on the subject :—

> Horses are subject to many diseases, the principal of which are *zahrbád,* a swelling caused by over-indulgence in green food. All the limbs swell, and unless taken in time it is likely to prove fatal. *Bhiláwa,* a berry, or *ajwain,* a seed, both of indigenous growth are said to be remedies for this disease. *Khúb* is an ailment in which the throat swells, and is probably strangles. It attacks foals and colts principally. A poultice of *samhálu* plant (vitex negundo) and cowdung is said to reduce the swelling. If not taken in time, the disease is a serious one. There is also a sort of paralysis known as *chandani* or *jhola* cured with *haldi* or turmeric. *Phila* is a sudden chill when heated, often causing death. *Kanar* or glanders is very fatal; *súl* or gripes and *khárish* or itch are common: the latter is cured with *tárámira* oil and sulphur.

SECTION B.—OCCUPATIONS, INDUSTRIES AND COMMUNICATIONS.

Occupations of the people.

Table No. XXIII shows the principal occupations followed by males, as returned in Table XVIIB at the census of 1891. The figures would perhaps have been more useful if they had shown the occupations of none but males over 15 years of age, but this information is not available by districts. Consequently the table, as it stands, shows also the occupation of infant males, which of necessity has been put down as that followed by their fathers. The census table above quoted shows the occupations of females as well, but this it has been thought unnecessary to abstract. Two-thirds of the males in towns are of the age of 15 and over, and three-fifths in the rural tracts, so a rough calculation can be made if it is desired to discover the occupations of males of that age. The figures in the table may be thus summarized :—

Agricultural	43·5
Pastoral	2·5
Domestic service	12·5
Artisans	15·9
Food and drink	9·6
Unskilled labour	5·1
Government service, Civil	4·8
Do. Military	1·5
Fakírs and mendicants	1·6
Commerce and transport	·9
Others	2·1

The classification must always be unsatisfactory, as explained in Chapter XII of the Census Report, on account of so many persons following several occupations distinct from each other, like the *kumhár*, who may be a potter, a brick-maker, a donkey driver, or a common carrier ; or the *Chuhra* who is both a scavenger and an agriculturist, and for this reason it is impossible to give an exact idea of how many should properly be classed as agricultural and non-agricultural. The *Chuhrás* form 12 per cent. of the total population, and very nearly all either combine agriculture with their legitimate occupation, or depend in great measure for their livelihood upon the yield of agricultural occupations. More detailed figures will be found in the original Census Table No. XVIIB, and abstracts Nos. 90 and 93 appended to the report of 1891.

The extent to which the people of the district are engaged in manufacturing industries may be gathered from Table No. XXIV. This shows that in the whole district there are only 10 silk factories, 9 cotton gins, 9 leather factories, and 8 shops (for they are nothing more) where *pashmina* and gold and silver brocading work is done. All these are in the Lahore city except some of the cotton gins. The largest of these outside Lahore are at Kasúr where 24 cotton gins are working, 38 hands being employed, and at Ráewind where 18 gins work and 35 hands are employed, of whom 18 are females. The outturn depends largely on the efficiency of the workmen, but from three to four maunds to each gin is considered a fair output for a working day of 12 hours. The charge for cleaning cotton is 7 or 8 annas a maund. The cleaned cotton is usually sent to Karáchi for export. The total number of workmen engaged in the mills and factories at work in the district is only 413 males and 100 females.

The number of men employed in small works or independent artisans throughout the district is 33,140. The following remarks refer almost entirely to the industries and manufactures carried on in Lahore city.

Formerly Lahore had a name for the manufacture of silk cloths such as *daryáie* and *gulbadan ;* they were made with a superior quality of silk thread from Bokhára which has now almost ceased to be imported partly on account of its heavy cost and partly because of a change in the fashion, men having almost given up wearing silk clothes now. The *daryáie* now sold is somewhat coarse and inferior and is worked in glaring colours : latterly, however, there has been an improvement in this respect, the red, green and yellow colours having been partially abandoned for grey, pink and brown. There are no silk manufactories on any large scale ; only a few small shops with 7 or 8 hands at work. *Phulkáris* or coarse cloth embroidered in silk are worked by women ; a few years ago a large European demand sprang up for these but now they are becoming less fashionable. *Patolis* or silk threads interspersed with gold and silver, used principally for *pyjama* strings (*izárbands*) were formerly somewhat of a speciality in Lahore, being exported from here to

Chapter IV, B.

Occupations,
Industries and
Communications.

Wool.

Jammoo and other Native States; they appear to be not so much in fashion now.

Local woollen manufactures properly speaking are confined to the coarse *loies* or blankets woven by means of the ordinary hand shuttle and *pashmina* made from the fine wool of hill goats known as *pashm* which is imported from Kábul, Thibet and Yárkand: the white *pashm* sells at from one to three rupees a ser, and black *pashm* is slightly cheaper. In Lahore itself the Kashmíri colony work a very good kind of *malida pashmína,* their *dhussa* sheets being superior even, it is said, to anything of the sort produced in Amritsar. Caps, coats and other clothes made of this *malida* and embroidered with silk find an extensive sale among the city people. Formerly a fair amount of Lahore made *pashmína* was exported to lower India; the demand is said to have decreased of late years.

Cotton.

The common manufactures of the local weavers, whose business still thrives in all villages and back streets of towns notwithstanding the cotton imports from abroad, are *khaddar, súsi, khárwa* and *lungis. Khaddar* is a very strong cloth made of home spun thread: it has different names according to its width, *chousi* being *khaddar* with four hundred threads in the width, *painsi* with five hundred, and *chassi* with six hundred. The last variety is the finest. *Susi* is a striped cloth, *khárwa* is a stout red cloth, and *lungis* are usually worked with a coarse blue thread which is very durable. The weavers are now trying to imitate English checks and have succeeded to some extent. *Durries* too are woven in Lahore; the designs are good but the workmanship is not equal to that of Umballa as regards either strength or neatness.

Gold work.

Gold lace (*gota*) is made by women at their houses from wire obtained from the *kundla kash,* whose trade it is to draw out very fine silver wire and guild it over with gold washing. Gold and silver leaf is prepared by placing the gold or silver between leathern pads and beating it very thin.

Other metal work.

Brass and copper are imported for making cooking and other utensils; spades and other agricultural implements are turned out in the city in considerable number. The iron-workers have mostly learnt their work at the Railway Workshops, and some few of them are fairly skilful in their business.

Woodwork.

The former native style of carving on a large and magnificent scale, of which the best specimens are to be found in old doorways and window frames, has now given way to more minute and artistic workmanship which expends itself chiefly in petty articles of ornament and luxury or in models of the old native productions. The present style is improving and extending rapidly under the influence of the Local School of Art, who are making it their object to keep the old native designs alive as far as the public taste and demand allow. The woodwork trade has become much more popular in Lahore of late years than it ever was before.

Lac work is a common source of livelihood in the city. Bangles of lac find an extensive sale, sets of twenty or twenty-five for each hand being fitted up and inlaid with gold leaf and *pot* (small imitation pearls). Small wooden toys also are made and covered with a coating of lac. The pottery of Lahore is poor compared to that of other places in the province, the only articles of glazed manufacture are *chilams*, cups, *hookahs* and flower vases.

Electroplating is coming in, but is badly done at present. Brick making which was always rather a speciality of Lahore has been improved lately in the factory started a few years ago near the Lahore civil station and known as the Brick, Tile and Lime Works. They are said to turn out a stronger kind of ordinary brick than the native kilns do, and a very fair description of roofing tiles.

The note furnished by Mr. Lockwood Kipling, Principal of the Lahore School of Art for the last edition of the Gazetteer has been revised and brought up to date by his successor Mr. F. H. Andrew who has very kindly supplied what follows:—

Extinct industries.

It is surprising to those familiar with the actual state of the Industrial Arts in Lahore, to see in catalogues of Indian Art collections in Europe, so many rare and beautiful objects ascribed to this city. Glass, enamels and arms elaborately wrought are among these. In some cases Lahore has evidently been written loosely for the Punjab at large; but in others a decayed if not extinct craft is indicated. It is doubtful whether any good enamel was ever wrought in this city, and the armourers to whom so many richly decorated weapons are attributed are represented now by two or three very old men. Gold embroidery naturally flourished where there was a Court; and the kindred wire-drawing business with it. The superiority of the Lahore *kandla kash* (silver ingot gilder) brought about by severe enactments and kept up by the guild, is now a tradition merely, and there are comparatively few workers in *tilla* or gold thread, although their number is increasing.

Glass.

Glass bangles are made by two or three workmen, but in no great quantity nor are the colours brilliant; while the manufacture of the kerosine lamp chimney, which at one time promised to become extensive, has fallen off, and is now confined to one man; Delhi having become the principal source of supply for the Punjab. Recently the Punjab Science Institute has been making some very good glass flasks, funnels, insulators, &c. But these are not made from the raw materials, broken glass being simply melted and blown; and in the case of the lamp chimneys the blowing and annealing are so imperfect that they usually fly into pieces directly they are used. The arts that have disappeared have been succeeded by trades of a more useful character, dependent rather upon the increasing prosperity of the people than on the luxuries of a limited class.

Vegetable oils, acids, soap and candles, printing and book-binding.

Among these may be mentioned the manufacture of vegetable oils by steam-driven machinery. Laboratories for the production of sulphuric and nitric acid, soap and candle making, letter-press printing and book-binding are in the hands of natives, and are flourishing.

Leather.

The leather trade is a distinctly improving one, and a large quantity of saddlery and shoes is annually turned out. Shoes known as "Gámi Sháhi" a thick and strongly built kind are a speciality of the place and are sent to most parts of the Punjab.

Chapter IV, B.

Occupations, Industries and Communications.

In cotton fabrics *khaddar*, worn largely by agriculturists all over the Punjab for the sufficient reason that its solid texture with the native nap unsinged renders it warm in winter, while it is not too hot for summer, and dun coloured *khes* are the only cloths made. The former is now principally made in Lahore for the cotton printers' use. The cotton printing of the Punjab, and particularly of Lahore, is remarkable for its strong rich colour and architectonic character of design, which make it perfectly adapted to decorative purposes. Several dyers show remarkable aptitude in applying their designs to *purdahs, dados*, floor cloths, &c., and the effect is always better on the coarse native woven cloths than upon English calico, which however is also very largely used and is cheaper. The trade in cotton prints rose steadily from the time of the Punjab Exhibition of 1881-82, and for a time a comparatively large quantity was exported to Europe and America. But the fashion for these prints having declined, the trade is now almost entirely confined to India, where it is a fairly steady one, owing probably to the cheapness and effectiveness of the prints, and to their suitability for interior decoration in this country. *Kaddar* is still made in households for presentation as wedding gifts. The women spin the thread and making it up into hanks hand it over to the weaver to weave. This being done they next give it to the dyer, who dyes it usually with *majit* (madder). A red ground with black pattern is considered the most auspicious treatment, and although in villages it is sometimes dyed black, in cities it is invariably red. This cloth is used too rather extensively by the *bhabaris* for embroidering *phulkáris.* These were formerly made exclusively for home use, but since the exhibition of 1881-82 so great has been the demand for them by Europeans that *phulkári* embroidering has become quite an industry; and there are regular traders who buy of the makers for retail.

The production of *khes* is not to be compared with that of some of the western districts, from which indeed rough cloths are occasionally imported. There is scarcely any muslin weaving, although there is a large consumption of imported muslin. A great deal of European cloth changes hands here, and a considerable quantity is used by cotton printers to make into *abrás* for ordinary use, or tinselled garments for wedding festivities. Much of the cotton grown in the district is locally consumed, and the greater part is ginned by the little hand machine which turns out about 24 lbs. of cleaned cotton in a day. But it says much for the enterprise of the Lahori, that a Sikh mechanic is the proprietor of a factory fitted with Oldham machinery.

It is contended by some workmen that the fine *pashmina* known as *malida* made in Lahore is superior to that of Amritsar, and this appears to be borne out by the fact that a large quantity is exported, and that the trade, which is generally in the hands of Kashmíris, is improving. *Chaddars topis, dhusás, patkás* and other articles are made, the two last being specialities of Lahore. Besides fine good coarse woollen blankets (*loies*) are made. The greater part of this hand-weaving both cotton and wool is entirely unnoticed by Europeans, very few of whom venture into the city, or thread the narrow alleys of such suburbs as Mozang. One slight indication of the extent of this domestic craft is afforded by the fact that the shuttle-maker's trade is as such small trades go, a busy one. At every fair one or two stands will be found where weaver's shuttles are sold. A good shuttle lasts for many years, and is carefully handled and cherished. Perhaps it is fair to conclude that hand-loom weaving after all is scarcely so dead as might be expected.

In silk there is a relatively large and prosperous trade. The ordinary Lahore *daryáie* is a stoutish, somewhat roughly woven and, considered as silk, lack-lustre fabric, narrow in width, and usually crude in colour. A thinner sort, similar to the silks used for linings, costs about 12 annas per yard; others are sold at a rupee and upwards. *Gulbadans* are striped fabrics, and were formerly woven much stouter than at present and in wider widths. But since they have gone out of fashion and are now almost exclusively worn by children, there is no object in adding to the cost of manufacture by making them wider than is absolutely necessary. *Dhúpchán* is the name given to shot silks, a changing effect of colour being given by a warp of one tint and a weft of another. Red and green are favourite colours for this combination. The greater part of these silks are for zanána use, the narrow widths and crude colours preventing their adoption by Europeans. *Susís* or fabrics of mixed silk and cotton do not seem to be regularly made.

Cotton.

Wool.

Silk.

The *iláqaband's* trade which in the time of Mahárája Ranjít Singh was an extensive one, is now probably of but small commercial importance, but recently the *patoli* worker has taken to making gold thread whips and knots, crowns, &c., for uniforms. Much taste and ingenuity are shown in such small articles as *pajáma* strings, ornaments, bed cords braids, tassels, &c., which make a considerable show in the bazár.

Patoli work.

Chapter IV, B.

Occupations, Industries and Communications.

The immense improvement noticed as taking place in carpentry and cabinet making ten years ago, has steadily continued, and within the last decade the production of not merely articles of utility, which have however also been produced in increasing numbers, but also of articles for decorative purposes, luxuries, has been remarkably large. While the beginning of the production of improved furniture might be traceable to the influence of the Railway Workshops, the inspiration for the articles of luxury may be traced to the Mayo School of Art, which, it is admitted, has had, and continues to have a decided influence on carpentry, as well as upon other branches of manufacture, such as cotton prints, metal work, &c. This is partly due to objects actually made in the schools, to designs and suggestions given to bazár craftsmen, and to its connection with exhibitions held at London, Paris, Melbourne, Lahore and Calcutta, for which it has acted as agent. Its aim is to recur as much as possible to the best types of indigenous design, and to make more widely known the actual state and capabilities of the arts of the province. In some branches the School of Art has been of great use and has both stimulated demand and increased production. A comparatively large trade is now being carried on in carved *pinjra* work, screens, brackets, overmantels, cabinets, &c., executed in deodar and shisham wood; and the majority of such articles would compare, for workmanship alone, most favourably with the cabinet work of Europe; while the designs are characteristic and frequently exceedingly good.

Woodwork, furniture, &c.

It may be safely said that the carelessness and want of neatness formerly complained of are very much less now than ten years ago; and the tendency is still to improve along these lines. So that with the continued and combined influences of the Railway Workshops, the Railway Technical School and the Mayo School of Art, the carpentry and cabinet making of the district should reach a very high level.

Carelessness and idleness are the faults most frequently complained of in connection with the men employed in the Railway Workshops, but it is doubtful whether the Punjabi is more averse to labour than the rest of the world, while it is certain that for generations his industry has been of a desultory and intermittent sort. The independent workman is frequently very laborious, but he works at his own hours. Sometimes in the hot weather he turns night into day; and social customs demand that he shall be free to take a day or two when he choses. So it is not unnatural that he should find the regular recurrence of the factory bell tiresome. The carelessness and want of neatness may perhaps be considered a local peculiarity, to some extent. The Punjab industrial and agricultural races when compared with those of the Deccan for example, seem to be much less neat and handy; while their implements are rougher, and their homes more untidy. But there is no denying that they sometimes show an energy and capacity not often found in the south. It is noticeable that much of the good furniture, which owing to the frequent changes among the Europeans who own it may be described as "in circulation" has been produced by solitary workmen usually under European direction, but occasionally carrying out their own designs.

It is a good sign that several of these men are now establishing something like shops with a view to offering a continuous supply of furniture, and those who have so far advanced beyond their former casual ways of business, are generally doing well; and there seems to be some hope of the carpenter and cabinet maker developing a capacity for small commercial transactions sufficient to emancipate him from the toils of the middle man.

It is, however, still a fact that the *kabáris* have most of the retail trade in their hands, and their shops offer a curious and unpicturesque combination of the suburban furniture shop, the marine store, and the old book stall. Some of the tradesmen employed what would in England be called "shop hands" who put together cheap cupboards and other articles of furniture in wood, cut from the outsides of deodár logs, and afterwards covered with cheap resin varnish.

Chapter VI, B.

Occupations, Industries and Communications.

One or two enterprising Sikh carpenters have started carriage and cart building, and are doing fairly well.

Metalwork. Copper. Brass.

The copper bázár in the city presents the usual busy and noisy scene. The greater part of the wares sold are imported. Roughly hammered and perforated copper *pándáns* from Lucknow, finely beaten plain copper *degchís* from Delhi and brass wares from other places in the Punjab are to be seen. Antimony bottles and other small articles are cast in Lahore, but there is not a large production of cast brass.

Silver and gold.

Hindús say it shows disrespect for the metal to wear gold ornaments below the waist. Silver should be used there. Similarly, many goldsmiths decline to work in silver as being *infra digni-tatem.*

It cannot be said that there are any characteristic ornaments of Lahore, but the elaborate ones usually made in large cities, such as *batua* a pretty triangular shaped scent bottle with an open work body and clusters of little bells, worn by newly married girls; *tád*, an armlet worn by women; *ghungriánwála bála*, ear-rings having little hanging balls attached; *tarági*, a waist girdle, &c., are made here. There are several silversmiths who show considerable skill in their work, if they are allowed to take their own time on it. But now that the *saráf* has become the middleman, and regularly employs silversmiths that he may supply his clients with ready made articles, perhaps there is a danger that less care will be shown in the work than was the case under the old system when the customer advanced a sum of money and was perforce content to wait until such time as it should please the artist to finish the ornament desired.

From one to four annas is the price per tola generally paid for silver work, while for gold the rate is from four annas to one rupee, and then alloy is frequently mixed with the gold. So that the goldsmith's trade is a distinctly profitable one.

Sale engraving.

There are a few *mohrkands* or seal engravers, and some of them work with great neatness. They never attempt glass engraving, for which their tools are perfectly suitable, and are content with a small but regular practice in signet rings and amulets.

Tin.

The pure metal has long been used for tinning copper, cooking and drinking vessels, but the import of sheet tin is not great, although increasing. The material generally used for an immense variety of articles, milk measures, culinary utensils, lamps, cash boxes, clothes boxes, &c., &c., is the kerosine tin; which when empty finds a ready sale in the bázár. The whitesmith is fairly expert, although his tools are not of the handiest and lead to a lavish use of solder. The kersoine tin flattened out is in favour also as a roofing material.

Electroplating.

There are only one or two men in Lahore who practise this comparatively new trade; and their work is generally inferior; showing too great an economy of the silver; so that it quickly rubs off. The electroplaters are mostly of the Chumar caste and their customers are nearly all Europeans, the native having at present no use for such an expensive luxury.

Blacksmithing and koft work.

This is not in a very flourishing condition and is limited to common lock making, repairs to carriages and carts, and little odd jobs generally. A very small amount of *koft* work is done by one family, although it was an art that was very largely practised in Ranjit Singh's time.

Native pictures.

A few men make a fair living by the production of pictures rudely done in water colours, of Hindu mythological subjects, which are to be seen at every local fair, and at certain suitable spots in the city, where a blank wall gives an opportunity for displaying the work. The prices are cheaper than those of the highly varnished chromo-lithographs of the same subjects that come from Germany.

Photography.

This has of late become a very popular amusement with natives, and they show remarkable aptitude for mastering the technique of the science. About half a dozen men have taken to it as a profession and are doing fairly well.

In the Mayo School of Art an effort is being made to introduce certain of the photo-mechanical processes for the reproduction of book illustrations, &c. Should this be successful, it is believed great benefits will accrue therefrom in the better production of text-books, school and ordinary literature locally produced; and in creating a new and popular industry, for popular it is bound to be.

Lahore has naturally been always a great brick-burning place, for there is not a stone to be found for many miles round. The old Brick-making. fashioned native brick is scarcely thicker than an English "quarry," but it was often so well made and burnt as to resist the alkaline efflorescence which is the bane of all buildings raised on this salt soil. Of late years, bricks of English sizes have been used, and the results in a technical sense are admirable.

The Railway Station buildings are excellent as brick work, and more recent buildings show a similar quality of workmanship. The Municipality and private firms are now producing first rate bricks in considerable quantities. The introduction in the plinth of new buildings of courses of glazed bricks to prevent the attacks of the destructive alkaline efflorescence has often been talked about, and it is surprising that the Public Works Department has not hitherto attempted any cure for a canker which seriously threatens the life of every building it raises. The practice of cutting and carving burnt brick, formerly common in some parts of England is here carried to unusual perfection : and finials, mouldings, columns and bases, and the small tabernacles in door jambs in which lamps are placed, are skilfully wrought. The work is often done with no other tool than a chopping instrument such as a *tesha* or adze.

The practice of constructing a latrine on the roofs of native houses, which, it is desirable to enclose for the sake of privacy, while securing ventilation has led to the manufacture of open grille work in large pieces cut through the green clay with oblique perforations in geometric or sometimes floral patterns. In an architectural sense nothing could be more decorative, but it is an element of native design, until recently, unaccountably neglected by our modern architects. The Executive Engineer, Lahore, has however recently introduced a press for making pierced bricks; and these bricks have been used with considerable success in some of the new buildings; notably in the new Jubilee Museum and Technical Institute.

Flooring tiles are made in large quantities, but they are uniformly bad, crooked, soft and ill-fitted together. A good flooring tile is Tiles. the great *desideratum* of Upper India, and it is hopeless to expect the ordinary clay of the plains to resist damp from below and wear from above. The refractory clay from Rániganj is now made into first rate tiles burnt at a great heat with coal; and possessing some of the qualities of Staffordshire tiles, nothing that can be done with more alluvial brick earth can ever rival such tiles.

The plasterer's business, considering the vast surfaces covered with the material, is in a backward and unsatisfactory condition. Other building trades. Two or three years play havoc with the work. The cause is the increased cost of labour which prohibits thorough grinding and workmanship. Another fault is that less fibrous material is now mixed in the plaster than formerly, so that it lacks tenacity, and bond.

In architectural woodwork the rebuilding of parts of the city consequent on the demolitions for the water-works showed that much of the skill which is so evident on the carved fronts of the last century still survives. This is due in great part to the fact that the elementary training of each youth who learns the carpenter's trade largely consists of practice in drawing and carving flowers and foliage relief.

Reference has been made to the Steam, Oil and Flour Mills established about ten years back in Lahore. The enterprise continues Oils, turpentine, varnishes. to be a successful one, the outturn of oil being now about 2,000 maunds per mensem; which is sold in the country and exported to Europe. The Company's capital is Rs. 1,70,000. All the oils seem of good quality, clear and free from impurities. Linseed oil varnish is manufactured and largely consumed by Government and Railways.

Turpentine is already distilled by natives in such quantities as to be sold at a cheap rate, from *ganda baroza*, the rezin of the deodar; and perhaps, of other needle woods in the hills. The distillation is not very perfect, and the spirit reserves the characteristic sweet odour of the rezin, but it is quite good enough

Chapter IV, B.

Occupations,
Industries and
Communications.

for painting purposes. Common *rál* or rezin varnish is made by painters ; but much time and labour are lost with imperfect apparatus in the preparation in small quantities of the superior *sundras* varnish.

Oil cake.

Rape and *til* cakes are sold in the country and linseed cake chiefly exported. Castor cake is exported and despatched to the North-Western Provinces and Bengal for manure. The Punjab farmers do not use it although it is a valuable manure.

Flour.

The outturn from the flour mills is about 300 maunds of flour and *atta* per day. In connection with the flour mill powerful hydraulic machinery is used for the manufacture of compressed food for cattle.

Candles and soap.

It has been found that the superior quality of Lahore made soap is of unusual excellence, and it is used in large quantities for washing wool, &c., in the Egerton Woollen Mill at Dhariwál. A native firm makes exceedingly good toilet soap from cocoanut oil, which is finding considerable favour. The trade in tallow candles too is a fairly thriving one ; but the kerosine oil lamp is rapidly supplanting both these and the dirty, smoky *shamadan* or *cherágh.*

Printing, lithography, book-binding, &c.

There is perhaps no one of the arts imported from England that has been accepted with more readiness than that of printing. Though capable of being treated so as to almost reach the dignity of a fine art, the business is in itself not very difficult to learn. There are several native presses where very fair work is produced, which however would be still better were better ink and paper used. Lithography though much used for the vernacular papers, &c., is in a poor way ; and anything pictorial produced by this process, is as a rule too bad for words. Some good work is occasionally done under the superintendence of the Mayo School of Art. A Bengali has just started a lithographic press which turns out work far superior to the older ones. He is also a very good die-sinker, the only one in Lahore. One man is making rubber stamps very successfully.

Book-binding has been learnt by men employed at the Railway, Jail, Government and Mission presses ; but it is generally lacking in finish, although steadily improving.

Chúnián and Kasúr.

In Chúnián and Kasúr fine leather and brass *huqás* are made ; excellent shoes and lacquered spinning-wheels. In the latter place very fine cotton *darris* are also made.

Course and nature of trade.

There are no statistics available for the general trade of the district and very incomplete figures for the trade of Lahore city even. The only returns available are of commodities which pay octroi duty on being brought within municipal limits. Particulars of these will be found in Chapter VI, Section A. The exports and imports of food-grains have already been noticed at page 174.

Prices of commodities and land.

Table No. XXVI gives the retail market prices of commodities for the last ten years.

The prices of land, sold or mortgaged, at different periods according to the sale and mortgage statistics furnished in Table XXXIV are shown in the margin, but the quality of land varies so enormously and the prices returned are so often fictitious that the

	Sales.	Mortgages.
1869 to 1878 ...	20	22
1879 to 1888 ...	29	26
1889 to 1891 ...	42	35

figures have little value save to show that the price of land has risen gradually and rapidly during the last twenty years. A more accurate estimate of the present true selling price of land in different parts of the district is given below :—

Chapter IV, B.

Occupations,
Industries and
Communications.

Prices of com-
modities and land.

Price per acre.

Lands round Lahore city ...	Irrigated ...	...	Rs. 500
	Unirrigated	...	„ 100
Other land in Lahore tahsíl ...	Irrigated ...	...	„ 100
	Unirrigated	...	„ 60
Land in Kasúr tahsíl	Irrigated ...	...	„ 80
	Unirrigated	...	„ 30
Land in Chúnián tahsíl ...	Irrigated ...	...	„ 60
	Unirrigated	...	„ 25
Land in Sharakpur tahsíl ...	Irrigated ...	...	„ 45
	Unirrigated	...	„ 10

The wages of labour are shown in Table No. XXVII for the last ten years. The figures are taken from Table No. 46 of the Annual Administration Report for the Province. 　　*Wages of labour.*

The local unit of area best recognised by the people is the ghumáo, which in the Bári Doáb portion of the district is equivalent to ·826 of an acre and in the Rechna Doáb portion to a full English acre. The complete table of areas is as follows :— 　　*Local measure-ment.*

1 Karam square	...	...	= 1 Sirsáhi.
9 Square sirsáhis	...	...	= 1 Marla.
20 Marlas	...	...	= 1 Kanál.
8 Kanáls	...	...	= 1 Ghumáo.

But in the Bári Doáb the karam is 60 inches or 5 feet and in the Rechna Doáb it is 66 inches or 5½ feet, so that each measure, that can be expressed in karams, means different areas north and south of the Rávi. On the north 8 kanáls make an acre ; while on the south an acre is equivalent to 9·68 kanáls and this is the figure that must be used as the divisor in reducing kanáls into acres. To convert ghumáos into acres south of the Rávi add two ciphers and divide twice by eleven : to convert acres into ghumáos multiply twice by eleven and reject the two last figures.

It is unfortunate that two standards of measurement should exist in the same district, and even in the same pargana ; but if the statute acre is adhered to in matters of calculation there will

---

*This does not refer to building land.

be little inconvenience, provided that the fact of the difference is borne in mind. The bigha, which is sometimes used by the people in speaking of the amount of land they hold, more especially in the highly cultivated portions of the district, consists of four kanáls or one-half of a ghumáo.

Local weights and measures.

The following tables give the local measures of weight and capacity :—

1	chhaták	= 5 Rs. weight.	2	duséris	= 1 chauséri.
2	chhatáks	= 1 adhpáo.	5	sérs	= 1 panséri.
2	adhpáos	= 1 pao.	2	panséris	= 1 dasséri.
2	páos	= 1 ádhsér.	2	dasséris	= 1 bisséri.
2	ádhsérs	= 1 sér.	2	bisséris	= 1 maund.
2	sérs	= 1 duséri.			

N. B.—Dasséri and *Bisséri* are not very common.

8	rattís	= 1 másha.	2	panjtolias	= 1 dastolia.
12	máshás	= 1 tola.	2	dastolias	= 1 bistolia.
5	tolas	= 1 panjtolia.	50	tolas	= 1 pachástolia.

There are different standards in the different parts of the district ; for instance in the Mangtanwála village, tahsil Sharakpur :—

1	adhpáo	= 1 chuhá.	16	topás	= 1 maund.
4	chuhás	= 1 paropi.	10	maunds	= 1 khalmár.
4	paropís	= 1 topá.			

In the village of Muridkí :—

1½	chhatáks	= 1 chuhá.	16	topás	= 1 maund.
4	chuhás	= 1 paropi.	2½	maunds	= 1 máhni.
4	paropís	= 1 topá			

In the Tappa village, tahsil Chúnián :—

1¼	ser	= 1 topá.	16	topás	= 1 maund.

In the Kanganpura ilaqa :—

14	sérs	= 1 topa.	16	topas	= 1 maund.

On the banks of the Sutlej, Chúnián tahsil :—

4	sérs	= 1 topá.	16	topás	= 1 maund.

On the banks of the Rávi :—

2	sérs	= 1 topá.	16	topás	= 1 maund.

In the Lahore villages in the Rechna Doáb :—

Chapter IV, B.

Occupations,
Industries and
Communications.

Local weights and
measures.

4 paropís	= 1 topa.	4 pais	= 1 maund.
2 topas	= 1 daropa.	12½ maunds	= 1 máhni.
2 daropas	= 1 pai.	¼ máhni	= 1 pand.

The *Lahori* or *Pukka* maund in use in the city in all trade transactions connected with the sale of raw silk, fur, potatoes, tobacco, milk, onions, tea and limes weighs 50 standard sérs. For sugar and dried fruits 42½ sérs is reckoned as a maund. In the sale of fresh fruit additional allowance of 30 per cent. is made, that is 130 count as 100.

The figures in the margin show the communications of the

Communications.	Miles.
Railways	126
Metalled roads ...	186
Unmetalled roads	862

district as returned in quinquennial Table No. I of the Administration Report for 1892-93, while Table No. XLVI shows the distances from place to place as authoritatively fixed for the purpose of calculating travelling allowance. Table No. XIX shows the area taken up by Government for communications within the district. Of the metalled roads 73 miles are within the municipal limits of Lahore.

Of river traffic there is little or none. Neither on the Sutlej nor on the Ravi is navigation easy enough to attract cargo boats, but on the latter timber is floated down from Chamba as far as Lahore when the river is in flood.

The Delhi-Peshawar branch of the North-Western Railway was formerly known as the Sindh Punjab and Delhi Railway as far as Lahore, and the continuation beyond Lahore which was laid down between 1876 and 1884 was the Punjab Northern State Railway. The contract of the Sindh Punjab and Delhi Company with Government expired on the 31st December 1884, from which date Government took over the line under its own management, and the Delhi-Peshawar Railway, with its branches and extensions, is now worked by the Public Works Department under the name of the North-Western Railway. The main line from Umballa running nearly due west crosses the Lahore and Amritsar border at the village of Wágha and preserving a westerly course to within a mile or so of Lahore, then takes a sharpish curve and two miles or less after leaving Lahore city has an almost direct northerly course, running parallel to and within a few hundred yards of the old Trunk Road from Lahore to Peshawar. A mile or mile-and-a-half from Lahore city it crosses the Ravi river by a bridge which formerly had 33 spans and a length of 3,218 feet. In the last year or two 15 spans on the right bank and three spans on the left have been closed, and the bridge has thereby been

reduced to only 15 spans over the channel proper, or to a length
of 1,456 feet. For the passage of the railway a new bridge
has been constructed alongside of the old on the basis of
the former piers which have been extended upstream, and the
old bridge is to be utilised as a road for wheeled traffic ; whether
this will ultimately bring about the abandonment of the present
line of road which lies over the bridge of boats a quarter of a
mile or more below where the railway crosses the river is not
certain. No such step is under contemplation at present. The
Mooltan and Karáchi branch of the North-Western system runs
nearly due south for a distance of 26 miles from Lahore as far
as Ráiwind ; from there it takes a half westerly turn and leaves
this district after a course of 66 miles on the further side of
Wán Rádha Rám station.

The Kasúr and Ferozepore branch leaves the Mooltan line at
Ráiwind junction, has stations at Rájajang, 3 miles from Ráiwind ;
Rukhanwala, 8 miles ; Kasúr, 16 miles and Gunda Singhwála, 23
miles. At the last named place the railway crosses the Sutlej
by the Gunda Singhwála bridge which was opened formally
by His Honor the Lieutenant-Governor of the Punjab in April
1887.

The table below shows the principal roads of the district
together with the halting places on them and the conveniences
for travellers to be found on each. The bridge-of-boats by which
the Lahore and Peshawar metalled road is carried across the
Rávi is maintained throughout the year. It rests on 37 boats
in all and is 987 feet in length. All wheeled traffic passing over
the bridge has to pay toll, the amount of which varies according
to the conveyance. The collection of the tolls is kept under
direct management ; the gross income therefore varies considerably : in the year 1891-92 it was Rs. 15,250, in the following year
it was Rs. 28,450. Against these receipts however a heavy
outlay of seven or eight thousand rupees is incurred.

Route.	Halting Place.	Distance in miles.	REMARKS.
Grand Trunk Road, Lahore to Peshawar.	Lahore	...	
	Sháhdara	4	G. T. Road. Sarái, encamping-ground, supply depôt, well. Road bungalow (*Bárádari* at head of boat-bridge).
	Muridke	12	G. T. Road. Sarái, encamping-ground, supply depôt, well. Civil rest-house.
	Khari	6	G. T. Road. District ends.

Chapter IV, B.
———
Occupations.
Industries, and
Communications,

Roads, rest-houses
and   encamping-
grounds.

Route.	Halting Place.	Distance in miles.	Remarks.
Grand Trunk Road, Lahore to Ferozepore.	Lahore	...	
	Kána Kácha	14	G. T. Road. Encamping-ground, supply depôt, well. Road bungalow.
	Luliáni	9	G. T. Road. Encamping-ground, supply depôt, well. Road bungalow,
	Kasúr	9	G. T. Road. Encamping-ground, supply depôt, well. Civil rest-house, road bungalow.
	Ganda Singhwála (on the banks of the Sutlej)	8	G. T. Road. Encampting-ground, supply depôt. well, saráI, canal bungalow. Railway station.
Kasúr to Ráiwind.	Kasúr	...	
	Rukhánwála	9	Unmetalled Railway station.
	Ráiwind	9	Metalled. Railway station, supply depôt, well, saráI with quarters for Europeans.
G. T. Road, Lahore to Amritsar.	Lahore	...	
	Chabíl or Munáwáu ...	10	G. T. Road. Encamping-ground, saráI, supply depôt, well. Police rest-house.
	Wagha...	8	G. T. Road. Canal rest-house. District ends.
Lahore to Harike.	Lahore	..	
	Haríke	47	Unmetalled, viá Mian Mír and Patti, well.
Lahore to Mooltan.	Lahore	...	
	Parade Chauburji ...	2	Metalled. Encamping-ground, well.
	Niáz Beg	6	Metalled for 4½ miles. Encamping-ground, well. Canal rest-house.
	Chúng...	5	Unmetalled. Police rest-house, encamping-ground, supply depôt, well.
	Manga...	12	Unmetalled. Police rest-house, encamping-ground, supply depôt, well.
	Bhái Pheru	10	Unmetalled. Police rest-house, encamping-ground, supply depôt, well.
	Saráí Mughal... ...	8	Unmetalled. Police rest-house, encamping-ground, supply depôt, well,
	Halla	8	Unmetalled. District ends.
Chúnián to Mooltan.	Chúnián	...	Civil rest-house, saráI, supply depôt, well.
	Wán Rádha Rám ...	15	Unmetalled. Encamping-ground, saráI with quarters for Europeans, supply depôt, well. Railway station.

Chapter IV, B.

**Occupations,
Industries and
Communications.**

Roads, rest-houses
and encamping-
grounds.

Route.	Halting Place.	Distance in miles.	REMARKS.
Chúnián to Feroze-pore.	Chúnián	...	
	Rájowál	12	Unmetalled. Encamping-ground, supply depôt, well.
	Khudián	6	Unmetalled. Encamping-ground, Police rest-house.
	Tárágarh	5	Unmetalled. Small encamping-ground, supply depôt, well.
	Ganda Singhwála ...	...	Unmetalled. Encamping-ground, supply depôt, well, sarái, canal bungalow, Railway station.
Chúnián to Chánga Mánga.	Chúnián	...	
	Chánga Mánga ...	10	Unmetalled. Sarái with quarters for Europeans, supply depôt, well, Railway station
Kasúr to Patti.	Kasúr	...	
	Khem Karn	6	Metalled. Canal bungalow.
	Valtoha	6	Unmetalled. Police rest-house.
	Patti	16	Do. do.
Amritsar to Ferozepore.	Sur Singh	...	Unmetalled.
	Álgún Hardo	8	Do. Canal bungalow.
	Khem Karn	11	Do.
	Ganda Singhwála ...	8	Do. (see above).
Lahore to Sháhpur.	Lahore	...	
	Mandiáli	10	Unmetalled. Road bungalow, En-camping-ground, supply depôt.
Lahore to Sharakpur.	Lahore	...	
	Sháhdara	4	G T. Road (see above).
	Burj Atári	7	Unmetalled.
	Sharakpur	10	Do. Civil rest-house. Sarái with supply depôt.
Sharakpur to Shekhú-pura.	Sharakpur	...	
	Shekhúpura ...	18	Unmetalled. Encamping-ground, supply depôt.
Chúnián to Kangan-pur.	Chúnián	...	
	Kanganpur	16	Unmetalled. Police rest-house.
Kanganpur to Ganda Singhwála.	Kanganpur	...	Police rest-house.
	Mokal	6	Unmetalled. Bárádari.
	Doburji	13	Do. Encamping-ground.
	Ganda Singhwála ...	13½	Do. (see above)

In addition to the above there are a large number of village cross roads, some of them kept up under the control of the Local Fund Boards, some mere village tracks. On the whole the roads in the district are not in good order. Outside the Grand Trunk Roads and Municipal limits the best roads in the district are found along the bank of the main branches of the Bári Doáb Canal across which bridges leading from

Chapter IV, B.
——
Occupations,
Industries and
Communications.

Roads, rest-houses
and encamping-
grounds.

Rest-houses.

one side to the other are thrown at intervals of two miles or so. The canal roads are not metalled but they are very well consolidated and usually overgrown with grass which offers most pleasant driving and riding. Table No. XLVI shows the distances from place to place in the district.

There are district rest-houses at Chúnián, Kasúr and Sharakpur; Police bungalows at Waltoha, Patti, Khudián, Kangánpur, Saráí Mughal, Bhái Pheru, Ráiwind Chung, and Mangtanwála. At Chánga Mánga, Umarabad and Murídkí saráí rooms are kept for District officers on tour. There are Public Works road rest-houses at Kahna, Luliáni, Kála Shah Káku and Mandiáli. The Canal Department has rest-houses at Wágah, Dogaich, Klás Mári, Niázbeg, Amar Sidhu, Her and Jaman in Lahore tahsíl ; at Khálra, Algon, Manihála, Patti, Pohuwind, Khem Káran, Rukhanwála, Husain Kanwan in Kasúr tahsíl ; at Bhamba, Gundián, Chánga Mánga, Kanwan, Ladi, Lole Jattán, and Mámuki Sharaf in the Chúnián tahsíl. These rest-houses are all fitted with the more necessary furniture, but with the exception of some of the District and Police rest-houses have no cooking utensils or servants.

During the cold weather months the river stream of the Sutlej and the Rávi, especially the latter, sinks very low and in many places people can cross on foot or on horseback. During the hot weather however and sometimes in the cold weather after heavy rain the rivers are impassable, except in the ferry boats, which ply from one side to the other. The following statement shows the number of minor ferries on the Rávi and their stations, with the number of boats maintained at each :—

No.	Name of Ferry.	Miles from point at which river enters district.	Number of boats maintained at each.
1	Dhana	1	2
2	Talwára Marl	4	2
3	Lakhodher	8	2
4	Karaul	9	8
5	Kadián	12	3
6	Faizpur	18	3
7	Saggián Atári	20	5
8	Sádhwar	21	2
9	Niáz Beg	22	2
10	Shahpur	24	2
11	Chung	28	2
12	Mohlanwál	30	2
13	Khudpur	32	3
14	Rángílpur	34	2
15	Mánga	38	2
16	Lakhanke	42	3
17	Maddrán	48	2
18	Malewál	50	2
19	Asal, Jajja and Naroke	54	2
20	Guruke Duln	57	1
21	Aujla and Alpa	62	2

Chapter IV, B.

Occupations, Industries and Communications.

River ferries.

The establishment maintained at each ferry consists of four boatmen from the 16th May to the 16th September when the river is in flood and of two boatmen for the rest of the year. The men and boats are provided by contractors who take the ferries under separate annual leases, and in return for monthly payments to Government, the amount of which depends on the results of the lease auctions held at the beginning of the year, are invested with the right to collect the ferry dues. The contractors pay their boatmen by a half share of the dues from 16th May to the 16th September and by a third share for the remainder of the year. The rates paid at the minor river ferries vary from one pie to one rupee according to the nature and weight of the animal or other article conveyed across. A foot passenger pays three pies, a sheep goat or pig one pie ; other animals pay in proportion to their size and weight, the charge for a beast laden being double what it is for one unladen. The villagers along the bank of the river usually compound with the contractors for fixed grain payments, entitling them to go and carry to and fro across the river as they will without charge.

The minor ferries were formerly under the management of the Deputy Commissioner : of late years they have been surrendered to the Local Boards in consideration of a fixed annual payment to Government equal to something less than the total net profits which Government had heretofore obtained from the ferries. At present the District Board pays to Government each year on this account Rs. 8,954. The income from the ferries varies. For the three years 1888 to 1891 it averaged over Rs. 11,000 ; in 1892-93, which was an exceptionally unfavorable year, the gross receipts only reached Rs. 8,063. The income depends principally on the quantity of water in the river during the year. If people can cross the stream by natural fords, it is not to be expected that they will use ferries for which they have to pay. Against their gross receipts the District Board incur expenditure on Ferry establishment, averaging nearly Rs. 800 per annum, the principal item of which is the Darogha of Ferries salary at Rs. 30 a month.

The Rájghát or Shahdara bridge-of-boats,

The chief road of communication across the Rávi in this district lies over the bridge-of-boats which is maintained throughont the year at Shahdára, two miles or so distant from the Lahore city. This bridge is constructed with planks laid over 31 large boats of the country pattern which rise and fall with the river flood. Straw is laid over the planks and the sides of the bridge are closed n with rails. A permanent establishment of 15 boatmen is retained on the bridge for its custody and maintenance in good repair. These are paid from Rs. 6 to Rs. 8 a month. The charges for transit are the same as for the minor ferries mentioned above. Carriages drawn by horses pay from one rupee to two annas according to the class of carriage. The collection of ferry dues in some years is kept under direct management of the District Officers, in other years it is leased out to a contractor : the former method is resorted

to if no contractor offers a high enough bid for the lease. **Chapter IV, B.**
There is a considerable expenditure on maintenance and repairs
of the bridge, and new boats are required every now and again. **Occupations, Industries and**
The income and expenditure of the last five years are shown **Communications.**
below :—

The Rájghát or Shahdara bridge-of-boats.

Years.							Income.	Expenditure.
							Rs.	Rs.
1888-89 ...	...	...	...	...	...	...	14,631	8,806
1889-90 ...	...	...	...	..	...	...	16,340	9,899
1890-91 ...	...	...	...	..	...	...	15,125	10,333
1891-92 ...	...	...	...	...	...	...	15,250	7,829
1892-93 ...	...	...	...	...	...	...	23,449	7,722
1893-94 ...	...	...	...	...	...	...	28,552	...

All the Sutlej ferries between this district and Ferozepore **Ferries on the Sutlej.**
are managed from the latter district. Nothing is known here
of their maintenance or income. The locality of each ferry is
indicated in the following statement :—

River.	Name of ferry in Ferozepore district.			Lahore village nearest to the ferry.	Tahsíl of Lahore district.
Sutlej ...	Harike ...	...	...	Harike	
	Rukanwála	...	...	Bandala Ghulám.	
	Masteke Pár	...	...	Masteke War.	Kasúr.
	Kandeke	...	...	Masteke.	
	Mamdot	...	...	Thatthi Faríd.	
	...	...	...	Doburji	
	Mattar ...	...	...	Dhingke.	
	Bahádarke	...	...	Saddar.	Chúnián.
	Panjgirain	...	...	Mokul.	
	Maddeke	...	...	Babuliána Hithár.	
	Megha ...	...	...	Shahbázke.	

The postal service in the Lahore district is good. Outside **Postal communication.**
Lahore itself there are six district sub-offices at Chánga-
Mánga, Chúnián, Kasúr, Mian Mír, Ráiwind and Sharakpur,
through which letters pass to and from the village post offices :
of these last there are in the district altogether 55.

The General Post Office which stands in Anárkali near
the Central Museum was built in 1849 and has since been added
to and improved. All deliveries in the civil station and city,
except in the Railway quarter, are made from the General Post
Office five times a day, except on Sundays and other general
holidays, when only one delivery is made. In the Railway
quarter the post is delivered from the Naulakha office, twice on
week days and once on Sundays. Besides these there are five
post offices within the walls of the city, one in Mozang village
which forms part of the civil station, and a sub-office near the

Chapter IV, B.
—
Occupations,
Industries and
Communications.

The   Telegraph
Office.

Charing Cross Hotel. None of these deliver letters but only receive. Also there are letter boxes everywhere, 18 in the city and 26 in the civil station.

Lahore is provided with first class telegraphic communication to the rest of India, duplex lines working to Calcutta, Karáchi, Simla, Agra, Quetta, Ráwalpindi and Peshawar.

The head office is a fine building very centrally situated at the junction of the roads opposite the Accountant-General's office (Sháh Chirágh). It was erected in 1882 and considerably enlarged in 1892. The main building affords accommodation for the Signal Office, the Assistant Superintendent's Office, the Telegraph Master in charge, and the Testing Telegraph Master; there are also two barracks accommodating twelve signallers each. The staff of the head office consists of one first grade Telegraph Master, three 4th grade Telegraph Masters, one Testing Telegraph Master, one Telephone Clerk and six ordinary Clerks.

There is also a sub-office at Mian Mir in charge of a Telegraph Master and worked by three military signallers.

Lahore is the head-quarters of the Lahore sub-division of Telegraphs which extends to Mooltan, Ferozepore, Montgomery and Jhang. The technical management of the Telegraph Offices along the Railways, within the limits named above is also under the Lahore Office.

Telephone   ex-
change.

The Telephone exchange is worked from the head Telegraph Office, and connects with the following offices :—Police exchange, Charing Cross, District Police Office, Government House, Public Works Secretariat. The Police exchange, Charing Cross, connects with the Central Jail, the Anárkali Police station, and the Police lines in the city. A single line connects the General Post Office in Anárkali with the Naulakha Post Office. There is also a Telephone exchange at Mian Mir connecting with the main offices of the military station.

CHAPTER V.

ADMINISTRATION AND FINANCE.

SECTION A.—GENERAL ADMINISTRATION.

The Lahore district is under the administrative control of
the Commissioner of the Lahore Division, whose head-quarters
are at Lahore. The ordinary head-quarter staff of the district
consists of the Deputy Commissioner (who is also Magistrate of
the District, Collector and Registrar), two Assistant Commissioners, and four Extra Assistant Commissioners, one of whom
is the Revenue Assistant, and another is the Treasury Officer. The other Assistants perform criminal, revenue and
miscellaneous executive work under the control of the Deputy
Commissioner, and also whatever civil judicial work may
be made over to them by the District Judge. An Assistant
Commissioner, if he can be spared, or if not, an Extra Assistant
Commissioner, included in the staff above stated, is posted
to the Kasúr outpost, which includes the charge of the two
tahsíls of Chúnián and Kasúr with Kasúr as head-quarters.
Each tahsíl is in subordinate charge of a Tahsíldár, who ordinarily exercises the criminal powers of a second class Magistrate, the civil powers of a Munsiff of the second grade, and on
the revenue side the powers of a second grade Assistant
Collector. Under him is a Náib-Tahsíldár with the same civil
powers, but with criminal powers of the third class only. The
village record staff working under a sadr kánúngo with one
Assistant is of the strength shown below :—

Tahsíl.	Office.	Field.	Patwárís.	Assistant patwárís.
Lahore	1	4	81	4
Chúnián	1	4	82	2
Kasúr	1	4	83	3
Sharakpur	1	3	70	2
Total	4	15	316	11

The chief Judicial officer is the Divisional judge, who
sits at Lahore and is also Sessions Judge, exercising civil and
criminal powers within the jurisdiction of the Lahore district.

The District Judge ordinarily does only civil judicial work,
original and appellate. There are four Munsiffs in the district,
one for each tahsíl, each with second class Munsiff's powers.
Those of the Kasúr and Chunián tahsíls hold their court at
the head-quarters of their respective tahsíls ; the Munsiffs of

Chapter V, A.

General Administration.

Cantonment Magistrate.

Honorary Magistrates.

Lahore and Sharakpur tahsíls both sit at the district head-quarters. A Small Cause Court Judge also sits at Lahore.

The Cantonment Magistrate at Mian Mir exercises criminal powers of the first class within the military cantonments and some civil judicial powers as well.

A bench of Honorary Magistrates has been invested with criminal jurisdiction of the second class within prescribed limits which, roughly speaking embrace the city; the sadr bázár of Anárkali and the north-west corner of the civil station. On this bench are eight Magistrates who can exercise the powers granted to the bench when sitting in pairs; while some have the privilege of exercising second or third class powers sitting individually. Three Honorary Magistrates have been given magisterial powers of the first class over the whole district and civil judicial powers up to certain limits as well, and three others exercise second class criminal powers within certain defined village limits. The number and value of civil suits regarding moveable and immoveable property and the number of revenue cases in the last ten years are given in Table No. XXXIX and details of criminal trials in Table No. XL.

Registration.

Four non-official Sub-Registrars have been appointed, who register deeds at Lahore, Kasúr, Chúnián and Sharakpur. At the three outlying tahsíls, in the absence of the Sub-Registrar, the Tahsíldár or Náib-Tahsíldár registers deeds in his capacity as Joint Sub-Registrar. At the sadr, if the Sub-Registrar is absent, the Deputy Commissioner, who is Registrar of the district, appoints a person to perform the duties, under the power invested in the Registrar by Section 12 of the Registration Act. The Cantonment Magistrate is *ex-officio* Sub-Registrar for Mian Mír cantonments. The number of deeds registered at each registration centre during the last ten years is shown in Table No. XXXIIIA.

Police.

The police force is controlled by a District Superintendent and one or more Assistants. The District Superintendent and one of the Assistants receive an extra allowance of Rs. 100 and Rs. 50, respectively, for the special charge of the city of Lahore. The strength of the force on 1st January 1894 is shown in the margin. In addition to this force there are twelve town-watchmen on Rs. 5 per mensem in

Class of Police.	Total strength.	DISTRIBUTION.	
		Standing guards.	Protection and detection.
District (Provincial).	875	212	663
Cantonment ...	67	...	67
Municipal ...	488	9	479
Canal	...	...	...
River	...	...	...
Ferry	...	...	...
Total ...	1,430	221	1,209

town Patti, with one daffadár on Rs. 8 and eight town-watchmen on Rs. 5 in Sharakpur.

Most villages have one or more chaukídárs, the smaller ones which are near one another often sharing a chaukídár between them. The number of these in each tahsíl is shown below :—

Lahore tahsíl	345
Kasúr tahsíl	303
Chúnián tahsíl	320
Sharakpur tahsíl	230

The figures for Lahore tahsíl include eleven daffadárs, all the larger villages having each a daffadár. The ordinary pay of a chaukidár is Rs. 3 per mensem. In some villages of Lahore tahsíl they get Rs. 4.

The head-quarters of thánás or principal circles of jurisdiction, and the chaukís or police outposts and roadposts are distributed as follows :—

Tahsíl Lahore.	Tahsíl Kasúr.	Tahsíl Chunián.	Tahsíl Sharakpur.
Police Stations.	*Police Stations.*	*Police Stations.*	*Police Stations.*
Lahore	Kasúr	Chúnián ...	Sharakpur S.
Anárkali ..	Patti	Bhái Phern	Mángtánwála.
Munánwán	Valtoha	Sarái Mughal	Murídkí.
Shahdára*	Luliáni	Kanganpur.	
Chuug	Khudián.		
Kána Kácha.			
Kálra†			
Raiwind.‡			
Mian Mír.			
Baki			
Outposts.	*Outposts.*	*Outposts.*	*Outposts.*
Nankána	None	Chánga Mánga ..	None.
Davipura.			
Wágha.			
Roadposts.	*Roadposts.*	*Roadposts.*	*Roadposts.*
Amar Sidhu	Ganda Singhwála,	Wan Rádha Rám	None.
Mian Mír Canal.			
	Municipal Police post.		
	Khem Karn.		

There is a cattle-pound at each *thána* and also at Chánga Mánga, Jhuggián, Nankána and Chhabil.

The district lies within the Eastern Police Circle of the Province under the control of the Deputy Inspector-General of Police at Lahore.

Certain men belonging to two tribes have been proclaimed under the Criminal Tribes Act. The tribes are the Sansís and the Mehtáms.

---

* Includes a few villages in Sharakpur tahsíl.
†   Ditto   Kasúr Tahsíl.
‡   Ditto   Chúnián and Kasúr tahsíls.
§   Ditto   Chúnián tahsíl.

The number of *Sansis* on the Register on 31st December 1893 was 245 males of and over the age of 12 years; females none.

The number of *Mehtams* on the Register on 31st December 1893 was 221 males of and over the age of 12 years; females none.

The *Sansis* live in different parts of the district in the jurisdictions of Sharakpur, Murídke, Mángtánwála and Shahdara; some are earning an honest livelihood but others have been giving trouble.

The *Mehtams* live in a village of the same name about three miles north-east of Sharakpur. They profess to be agriculturists, but the greater number of them are dependent for their living on the sale of wood and grass, while others go out as field labourers.

Owing to their thieving propensities they were registered under the Criminal Tribes Act in 1888.

There are three gaols at Lahore, the District Gaol, Female Penitentiary, and the Central Gaol, under the management of the same Superintendent, but each possessing a separate subordinate establishment of its own. Tables Nos. XLII, XLIIA, and XLIIB. show the convicts in gaol for the last five years.

The Lahore District Gaol is built for 607 prisoners, and in 1892 had an average daily population of 537. It receives the male prisoners of the Lahore district only. The usual gaol industries are carried on in it and a considerable number of prisoners are employed on extra-mural works, such as brick-making, &c. The cost of its maintenance is Rs. 27,556 per annum, or Rs. 51-5-0 per prisoner. Its income from manufactories was Rs. 4,532 in 1892.

The Lahore Female Penitentiary is built for 296 prisoners. It receives female long-term and life-prisoners transferred from all parts of the Punjab, and all the female prisoners from the Lahore district. In 1892 it had an average daily population of 124. The industries carried on are very insignificant—knitting, sewing, carding, wool, &c. The cost of its maintenance is Rs. 9,646 or Rs. 77-12-10 per prisoner per annum.

The Lahore Central Gaol covers 33 acres of ground, and is built on the radiating principle. It consists of two octagons, each containing eight compartments radiating from a Central watch tower, from which a full view of the whole prison can be obtained. At the divergence of the two octagons is placed the hospital, three barracks *en echelon*, in an enclosure of its own. The octagons and hospital enclosures are surrounded by iron railings, so that free circulation of air all over the prison is not interfered with. In addition to these, but outside the great wall is an enclosure containing 100 solitary cells, and beyond this again is a second enclosure containing two large wells with appliances for drawing water by manual labour: the water is pumped up into four large tanks containing 24,000 gallons, and from these is distributed by means of pipes and hydrants to all parts of the jail. This system of water supply was introduced for the first time in 1891 at a cost of about Rs. 56,000 and has been most effectual in improving the health of the gaol which was suffering from the contamination of the numerous shallow wells distributed over the gaol enclosure : these wells have now all been closed and built up. A third enclosure has also been added to the gaol, comprising a Juvenile ward capable of containing in separate cubicles as many as 58 prisoners.

The various store-rooms for food, clothing, raw material, &c., &c., are placed outside the railings of the octagons. The whole area of the prison is planted with grass and trees, and is enclosed within a mud wall 18 feet in height, and approached through two gates and a long narrow passage. Each octagon forms a separate and complete prison, having its own workshop, so that dangerous characters need not be taken out to work. The buildings are constructed entirely of sun-dried bricks set in mud, with tiled roofs. There is also a small prison for Europeans consisting of one large ward and three smaller ones, with rooms for dressing and bathing attached. The gaol is built for 1,308 prisoners, but the average daily population in 1,892 was 1,281. There is tent accommodation for 1,600 persons, which is maintained to serve in the event of the prisoners having to be moved into camp on the outbreak of an epidemic. The Central Gaol receives long-term male prisoners only, transferred from almost all parts of the Punjab. The prisoners are encouraged to good conduct and industry by a system of marks under which they obtain rewards—such as interviews with their friends, promotion to offices in the prison, gratuities and small remissions of their sentences.

There is a school in the gaol under the supervision of the Educational Department, to which teachers selected by that department are appointed, and which all prisoners under 24 years of age are required to attend. During the year 1892, 69 prisoners who could neither read nor write on admission learned to do both a little, and three to read and write well.

Labour is divided into three classes—hard, medium and light. Every prisoner must, according to the length of his sentence pass a certain time in each description of labour, and his removal from one stage to another depends upon his conduct. Prison labour consists of weaving blankets and cloths of various kinds, pottery, paper-making, the making of mats and floor cloths (*darris*), both of cotton and grass, weaving carpets similar to Persian ones, tent-making, and lithographic printing. A large number of carpets are exported to England, France and America. There is a large lithographic press fitted with express machines of the best type : the work in this department is done entirely by prisoners ; who print forms, Circulars and Registers for the Judicial Courts, Dispensaries and Gaols of the Province.

Chapter V, A.

**General Adminis-
tration.**

Gaols.

The average net profit of the whole manufactory for the last five years was Rs. 27,433 per annum.

The cost of maintaining the Central Gaol is a little less than one lakh of rupees per annum, or Rs. 76 per prisoner. The whole institution is under the charge of a special officer designated the Superintendent, who resides in quarters provided for him outside the prison. There is a European Deputy Superintendent, and for the native prison, a native jailor and staff of warders. For the European gaol there are two European warders and various other officials, who are provided with quarters.

The gaol guard is formed of reserve prison warders who are all pensioned soldiers : there is one head reserve warder with 39 warders and 2 orderlies, who are regularly drilled and trained in the use of firearms. The men are armed with breech loading Snider carbines and those in the hands of the sentries on duty are loaded with buck shot.

The Superintendents of the Central Gaol have been as follows since the year 1858 : —

Dr. Dallas	...	...	...	1858 to 1862.
„ Penny	...	...	...	1863.
„ Gray	...	...	...	1864 to 1867.
„ Henderson	...	...	...	1868 to 1870.
„ Lethbridge	...	...	...	1871.
„ Warburton	...	...	...	1872-73.
„ Henderson	...	...	...	1874.
„ Stephen	...	...	...	1875-76.
„ Dickson	...	...	...	1877-78.
„ Stephen	...	...	...	1879-80.
„ Dickson	...	...	...	1881-82.
„ Coates	...	...	...	1883-84
„ Dickson	...	...	...	1885-1893.
„ Braide	...	...	...	1894.

The *thaggi* school of industry.

When the British Government was established in the Punjab one of the first things done was to extend to this Province the agency for the suppression of *thaggi* and dacoity, which had proved so effective in other Provinces and the head-quarters of which were at Jubbulpore. The system pursued in the Punjab was the same as that in force at Jubbulpore. Men who had been convicted of *thaggi* and sentenced to transportation or to death for numerous murders had their sentences held in suspense on condition that they assisted in the detection of other gangs of *thugs*. These men, some sixty in number, were located, together with their wives and families, in an old native building called Lehna Singh's Chauni, and were to all appearance gentle characters, fond of pigeons, rabbits, and other pets, and by no means so terrible as the police reports showed them to be. They were placed under restraint merely sufficient to prevent their escape, and were employed in the manufacture of tents. Their dietary was not fixed on penal principles, each man receiving a monthly allowance for the purchase of food. If they worked over hours, they received

extra pay, and their families were paid for any work done by
them. When the authorities desired to use any one for detective purposes, he was despatched abroad under proper escort.

In 1863, after the introduction of the new system of police,
the maintenance of a special detective agency for the suppression of *thaggi* was abandoned as no longer necessary, and the
thugs then in custody were made over to the prison department,
as they could not safely be let loose upon society. The jail
department had to provide quarters for these men, and a building
on the plan of a native *sarai* was erected at a cost of Rs. 8,000,
in which the *thugs* and their families were located. A large
workshop for tent-making was provided, but no change was
made in the system of management or employment, and the
whole institution was placed under the supervision of the Su-
perintedent of the Lahore Central Prison. The *thugs* are gradually dying off, and their places not having been supplied by
fresh admissions, there remain now in this institution only one
old man and three widows, who in all human probability will
last but a short time longer, and then this memorial of one of
the most marvellous and detestable of criminal organizations
will cease to exist in the Punjáb. Their maintenance, including
that of the widows, amounted to about Rs. 192 in 1892.

The segregation of the insane and the alleviation of their
condition by suitable treatment is essentially a modern idea,
and it is not therefore surprising that a Lunatic Asylum was
unheard of in the Punjab until its suggestion by Dr.
Honigberger, State Physician, during the regency of Mahárája
Dulíp Singh, who thus describes its origin in his *Thirty-five
years in the East* (pages 150—153) :—

"Major MacGregor, the Director of the Police at Lahore, on passing the
bázár on horse back, was one day stopped by a woman who was believed to be
insane. On account of this accident the Resident issued an order that the
Darbár should establish an asylum for such persons. I was consulted upon
the subject, and it was resolved that such patients should be received into my
hospital. Accordingly, many lunatics were brought there, and they were
generally followed by a great many curious spectators. I succeeded in curing,
in the course of two months, the first five individuals under my superintendence,
which fact I communicated to the Rája Tejá Singh, and he ordered me to present
them to the assembly at the Residency of Anárkali, which I did. But they
manifested no desire to see them, and looked upon the matter with indifference.
The indifference shown to me, however, in the Residency did not prevent me
from presenting the restored lunatics to the Native *Darbár* at the fortress, and I
was ordered to send them to their respective homes."

In May 1849 the Board of Administration placed the
superintendence of the Lunatic Asylum under the Presidency
Surgeon Dr. Hathaway, to whom Dr. C. M. Smith succeeded
in 1852, and Dr. Scriven in 1870 ; Dr. Fairweather was
Superintendent in 1881 and Dr. Gray in 1882. Dr. Center held
charge from 1884 till 1892, when he retired from the service
and Dr. Coates took over charge.

The Central Lunatic Asylum was at first located in the
city ; in 1853 it was moved into the Anárkali barracks, vacated

when the troops were transferred from Anarkali to Mian Mir in 1851 ; later on as the number of lunatics increased, it was located a little way outside the civil station on the Amritsar road, where it still stands to the north of and out-flanked by the Railway Station and barracks, on a rising and fairly drained ground. The site is not well suited for its purpose ; when first chosen, it was at a considerable distance from any dwelling house. Now, however, a large suburb extends in that direction. The asylum consists of five large walled courts, each resembling somewhat a native *sarai* with dwellings occupying two sides of most of the courts. Of these courts one is used for the general male ward, a second for workshops hospital and a few male lunatics, and a third for the female ward and hospital. The fourth is employed for the detention of criminal lunatics, and the fifth court is used solely as a garden. There are two smaller courts outside used as a quarantine ward for new arrivals, male and female ; also a *post mortem* room in a detached enclosure, and separate buildings for the Resident Assistant Surgeon and matron. There is a detached house for European lunatics outside the asylum walls : it has accommodation for two lunatics but is seldom used. The asylum buildings are calculated to accommodate 290 inmates, 48 females and 242 males : there are seven solitary cells, and cells for 55 criminal and dangerous lunatics, barracks for 95 ordinary male lunatics and for 52 convalescents ; also room for 33 patients in the hospital for male lunatics. The daily average number of patients for the last five years was 242—194 males and 48 females ; of these 43 males and 2 females were criminals. The number of criminal lunatics is increasing steadily.

The average expenditure on the asylum for the last five years was Rs. 28,011, or nearly Rs. 116 per head. The establishment consists of a Superintendent who is the Civil Surgeon of Lahore, a Deputy Superintendent, a native doctor and a compounder for the entire hospital. On the male side there is a head warder and 26 other permanent warders, besides three temporary warders employed when the asylum is full ; while in the female side there are one matron, one head female warder, and three female warders. Cases of great maniacal excitement frequently occur among the criminal lunatics, for which padded rooms and separate cells are provided. Of the alleged causes of insanity amongst natives, hemp and its preparations appear to be by far the most prolific, but the enquiries on which the causes of madness are recorded are as a rule totally insufficient, and probably 90 per cent of the cases of madness ascribed to consumption of *bhang* or *charas* were wrongly recorded so. There are many cases of epileptic mania, and of congenital deficiency of intellect. Melancholia is not uncommon, but it may possibly be characteristic of the Punjab temper in matters of faith that it more frequently arises from grief than from religion. The asylum is conducted on the non-restraint system and all who are able are encouraged to work in the garden, or in weaving, making string and keeping the premises clean. Nothing but want of funds has prevented the Government from building a new asylum long before this ; the present building has frequently been reported as both unsafe and unhealthy.

In 1877, the Diocese of Lahore was constituted as a Memorial to the Most Reverend Dr. Milman, Bishop of Calcutta, and Metropolitan of India, whose death at Rawalpindi, was humanly speaking, in a large measure due to overwork, consequent on the unwieldy size of the three Dioceses of Calcutta.

The Diocese of Lahore has been taken, partly from that of Calcutta, partly from that of Bombay. It includes the Provinces of the Punjab, Sindh, and British Baluchistan, and to the north and west is coterminous with our North-West Frontier.

In December 1877, Dr. Thomas Valpy French was consecrated first Bishop of the Diocese. He resigned the Bishopric in 1887, and the present Bishop, the Right Reverend Henry James Matthew, D.D., was consecrated as his successor. In accordance with the sanction of the Letters Patent the Bishop appoints an Archdeacon for the Diocese, who holds Archdeaconal jurisdiction within the boundaries of the Diocese as given above, under the title " Archdeacon of Lahore." The present Archdeacon, the Venerable A. N. W. Spens, is the third holder of the office since the foundation of the diocese, and was appointed in 1892, in succession to the Venerable W. H. Tribe, M. A.

In 1880, that portion of the Punjab which extends northwards from the River Sutlej (inclusive of Ferozepore) was formed into a Vicariate separate and distinct from that of Hindustán. The Right Reverend Dr. P. Tosi was appointed Bishop and Vicar Apostolic of the Punjab. In 1886 that same portion of the Punjab was constituted a Diocese under the title of the Diocese of Lahore. The Right Reverend Dr. Godfrey Pelckmans was consecrated Bishop of Lahore on the 13th August 1893.

The following is a list of the principal churches in Lahore :

The Cathedral Church of the Resurrection in the centre of the civil station.

The Roman Catholic Cathedral Church of the Immaculate Conception in Anarkali under the supervision of the Roman Catholic Bishop of Lahore.

The Presbyterian Church belonging to the American Mission situate near the Accountant-General's Office.

The Railway Church in Naulakha near the Railway Station in charge of a Chaplain connected with the Church Missionary Society.

St. Mary Magdalene's Church at Mian Mir under the Chaplain at Mian Mir.

There are also several other Native Christian churches which are now likely to increase in number.

Table No. **XXXVIII** gives separate figures for the last ten years for each of the hospitals and dispensaries now open in the Lahore district. The Mayo hospital, opened in 1871, is a Provincial institution for native patients as the Albert Victor Hospital, opened in 1892, is for European patients. The staff of these two hospitals consists of two visiting Surgeons and two visiting Physicians ; with two House Surgeons, an Apothecary and four Medical Officers for out-patients. During the year 1893 the total number of patients treated in both hospitals was as follows :

Out-patients	...	...	...	52,947
In-patients	...	...	...	3,902
			Total ...	56,849

The daily average number under treatment was 155·75. In the course of the year 1,611 major and 9,443 minor operations were performed. The expenditure for 1893 was as shown below :—

				Rs.
Establishment	...	...	...	12,538
Diet of patients	...	...	...	7,870
European medicines	...	...	...	2,227
Country medicines	...	...	...	409
Miscellaneous	...	...	...	8,274
Buildings and repairs	...	...	...	3,368
			Total ...	34,686

The Lady Aitchison Hospital for women faces the Mayo Hospital across the road. The movement towards providing special hospital arrangements for women in Lahore was commenced in 1885, when the Municipal Committee obtained the services of Dr. Elizabeth Bielby as Physician to a woman's hospital. At first the only accommodation was a small dispensary in the Anárkali bazár, where for a time very few patients attended. Subscriptions were invited for the erection of a proper hospital, and the foundation stone of the present building was laid by Lady Aitchison on the 15th of February 1887. It was opened in November 1888 by the Countess of Dufferin. Of late years the number of patients has been rapidly increasing, and in the last year (1893) the daily average of out-patients was 105½ and of in-patients 23½. The hospital staff includes, besides Dr. Bielby, a House Surgeon and a Head Nurse who has been trained in the hospital : there are also six English speaking nurses, and six native *dáies ;* the latter being employed principally on going out to nurse in private families at fixed charges. The hospital is supported chiefly by contributions of Rs. 500 per mensem from the Lahore Municipal Committee, Rs. 300 per mensem from the Punjab Government, Rs. 200 per mensem from the Central Branch, and Rs. 72 per mensem from the Punjab Branch of the Countess of Dufferin's fund. All surplus funds are invested in Government paper for the endowment of the hospital.

Besides the above hospitals, there is in the city of Lahore a dispensary recently established by the Municipal Committee and in charge of a Hospital Assistant. A Railway Hospital in Naulakha with a subsidiary dispensary in the city.

Outside the city in the district there are four dispensaries; situated respectively at Kasúr, Patti, Chúnián, and Sharakpur. That at Kasúr is in charge of an Assistant Surgeon: the other three are looked after by Hospital Assistants. All these institutions are popular and the people resort to them freely: in the year 1893 the number of cases treated at these dispensaries were 995 in-door and 53,000 out-door patients.

Within the municipal limits of Lahore and six minor municipalities the management and expenditure of local funds is vested in the town or Municipal Committee, consisting principally of elected and partly of nominated members. Detailed mention of these Municipal Committees and their working will be found in Chapter VI. Outside municipal limits all local funds are administered by Local Boards whose jurisdiction is conterminous with tahsíl limits and who are subject to the control of the District Board, which is composed of members deputed by nomination or election from the Local Boards. As mentioned above there is one Local Board to each tahsíl. The constitution of each is shown in the following statement:—

Tahsil.	NUMBER OF MEMBERS.				President.
	Ex-officio.	Nominated.	Elected	Total.	
Lahore ...	1	1	14	16	Tahsíldar.
Kasúr ...	2	3	12	17	Assistant Commissioner.
Chúnián ...	1	3	12	16	Tasíldár.
Sharakpur ...	1	2	10	13	Tahsíldár.

The Tahsíldár is in each case ex-officio president except in Kasúr where the Assistant Commissioner or Extra Assistant in charge of the outpost is president ex-officio. All nominated or elected members hold office for not more than three years, the dates from which their appointment or election is held to commence being so arranged that only a certain proportion of members vacate office each year.

Chapter V, A.

General Adminis-tration.

Local and District Boards.

The District Board is composed of 25 delegates elected from the Local Boards, 4 nominated delegates, and 4 *ex-officio* members. The Deputy Commissioner of the district is *ex-officio* President. The Committee holds its meetings in the Jubilee Town Hall of Lahore and is supposed to convene once a month.

The following matters are under the control and adminis-tration of District Board within the area subject to its authority :—

(1)   The management of all property vested in the District Board.

(2)   The construction, repair and maintenance of public roads and other means of communication.

(3)   The establishment, management, maintenance and visiting of public hospitals, dispensaries, saráis and schools, and the construction and repairs of all buildings connected with these institutions ;

(4)   The training of teachers and the establishment of scholarships ;

(5)   The supply, storage and preservation from pollution of water for drinking, cooking and bathing purposes.

(6)   The planting and preservation of trees.

Duties of the Local Boards.

1. The Local Boards have power to sanction plans and estimates of works and repairs involving an expenditure not exceeding Rs. 300 ; works and repairs exceeding that sum require the sanction of the District Board.

2. The civil charges under the heads—

> Educational,
> Medical,
> Arboriculture,
> Miscellaneous,

are under the control of the Local Boards throughout their respective jurisdictions ; alterations in existing charges are subject to the sanction of the District Board.

3. The management of local properties and ferries within their respective jurisdictions is in the hands of Local Boards.

The channel of communication between the Local and District Boards is the Secretary to the Local Funds. Mr. D. Johnstone at present fills the post in an honorary capacity.

Income and ex-penditure of the District and Local Boards.

Table No. XXXVI attached to this work shows the annual income and expenditure of the District Funds during the last ten years. Their receipts are made up principally from the local rate which is levied at the rate of Rs. 10-6-8 per cent. on the land revenue. A large share of the income goes to objects of compulsory expenditure, such as education, hospitals, and contributions to Provincial purposes. The surplus available for such necessary matters as the repair of roads and bridges is far too small for the requirements of the district. Consequently the communications in charge of the Local Boards are not as well maintained as one would expect to find in so important a district.

SECTION B.—EDUCATION.

PART I.—SCHOOLS.

Table No. XXXVII gives figures for the Government and Aided High, Middle, and Primary Schools, English and Vernacular, for boys and girls. The district lies within the Lahore circle which forms the charge of the Inspector of Schools at Lahore.

There are five high schools for boys ; one the Central Model School at Lahore, purely a Government institution ; this is noticed separately below ; another the Municipal Board High School at Kasúr supported partly from provincial, partly from Local Funds and partly from tuition fees. The third is the Mission High School at Lahore, maintained by the Presbyterian Mission, and supported largely from Provincial and Local Funds and therefore classed as an " Aided " School. The remaining two high schools are " Unaided." One is the Dayanand Anglo-Vedic School maintained by the Lahore Arya Samáj. This has made remarkable progress since its foundation in 1886. At present it is the largest high school in the district, well managed and with all its classes filled. Its numerical strength is 660. The success of its students in the Matriculation and Middle School Examinations compare favorably with the results shown by the best schools in the Province. Almost all the students read Hindi and a large proportion of them learn Sanskrit. There are very few Muhammadans on the school roll. The other " Unaided " high school is the *Madrassah-ul-Musalmin*, specially maintained for the education of Musalmáns. The number of students in this at the end of last year was 759. Every pupil is taught Arabic. In the Entrance Examination of March 1893, out of 26 students who entered, 19 were passed and of 50 that entered for the Middle School Examination, 13 were passed.

There are seven Anglo-Vernacular Middle Schools altogether ; two of these are Municipal Board Schools at Chúnián with about 500 students ; three of them are " Aided," namely, the Aitchison School, the Mission Night School, and the Mian Mir Cantonment School ; the remaining two are " Unaided" one being maintained by the *Sanátan Dharm Sabha* of which mention was made at pages 90 and 91 and the other the Lyall School. Beside these there are six purely Vernacular schools located at the villages of Khem Karn, Súr Singh, Patti, Sharakpur, Badhéna, Bághbánpura. The last named has been known for several years past as the best Middle School in the district.

Chapter V, B.

Education.
Part I—Schools.

Primary Schools.

There are in all 67 schools in which education is given in Vernacular up to what is called the Primary Standard : 45 of these are located in the villages shown below separately for each tahsil :—

Lahore.	Kasúr.	Chúnián.	Sharakpur.
Shahdra ...	Luliáni ...	Khudián ...	Labanwála.
Dholanwál ...	Wán ...	Shámkot ...	Tapiála.
Niyáz Beg ...	Sidhwán ...	Kanganpur ...	Kot Pindi Dás.
Burj Atári ...	Mari Megha ...	Bahrwál ...	Rihán.
Khánpur Shahpur	Gharyála ...	Kila Dharm Singh,	Khánpur Kalán.
Khudpur ...	Sobráon ...	Tujja ...	Mallian Kalán.
Icchra ...	Sehjra ...	Bahrwál ...	Kuthiála.
Kána Kácha ...	Waltoha ...	Bughiana ...	Mangu Táru.
Lakhoke ...	Mahalum ...	Tambar.	
Hudiára ...	Rájájang ...	Bháiphern.	
Manihála ...		Bhuchoke.	
Bhasín ...			
Awán Dhayáwála.			
Lakhodher.			
Kamánh.			
Fatehgarh.			

The above include seven zamíndári schools in which special arrangments are made for teaching agriculturists. In addition to the above there are four Primary Schools maintained in Lahore city by the Municipal Committee. Gurmukhi Branch schools are established by local bodies in localities where they appear needed. In all such schools the scholars are taught both Punjábi and Urdu to the standard of the Lower Primary examination, so that they may be able on completing their course to join an Upper Primary Department of the ordinary type. There are also many Indigenous Schools in the district; chiefly Musalmán, and in these the Kurán and its Traditions are carefully taught.

Female education.

There are 33 Girls' Schools with 1,297 scholars in the district, of these 28 are aided, all under the management of one or other of the three societies, the Punjab Association, the Indian Female Normal Society, and the American Presbyterian Mission. The Punjab Association consists of a central institution known as the Victoria School and nine Primary Branches, the whole numbering 550 scholars and increasing rapidly. The Victoria School is located in the large and beautiful building known as Nao Nihal Singh's Haveli, which has been lately restored. It teaches up to the Middle Standard in the three Vernaculars— Urdu, Hindi, and Punjabi, and also in Persian and Sanskrit. The teachers are, with the exception of the Sanskrit master, all native women. The School is presided over by a Bengali lady who was educated in England. The pupils include the daughters of many of the educated Hindús of the professional classes, though these usually leave at an early age to be married. The Musulmáns of the upper classes have not got over their objection to sending their daughters to school, though every arrangement is made for maintaining strict *parda*. The school includes a training class for teachers which has supplied several teachers for the Victoria School itself and for its branches.

The Indian Female Normal Society maintains the Boarding School for Native Christians, formerly known as the Indian Female Normal School and now as the Lady Dufferin School. It is an Anglo-Vernacular High School, teaching up to the Entrance Standard and numbers nearly 100 girls of the better class of Native Christians. In connection with this Society there are also several Musalmán schools in the city, with 170 pupils or thereabouts.

The American Presbyterian Mission maintains a few Primary Schools in the city, the scholars in which number about 300 ; the majority learn Gurmukhi, only a few learning Urdu.

Outside the three societies named above very little is done for female education in this district. The Municipal Committee of Lahore has a small school at the Bháti gate attended by Musalmáns of the lower class ; and there is a Primary Board School at Kasúr, which is attended by the daughters of some of the leading Musalmáns in the town, an unusual state of things. At Clarkabad there is an Industrial School, mainly for the children of the lowest class of Native Christians, who are sent there from the mission stations of adjacent districts. This is an ordinary Primary School in which a certain amount of spinning, cooking and household work is taught. A few Girls' Schools are supported by the Arya Samáj and the Anjuman Islámia of Lahore, not under Government inspection; consequently their statistics are not known. The Anjuman's schools are, it is believed, chiefly devoted to instruction in the Kurán. In all these female schools, speaking generally, the Musalmán girls are taught Urdu, but the Hindu girls of all castes are taught Gurmukhi or Hindi.

The foregoing remarks refer only to native schools. There are besides in the city of Lahore five European schools for boys and three for girls. The High School has 61 boys on its rolls, of whom 7 are at present being taught up to the " High " standard, 21 up to " Middle " standard, and the remainder up to " Primary." The Railway Night School which educates sons of Railway employés up to the Middle standard, has 26 scholars ; the Cathedral Orphanage Middle School 27 ; Donald Town School 45 ; and St. Anthony's School 34. The last two teach up to the " Primary " standard. The three European Girls' schools are the Cathedral High School with 30 scholars, the Convent School with 80, and the Cathedral Orphanage with 28. These three all teach up to the " Middle " standard.

Of all the schools to which reference has been made above the only one which requires more detailed mention than has already been given is the Central Model School, spoken of on page 215 as being purely a Government institution. It is in fact the only Government *High School* in the Province and appears to have taken the place of what was before known as the *Lahore District School.* The building is attached to the Central Training College and as the School teaching comprises all stages from the Infant to the Entrance standard, it comes in useful as a practising institution for the teachers under training in the College.

The management of the school is vested in a Headmaster on Rs. 300 a month, under the direct control of the Principal of the Central Training College.   The other school staff consists of nine assistant English masters on monthly salaries ranging from Rs. 160 to Rs. 30, two English writing masters on Rs. 35 and Rs. 30; two science masters on Rs. 70 and Rs. 45 ; two mathematical teachers on Rs. 45 and Rs. 35 ; four Oriental teachers on Rs. 80, Rs. 45, Rs. 40 and Rs. 30 ; two Sanskrit teachers on Rs. 50 and Rs. 40 ; six Vernacular teachers on salaries ranging between Rs. 25 and Rs. 15 ; one drill master and one gymnastic master on Rs. 20 and Rs. 15 respectively.

The subjects taught in the school are :—English, Persian, Sanscrit, Arabic, Hindi, Gurmukhi, Urdu, Mathematics, History and Geography, and Natural Science.

The following figures show the working of the school for the last five years :—

Years.	Expenditure.	Number of students.	RESULTS.				
			Number who passed the Entrance Examination of the Calcutta University.	Number who passed the Entrance Examination of the Punjab University.	Number who passed the Middle School Examination.	Number who passed the Upper Primary School Examination.	Number who passed the Lower Primary School Examination.
1888-89	5,339	287	...	11	14	21	31
1889-90	5,559	271	5	6	10	15	34
1890-91	6,247	231	6	4	13	16	24
1891-92	7,279	750	6	55	31	65	42
1892-93	18,070	629	8	47	29	59	42

Quarters are provided for resident pupils at present in a hired building. A regular boarding house is shortly to be built.

It is unfortunate that the school has no feeders of its own n the city ; when the old Municipal Board School was amalgamated with this in 1891, the Branch Schools of the former were retained under the management of the Lahore Municipality. It should be noted that the sudden increase of expenditure shown against the year 1892-93 is due to a large increase in the number of students consequent on the amalgamation of 1891 above referred to.

There are in Lahore two Government Training Institutions, the Central Training College and the Normal School. The former is managed by the Principal subject to the general control of the Director of Public Instruction. The Principal is assisted in his duties by the Assistant Superintendent, two Assistant Masters who may be required also to translate, compile and examine Text books, a Science master, and a Maulvi who also teaches in the Central Model School. Similarly a Gymnastic master gives instruction in the latter as well as in the Training College. There is an Anglo-Vernacular as well as a Vernacular Department. The former is subdivided into a senior and a junior class. The Vernacular Department consists of one class only, called the Senior Vernacular class.

The Lahore Normal School dates from the first establishment of the Education Department in the Punjab in 1856. Its first object was to train teachers for Vernacular Schools of all grades. The system was devised with the view of adding to the general knowledge of the indigenous teacher, who, whilst tolerably well acquainted with Persian, and possessed of some local influence in his village, which it would have been unwise to sacrifice, was absolutely ignorant of geographical and other subjects, and has never seen practised before him any better method of instruction than the traditional and laborious system of repeating by rote. In 1866 the Director of Public Instruction established an honor class in connection with the instruction, with a view to create a supply of Vernacular teachers of a higher stamp. The scheme was modified in 1868, and again in 1872. Since the opening of the Central Training College in 1881, the business of the Normal School has been confined to the training of teachers for the Vernacular Primary Schools. On the establishment in 1889-90 of the Zamíndári Schools for the benefit of those members of the agricultural classes who work in the fields with their own hands, a corresponding zamíndári class was opened in the Normal School with the object of training teachers for the Zamíndári Schools. The students attending this class receive instruction in Urdú, Hindi, Punjabi or Pashto, Arithmetic on native methods, and in the method of teaching and school management. They undergo a special examination which is so arranged as to enable them to appear in the Junior Vernacular Certificate Examination if they wish to do so. A small addition to their ordinary salary is to be allowed to certificated teachers in charge of Zamíndári Schools and this, of course, acts as an inducement to Normal School students to join the zamíndári class. The test for admission into a Normal School is the Middle Schools Examination. The nominations are made by the Deputy Commissioner and the Inspector of Schools. The course of instruction extends over one year, at the end of which the students are examined for the Junior Vernacular and Zamíndári certificates. The subjects of examination for the junior vernacular certificate test are the same as for the Middle School Examination in Vernacular, with the addition of the method of teaching and school management. Provisional Junior Vernacular 2nd grade certificates are awarded to all candidates who pass the corresponding examination. The school was formerly held in the Hazúri Bágh, but in 1880 was removed to a building known as the Tosha Khána, to make way for the Central Training College. Since the amalgamation of the Central Model School attached to the Central Training College with the Municipal Board School, held in a building close at hand, and the placing of the whole under a European Master in October 1891, the Normal School has been given rooms in the Central Training College building. The school staff consists of a head master, a second master, an Oriental teacher, a Hindi and a Punjabi teacher, and a gymnastic master under the superintendence and control of the Principal of the Central Training College. The practising Model School which formerly existed only in name has since 1886 been systematized and placed on a statisfactory basis, with a sufficient supply of efficient teachers. The students continue to reside in the Hazuri Bágh and in the Tosha Khána, the latter place having been occupied by them since the removal of the school to the Central Training College building in 1891. The statement given below shows the numbers and expenditure for five years. The cost is defrayed principally from the provincial revenues :—

Year.	Number of pupils at the close of the year.	Number of pupils on the rolls monthly.	Number of successful candidates	Annual expenditure.
				Rs.
1888-89	52	62	20	7,877
1889-90	61	62	23	7,916
1890-91	58	65	44	8,340
1891-92	50 Junior Vernacular, 17 Zamín-dári.	81	23 Junior Vernacular. 8 Zamín-dári.	8,518
1892-93	64 Junior Vernacular. 22 Zamín-dári.	72	50 Junior Vernacular. 9 Zamín-dári.	7,424

The Aitchison College was founded in November 1886 ; its objects are the education of (a) relatives of Ruling Chiefs ; (b) youths of good family ; (c) Wards of Court if eligible under (a) or (b). The teaching embraces all standards from the Primary upwards. There are at present 78 boys on the rolls, of whom 32 are being taught in the Primary School, 26 in the Middle, 13 in the High Department, and 7 in the Lahore Government College course. Last year 5 of the College students appeared in the Intermediate Examination and 4 passed. For the Entrance Examination 5 went up and 3 passed. In the Middle School Examination 11 entered and 7 passed : 3 passed in the upper Primary, 6 out of 8 in the lower Primary, and 6 out of 7 by the Infant standard. The education given at this institution therefore may be said to be highly satisfactory of its kind. Special attention is given to English and to English pronunciation. The school is excellently provided with class rooms, with a chemical laboratory and with a speech room. There is ample recreation ground all about the different buildings and there students are encouraged to play all sorts of English games, especially cricket and tennis, in which some of them excel. There is boarding-house accommodation for all. The supervision is good, every possible care being taken to keep the boys from bad habits and moral contamination. The late General S. Black was president of the Aitchison College from 1886 to 1892. In succession to him Colonel Sir Benjamin Bromhead obtained the appointment.

The chief institution for technical education is the " Mayo School of Art " founded in 1875 in commemoration of the late Lord Mayo, Viceroy and Governor-General of India. The object of the school is to give instruction in architectural drawing and designing, painting, modelling, moulding, stone and wood carving, &c., with special reference to the artistic industries indigenous to the Punjab and to the Architectural and Decorative styles of art peculiar to this part of India. There is a class for elementary instruction in engineering, maintained in connection with the Punjab University and open to all students who have passed the Entrance Examination. Besides this there are three main sections of the school, devoted to construction, to decoration, and to modelling. All candidates for admission to the school are expected to show some aptitude for the study of art in some form, and they are kept on two months' probation before definitive enrolment. The general age of admission is from 14 to 16 years. The school is located near the Anárkalli Gardens. An account of the building will be found in Chapter VI. The institution is supported by Government and is under the control of the Director of Public Instruction. The staff of the school consists of the Principal, Vice-Principal, five trained Assistants, and a Registrar. The average number of pupils during the last five years has been 114, and the expenditure in the last year, 1893, amounted to Rs. 23,060.

Chapter V, B.

Education.
Part I—Schools.

Railway Technical
School.

The Railway Technical School is intended for the sons of artisans employed in the Lahore Railway Workshops. It is an industrial school, established in February 1889 with the object of providing a suitable education for the sons and nearer relatives of artisans. It is supported entirely by Government and is under the control of the Director, Public Instruction, and a Committee. The school included 275 scholars at the end of last year.

Veterinary College.

A full account of this institution has been given in Mr. Ibbetson's provincial volume of the Gazetteer. The total number of students is limited to 60 but a larger number are sometimes admitted. The teaching staff at present comprises the Principal of the College, one European Professor, and four native assistants. But a proposal is now before Government for an additional European Professor. The following table shows the hospital work done in the College during the last three years :—

| YEAR. | EQUINE PATIENTS. | | BOVINE PATIENTS. | | Total patients. | Examination of horses for soundness. |
	In-door.	Out-door.	In-door	Out-door		
1890-91 ...	352	471	28	489	1,340	11
1891-92 ...	421	795	21	796	2,033	75
1892-93 ...	447	896	20	784	2,147	61

Many of the cases which now come to the College are said to be of a particularly difficult nature, animals being frequently brought from long distances after other treatment has been tried and failed.

The large majority of cases that come for treatment are bowel complaints, lameness and wounds and contusions.

Kasúr School of Industry.

In 1874 a School of Industry was established at Kasúr by the Anjuman-i-Kasúr, and an attempt was made to maintain an institution in which instruction of a practical nature in the principal branches of native handicraft should be given to the youth of the place after they had left school, and by means of which improvement might be effected in the native methods of manufacture and in the quality of articles turned out. The institution was partially supported by grants from District and Municipal Funds. A large building was constructed with a spacious courtyard at a cost of Rs. 3,465 collected privately for the erection of a memorial of His Royal Highness the Prince of Wales visit to Lahore in 1876. In this building the work of the school was carried on. Carpet making, cloth weaving, leather work, needle work, carpentry, metal work were all taught, the teaching staff were paid as much as Rs. 82 per mensem, and the daily attendance of pupils averaged 30 for many years. Some of the pupils received scholarships of Rs. 2 or Rs. 2-8-0 a month. *Lungis, daris* and carpets made at this school were in great request. The school was thriving for some time, but from 1882 when Kádir Bakhsh Khan, Extra Assistant Commissioner, who had taken the greatest interest in the institution, was transferred from Kasúr, the prosperity of the school rapidly declined. The management grew worse and worse, subscriptions due were not collected, and the manufactures that were sold were not paid for. In January 1887 the District Board ceased to pay its yearly subscription of Rs. 32, and the Municipal Committee of Kasúr shortly after stopped its annual grant of Rs. 60. The establishment, however, was still retained and the scholarships continued to be paid ; the school finances were found to be in great disorder when Kádir Bakhsh Khan returned to Kasúr in 1888 : he reduced matters to some order for a time, cutting down unnecessary expenditure and dismissing superfluous establishment; but on his death in 1890 the school affairs once more fell into mismanagement, and gradually the institution ceased to exist. The building at present stands almost deserted. Four or five of the looms are worked by private enterprise, the workers paying a small rent to the Anjuman for the use of the looms. The library formerly belonging to the school has been transferred to the High School of Kasúr, where additions are being made to it year by year.

Chapter V, B.
——
Education.
Part II—Punjab
University.
Kasur School of
Industry.

THE PUNJAB UNIVERSITY AND COLLEGE INSTITUTIONS RECOGNISED BY IT.

PART II.

In bringing the above mentioned Institutions into one part together it may perhaps be useful to explain that the Punjab University is merely an examining body and the colleges recognised by it are those which prepare students for its examinations. For the notes that follow on the University, the Oriental College and the Law School, the public are indebted to Dr. M. A. Stein, the present Registrar of the Punjab University and Principal of the Oriental College. The account of the Government College has been taken mainly from the Provincial Gazetteer edited in 1888-89, subject to corrections and additions kindly made by Mr. William Bell, Principal of the College.

The University of the Punjab was constituted in the year 1882 by Act XIX of the Governor-General of India in Council " for the purpose of ascertaining by means of examination the persons who have acquired proficiency in different branches of Literature, Science and Arts," and was invested by the same Act with the power of conferring upon them academical degrees, diplomas and other distinctions.

The history of the movement which led first (in 1869) to the establishment of the Punjab University College and subsequently to the raising of this Institution to the status of an University, has been fully set forth in Section B. of the VI chapter of the Provincial Gazetteer 1888-89, (pages 166-75). There also a detailed account will be found of the organisation given under the above Act to the newly founded University, as well as of the chief Statutes and Regulations adopted by the governing body of the University on its constitution.

In the following notes it is intended to record briefly the chief events which have marked the development of the University during the first decade of its existence, and to supply information as to the scope and extent of the work done by the University in the cause of higher education during the last academical year 1892-93.

During the first two years after the constitution of the University, the labors of the Senate were chiefly directed towards the framing of revised rules and regulations for the several examinations leading up to its Arts and Oriental Degrees. The establishment of two separate Faculties of Arts and Oriental Learning by the Act of Incorporation made it possible to provide for instruction and examination through the medium both of English and the Vernacular Languages of the Punjab. Other principles kept prominently in view were : that the number of obligatory subjects in any examination should be as few as possible consistently with the attainment of a proper eductional standard ; that provision should be made for an oral as well as written examination wherever this could be done with advantage, and that the conduct of all examinations be entrusted as far as practicable, to persons who had not been engaged in teaching the candidates.

One of the Institutions to be maintained under the Statutes by the Univeristy is the Oriental College : special rules were prepared for its management, by which this Institution was placed under the control of a permanent Committee of the Senate. In 1885 Regulations were also framed for the other teaching Institution maintained by the University, the Law School, the examinations connected with its course having been recognised by the Chief Court as the compulsory tests for admission to legal practice in the Province.

The University having entered into possession of the various Endowments and Trusts previously held by the Punjab University College, it soon became necessary to provide rules which would ensure the proper administration of the University finances and the application of the different Trusts to their specific objects as originally intended by the donors. The financial rules passed in 1886 have, with some subsequent modifications, been found sufficient to effect this purpose. In the same year detailed regulations were adopted relating to the award of Arts Scholarships by the Government and University, which placed the conditions of their award and tenure on an uniform basis.

In view of the elevation of the Lahore Medical School into a Medical College with an increased professorial staff, the University was empowered in 1887 by the Supreme Government to grant the Degrees of Bachelor and Doctor of Medicine.

In the following year the constitution of the Syndicate and Faculties was thoroughly revised on the lines of a memorandum drawn up by the Vice-Chancellor, Dr. W. H. Rattigan. The new rules adopted made the Syndicate a real Executive Committee of the Senate, elected on representative principles. The Faculties were provided with a constituted Head, the Dean, responsible for the transaction of business, and a Board of Studies was created within each Faculty with power to exercise special control over all questions connected with the standard of examinations. The reforms in the organisation of the Oriental College effected in 1888 have been noticed in the remarks on that Institution ; they were accompanied by certain changes in the Regulations for the Oriental Language Examinations, which fixed proper tests either in English or in General Knowledge for those Oriental Titles Candidates who wished to qualify for diplomas. In the same year the Senate established conditions for the management of the munificent endowment made by Seth Rám Rattan, R. B., with a view to the encouragement of Sanskrit studies in the Punjab.

During the Academical year 1889-90, important modifications were made by the Senate, on the basis of certain proposals of the General Educational Conference of 1889, in the Regulations affecting the pass percentages and standards of the several Arts and Oriental Faculty Examinations. The changes adopted after careful consideration were, it was thought, calculated to facilitate the admission of students to University studies while preserving standards for examination which were likely to maintain the reputation of the University. The important and long pending work of the separation and adjustment of the accounts of the numerous Special Trusts and Endowments was brought to a satisfactory conclusion in the same year. A full report on the state of the various endowments was submitted to the Senate after a thorough scrutiny of the Funded Account Books since the date of the Foundation of the University, and it thus became possible for the first time to lay down distinct rules for the future management of each individual Trust. In order to meet the excess cost incurred by the Oriental College in providing tuition in Classical Languages to students of the Government College, the Local Government liberally sanctioned on the application of the University, an additional grant of Rs. 3,120 per annum. The Endowment Funds of the University received in 1890 a very considerable addition by the munificent gift of Rs. 50,000 offered by His Highness the Mahárája of Patiala for the establishment of University Scholarships in honor of His late Royal Highness Prince Albert Victor's visit to the Punjab.

The Supreme Government having, on application of the University conceded to it the privilege of granting Law Degrees, detailed Regulations were framed in 1891 for the Examinations for Bachelor of Law and Doctor of Law Degrees, which subsequently received the sanction of the Supreme Government.

In connection with the adjustment of the Trust Accounts effected in the previous year, the Financial Rules of the University were thoroughly revised in order to ensure for the future the proper separation of the Current from the Special Trusts and General Endowment Accounts, and a Board of Accounts was constituted to act as a consultative body on all financial matters. The Local Government liberally responded to an application of the University by sanctioning an additional grant of Rs. 2,400 per annum for the improvement of the Law School.

In 1892 the Syndicate and Senate devoted much consideration to proposals connected with the institution of Examinations in Science. The Supreme Government having invited the co-operation of the University towards establishing an alternative Entrance Examination which would lead to a bifurcation of studies in secondary schools, it was thought that the object in view could be attained only by establishing on the Science side an alternative to the existing Entrance Examination of the Arts Faculty which would lead up to a higher University course and a Degree in Science, respectively. The Senate accordingly adopted a scheme providing for an Entrance Examination in Science and the institution of an Intermediate Examination in Science leading up to an Examination for the Degree of Bachelor of Science. These recommendations were agreed to by the Local and Supreme Governments and full Regulations have since been framed and sanctioned to give effect to them.

The rules relating to the various Readers and Translators on the Endowments of the University were subjected to a thorough revision in order to bring the conditions of award and the duties connected with these posts into close agreement with the original objects of the Endowments. The Regulations for the several Oriental Language Examinations also underwent revision in 1892 and amendments were effected in the Rules relating to the admission to the various Arts Examinations.

During the year 1893 the Board of Accounts was able to report a considerable improvement in the financial position of the University owing mainly to the steady increase in the number of candidates offering themselves for the Examinations of the University, and to recommend in connection therewith a substantial increase in the remuneration given to its Examiners. The Board's recommendation was adopted by the Senate, and it is satisfactory to note that the scale of remuneration now offered bears favorable comparison with those of other Indian Universities.

Rules were framed in the same year for the re-examination, under certain conditions, of Answer papers at the University and

Middle School Examinations. .The Medical Degrees, Diplomas and Licenses granted by the Punjab University were recognised by the General Medical Council of the United Kingdom, the University of Oxford having already sometime previously admitted the Punjab University to the privileges of a Colonial University under its Statutes.

The following statements will illustrate the actual working of the University and the extent of its operations in the Academical year ending 30th September 1893.

At the proper University examinations held during the year in the Faculties of Arts, Oriental Learnings, Law and Medicine, not less than 2,111 candidates presented themselves. In addition to these 5,183 candidates who appeared at the Punjab Middle School Examination of that year, were examined through the agency of the Punjab University. The total amount of fees realised from the candidates was nearly Rs. 76,000, this sum forming the most important item on the receipt side of the University Budget.

The tabular statement recorded below shows the number of candidates who appeared at the several University examinations and the results. The corresponding figures for 1883 are shown with the object of affording a comparison with the University's examination work in the first year of its existence; they will best indicate the progress since made in extending the University's operations :—

Name of Examination.	1883.		1893.	
	Number of candidates.	Number passed.	Number of candidates.	Number passed.
Oriental and Arts Faculties—				
Entrance, Oriental	74	20	21	15
Do. Arts	312	103	1,296	803
Intermediate, Oriental ...	8	3	3	2
Do. Arts	42	18	222	149
Degree of Bachelor, B. O. L.	3	1	6	3
Do. do. B. A. ...	17	6	126	51
Degree of Master, M. O. L. ...	3	3	1	1
Do. do. M. A. ...	5	3	12	7
Oriental Languages—	330	213	273	98
Additional Test in English ...	...	...	10	9
Law Faculty—				
Preliminary	...	...	35	23
First Certificate	100	24	9	6
Licentiate	65	27	14	8
Intermediate in Law... ...	...	...	14	3
Bachelor of Laws	...	...	1	1
Faculty of Medicine—				
First Examination for L. M. S.	11	5	37	12
Do. do. M. B...	...	...	5	1
Second Examination for L. M. S.	12	4	24	14
Do. do. M. B.	...	...	2	1
Faculty of Civil Engineering—				
First Examination	7	3	...	...

The number of individual examiners employed in the University examinations of 1892-93 was 185 and remuneration to the total amount of over Rs. 18,000 was paid to them.

The collegiate institutions recognised by the University in the year 1893 were the following :—

A.—In the Oriental Faculty—

> The Oriental College, Lahore.

B.—In the Arts Faculty—

> *i.* The Government College, Lahore.
>
> *ii.* The St. Stephen's Mission College, Delhi.
>
> *iii.* The Mission College, Lahore.
>
> *iv.* The Municipal Board College, Amritsar.
>
> *v.* The Dayanand Anglo-Vedic College, Lahore.
>
> *vi.* The Scotch Mission College, Siálkot.
>
> *vii.* The Mahendra College, Patiála.
>
> *viii.* The Egerton College, Baháwalpur.

C.—In the Law Faculty—

> The Law School, Lahore.

D.—In the Medical Faculty—

> The Medical College, Lahore.

The Oriental College and Law School are directly connected with the University and supported entirely from its funds, endowed or unendowed.

Besides the above two Institutions, the University gives its help towards the maintenance of *Yunáni* and *Vaidya* classes for the teaching of the Indian system of Medicine, attached to the Medical College, Lahore, and of the Civil Engineering class placed under the superintendence of the Principal of the Mayo School of Art by providing the salaries of the Lecturers (3), employed in these classes.

Scholarships to the amount of Rs. 300 are awarded by the University to, and enjoyed by, students in the various Institutions recognised.

Six Readerships and Translatorships are maintained on the several Endowed Trusts on a total expenditure of Rs. 5,416 during the year. Four Readers and one Translator are attached to the teaching staff of the Oriental College, and one Reader is employed in the instruction of the Engineering class at the Mayo School of Art.

The Senate under the Chancellorship of His Honor Sir Dennis Fitzpatrick, K. C. S. I., Lieutenant-Governor of the Punjab, and the Vice-Chancellorship of the Hon'ble W. H. Rattigan, LL. D., (first appointed in 1887), consisted at the close of the year 1892-93 of 135 Fellows, constituted in six

Faculties under their respective Deans.   The Syndicate was
composed of 18 representatives of Faculties presided over by
the Vice-Chancellor.   A full list of the Fellows named in the
Schedule to the Act of Incorporation appointed by the
Chancellor or nominated by the Senate, will be found in the
University Calendar, where also Succession Lists are given of
the Chancellors, Vice-Chancellors and other officers of the
University.

Chapter V, B.
—
Education,
Part II—Govern-
ment College.

The receipts and disbursements of the several accounts of
the University for the year ending 31st March 1893 are shown
below :—

	Current Account.	Special Endowed Trusts.	Unendowed Special Trusts.	Total.
	Rs. A. P.	Rs. A. P.	Rs. A. P.	Rs. A. P.
Receipts ...	1,42,036 14 11	11,679 10 5	1,550 0 0	1,55,266 9 4
Expenditure ..	1,26,136 7 9	12,178 4 0	1,617 7 4	1,39,932 3 1

The total amount of the Government securities held by the
University on the 13th March 1893, aggregated to the nominal
value of Rs. 4,71,900.   Out of this amount Rs. 2,82,300
belonged to 27 separate Endowed Trusts founded for the
maintenance of Readerships, Exhibitions, Scholarships, Prizes
and Medals.

This College was founded in 1884.   Its purpose is to afford
the means of a University education to all in the Province who
may desire this ; but the fees are higher than in any other
Collegiate institution in the Province.   Only such as have
passed the Entrance or Matriculation Examination are admitted,
and these are prepared for the University degrees in Arts.
Previous to the establishment of the Punjab University College
in 1870, only the courses of the Calcutta University, to which
this College is affiliated, were followed.   From 1870 till 1882
when had been the "Punjab University College" became
the " Punjab University," with powers to confer degrees, an
attempt was made to meet both the Calcutta and the local
standards ; but now the course of instruction has been made
to conform exclusively with the schemes of the new Punjab
University.   There are three distinct courses of study—the
Intermediate Course, extending over two years from the date
of matriculation, and embracing at least four and not more
than five subjects ; the *B. A. Course,* also of two years, embracing three subjects ; and the *M. A. Course,* of one or two years
in the entire field of one branch of literature or science.   The
subjects in which instruction is given are : (1) English, the

Government
College

Language and Literature; (2) Arabic, Sanskrit and Persian; (3) History and Political Economy; (4) Mathematics; (5) Mental and Moral Science; and (6) Physical Science.

The College building is situated in Anárkali on an elevated site to the north of the public gardens and adjacent to the District courts. It is an imposing structure, of gothic style, with a large centre clock tower. Besides the Government College, the building accommodates the classes of the Oriental College and School. These occupy part of the north-east wing, the rest of the building being set apart for the Government College. This block contains a large hall, used for examining and Convocation purposes, six large and three small class rooms and a Professor's common room. The cost of the building was Rs. 3,20,605, which was met from Provincial Funds.

The College is supported entirely by Government, and is under the control of the Department of Public Instruction. The staff consists of a Principal, who is responsible for the management of the institution, and who is also Professor of English Literature and History; of four Professors, to whom the subjects of Mental and Moral Science, History, Mathematics and Physical Science are entrusted; of four Assistant Professors, and a Maulvi and Pandit. The Oriental teaching is provided by the Oriental College.

From the figures given below, it will be seen that the average attendance in the College for the last five years has been 135 and the average annual cost Rs. 49,143 :—

Years.						Average attendance.	Average cost.
							Rs.
1888-89	...	...	...	...	...	137	45,716
1889-90	...	...	...	...	...	115	52,907
1890-91	...	...	...	...	...	113	48,809
1891-92	...	...	...	...	...	139	48,871
1892-93	...	...	...	...	...	171	49,415

The number of students on the roll in 1893 was 171, of whom 68 were reading the intermediate course, 89 for the B. A. and 14 for the M. A. degree. The following table gives the number of passes from the College by the University examinations for the last five years, showing an aggregate for the period of 103 by what is now the Intermediate Standard, 84 by the B. A. and 11 by the M. A.

Years.	First Arts and Proficiency.	B. A. and High Proficiency.	M. A. and Honors.
1888-89	21	7	2
1889-90	25	20	...
1890-91	12	19	2
1891-92	20	22	2
1892-93	25	16	5

The College has attached to it a library containing 1,360 volumes. In connection with the teaching in Physical Science, there is a well-stocked museum of apparatus, as well as a collection of minerals, rocks and fossils presented by the Geological Department. There is a Debating Club connected with the College which meets every Saturday for discussion of matters of scholastic and practical interest.

The College now possesses a large boarding-house, the finest in the Province, built at a cost of over Rs. 40,000. It is within the College precincts and contains accommodation for about 120 boarders. The senior boarders are provided with separate rooms, while the juniors occupy dormitories having each places for eight persons. Attached to the boarding-house are baths for Hindús and Muhammadans, nine kitchens, and a spacious football ground, as well as a cricket ground and tennis courts. The old Presbyterian Church in the College ground has been purchased by Government at a cost of Rs. 15,000 and converted into a gymnasium fitted with apparatus and appliances of the best modern kind. Drill and gymnastics are taught daily by a paid instructor.

The neighbouring building formerly used as the office of the Excise Commissioner has been remodelled and is now set apart as an official residence for the Principal of the College. This enables him to superintend the boarding-houses and to look after the general welfare of the students more efficiently than was possible under the old arrangements.

The Oriental College was established by the Senate of the Punjab University College in 1870 for the purpose of teaching the Classical Languages and Literatures of the East and imparting higher instruction in Western Sciences through the medium of the standard vernaculars of the Province. In 1882 the institution was taken over by the newly constituted Punjab University which has since maintained it in accordance with the provisions of its Statutes. A School Department was attached to the College for the purpose of training students for the lowest

The Lahore Oriental College.

test of the Oriental Faculty and subsequent admission to the College.

In the year 1884 the tuition in Oriental Languages of the students reading for Arts Faculty Examinations in the Government College was entrusted by the Local Government to the Oriental College.

In 1888 a thorough re-organisation of the Oriental College and School was effected. The *Yunani* and *Vaidyá* classes and the Engineering class previously accommodated in the Oriental College, were transferred to the Medical College and School of Art, respectively. In accordance with recommendations of a special Sub-Committee of the Syndicate, the classes preparing for the various Oriental Titles Examinations of the University were strictly separated both in College and School from those which read for the Arts Courses of the Oriental Faculty leading up to the B. O. L. Degree. Tuition in the English Language was organised for all students attending the Oriental Titles classes in order to enable them to acquaint themselves to some extent with the results of Western philology, and to qualify for the additional test which was established in that year for candidates wishing to obtain Diplomas of Oriental Titles.

The object of the Oriental College as re-organised on the above lines, is: (a) to impart a knowledge of the Sanskrit, Arabic and Persian Languages and Literatures on a sound basis and in accordance, as far as circumstances will admit, with the historical methods of European philology, to students who wish to prepare themselves for the Proficiency, High Proficiency and Honors Examinations of the Punjab University in these Languages, and to train them eventually to act as efficient teachers of these Classical Languages ; (b) to give instruction to students who after acquiring a sufficient acquaintance with the subjects of Mathematics, General Knowledge, &c., through the medium of the Vernacular (Urdu or Hindi) pass the test of the Entrance Examination of the Oriental Faculty of the Punjab University, and wish to pursue their studies for the Degrees of Bachelor and Master of Oriental Learning taking up Arabic or Sanskrit as their Classical Language ; and (c) to prepare students for the Proficiency and High Proficiency Examinations in Gurmukhi of the Punjab University by giving them a scholarly knowledge of the historical development of the Punjabi Language and the Literature contained in it. The costs of instruction in the last named Department are provided by the Patiála-Gurmukhi Endowed Trust.

The College is managed by a special Committee composed of Fellows of the University presided over by the Vice-Chancellor and under the control of the Syndicate and Senate. The teaching staff consists of a Principal who is also Professor of Sanskrit five Pandits, five Maulvís, three Munshís, two English, two Urdu, one Hindi and two Gurmukhi teachers. Five of the

Readers and Translators on the Endowments of the University are also employed in the instruction of the Oriental Degree and Government College classes.

The total expenditure in connection with the Oriental College and School during the year ending 31st March 1893 aggregated Rs. 32,779, of which Rs. 21,189 were spent from the Oriental College Budget on account of salaries of staff, &c., Rs. 10,634 from the University Budget on account of Endowed Readerships, pay of Assistant Professors and scholarships, and Rs. 956 from Provincial Funds on account of Government scholarships. Rupees 27,632 represented expenditure upon the College, Rs. 5,147 represented expenditure upon the School.

Towards the expenditure against the Oriental College Budget Rs. 3,120 were contributed by the special Government grant which had been sanctioned with effect from the 1st April 1890 by the Local Government to meet the actual expenses connected with the tuition of Government College classes in Oriental Languages.

The number of students on the roll on the 31st March 1893 was 72 in the College and 50 in the School Department. The number reading for the various examinations were as shown below :—

COLLEGE DEPARTMENT.

M. A. Degree	... 2	Honors in Sanskrit	... 4	Honors in Persian	... 6
M. O. L. „	... 2	High Proficiency in Sanskrit 9	High Proficiency in Persian 7
B. O. L. „	... 8	Honors in Arabic ... 14	Honors in Gurmukhi 5
The Intermediate Examination .. 4	High Proficiency in Arabic 9	High Proficiency in Gurmukhi... ... 2

SCHOOL DEPARTMENT.

Entrance Examination (Oriental Faculty), 11 | Proficiency in Arabic... 7 | Proficiency in Gurmukhi, 5.

Proficiency in Sanskrit, 20. | Do. in Persian, 7 |

In addition to students actually belonging to the Oriental College, 114 students of the Government College, Lahore, who were reading for Arts Examinations, received in the year 1892-93 instruction in Oriental Languages from the staff of the Oriental College, seven teachers (among them the Principal) taking part in the tuition of these classes.

The following statement shows the number of students of the Oriental College who passed the various University Examinations during the last five years and the average percentages of passed candidates for each year :—

	1888-89	1889-90	1890-91	1891-92	1892-93	Aggregate for five years
Percentage of passed candidates	67·7	71·4	72·4	82·8	66·1	
Total number of students passed	43	40	42	47	39	211
GURMUKHI — High Proficiency or Vidyán	3	2	2	3	1	11
Proficiency or Buddhimán	1	3	2	1	2	9
Special Examination — English language	...	...	...	2	7	9
PERSIAN — Honors or Munshi	7	3	1	3	5	
High Proficiency or Munshi Alim	1	2	3	3	1	10
Proficiency or Munshi	1	1	3	1	1	7
ARABIC — Honors or Maulvi Fazil	3	3	6	5	4	21
High Proficiency or Maulvi Alim	5	6	6	5	4	26
SANSKRIT — Honors or Shastri	...	2	2	3	1	8
High Proficiency or Vishárada	5	2	3	2	1	13
Proficiency or Prajna	5	2	6	5	4	22
ORIENTAL FACULTY — M.O.L. and M.A. Examinations	...	2	...	1	1	4
B.O.L. Examination	2	3	2	1	2	10
Intermediate Examination	3	2	3	5	2	15
Entrance	2	3	4	2	1	12

With regard to the results of the tuition given by the Oriental College to students of the Government College, it may be
noted that 87·2 per cent. of all Government College students who
appeared in the Intermediate and B. A. Examinations of 1893
passed with success in the Oriental Classical Languages in which
they had received tuition from the Oriental College staff.

The system of house examinations in College and School,
as introduced in 1888, is supplemented by an annual examination for the first year classes. The award and tenure of
stipends has been made in every case strictly dependent on
the results gained by individual scholars in these house examinations.

The library of the College which has been considerably
enlarged since 1888 is chiefly intended to provide the College
with critical editions of Oriental Classics and with such modern
works dealing with the several departments of Oriental studies
as would help the teachers and students to acquaint themselves
with the results obtained by Western philological and historical
research.

The Law School was founded by the Punjab University
College in the year 1870 with the view of imparting legal knowledge to candidates preparing for the Mukhtárship and Pleader-
ship Examinations. Since the year 1882 the Law School has
been maintained and controlled by the Punjab University which
obtained the power of granting licenses and Degrees of Law.

Candidates who have passed the Entrance Examination of
the Punjab University, or who have obtained the special permission of the Chief Court, are admitted in the Law School.
After one year's attendance and on their passing the Intermediate Examination they are allowed to appear at the Preliminary Examination in Law, and on their passing this examination
they are admitted to the second year class. After a year's attendance and on their passing the First Certificate Examination
in Law they are admitted to the third year class in which they
are prepared for the Licentiate in Law Examination.

Similarly, a graduate who has passed the Preliminary and
Intermediate Examinations in Law is eligible to appear at the
LL. B. Examination after a total attendance of three years at
the Law School.

The staff of the Law School for 1893 consisted of a Law
Lecturer, two Assistant Law Lecturers and two Law Readers.

The expenditure during the year ending 31st December
1892 amounted to Rs. 7,440-7-4 as against Rs. 6,271-1-0 in the
previous year.

The income of the Law School consists of admission,
tuition and examination fees. The receipts realised from 1st
October 1892 to 30th September 1893 amounted to Rs. 5,252
as against Rs. 4,645-8-0 in the previous year.

Chapter V, B.

Education.

Part II—Medical College, Lahore.

In the various Law Examinations for 1892 the following number of candidates passed from the Law School:—

Licentiate Examination 7	Preliminary Examination ... 23
First Certificate Examination ... 5	Intermediate Examination ... 3

Medical College, Lahore.

The Medical College was founded in 1860 with the object of training natives of the Punjab as medical practitioners; it having been found that Bengalís were not so acceptable to the people of the Punjab in the capacity of medical men as their own fellow countrymen. Doctor J. B. Scriven was the first Principal, and with him were associated Doctor Manners Smith, Civil Surgeon of Lahore, and Doctor Burton Browne, who succeeded to the Principalship in 1872. The College was first located in an old barrack on the site at present occupied by the Government College, and attached to it was a hospital constructed out of a building formerly used as a stable in the Tibbi bazár. In 1870 the Mayo Hospital took the place of the rude structure formerly in use, and in 1883 the present College buildings were completed and opened. These buildings are situated on the south side of the Mayo Hospital in the same enclosure and are in the same architectural style. They consist of a large one-storied building composed of a central block and two wings at right angles. In the central block are the large library hall, and three lecture theatres, with the Principal's office. In the west wing were at first the dissecting room and anatomical museum, but within the past two years the dissecting room has been removed to a large and handsome building erected on the site formerly occupied by the Christian Free School of Lahore; the accommodation thus released has been occupied by zoological and pathological museums and laboratories. In the east wing are the chemical laboratory and museum. The cost of the original College buildings was Rs. 1,15,000 and the new dissecting room in which there is accommodation for 500 students with a lecture room and museum attached, cost Rs. 41,000.

The College contains two classes of students, viz., those reading for a University degree or diploma in medicine, and those who are being trained as Hospital Assistants; the latter are taught in the vernacular and constitute what is termed the "Hindustáni" class, whilst the University candidates form the "English" class. The number of students under instruction in 1893 in each of these classes was as follows:—

English class 200
Hindustáni class 298
Total 498

The expenditure on the College during the year 1892-93 was Rs. 98,825. The staff consists of the Principal assisted by seven Professors in the English class and four teachers in the Hindustáni class.

Since its foundation the College has educated 187 Licentiates in Medicine, 4 Bachelors of Medicine and 653 Hospital Assistants, the majority of whom have been employed by Government. The lectures delivered in the College are now recognised by most of the English licensing medical bodies.

The Daya Nand Anglo-Vedic College was established in honour of Swámi Daya Nand Saraswati with the following objects :—

Daya Nand Anglo-Vedic College.

(*a*) To encourage, improve and enforce the study of Hindi literature.

(*b*) To encourage and enforce the study of classical Sanskrit and of the Vedas.

(*c*) To encourage and enforce the study of English literature and sciences, both theoretical and applied.

(*d*). To provide for technical education in the country.

The College is situated next to the Lahore Government College. It cost about Rs. 41,000 to build and was opened on 1st June 1886. It is supported by means of subscriptions and endowments contributed by members of the Arya Samáj and the income from tuition fees. The amount of endowment for the maintenance of the institution at present in the hands of the Managing Committee is little short of a lakh-and-a-half. The College prepares boys for the Middle School, Entrance and Intermediate in Arts Examinations and teaches English, Sanskrit, Persian, History and Philosophy, Physical Sciences going up to the B. A. Standard. The College has been steadily increasing in numbers, and at the close of the year 1892-93 contained 212 students. Of these 190 were in the Intermediate and 22 in the B. A. class.

This institution was first established in the year 1866, but three years later was closed again chiefly owing to the death of the Rev. Mr. Henry, the Principal. It was re-opened in 1886, and since then has been sending candidates to the Intermediate and B. A. Examinations of the Punjab University.

Mission College, Lahore.

The present College buildings and boarding-houses were completed in 1889 at a cost of Rs. 60,000 or more on land granted by the Punjab Government, who also gave a building grant of Rs. 20,000. The institution has no endowment, either for its maintenance or for scholarships and prizes but a large number of its students are the recipients of Government, Municipal or University scholarships. Boarding-house accommodation is provided for about one-half the whole number of students in attendance, which in 1893 was 235 ; of these 126 were Hindús, 58 Muhammadans, 27 Sikhs, 24 Christians.

SOCIAL AND EDUCATIONAL.
PART III.

The following brief account of the leading societies at present in existence in Lahore is inserted here under Education, as their objects are mainly educational.

Sat Sabha, Lahore.—This Sabha was founded in 1866. Its object is the diffusion of useful knowledge through the medium of the Punjábi language and the reformation of the moral and social condition of the Hindu community.

Anjuman-i-Islámiya, Lahore.—The Anjuman-i-Islámiya was established in 1869, and interests itself in all questions affecting the Muhammadan community. Its chief aims are to popularize the measures of Government affecting Muhammadans, and to represent to Government the views of that community.

Guru Singh Sabha, Lahore.—This society was founded in 1879. It has for its special object the representation of Sikh interests, the encouragement of the Punjábi language, and the maintenance of Sikh doctrines and customs.

Arya Samáj, Lahore.—This Samáj was founded in 1879. It has for its main object the revival of the Vedic religion and the spread of Sanskrit learning. It maintains a College at Lahore, called the Daya Nand Anglo-Vedic College, which is one of the most interesting educational enterprises in Northern India. The society has numerous branches. It issues an organ in English called the *Arya Patrika.*

The Khálsa Diwán, Lahore.—This society was established in 1883. Its chief aims are the diffusion of useful knowledge among the Sikh community, the improvement of Punjábi literature, the extension of female education, the religious instruction of Sikh youths to unite the Sikh community into a whole, and to inculcate loyalty to the British Government. It has various branches throughout the province. It started recently the Khálsa College, a movement which is likely to result in complete success.

The Indian Association, Lahore.—This society, which is a branch of the National Indian Association, Calcutta, was established in 1883. Its chief objects are political advancement and social reform.

The Punjab Association, Lahore.—This association, which was established in 1886, is a branch of the society in London, known as the National Indian Association. The objects of the Association are (1) to co-operate with all efforts made for advancing female education and social reform in India, especially in the Punjab; (2) to promote friendly intercourse between the English people and the people of India. The Association publishes in English and Urdu a monthly journal called the *Punjab Magazine.*

Anjuman-i-Himáyat-i-Islám, Lahore.—This Anjuman was established in 1886. Its objects are to discuss and publish the principles of Islám, to teach the Muhammadan religion to boys and girls, so as to save them from the influence of other religions and to support poor and orphan children. It maintains a large school in connection with which College classes have recently been opened and publishes text-books for Islámiya schools.

The Punjab Science Institute, Lahore.—This society was founded in 1886, owing chiefly to the efforts of Professor J. C. Oman. Its chief objects are the diffusion of scientific knowledge and the encouragement of technical education in the Punjab. It gives popular lectures in science throughout the year in both English and the Vernacular.

SECTION C.—MILITARY.

The principal Military station in the district is the cantonment of Mian Mir, the head-quarters of the Lahore Division, situated about four miles to the east of the civil station and seven from the fort of Lahore. The locality was selected in 1851-52, when it was decided to abandon the former cantonments at Anárkali on account of their unhealthiness. It has two railway stations—Mian Mir East, on the line from Lahore to Delhi, and Mian Mir West, on the line from Lahore to Mooltan. The ordinary garrison of Mian Mir consists of two Batteries of Royal Artillery, one regiment of British Infantry, one of Bengal Native Infantry, and one of Punjab Pioneers. Lahore is held by detachments of Royal Artillery and British and Native Infantry from Mian Mir.

The total strength of the garrison at present is as shown in the margin: this includes 201 men on detachment at Amritsar.

Station.	Staff and Regimental Officers.	Artillery.	Ammunition establishment.	Native Cavalry.	British Infantry.	Native Infantry.
Mian Mir	88	214	392	625	901	1,771
Fort Lahore	3	...	...	...	82	53
Total ...	91	214	392	625	983	1,824

The Transport establishment authorised for Mian Mir Depôt and the two Field Batteries of Royal Artillery is shown below:—

Detail.	Elephants.	Pack mules.	Hired camels.	Draught and grass mules.	Siege train bullocks.	Draught bullocks.	Mule carts.	Bullock carts.	Jamadárs and Daffadárs.	Salútrís.	Artificers.	Other camp followers.
Mian Mir Depôt and Field Batteries.	22	200	312	150	160	148	31	180	23	2	12	287

Chapter V, C.
Military.

Besides the above the following ambulance transport is authorised to be maintained at Mian Mir :—

Field dandís	...	...	...	80
Ambulance tongás	...	...	...	48
Field stretchers	...	...	...	68
Bearers	...	...	...	300

men with 6 mates and 3 sardárs.

Mian Mir has, from the first, been conspicuously unhealthy as a station for troops.

Volunteers.

The 1st Punjab and North-Western Railway Volunteer Rifle Corps have their head-quarters at Lahore.

The Administrative Battalion 1st Punjab Volunteers consists of the Punjab Light Horse and three companies of Rifles, of which " A " and " B " companies are mainly composed of Clerks in Government employ, with a small sprinkling of the Mercantile community.

" C " company consists of the Educational staff and pupils of the Boys' High School and Cathedral Orphanage.

The strength of the 1st Punjab Volunteers as it stood on the 1st January 1894 is shown in the statement in the margin. There are also 25 Reservists in Lahore.

Troop or Companies.	Officers.	Non-Commissioned Officers.	Volunteers.	Total.
Punjab Light Horse ..	2	3	37	42
" A " Coy. ...	3	7	91	101
" B " ,, ...	6	3	71	80
" C " ,, ...	2	3	42	47
Total ...	13	16	241	270

The Punjab Light Horse Corps is of quite recent formation, having been sanctioned by the Government of India in 1893. At present the corps consists of about 50 members, Mr. Arthur Grey being the Commandant; they recruit entirely from Europeans, the names being first approved by a committee appointed by the corps. Their head-quarters are in Lahore, separate from those of the 1st Punjab Volunteer Rifles, with which the Punjab Light Horse are linked only for administrative purposes. A Sergeant Instructor is attached to the Corps; drill exercises are held every morning and regular parades twice a week. The corps is at present entitled to one Lieutenant and one Sub-Lieutenant as well as the Commandant.

The North-Western Railway Volunteer Rifles are nearly all Railway employés and have three companies at head-quarters at Lahore. On the 1st January 1894 the strength of these three companies and head-quarter staff was 11 officers, 45 non-commissioned officers and 257 privates. The corps has an Adjutant, and the Director-General of Railways is the Honorary

Colonel. The Commandant is the Manager of the North-Western Railway, and the Field Officers are Heads of Departments, the Company Officers being the District officers of the line.

The corps is completely equipped for service and has great-coats, havresacks and water-bottles.

The corps has eight out companies quartered at different places on the North-Western Railway.

The funds of the corps are in a very flourishing state, nearly every member earning the capitation grant every year. It contains some of the most famous rifle shots in India, and has won the Inter-Regimental Cup, B. P. R. A. four times in the last six years.

SECTION D.—REVENUE.
PART I.—LAND REVENUE.

Land Revenue.

The system in force for taxing the land under the Muhammadan rule is not clearly known. During the Sikh *ráj* the State's share of all ordinary crops was fixed at one-fourth : this was taken in kind either by the system of *kankut*, which was a rough appraisement of the outturn before the crop was cut or by division after the crop was harvested. The Government share of the produce was usually sold in the village at current bazár prices. On special crops such as sugar-cane, cotton and tobacco the revenue was often taken in cash : that is the cultivator either paid eight annas a kanal ou the area actually cropped or Rs. 12 a well in lieu of all demands on account of such special crops. Much of the district was then granted in jágír to powerful Sikh feudatories who had the right of collecting and keeping the full Government demand on the tract assigned. The land retained by the State for its own benefit was either farmed out to lessees or managed directly under the State through paid revenue agents. In either case extortion was the rule and the people had to pay numberless extra imposts over and above the legitimate state demand.

Settlement of Land Revenue.

Immediately after annexation in 1849 a summary settlement was effected by Captain Tytler at cash rates ; based on a rough valuation of the kind rents taken by the Sikhs subject to a deduction of 10 per cent. For want of reliable information and experience as to the true productive capacity of the land Captain Tytler pitched his assessments somewhat high. Prices at that time were ruling low, and the new assessments were immediately followed by a failure of the rains. Consequently the people felt this unaccustomed system of cash payments extremely burdensome and many of them left their villages and lands sooner than submit to it. Three years later operations for a regular settlement commenced. Large reductions were granted at once and the people were gradually induced to return to their homes. Mr Egerton had charge of the settlement of the Cis-Rávi portion of the district as it now is, and Mr. Morris of the Trans-Rávi portion, much of which was at that time included in the Gujrán-

wála district. The settlement occupied four or five years,
and was concluded in 1858. In that time the boundaries of
mauzas or revenue paying units were carefully demarcated for
the first time. All land under cultivation was measured. The
rights of ownership or occupation were enquired into and recorded, and distinctions drawn between tenants with or without
rights of occupancy. The ultimate assessments of the first
regular settlement showed a reduction of 11 per cent. on the
summary demand of 1851 for the whole district, which was constituted in its present boundaries immediately after settlement
operations were concluded. The pitch of Mr. Egerton's assessments varied from less than eight annas an acre of cultivated
land in the Mánjha uplands to one rupee or more in the
river tracts. Mr. Morris's assessments in the Trans-Rávi portion of the district averaged as high as Re. 1-7-0 the acre.
The cause of the latter assessments being so high comparatively
to those in the Cis-Rávi tract dated back to the original summary
assessments. The Trans-Rávi cultivation is carried on mainly
by well irrigation, the profits from which there was at that time
a tendency to exaggerate. Moreover much of the land on that
side of the river then received excellent inundation partly from
the Rávi and partly from the Deg stream. Even as early as
1856, owing to the widening of the Rávi bed, and the increasing
appropriation of the Deg water by villages situate along the
stream before it reaches Lahore district, this natural inundation was showing a marked falling off. Mr. Morris marked his
sense of the previous assessments having been excessive by
partial reductions, but from one reason or another failed to give
sufficient relief. Shortly after his assessments were announced
twelve estates were thrown up by their owners and had to be
farmed out for a time. Further reduction of revenue was found
necessary in a considerable number : and many continued to
pay a revenue which was above the value of the share of produce to which Government was theoretically entitled.

The first regular settlement was sanctioned for a term of
ten years. In 1860 a severe drought set in which lasted nearly
two years. Prices rose very high in 1861, wheat going up to 16
sérs the rupee. Relief came in 1862 and seasons continued
favourable until 1869 when a second drought occurred hardly
as severe as that of 1860-61.

The revision of the regular settlement was commenced by
Mr. Saunders in 1864 and completed in 1868 under the
supervision of Mr. Prinsep, Settlement Commissioner. New
maps and records were made for each estate. Assessment circles
had been arranged at the previous settlement and revenue
rates framed for each circle ; but Mr. Egerton had assessed
considerably below his circle rates and Mr. Morris also, though
to a less degree. Mr. Saunders retained the former arrangement of assessment circles, and for dry cultivation assumed
revenue rates very little different from his predecessor's,
but under Mr. Prinsep's directions lightened the assessments

on wells, abandoning the system before in vogue of assessing well-irrigated land with an acreage rate, in favor of imposing a lump sum on each well. This lump sum known as well *abiána* was varied from circle to circle but was uniform for all wells in each circle. The highest *abiána* was Rs. 20 in the immediate vicinity of Lahore where water is near the surface and well cultivation is very profitable; and the lowest was Rs. 6 a well in the western portion of the Mánjha where the water-bearing stratum lies very deep and wells are most expensive both to build and to work. Besides framing revenue rates Mr. Saunders also made calculations of the value of the produce grown in each circle, the principle of assessment then being apparently that Government was entitled to take one-sixth share of the gross produce. These estimates however were based on very unreliable *data*, both as regards the area ordinarily cropped and the assumed rates of yield : nor does Mr. Saunders appear to have paid much attention to them : for the total amount of those estimates for the district was Rs. 9,94,000 while his revenue rate estimate came to less than Rs. 7,40,000 and his actual assessments to Rs. 6,79,000 only. The impression left by Mr. Saunders' village assessments and the notes he left behind him is, that his conclusions as to what each village could pay were based on the revenue it had hitherto paid and on the progress it had made since the previous settlement. Relying on his predecessor's assessments as absolutely correct at the time they were made he increased or reduced according as the estate's resources had improved or deteriorated. The result of his settlement therefore was to leave the pitch of assessment very much as it had been before : the actual increase of revenue fixed by Mr. Saunders over the previous demand was hardly proportionate to the mere increase of cultivation alone that had taken place between the two settlements, setting aside all improvement in respect of other resources, such as artificial irrigation, rise of prices, and extended markets and communications. The following statement shows the revenue assessed on the district at each of the settlements noticed above, the incidence of each fresh demand on the cultivated area of the time, and the percentage of decrease or increase resulting from each new assessment :—

		Initial assessment.	Progressive after ten years.	Total.	Percentage of decrease or increase.	Incidence on cultivated area of initial assessment.
		Rs.	Rs.	Rs.	Rs.	Rs. a. p.
Summary Settlement, 1851	...	6,03,736	...	6,03,736	...	0-12-6
Regular Settlement, 1856	...	5,45,917	...	5,45,917	−11	0-11-8
Revised Settlement, 1868	...	6,78,755	46,942	7,25,697	+22	0-11-6

The progressive increases were intended to provide for probable extensions of cultivation in estates with a large amount of waste. Some were to come into effect after five years, some after ten years. The Government was of opinion that Mr. Saunders' whole assessments were extremely moderate and that well-irrigated lands had been treated too leniently under Mr. Prinsep's system, revenue having been sacrificed that was fairly due to Government. Partly on this account and partly in view of the rapidly increasing value of land and agricultural produce, the Punjab Government in their review of the settlement proceedings expressed their opinion that it would be inexpedient to sanction the settlement for the term of 30 years as proposed by Mr. Saunders and held that ten years would be sufficient. Subsequently however it was discovered that the Settlement Commissioner had been authorized to announce, and did announce, that that settlement was to be made for 20 years. It was therefore deemed right by the Government of India, notwithstanding the lightness of the assessment, to sanction the settlement for that term, and orders were issued accordingly.

The announcement of the new assessments in 1868 was followed early by a severe drought which lasted nearly two years and then succeeded several seasons of short rainfall. The middle years of the term of revised settlement were fairly favourable to the cultivators, the latter years were generally marked by inadequacy of the rainfall. From the very commencement the Bári Doáb Canal was being rapidly extended over the Mánjha tract and in the western portion of the Sutlej Hithár irrigation from the inundation canals was spreading more slowly : the latter though not nearly so beneficial to the lands irrigated as the former, was very lightly taxed with canal revenue rates. In all such irrigated tracts therefore the improvement of resources and the accompanying extension of cultivation taking place year by year took away all possibility of the revised assessments proving oppressive. Elsewhere in the Cis-Rávi portion of the district the revenue demand was found fair enough as a general rule and heavy only in certain individual estates : north of the Rávi however many villages had considerable difficulty in meeting their revenue liabilities unless the season's rainfall was favourable above the average.

Second revision of settlement. ·

The revision of Mr. Saunders' assessment of 1868 was made between 1891 and 1893, settlement operations having been begun in the summer of 1888. The entire district, excepting some of the Government rakhs was re-surveyed and the land records were brought up to date. These latter operations were not concluded till the spring of 1893. To avoid waste of time and undesirable protraction of the settlement proceedings, assessment proposals were submitted and sanctioned for each tahsíl before all measurements and records were complete. As sanction to the proposals for each tahsíl with emendations was received individual village assessments were fixed and announced : the distribution of the village demands was then made on the village areas as then known. Subsequently however when new records for all estates were complete in 1893 the village assessments were re-distributed afresh over the areas ascertained from the newly completed measurements. The principle laid down for assessment at this second revised settlement was that the new demand should not exceed half the landlord's net assets as ascertained from estimates made of the value of the gross produce, and from cash and kind rents found to be paid. The reasons for taking an increase on the previous revenue demand of the district were first an extension of the area under cultivation by about 33 per cent. on that shown as cultivated in the records of 1868; secondly a rise of prices estimated by the Settlement Officer to be between twenty and twenty-five per cent., thirdly the admitted inadequacy of the previous assessments, particularly on irrigated soils. The leniency of Mr. Saunders' assessments on well-irrigated land has already been adverted to. No provision existed in 1868 for assessing canal irrigation to land revenue in excess of that found suitable for dry cultivation; it was considered that the landlord's extra profits arising from such canal irrigation should be left to the Canal Department to tax as they might see fit, and to this end it was settled by the Government in 1868 that all land actually irrigated in any one harvest should pay in addition to the water-rates which generally varied according to the crop irrigated a fluctuating water-advantage or owner's-rate as it was sometimes called: its amount varied from 8 annas to Re. 1-8 according to the locality and the nature of the irrigation. While the recent settlement was in progress, in 1891 the system of Bári Doáb Canal rates underwent a reform. The old water rates or price of the water were raised; the new rates were taken slightly higher than the former water-rates and the water-advantage rates combined : and orders were issued on the land revenue side in supersession of previous instructions that all land classed in the village records as canal irrigated (*nahri*) should be rated and assessed higher than lands not enjoying canal irrigation. The result of this reform was that the dry rates of the previous settlement, low as they had always seemed by comparison with rates current in other adjacent tracts, yet when extended to the new and hitherto unassessed area under cultivation, were found sufficient, with the addition of a small extra wet rate on all land under canal irrigation, to create a large increase of revenue : consequently in view of the undesirability for political and economical reasons of taking suddenly too large an increase, it was not found possible in the Bári Doáb to raise the dry or well-irrigated rates of the former settlements to any great extent. In the Sutlej Hithár for irrigation from the inundation canals the former water-rates were increased and the water-advantage or owner's-rate was slightly raised, the result of which was, to raise the total canal payment by 62 per cent. Land revenue on canal-irrigated land here was to be assessed on the same principles as unirrigated land : indeed in this case owing to the large increase in the canal payments on such land and to the absolute dependence of the soil once irrigated from the inundation canals on the continuance of the irrigation it was deemed advisable to put a slightly lower rate on land under irrigation from such canals than was deemed suitable for unirrigated land. The revenue-rates sanctioned for each assessment circle and for each class of land, irrigated or unirrigated, are stated in the Settlement Report of 1893. The final increase of revenue obtained in each tahsíl and the incidence of the old and new assessments on the existing cultivated areas are shown below :—

TAHSIL.	REVENUE IN THE YEAR BEFORE REVISION.		REVENUE NEWLY ASSESSED.		Percentage of increase.
	Total.	Incidence on cultivated area per acre.	Total.	Incidence on cultivated area per acre.	
	Rs.	Rs. a. p.	Rs.	Rs. a. p.	
Lahore	2,21,440	0 14 6	3,13,710	1 0 0	41
Kasúr	1,92,585	0 7 5	3,00,336	0 11 6	56
Chúnián	1,68,769	0 7 5	2,21,976	0 9 2	32
Sharakpur ...	1,39,849	0 15 2	1,41,259	0 15 1	1
Total District ...	7,22,643	0 12 4	9,77,281	0 12 8	35

The above figures do not include anything for canal owner's rate which on land irrigated from the Sutlej Inundation Canals has been estimated to yield Rs. 27,000.

In addition to the land revenue shown above, a further sum is levied from the landowners on account of rates and cesses which altogether make up an increase of Rs. 20-6-8 per cent. on the fixed revenue. These rates and cesses are as follows :—Rs. 10-6-8 per cent. for local rates, Rs. 5 per cent. for lambardári cess and Rs. 5 per cent. for patwáris' cess. Besides these in some villages, which at present form the majority, another cess of one per cent. is taken for payment of a village officer known as the Ala Lambardár or chief headman. This appointment, however, has now fallen somewhat out of date and is regarded by most revenue officers as unnecessary. It has, therefore, been abolished for the future in all villages where its usefulness could not be ascertained, though the abolition is not to come into effect until the present holder is dead. Thus, the Ala Lambardári cess will continue to be levied in fewer and fewer villages as years go on. Including cesses then the total fixed demands for which landowners are responsible to Government in the present year 1892-93 are shown below for each tahsíl :—

Tahsil.	Fixed land revenue.	Rates and cesses varying between Rs. 20-6-8 and Rs. 21-6-8 on land revenue.	Total.
	Rs.	Rs.	Rs.
Lahore	2,17,395	64,472	2,81,867
Kasúr	2,73,169	61,875	3,35,044
Chúnián	1,91,799	44,886	2,36,685
Sharakpur	1,17,152	29,439	1,46,591
Total ...	7,99,515	2,00,672	10,00,187

The cultivated areas upon which the present revenue is collected are shown in Table No. XIV which purports to be a statement of surveyed and assessed area, including waste as well as cultivated. Ordinarily the village assessments were not increased on account of the existence of waste. Many estates, especially in Chúnián and Sharakpur tahsils, include large areas not under cultivation which *primâ facie* should strengthen their resources materially and form a valuable additional asset, whether they be regarded as grazing ground for cattle or as new land to be brought under the plough as necessity may arise. As grazing grounds they are no doubt useful for the village cattle, but by the custom of the country the village menials to whom most of the stray cattle belong get their grazing free, and consequently the owners make no actual profit off such waste land though of course they benefit in some degree by having superfluous grazing land for their own cattle. As affording opportunity for extension of cultivation the existence of superfluous waste land is in some degree a source of strength to the estate, but unless irrigation can be secured for the new land, extension of cultivation in reliance merely on the precarious rainfall of this district only adds to an insecure area already large enough. Moreover the declared Government policy is to assess existing assets and not prospective profits. Only in Sharakpur tahsil in the Bár tract, where waste land is very extensive and the people are many of them graziers living more on the profits derived from their cattle herds than on the produce of their land, was land revenue avowedly assessed on the waste land.

In the civil station of Lahore, however, there was at the time of the British occupation a quantity of waste broken ground apparently unclaimed by any one. As the number of European residents in Lahore increased, houses were required and more and more of this land was taken up for building sites. At the revised settlement of 1868 under orders

Chapter V, D.

Part I—Land Revenue.

Second revision of settlement.

conveyed in Punjab Government printed letter No. 448 of the 24th March 1869 all land taken up for building purposes up to that time in the civil station of Lahore was assessed at Rs. 5 per acre; this sum, however, was to be inclusive of cesses. At the recent revision of settlement it was found that 1,026 acres of land had been built upon altogether : some of this had been assessed in 1868, some had been built upon since and had so far escaped assessment. Thereupon all land actually under buildings or compounds in the civil station was assessed at Rs. 5 an acre inclusive of cesses and a provision was sanctioned for the assessment at the same rate of all land in future taken up within the limits of the civil station for private building purposes.

Crown lands of Kasúr.

The lands belonging to the township of Kasúr comprising slightly over 8,000 acres were confiscated by the Sikh Government when the city of Kasúr was taken from the Patháns and had not been disposed of by them when the Government passed from the hands of the Sikhs to the British. At regular settlement the proprietary rights were still retained by Government and the land was leased out at a fixed sum to farmers who made what they could out of the tenants. In 1873 the estate was remeasured and a record of rights was prepared. Five hundred acres had then been granted out of the estate to two native gentlemen of Kasúr. The rest of the land was held by occupancy tenants or by tenants without rights of occupancy, the latter having far the larger share of the land. The revenue assessed on the estate in 1868 fell on the land at the rate of 4 annas 9 pies per ghumao, and totalled Rs. 1,524 which was to be increased to Rs. 1,800 after ten years. At the recent settlement a fresh record of rights was prepared for the estate. It was found that the amount of land in the hands of private alienees who had received it in grants from the Government at different times was 1,001 acres. The area under occupancy tenants' holding under Section 5 of the Land Revenue Act was found to be 431 acres cultivated and 38 acres uncultivated, while occupancy tenants under Section 6 were holding 1,412 acres cultivated and 27 acres uncultivated. All the above land was ordered to be assessed at the revenue-rates fixed for the estate, namely Re. 1-4-0 the acre on lands under sweet wells, Re. 1 the acre on lands under saline wells, 10 annas the acre on canal-irrigated land, 7 annas on unirrigated land. But occupancy tenants under Section 5 have to pay in addition 6 annas in the rupee of revenue and those under Section 6 have to pay 12 annas in the rupee additional.

Tenants-at-will were ordered to pay generally Rs. 2 an acre on all irrigated land and Re. 1-4-0 on unirrigated land, these rates being taken as a standard, and leases for 10 years were to be given to all such tenants. Cesses were to be paid on a portion only of the rents. The area in occupation of tenants-at-will was found by measurement to be 3,270 acres cultivated and 143 acres uncultivated. Four lessees were in possession of

515 acres under leases granted in 1887 and expiring in 1897, or a year later. The question of treatment to be extended to these lessees will be settled when the leases fall in. Formerly certain land in this estate had been granted in jágír to the Municipal Committee ; this has now been resumed. All plots of land of the class hitherto recorded as under *Qábizán*, the total area of which aggregated 107 acres, have been made over to the care of the Municipal Committee, Government being recorded as owner. Formerly no trees on any part of these crown lands could be cut down without permission of the officer in charge, and this restriction is still maintained. The total income from the crown lands of Kasúr, the area of which, including 872 acres waste, is 6,521 acres, comes to Rs. 7,008, of which Rs. 3,350 is on account of land revenue proper, Rs. 523 is additional rent paid by occupancy tenants and Rs. 3,135 is rent paid by tenants-at-will over and above the land revenue due on their holdings.

Table No. XXX shows the number of villages, parts of villages and plots, and the area of land of which the revenue is assigned, the amount of that revenue, the period of assignment, and the number of assignees for each tahsíl, as the figures stood in 1893. It will be understood that this only shows assignees of *land* revenue, and excludes *inámdárs*, &c., who receive out of the revenue of certain villages fixed sums bearing no relation to any ascertained area of land. If these *inúms*, &c., are included, the total amount of land revenue, which is assigned to others, and does not reach the Government Treasury, is Rs. 1,43,363 or 15 per cent. of the whole demand. The principal assignments, some of which have already been noticed in Chapter III, are as follows :—

Rája Harbans Singh, Rs. 4,459 ; Rája of Kapurthalla, Rs. 5,651 ; Sardár Sarúp Singh, Rs. 7,703 ; the *Bhai* family of Lahore, Rs. 8,346 ; Nawáb Ghulám Mahbúb Subháni, Rs. 7,683 ; Sardár Bhola Singh of Todipur, Rs. 2,497 ; Sardár Sangat Singh of Algon, Rs. 2,834 ; Mahánt Hari Dás of Bháipheru, Rs. 3,088.

The areas upon which the present revenue is collected are shown in Table No. XIV, while Table No. XXIX shows the revenue actually realized from land and in connection with land administration during the 11 years ending 1892-93 with full details.

The statistics given in Table No. XXXI showing balances, uspensions, remissions and advances under the Land Improvement and Agriculturist Loans Acts throw some light on the working of the last settlement.

Table No. XVII shows the area of rakh land owned by Government and the income obtained in 1892-93 on the rakh land granted out under cultivating leases ; the total area available for such leases under the Collector's control is 20,636 acres ; of this a large area, including 5,676 acres of waste land, have been granted on leases of 10 years or more ; the balance are given on yearly leases.

Chapter V, D.

Part I—Land Revenue.

Table No. XVII A gives some detail of other land owned by Government, not included in the rakh statement Table No. XVII.

Nazúl properties.

The principal *nazúl* properties consist of ancient buildings and cultivated and waste lands near Lahore. The following is a list of all the chief buildings situate in the district possessing any historical interest.

1. The tomb of Jahángír at Shahdara.
2.   „   of Asaf Jah at   „
3.   „   of Núr Jahán at   „
4 A domed building known as Nátch Ghar at Núrpur, let to North-Western Railway at an annual rental of Rs. 48.
5. The domed tomb of Bahádur Khan near Achintgarh.
6. The domed tomb of Ali at Achint-garh.
7. The domed tomb of Chisti on the Shálámár road.
8. The domed tomb of Sardár Fateh Singh at Achintgarh.
9. The domed tomb of Hazrat Ishán at Begampura.
10. Domed building known as Saru-wála at Begampura.
11. Domed tomb of Dái Angan.
12.   „   of Banglíwála.
13.   „   of Hakay Khan at Bághbánpur.
14. Domed building known as " *Maga-zinewála* " on the Mooltan road in Anárkali.

All the above, with the exception of No. 4 are unoccupied, and are maintained by the Government at an estimated cost of Rs. 100 per annum with the exception of the tomb of Jahángír and the Shálámár gardens which are maintained by Public Works Department under the supervision of the Executive Engineer, Lahore Provincial Division. The following is a list of the *nazúl* buildings requiring mention situate inside the city of Lahore :—

1. A Burj over the Roshnái gate.
2. The Haveli Nakáinwáli.
3. Hammám Wazír Khan.
4. Haveli Nau Nihál Singh.
5. The large Haveli of Suchet Singh.
6. The small   do.   do.
7. Tavela Suchet Singh.
8. Haveli Ganpat Rái.

Of the above No. 3 is used as an Octroi post and School, No. 4 as a Girls' School, Nos. 5 and 6 as the Lahore tahsíl, No. 7 as Munsiff's Court and No. 8 has been made over to the Municipal Committee on a yearly rental of Rs. 12 only.

The following as a list of the *nazúl* buildings situate outside the city of Lahore—

1. *Bárádari* of Mahárája Sher Singh in Shah Bilával.
2. *Sardi* at Shahdara.
3. Chauburji in Náwakot.
4. Gateway to the Gulábi Bágh near Begampura.
5. Gateway in Achintgarh.
6. *Bárádari* on the bank of the Rávi near Tárgarh, used as a road bungalow.
7. Barracks in Anárkali.
8. Chauburji in Anárkali.

In addition to the above there are 13 others of no particular interest, wholly or partially in ruins ; all of them are unoccupied except the one known as Gumbaz Mír Mannun which yields a yearly rental of Rs. 15 only. Of the above eight buildings No. 6 is used as a road bungalow, No. 7 for the offices of the Director of Public Instruction, Inspector-General of Jails, Sanitary Commissioner and the Government Advocate. No. 8 is occupied by the Punjab Public Library.

The *nazúl* buildings in Kasúr are—

1. Díwán Khana.
2. The domed building used as the court house of the Assistant Commissioner in charge of the Kasúr Subdivision and as a rest-house.

There are sixteen other buildings either wholly or partially in ruins, and of no particular interest. Of these only four buildings yield a yearly rental of Rs. 15 only.

There are about 4,148 acres of *nazúl* land, of which 2,452 acres are cultivated and 1,696 acres waste, chiefly situated in Anárkali and Lahore. The land in Anárkali is given out on rent at annual rates varying from Rs. 24 to 48 per acre. The question of increasing the rent on lands in Anárkali is under consideration. On some plots there are orchards and gardens, which are leased for a term of five years. The cultivated lands are now generally leased for one year. All the tenants are at will, and can be ejected within the period of their leases. The total yearly income derived from the *nazúl* lands and gardens amounts to Rs. 3,676, of which Rs. 2,005 is derived from the rent of land in Anárkali.

Notice of the rakh or forest lands has already been made in Chapter IV A. The number and area of rakhs which have not been leased out for cultivation and are still in the true condition of forest land are shown in the marginal statement.

Name of Tahsíl.	Number of forests.	Area in acres.
Lahore	22	31,086
Chúnián	34	123,654
Sharakpur ...	18	72,832
Total ...	74	227,572

The following tables give a detail of the rakh land in each tahsíl and show the departments under which they are managed. That under district management is no longer forest, having been mostly broken up for cultivation :—

TAHSIL LAHORE.

Rakhs under the Forest Department.

No.	Name of rakh.	Area in acres.	No.	Name of rakh.	Area in acres.
1	RESERVED FORESTS Shahdara plantation—		6	Rakh Jhedu	471
	Shahdara		7	Ladheke	1,958
	Jhuggián	1,396	8	Khana Nipál	449
	Mahmúd Buti ...		9	Sultánke	451
2	Sádhánwáli—		10	Pajián	433
	Tukra Wazír Khan				
	Do. Himmat Singh		11	Katarband	48
	Do. Chak Muhammad Bakhsh	349	12	Faizpur	217
	Do. Káhan Singh		13	Terah	1,298
3	Karol plantation ...	23			
4	Jhok	2,976			
5	UNRESERVED RAKHS Korutana	359		Total ...	10,428

Rakhs partly under the Forest Department and partly under the District management.

No.	Name of rakh.	Area in acres under Forest Department.	Area in acres under the District management.
1	Bhangali	109	
2	Dera Chabil	781	
3	Kot Lakhpat	3,263	Reputed area 2,482 acres. Most of the land granted and broken up for cultivation.
4	Lakhowál	808	
5	Chandrai	1,851	
6	Rodeshah	222	
	Total ...	7,034	

Rakhs under the District management.

No.	Name of rakh.	Area in acres.
1	Bhasin	
2	Chabil Tulspur	
3	Ráiwind Jadíd	
4	Sheikhkot	Reputed area 3,139 acres. Land mostly granted out and broken up for cultivation.
5	Awán	
6	Lidhar	
7	Julliána	
8	Diál	
9	Dhalla	

Rakhs under the management of Military Department.

No.	Name of rakh.	Area in acres.
1	Baikuntha	4,387
2	Padri	490
3	Dahuri	763
4	Bhangali	3,891
5	Terah	4,093
	Total	13,624

Tahsil Kasur.

Rakhs under the District management.

No.	Name of rakh.	Area in acres.
1	Rakhanwála	⎫
2	Kasúr	⎪
3	Katloi	Reputed area 1,116 acres. Land mostly granted out and broken up for cultivation.
4	Vaigal	⎬
5	Algon	⎪
6	Kotli Súr Singh	⎭

Tahsil Chunian.

Rakhs under the Forest Department.

No.	Name of rakh.	Area in acres.	No.	Name of rakh.	Area in acres.
	RESERVED FORESTS.		16	Thatti, No. I	644
1	Chánga Mánga Plantation	10,132	17	Do. No. II	531
2	Gandián	4,762	18	Halla	6,082
3	Jalloke	3,047	19	Harse Ghuman	7,646
4	Shahpur	2,232	20	Bherwál	4,755
	UNCLASSED FORESTS.		21	Naroke	1,924
5	Mudke	1,127	22	Hadjra	6,858
6	Theh Sheikh	718	23	Wairar Pattoke	17,606
7	But	428	24	Rosa	6,935
8	Bhoneke	2,392	25	Chúnián	1,778
9	Theh Chor	4,970	26	Shamsabad	1,617
10	Bhugiána	4,903	27	Deosiál, North	2,464
11	Ráwal Jhangar	498	28	Do., South	2,334
12	Naul	460	29	Wán Rádha Rám ...	9,424
13	Shah Ináyat	2,344	30	Mundeke	638
14	Dubli	1,452	31	Dhala	5,340
15	Dhig	1,932		Total ...	117,973

Rakhs partly under the *Forest Department* and partly under the District management.

No.	Name of rakh.	Area in acres under Forest Department.	Area in acres under District management.
1	Bhail Bhuchoke	3,468	Reputed area 4,053 acres. Land mostly granted out and broken up for cultivation.
2	Pannar	298	
3	Aulakh	1,910	
	Total ...	5,676	

Rakhs under the District management.

No	Name of rakh.	Area in acres.
1	Bhamba	Reputed area 6,793 acres. Land mostly granted out and broken up for cultivation.
2	Nathoke	
3	Handal	
4	Sarai Chhimba	
5	Khanke Maur	

Tahsil Sharakpur.
Rakhs under the Forest Department.

No.	Name of rakh.	Area in acres.	No.	Name of rakh.	Area in acres.
1	Mádho Dás	2,782	10	Khuni Chak	72
2	Malikpur	1,883	11	Kuthiála	9,825
3	Thatta Chor Shah ...	593	12	Báoli Lahna Singh ...	12,237
4	Ratoana	1,848	13	Chhaoni	4,925
5	Kangriwála	1,140	14	Dhanoha	483
6	Mahandevi	15,881	15	Kalpi	299
7	Kapi	2,441	16	Bhagtera	2,449
8	Khaira	2,619	17	Mandiánwála	201
9	Marh	4,023	18	Bhagour	11,017
				Total	74,718

Rakhs under District management.

Chapter V, D.

**Part II—
Other Sources of
Revenue.**

Rakhs or forest
lands.

No.	Name of rakh.	Area in acres.
1	Nurewál	⎱ Reputed area 3,053 acres. Land
2	Bhaghiárwála	⎰ mostly granted out and broken up for cultivation.

PART II.— OTHER SOURCES OF REVENUE.

The other direct sources of Government income beside land revenue are stamps, registration, excise and income-tax.

The income from the sale of stamps in this district is stated for the last ten years in Table No. XXXIII. Lahore ranks highest of all the districts in the Punjab as regards stamp income. The returns generally speaking show a gradual increase year by year. The income from judicial stamps in 1890-91 was abnormally high owing to more than Rs. 40,000 Court-fee stamps having been filed in one single suit, a large succession case involving the estate of the late Rai Bahádur Mela Rám. The present number of stamp vendors in each tahsíl is shown below—

Name of tahsíl.	Court-fee stamp vendors.	Number of non-judicial stamp vendors.
Lahore ... ...⎰	District Court ... ... 1 Chief Court ... ... 1 Munsiff's Court... ... ... 1 Small Cause Court ... ... 1 Honorary Magistrates' Court . 1 Cantonment Magistrate's Court 1	96
	Total .. 6	
Chúnián ... ...⎰	Tahsíl ... ... 1 Kot Rádha Kishen (Honorary Magistrate's Court) ... ⎰ 1 Kila Dharm Singh (Honorary Magistrate's Court) ... ⎰ 1	67
	Total ... 3	
Kasúr	Tahsíl 1	64
Sharakpur	Do. 1	28

The number of deeds registered in the last ten years and the value of the property affected in rupees are exhibited in Table No. XXXIII. Since the year 1882-83 up to the present the number of deeds registered has increased 27 per cent. and the value of property affected has risen 82 per cent. In the same period the income from registration has risen from Rs. 11,708 in the year 1882-83 to Rs. 16,354 in the year 1891-92. The Lahore district ranks fourth among the districts of the Province as regards registration income and sixth as regards the number of deeds registered. The Deputy Commissioner of the district is Registrar. Formerly the main body of the registration work was done by the Treasury Officer as Sub-Registrar at head-quarters and by the Tahsildárs as Sub-Registrars at tahsíls. In 1884 a non-official Sub-Registrar was appointed at head-quarters to do all the registration work, except what the Registrar has to take according to rule; he receives a fixed proportion of the fees. Similarly at the outlying tahsíls non-official Sub-Registrars have been appointed in recent years with the view of relieving the Tahsíldár of registration business.

The Excise administration concerns itself with (1) imported European spirits and fermented liquor, (2) fermented liquors manufactured at licensed breweries in India, (3) spirits passed from distilleries in India worked according to the European method, (4) country spirits or spirits manufactured after the native method, (5) opium, (6) hemp drugs. These are sold wholesale or retail. On the wholesale vend of spirits or liquors a low fixed fee is charged. The fees for retail sale are generally fixed by competition; shops are allowed to be opened wherever they appear to be wanted and no objection exists, and the lease of the right to sell spirits, liquor or drugs at each shop, as the case may be, for the term of one year, is sold by auction. Sometimes tenders for leases of certain shops or groups of shops are accepted, and the auction system is dispensed with. The numbers of retail shops for sale of country spirits, European liquors, opium and other drugs that have been maintained in this district during the last ten years are shown in Table No. XXXV. The opium and drug licenses have always been granted together here: the shop licensed to sell the one is licensed to sell the other. Of the European liquor shops a small proportion are licensed to sell rum only. In addition to the license fees for their sale rum and country liquor are also charged with still-head duty, the former paying Rs. 4 an Imperial gallon on issue from the place of manufacture and the latter Rs. 3 an Imperial gallon of proof liquor and Rs. 2-8-0 for liquor under proof. The rum is principally manufactured at the Rosa distillery of the Shahjahánpur district of the North-West Provinces. The country spirits are manufactured in the central distillery at Lahore, where at present as many as 18 stills are working. The total amount of country liquor manufactured at this distillery in 1892-93 was 30,773 gallons, of which more than half went to shops situate in the Lahore city or cantonments, 4,049 gallons to the villages of Lahore tahsíl, 6,673 gallons to Kasúr tahsíl, 3,399 to Chúnián tahsíl, and 532 gallons to Sharakpur tahsíl. The Jats of the Kasúr Mánjha are large consumers of country spirits. The amount exported away from the district was only 422 gallons. As regards consumption of country spirits the Lahore district stands first of the districts of the Province, Amritsar with its large city population coming next. In consumption of imported liquors and spirits manufactured in India after the European method. Lahore comes second to Ráwalpindi which has a very large cantonment.

Opium consumption.

There are four kinds of opium at present consumed in the Lahore district : (1) Gházipur opium supplied from Bengal to the Government of the Punjab at a cost of Rs. 7-4 per sér plus cost of carriage to the Punjab and sold here at Rs. 13 a sér from the Government Treasury, (2) Málwa opium which can be bought at Ajmer for about Rs. 6 or 7 a sér and at present pays Rs. 3 a sér duty on importation into the Punjab, (3) hill opium imported free of duty from Kashmír and the Hill States round Simla, (4) Punjab grown opium which pays an acreage duty varying from Rs. 2 to Rs. 4 an acre in different districts. The acreage rate in this district is Rs. 4, and the area at present put under poppy cultivation is hardly over 300 acres. Formerly the Punjab grown opium was consumed in the Lahore district almost to the exclusion of any other kind. Now the Gházipur and Málwa kinds are increasing in popularity and have been much used during the last two years in preference to Punjab opium. The Jat agriculturists of the villages consume opium to a considerable extent. Of drugs *charas* is smoked mainly by the lower classes in the towns and by Fakírs ; it is imported from Yárkand under regulations enforced by a system of passes. *Bhang* is an infusion prepared by soaking the dried hemp leaf for a time in water : the kind of hemp used for this purpose grows wild in the submontane tracts of the Himalayas. The mixture is drunk largely by all classes in the hot weather, not always for its intoxicating properties, but often as a mild pick-me-up, just as Europeans might drink a whisky peg. This district ranks seventh in the Province in the consumption of opium and its preparations and eighth in the consumption of hemp drugs. During the last ten years the total Excise revenue of this district has increased by nearly a lakh of rupees, but the increase has occurred almost entirely under rum and country spirits, the improved revenue from which is due not to extended consumption so much as to stricter administration of the Excise laws. Only in recent years has it been found possible to check the illegal distilling which the Mánjha Jats had been used to carry on freely to the great detriment of the Government revenue.

Income tax collections.

In Table No. XXXIV are shown the number of assessees taxed in each class paying a separate tax, and the amount of tax collected from them during the last six financial years. In Table No. XXXIV A are furnished corresponding details for each tahsíl and each of the three principal towns of the district in the year 1891-92. The tahsíl figures are inclusive of those shown separately for their respective towns. Outside the towns petty municipalities and larger villages the rural tracts pay very little towards the income tax. In most villages the petty trader or grocer makes very small profits ; and the money-lenders are so secret in their loan transactions that their full real income seldom comes under taxation. The

Chapter V, D.

Part II—
Other Sources of Revenue.

Canal irrigation.

Bári Doáb Canal.

number of incomes assumed for the purposes of the income tax to be over Rs. 1,000, in villages as distinct from towns and minor municipalities, is 25 in Lahore tahsíl; 18 in Kasúr tahsíl; 7 in Chúnián tahsíl; and 11 in Sharakpur tahsíl.

The revenue derived by the Government from canal irrigation is the balance of profit left after deducting very heavy expenditure from very large receipts. The two systems of canals at work in this district are the Bári Doáb Canal which flows perennially and the Upper Sutlej Inundation Series which flow only during the hot weather months while the Sutlej river is in flood.

A full account of the Bári Doáb Canal will be found in Chapter VIII, Section E, of the Provincial Volume of the Gazetteer, which should be referred to for detailed information regarding the history of the canal. The original project for the canal was drawn up in 1850, shortly after annexation. Some modifications of the original design were found to be necessary, and a revised estimate was submitted in 1856. The canal was formally opened in 1859, and irrigation commenced in the following year.

The head works are situated on the left bank of the river Rávi near Mádhopur, in the Gurdáspur district. Considerable engineering difficulties were here encountered, owing to the Chakki and other hill torrents and natural drainage lines crossing or approaching near to the line of the canal, but these have been successfully surmounted. The canal runs in one channel for 30 miles, after which, near to the civil station of Gurdáspur a branch is taken off, which, seven miles further on, is divided into the Sobráon and the Kasúr Branches.

The branches of the Bári Doáb Canal operating in the Lahore district are—

    (i) the Lahore Branch;
    (ii) the Main Branch Lower;
    (iii) the Kasúr Branch;
    (iv) the Sobráon Branch.

Taking these in the order named, No. (i) leaves the Main Canal at Aliwál in the Gurdáspur distri ct, and passing through the Amritsar district reaches the Lahore tahsíl just beyond Attári in its 40th mile; then trending south-west it passes between Mián Mír and Lahore and ultimately tails into the Rávi near Niázbeg in its 63rd mile. This branch has eight distributaries working in the Lahore district; among these being the Shálamár Rájbaha which follows the alignment of the old Hansli Canal, constructed during the Mughal dynasty for the supply of the fountains in the Royal gardens, still known as the Sháhibágh, near Bhágwánpura. The Main Branch Lower (ii) also leaves the Main Canal at Aliwál, and, running down the Doáb fairly parallel to the Lahore Branch, enters the Lahore district in its 41st mile near the village of Chína. Its course then for 23 miles nearly coincides with the boundary of the Lahore and Kasúr tahsíls, to opposite the Railway Station of Ráiwind ; and thence, passing through the heart of the Chúnián tahsíl, it terminates at Chánga Mánga in its 94th mile, with an escape channel back to the Rávi at Alpah. This branch is the most important so far as the Lahore district is concerned, since it traverses the richest parts of the Mánjha, which is served by no less than 13 distributaries, with a combined length of 227 miles. Some of these Channels carry high supplies, and, except that they irrigate direct, might well be termed branches ; such are the Basarki Rájbaha with 240 cubic feet per second of full supply, the Bhuchar Rájbaha with 220 cubic feet, the Thamman with 240 cubic feet. Both the Main Branch Lower and the Lahore Branch Canals were first opened in April 1859, and irrigation commenced in 1860-61.

The Kasúr Branch (iii) was opened in 1878. It enters the Kasúr tahsíl in its 59th mile and terminates 10½ miles lower down in the Kasúr nalah, near the village of Algáon. It performs irrigation through the agency of the Khem Karan Rájbaha and its Branch, which are capable of conveying 266 cubic feet of water per second. The Rasúlpur Rájbaha, another large distributary of the Kasúr Branch, likewise does some irrigation in the tahsíl.

Finally, the Sobráon Branch (iv) (opened at the same time as the Kasúr Branch) passes through the Amritsar district parallel to the Kasúr Branch, and about 8 miles further east, and just touches the Lahore district at the town of Patti, where the canal debouches into a natural drainage channel, having expended itself in supplying the distributary channels above, only two of which, and these only in the latter half of their courses, provide irrigation in the Kasúr tahsíl.

The number of villages within the Lahore district that are served by each of the above-named branches of the Bári Doáb Canal are shown below—

Lahore Branch	...	...	...	...	...	177 villages.
Main Branch Lower	...	...	...	...	242	,,
Kasúr Branch	...	...	...	...	...	80	,,
Sobráon Branch	...	...	...	...	...	11	,,

It is understood that a considerable extension of irrigation from the Main Branch Lower will shortly be effected by opening a new distributary from it on behalf of the dry tracts in the western portion of the Chúnián Mánjha.

For administrative purposes the canal is worked in three divisions, each under an Executive Engineer. The Kasúr and Sobráon Branches are in the 1st Division, the Lahore Branch is in the 2nd Division, and the Main Branch Lower in the 3rd. The head-quarters of all three divisions are at Amritsar, where also is the office of the Superintending Engineer, to whom the executive officers are subordinate.

Chapter V, D.

**Part II—
Other Sources of
Revenue.**

Bári Doáb Canal
assessments.

Until recently there were two sets of canal assessment rates in use on the Bári Doáb Canal, one the water or crop rate varying with the crop grown and intended to fall on the cultivator or tenant's increased receipts due to the canal irrigation, the other the owner's rate varying in this district from Re. 1-8-0 to 12 annas an acre of land actually irrigated, and intended to fall on the owner's share of increased produce obtained by aid of the canal irrigation. The latter rate was introduced in 1868 at the revision of settlement. In practice it was not found to fulfil its object except where the owner was himself cultivating the land. Where the canal-irrigated land was in the hands of a tenant, the general competition for such land enabled the owner to get a much higher rent than he could have done if the land had not been canal-irrigated, and the tenant was also left to pay the owner's rate as well as the crop or water-rate. From this condition of things the Canal Department drew the just conclusion that their crop or water-rates were not high enough in comparison with the benefit derived from the irrigation. Moreover the double charge of the two rates had proved troublesome from an account point of view. It was therefore decided to abolish the owner's rate, which had failed to accomplish its purpose and to raise the crop or water-rates slightly above what the old crop rates and owner's rates combined amounted to. At the same time in supersession of the principles hitherto followed of assessing canal-irrigated land no higher than ordinary unirrigated land in its neighbourhood, orders were issued that all lands benefiting from canal irrigation should, in addition to the ordinary unirrigated rate, pay a *nahri parta* or canal enhanced rate, credit for the proceeds from which should be given to the Canal Department.

The schedule of canal water or crop rates was revised by Notification No. 2621 I., dated 10th June 1891. The rates now levied on the Bári Doáb Canal are as follows :—

Class.	Crop.	Flow.	Lift.
		Rs. a. p.	Rs. a. p.
I	Sugarcane and water-nuts	7 1 0	3 8 6
II	Rice	6 0 10	3 0 5
III	Orchards and gardens ; tobacco, poppy, and other drugs ; vegetables ; melons	4 8 8	2 4 4
IV	All dyes, fibres, and oil-seeds ; all rabi crops, except gram and *masar*	3 12 6	1 14 3
V	All kharíf crops not specified above ; gram and *masar* ; all fodder crops	2 12 5	1 6 2½
VI	Special rate which may be made applicable to channels selected by the Local Government. A single watering before ploughing for rabi followed by a rabi crop	2 0 4	1 0 2
VII	A single watering before ploughing not followed by a crop. Crops grown on the stubble of a previous crop	1 0 2	0 8 1

The nature of the cropping on the Bári Doáb Canal irrigated lands is indicated in the following percentage statement :—

Chapter V, D.

Part II—
Other Sources of
Revenue.

Bári Doáb Canal
assessments.

1	2
Name of crop.	Percentage of area sown.
Sugarcane	1
Rice	5
Maize	7
Cotton	7
Jowár	2
Other kharíf crops	10
Wheat	47
Barley	1
Gram	8
Other rabi crops	12
Total	100

The realizations under the rates shown above during the last three years are stated below—

1	2	3	4
	REALIZATIONS IN RUPEES.		
YEARS.	Kharíf.	Rabi.	Total.
1891-92	3,60,954	7,07,360	10,68,314
1892-93	4,46,520	6,15,966	10,62,486
1893-94	3,71,425	Not yet known.	...

The credit sum estimated to be due to the Canal Department on account of *nahri parta* under the recent assessments of land irrigated from the Bári Doáb Canal is Rs. 94,000. At present land revenue assignees receive Rs. 5,594 on account of *nahri parta* on their jágír holdings, in accordance with existing orders on the subject.

Chapter V, D,
—
**Part II—
Other Sources of
Revenue.**

Upper Sutlej In-
undation Canals.

The Upper Sutlej series of canals consists as far as the Lahore district is concerned of the Katora, Khanwah and Upper Sohág Canals. The Katora Canal issues from the Sutlej river near Ganda Singwála in the Kasúr tahsíl. From there the canal cut passes through the south-western portion of Kasúr tahsíl, irrigating at present not more than 12 or 15 hundred acres before it reaches Khudián situate in the Chúnián tahsíl near its border with Kasúr. Here the main branch breaks up into three large distributaries, which during the hot weather months give abundant irrigation to the Chúnián Hithár. To the south of the Katora Canal in the Chúnián tahsíl are the two other inundation canals, the Upper Sohág and Khanwah, which take off from the river within the limits of the Chúnián tahsíl some way below the Katora head. At present the total area irrigated by these canals within this district is between 40 and 50 thousand acres situate in 157 estates : more than two-thirds of this irrigation is done by the Katora Canal. The other two are very variable and as far as the Lahore lands are concerned, may irrigate one year double what they do another. As a matter of fact they are intended more for the benefit of the adjacent district of Montgomery than for that of Lahore.

The former rates charged for irrigation from these canals were a crop rate of 8 annas an acre for flow and 4 annas for lift ; and a water-advantage or owner's rate of 8 annas an acre on all land coming under irrigation any harvest, except that on the second cropping under irrigation in one agricultural year only 4 annas an acre was taken. In 1892 the scale of crop rates was revised, the former scale being thought too low. The new rates as finally sanctioned to come into effect from April 1893 are shown below :—

	Rs.	A.	P.
Class I.—Rice, gardens, chillies	2	4	0
Class II.—Cotton, sugarcane, melons, hemp and till.	1	8	0
Class III.—All other autumn crops not otherwise mentioned.	1	2	0
Class IV.—All rabi crops, fallow lands, lands ploughed but not sown.	0	8	0

The canal water-advantage rate was raised to 12 annas an acre to be levied on all land actually irrigated in the kharíf or rabi harvest, but not to be levied more than once in the year, whether the land bears one crop or two crops under the irrigation. The new water-advantage rate came into effect from the autumn of 1892.

The result of these changes in the rates was to increase the annual gross revenue from the Upper Sutlej inundation canals in the Lahore district by 80 or 90 per cent. The receipts derived from the irrigation of each canal in the Lahore district during the last three years are shown below :—

	1891-92.		1892-93.		1893-94.	
	Water-rate.	Water-advantage rate.	Water-rate.	Water-advantage rate.	Water-rate.	Water-advantage rate.
	Rs.	Rs.	Rs.	Rs.	Rs.	Rs.
Katora	15,393	14,231	18,850	26,386	28,829	24,355
Khanwah	883	805	1,681	1,511	3,127	3,892
Upper Sohág ...	2,107	2,075	4,116	6,024	2,215	2,920
Total ...	18,383	17,111	24,647	33,921	34,171	31,167

The nature of the cropping on land irrigated from these inundation canals is indicated in the following percentage statement :—

	Percentage of crop on area sown.
Rice	12
Maize	4
Cotton	4
Jowár	5
Other autumn crops	23
Wheat	24
Barley	2
Gram	18
Other rabi crops	8
Total	100

CHAPTER VI.

TOWNS, MUNICIPALITIES AND CANTON-MENTS.

SECTION A.—ANCIENT LAHORE.

I—History of Lahore City.

Chapter VI, A.
———
Ancient Lahore.

The city of Lahore.

Lahore is a city which may claim the attention, not only of the student of the history and antiquities of India, but also of the general reader. It is situated in a region interesting to all, as the classic ground of Alexander's conquests ; it is important in early Indian history, as the focus of the earliest struggles between Hindúism and Muhammadanism, and the centre of a confederation which, for upwards of two centuries, successfully withstood the progress of Islám. The name of the city is associated with every Muhammadan dynasty of Northern India from the Ghaznivides to the Mughals, sometimes as the seat of Government, and always as a place of importance. In the history of the Sikhs, it is distinguished as the scene of Arjun's martyrdom and as the capital of the kingdom founded by Ranjít Singh. Lastly, it is at the present time the chief city of a province containing within its limits perhaps the most martial population of India. Historians and poets of the East and of the West have united in celebrating the extent and eulogizing the splendour of Lahore. Abulfida, in the fourteenth century, had read of it in the pages of Ibn Alatir as "a city great among the cities of India." Abul-fazl, in the sixteenth, describes it as the "grand resort of people of all nations." "If Shíráz and Ispahán," says an old local proverb, "were united, they would not make one Lahore." The traveller Thevenot, who saw it in A.D. 1665, the period of its decline, states that a short time before his visit the city with its suburbs covered an area of three leagues in length. Bernier notes the magnificence of its palace, the length of its streets, and the height of the houses as compared with those at Agra or at Delhi. Our own Milton places Lahore among the—

> Cities of old or modern fame, the seat
> Of mightiest empires,

which met the eyes of the repentant Adam from the hill of Paradise,* and Moore has built up amid the "palaces, domes and gilded minarets" of Lahore, "a city of enchantment" sacred to the loves of Lála Rukh and Ferámurz.

Legendary history.

By local Hindu tradition the origin of Lahore, like that of most of the princely houses of India, is traced to Ráma, king

———
* Paradise Lost, Book XI, 1, 337—341.

of Ayodhya (Oude), the hero of the Rámáyána, whose two sons *Lav* or *Loh*, and *Kash*, are said to have founded the neighbouring cities of Lahore and Kasúr.   But it is not merely in local tradition that Lahore is made illustrious ; its name is celebrated in the legends and *quasi*-historic traditions of comparatively distant localities as the scene of the battles and chivalry of heroic times, and the metropolis, in a Greek sense, of other ancient Hindu States.   In the *Rája Tarangini* the ancient chronicle of Kashmír, Lahore is mentioned as a dependency of the great Lalitaditya. In the *Desh-vi-bhága*, a compilation from the Puránas, drawn up by order of the learned Rája Jai Singh Sawáí, of Jaipur, it is recorded that, at the end of the Dwápar or Brazen Age, Bhím Sen fought Ban Mal, Rája of Lahore, a mighty prince, with an army of 10,000 horsemen, and after a conflict of three days' duration, took him prisoner and made his kingdom tributary.   Again, in the ballad poetry of the northern border, " the forest near Lahore," then called Udenagar, figures as the battle-ground where Rasálú, son of Sál Váhán, the eponymic hero of Siálkot, fought and slew the monster *Rákhas*.   Again, to descend to more historic times, in the annals of the Mewár State, in Ráj-pútána, the founder of the royal line is recorded to have been Kanaksen, a Solar Rájpút prince, who migrated from Lahore. Moreover, the Solankhi tribe of Analhára Pattan and the Bhátís of Jaisalmer, whose name is still borne by one of the city gate-ways, point to Lahore as the seat of their earlier location.

On the other hand, there is a Muhammadan tradition that the present city and fortress of Lahore were founded by Malik Azáz, the friend and counsellor of Mahmúd of Gházni, and his tomb by the Taksáli gate is still revered by Musalmáns as the burial place of the Oekist of Lahore.

These two traditions may be reconciled by supposing that the original Hindú city of Lahore did occupy exactly its present site, or that the city had been deserted or destroyed before its final capture by the Muhammadans, and was founded by them *de novo*.   There are reasons which make it probable that both these suppositions are correct.   It is probable that there was an older city of Lahore somewhere in the vicinity of the existing village of Ichra, or about three miles from its present site.   In the first place, there is a tradition among the inabitants of villages of Ichra and Muzang to this effect ; in the next place, the old name of Ichra was Ichra Lahore, which is still to be found, it is said, upon old documents ; and lastly, the oldest and most sacred Hindú shrines are to be found in this locality.

These stories cannot indeed be considered history, but they show the intimate connection of Lahore with the semi-mythic period of Indian history.   Numismatic researches tend to show that Lahore formed a portion of the kingdom of Memandi and his successors, that it fell successively into the hands of the Scythic dynasties of Azes, Kadphises, and Kanekís, and subse-quently, under the rule of a Sassanian dynasty of princes who

Chapter VI, A.

Ancient Lahore.

Legendary history.

Muhammadan local tradition.

How reconcileable.

Chapter VI, A.
———
Ancient Lahore.
How reconcileable.

reigned between the fourth and seventh centuries A. D. It is possible that Kanekís, whose date is given by Prinsep as about 100 A. D. is the same as the Keneksen of the Mewár chronicle, and the Kanishka of the annals of Kashmir, in which case Lahore must have been the capital of the third Scythian dynasty. From the above and other similar traditions of Rájpút origin it may be inferred that the founders of Lahore were of the Rájpút race, and that the city was probably the capital of one of the earliest of the Rájpút States esablished in the west of India ; and this inference is corroborated by the fact that, at the earliest dawning of reliable Indian history,—the period of the Musalmán invasions in the seventh and tenth centuries,—we find Lahore the capital of an important Hindú principality, exercising a kind of feudal superiority over other States.

Name of Lahore.

The name "Lahore" (which is of course connected with the name of its mythical founder, the son of Ráma) is not peculiar to the capital of the Punjáb ; there is a Lahore in Afghánistán, the seat of an old Rájpút colony ; another in the Peshawar district, another in Hindústán Proper, and a *Lohár* in the Mewár State of Rájpútána. It appears in Muhammadan writers under the varied forms of *Lóhár, Lóher, Laháwar, Lehówa, Luháwar, Loháwar, Laha-núr,** and *Rahwar ;*† in the chronicles of Rájpútána it is mentioned under the the name of *Loh-kot ;* and in the *Desh-ví-bhága*‡ before mentioned, it is called *Lav-pur.* *Lóh-awar* is the oldest, and probably the most correct form of the name, as it is the form under which it appears in the writings of Abu Rihán al Barúni, a contemporary and companion of the Emperor Mahmúd of Gházri, and one who is known to have been well versed in the literature of the Hindús. The termination *áuar* is no doubt a corruption of the colloquial Sanskrit *awarana,* meaning a "fort" or "enclosure," which is found as a termination in the names of many other Rájpút cities,—as, for example, *Peshawar, Rájáwar* (commonly called *Rájore,* and *Sonáwar. Loháwar,* therefore, may signify *Fort of Loh,* and the name may thus correspond in signification with the *Loh-kot* of the Rájpútána chronicles, and give a key to the legend respecting its foundation.

Date of foundation.

The exact date of the foundation of Lahore is, as may be supposed, impossible to discover ; but we may make an approxi-

---

* In this form it occurs in the writings of Amír Khusrau of Delhi, one of the fathers of Urdu literature, who wrote at the latter part of the thirteenth century—

Az had Samání tá Lahá-núr.
Hech imárat nest magar dar Kasúr.

Also, in the records of a Muhammadan shrine, near Lahore, founded in the time of Bahlol Khán Lodi. *Lahá-núr,* is a corruption of *Lahá-nagar ; núr,* in fact, is still the Dakhani form of *nagar,* and appears in the names of other cities, *e.g.*—Kalánore, Kanánore.

† *Ráhwar* is probably a Muhammadan corruption, suggested by the fact that during the Pathán and Moghal dynasties, Lahore was the terminus of the great imperial road from Agra.

‡ An anonymous writer in the "Annual Register" for 1809 states that he was told at Lahore that the ancient name of the city was *Alla-núr.*

mate guess at the period of its rise to importance from the following considerations. We have already seen that Lahore was founded and had risen to be the capital of a great kingdom *before* the end of the seventh century of the Christian era. On the other hand there are reasons for believing that the city, if it existed, was a place of no importance up to at least the first century.. In the first place, there is no mention of Lahore, nor of any city with which it may be fairly identified, in the writings of the Greek historians of the expedition of Alexander to the East. Burnes would identify it with *Sangála*,* a city mentioned by Arrian as the stronghold of the *Kathœi* or *Katheri*, who occupied the region in which Lahore is situated. But the position of Sangála—three marches from the Rávi—would appear fatal to such a position. Yet there can be no doubt that Alexander crossed the Rávi in the vicinity of Lahore, and must in all probability have passed the site of the modern city. If, therefore, any place of importance had existed at the time, it would doubtless have been mentioned. In the next place, no city answering in name or description to Lahore occurs in Strabo, who wrote between B.C. 66 and A.D. 24, and describes with some particularity the region of Kathæa; nor does it appear in Pliny's description of the royal road between the Indus and Allahabad, which must have been written between A.D. 22 and A.D. 79. Lastly, no coins of the Indo-Bactrian or Indo-Scythic dynasties have been discovered at Lahore, although the locality formed a portion of the kingdom of Manander and his successors, and probably also of the Scythic dynasties of Azes, Kadphises, Kanekis. It may be therefore so far concluded with some degree of confidence that Lahore must have been founded *between* the first and seventh centuries of the Christian era.

But, further in the Geography of Ptolemy,† who flourished at Alexandria about A. D. 150, mention is made of a city called *Labokla*, situated on the route between the Indus and Palibothra, in a tract of country called *Kaspeiria* [Kashmir?]. described as extending along the rivers *Bidástes*, (Jhelam), *Sandabál* (*Chandr, Bhága*, or Chenáb), and *Adris* (Rávi). This place Wilford would identify, from its name and position, with Lahore, and the identification is made more probable by the recent discovery by Major-General Cunningham of the *Amakátis* of Ptolemy, a city placed by him in the immediate vicinity of *Labokla*,

Chapter VI, A.

—

Ancient Lahore.

Date of foundation.

---

* The identification of this place is a *vexata quæstio* amongst Punjábi antiquaries. Wilford would identify it with Kalanore ; Masson with Haripa ; others with Sangla, one of an isolated group of rocks on the border of the Jhang and Gujránwála districts, about 63 miles from Lahore. Elphinstone, the Settlement Officer of the Montgomery district, would identify it with a locality in that district, still bearing the name, situated within a reasonable distance of the Rávi, and within the local limits of the *Kathia* tribe, the representatives of the ancient *Kathaioi*. But see Archæological Survey Report and *Gazetteer* of the Montgomery district.

† Lib. vii § 46 § 48.

Chapter VI, A.

Ancient Lahore.

Date of found-
ation.

in the ruins of *Ambá Kápi*,* about 25 miles from Lahore. Lastly if Tod's Chronology is to be trusted, we have a further proof that Lahore must have been a place of some importance at the time Ptolemy's Geography was written, in the fact that the middle of the second century is assigned by Tod as the date of the migration of Prince Keneksen from Lahore. However this may be, we may fairly infer as much from the mere mention of the city by the Greek geographer, and approximately fix the date of Lahore's foundation at the end of the first or the beginning of the second century of our era.

Lahore before the
Muhammadan in-
vasion.

Beyond the fact of its Rájpút origin, hardly anything can be recorded with certainty of the history or even of the existence of Lahore until the period of the Muhammadan invasion. In the *Tabula Peutingeriana*, a valuable itinerary of the Roman Empire, supposed to have been drawn up about A. D. 230, mention is made of a city named *Tahora*, situated on the route from the Indus to the Ganges, which so far corresponds in position with Lahore that it is made to follow on the list of a city named *Spatúra*, on the river Chenáb. The former Major-General Cunningham would identify with Lahore; but Wilford prefers *Tihára*, an ancient city on the Sutlej, mentioned in the *Mahábhárata*; and philologically the latter identification would appear most probable, as the Sanskrit *á* is frequently represented (as before observed) by the Greek or Latin *o*; but the interchange of *t* and *l* is contrary to analogy. A far less dubious mention of Lahore is found, as pointed out by Major-General Cunningham, in the itinerary of Hwan Thsang, the Chinese traveller, who visited the Punjáb A. D. 630. He speaks of a large city, containing many thousands of families, chiefly Bráhmins, situated on the eastern frontier of the kingdom of *Cheka*, which, he says, extended from the Indus to the Beás. From this city he proceeded eastward to *Chíná Pati*, and thence to *Jálandhara*, the modern Jullundur. Now Jullundur is situated almost due east of Lahore, and midway between the two cities is a village called *Patti*, to this day. There can be little doubt, therefore, that the great Brahmanical city of Hwan Thsang was the city of Lahore.

It is probable that at Lahore, as in most Eastern States, there were frequent changes of dynasty. The earliest princes were perhaps Rájpúts from Ayodhya of the same family as those who reigned in Guzerát and Mewár. Subsequently—but when, it is impossible to say—the sceptre seems to have passed to the hands of Rájpúts of other tribes, such as the Solankhe and the Bhátís. At the period of the first appearance of the

---

* The fact that the accent of *Amákátis* is contrary to analogy, on the penultimate, seems to show that, in the Greek some stress was laid on that syllable which would have been the case if it had been originally written as two words, *Amakátis*; further the Sanskrit *á* is not unfrequently represented in Greek by an accentuated *á*; for instance, *Chandra Bhága* is rendered *Sandabál*; Vyàsa as *Bibásis*. The transmutation of the *p* sound into the dental has its analogy in the change of the Latin *Attus* into *Appius*, or the Sanskrit *Iravati* into *Adris*.

Muhammadans, Lahore was in the hands of a "Chauhán prince of the family of Ajmer," and during the later invasions of the tenth century the reigning family is Brahmanical. There are also reasons for believing that, either owing to change of dynasty, or to its exposed position on the high road from Afghánistán to India, the city of Lahore, before its occupation by Mahmúd of Gházni, had been deserted; and that in *Ferishta*, the Muhammadan historian, there is a confusion between Lahore the *City*, and Lahore the *Province*. It is, in the first place, expressly stated in the *Hadiqa tul aqlím* of Murtaza Husain, that before the Muhammadan invasion the seat of Government was transferred from Lahore to Siálkot, or *Sálvahnpur* and not re-transferred until the period of the Gháznivide Emperor Masaúd II. Such would also appear from the traditions of the Bhátís, which speak of *Sálvahnpur* as the capital city, when they were rulers of Lahore. Then again, Al Barúni, who speaks from personal knowledge of the locality of modern Lahore at the time of Mahmúd of Gházni's invasion, mentions Lahore, not as a city, but as a region, of which the capital was *Mádhokaur*. Now *Mádhokaur*, might easily, from the similarity between *h* and *n*, and *r* and final *t*, in the Arabic character, be corrupted from *Mankot* or *Mandúhkot*, a place near Siálkot. The supposition is rendered more probable by the fact that, in after times, Sher Sháh, the so-called usurper,—but, as will be hereafter pointed out, in reality the representative of the anti-Moghal, or anti-foreigner party,—seriously contemplated removing the seat of Government from Lahore, which had become associated with Moghal supremacy, to this very place, the capital of the last native dynasty. If such be the case, it will serve to explain the otherwise remarkable fact that no mention of Lahore is to be found in the Geography of Masúdi, the Herodotus of the Arabs, who wrote in the tenth century, and himself sojourned at Mooltan, or within little more than 200 miles from the modern city of Lahore.

Such are the somewhat barren results of inquiries into the pre-Muhammadan history of Lahore. They may be briefly recapitulated as follows:— That the city of Lahore, formerly Loháwar, and possibly the *Labokla* of Ptolemy, was founded by an ancient Rájpút colony some time between the first and seventh centuries of our era, probably as early as the beginning of the second; that it soon rose to be a place of importance, the parent of other colonies, and eventually the capital of a powerful principality, to which it gave its name; that, whether owing to change of dynasty, or to its exposed position on the high road from Afghánistán to India, it was subsequently deserted, and the seat of Government was removed to Siálkot or its vicinity, where it remained until the period of the invasion of Mahmúd of Ghazni in the beginning of the eleventh century; that the conqueror re-occupied the deserted city, and established a garrison in a fort, built possibly, like the *Purána Qila* at Delhi, on the ruins of the old Rájpút stronghold.

Chapter VI, A.
—
Ancient Lahore.

Subsequent history.

City buildings.

The foregoing pages have given in brief outline what little is known of the early history of the city itself. Its later fortunes were bound up with those of the province of which it became the capital, and will be found briefly narrated in Chapter II. The following pages trace the architectural history of the city, and show its state at various periods.

Modern Lahore falls far short of the glowing descriptions given by early writers, and quoted in the preceding pages. In size and populousness it is far inferior to Lucknow, Delhi, Agra, and even to Amritsar. The circuit of its walls does not exceed three miles, and its population, at the last census, was given at about 107,0C0. The streets are narrow and wormlike, and the general aspect of the city, with the exception of its northern front, is neither imposing nor picturesque. But a closer acquaintance with the city and its environs will tend considerably to modify the first impression and give some colour to the extravagant descriptions referred to above. That Lahore formerly covered a far larger area than it does at present is at once apparent from the number and extent of the ruins which cover the face of the surrounding country. From the city walls to Shálámár, Mian Mir and Ichra—a circle with a radius of some three or four miles—one is constantly coming across crumbling mosques, tombs, gateways and gigantic mounds. Some conception of the extent of Lahore in its palmier days, as compared with its present state, may be formed from the fact that of thirty-six *guzars* or quarters into which Lahore is known to have been divided, only nine are included within the area of the modern city ; but a more vivid picture of the desolation which has passed over Lahore will be obtained by a view of the surrounding country from a minaret of the Imperial mosque or of the mosque of Wazír Khán.

Some have supposed that the actual city, that is, the inhabited portion of Lahore, never extended beyond its present limits, and that the mass of débris which everywhere meets the eye is composed entirely of the remains of tombs and garden walls. The supposition may be proved to be erroneous, not only by the evidence of eye-witnesses, Native and European, such as Bernier, Tavernier and Thevenot ; but also from the existence among the débris of numerous small wells, such as are constructed in the private dwelling-houses of a closely-packed city and from the position of the large ruined mosque on the right-hand side of the Amritsar road, known as the *Idgah*, or place of asssembly upon Muhammadan feast-days. Such buildings are almost always erected in the immediate outskirts of a town ; it may be inferred, therefore, that when this mosque was built the city extended as far as its immediate vicinity : but the city is now nearly three miles off, and the building has long ceased to be the rendezvous of the faithful on their holy days. Again, we have a casual notice, in a Muhammadan writer of Akbar's time of a certain *guzar* or quarter, which is now desolate and upwards of a mile from the city, as being the most populous quarter of

Lahore; and lastly, we have the analogy of other eastern cities, such as Kábul, Tabriz or Ispahán, where the suburbs, that is the portion of the city beyond the walls, are far the most extensive and important parts of the town. Upon the whole it may be considered probable that in its best days, that is during the reign of Sháhjahán, the city must have had a circuit of some 16 or 17 miles. The portion of the city outside the walls probably consisted of numerous thickly inhabited spots connected with the city gates by long *bázárs*. The intervals between these different quarters were filled up with tombs, gardens and mosques, whose remains now form a conspicuous feature in the aspect of the environs of Lahore. The *Moti Mahal* or " Regent-street " of old Lahore is said to have been in the vicinity of the present civil station, and to this day coins and remains of jewellery are occasionally picked up in that locality after heavy rains.

It is easier to form an idea of the size and extent of the old city of Lahore than of its magnificence. Few cities have suffered more from desolating hordes and from anarchy than Lahore during the last 120 years previous to the inauguration of English rule. Eight times did the troops of Ahmad Shah Duráni pass through Lahore : Mahrattás and Sikhs have done their work of destruction, and the buildings, being for the most part built of brick, have perished and are perishing rapidly from mere exposure. But it is certain, from the accounts we possess and from the absence of any but insignificant specimens of Hindu and Pathán remains, that until the period of the Moghal dynasty, the city had no architectural pretensions : on the other hand, in the number and importance of its tombs, the profuse use of glazed tiles and enamelled frescoes as an architectural decoration, the recurrence of the bulb-like dome and semi-domed gateway we have all the characteristics of the Moghal or what may be termed the florid style of Indo-Muhammadan architecture, standing perhaps in a similar relation to the Pathán to that which the decorated style of English architecture bears to that termed semi-Norman. As far as can be judged from existing remains, Lahore can never have equalled Delhi in its public buildings, though the superior size of its private edifices would indicate the existence of more private wealth. Still, in the tomb of Jahángír the palace of that Prince and of his successor Sháhjahán, the mosque of Wazír Khan, the Pearl mosque, the gardens of Shálámár, and the Bádsháhi or Imperial mosque of Aurangzeb, will be found no mean specimens of architecture ; and on its north-eastern side, where the mosque of Aurangzeb, with its plain white domes of marble and tall unadorned *minárs*, the mausoleum of Ranjít Singh, with its curvilinear roof, projecting balconies and details, half Muhammadan, half Hindu, and lastly, the once brilliantly enamelled front of the palace of the Moghals stand side by side overlooking a broad and grassy plain,—Lahore can, even now, show an architectural *coup d'oeil* worthy of an imperial city ; and could we but imagine the same palace-front,

Chapter VI, A.
————
Ancient Lahore.

City buildings.

undisfigured by Sikh and English additions, with its coloured frescoes fresh and vivid, the river flowing at its base and eastward, as far as the eye could reach, a massive quay of masonry, with flights of steps at intervals and gardens extending to the water's edge, the now deserted suburbs filled with a thriving population and interspersed with tombs and *bárádaris* rising amid luxuriant gardens, whose gates glittered with many-coloured porcelain, we should form a conception of what we have reason to believe Lahore really was in the period of its prime.

Lahore of the Hindu period.

There are no architectural remains of the old Hindu city of Lahore,—a circumstance which might well be explained by the absence of stone material, and the numerous destructive invasions to which the city has been subjected; but it is not necessary to resort to this explanation, for the fact is in accordance with what all Indian architectural researches tend to show, namely, that the northern Hindu race was not, until a comparatively late period, in the habit of building temples, or durable edifices of any kind. Even at Delhi, the seat of Hindu dynasties from upwards of a thousand years before Christ to more than a thousand years after the Christian era, and where there is abundance of stone, no specimens of Hindu architecture exist dating earlier than the tenth or the eleventh century. There are some grounds for supposing that the old Hindu city of Lahore did not occupy exactly the site of the modern city. Tradition points to the vicinity of Ichra, a village about three miles to the west, as the site of old Lahore. The name of the village was formerly *Ichra Lahore*, a name still to be found, it is said, upon old documents and occasionally adopted in *hundís*, or native bills of exchange, drawn upon Lahore. Moreover, some of the oldest and most sacred Hindu shrines are to be met with in this locality.* Should such be the case, it is not improbable that the gateway of the present city, known as the *Láhori* or *Lohári* gateway, was so called as being the gateway looking in the direction of *Loháwar* or old Lahore, just as the Kashmíri gate looks towards Kashmir, and the Delhi gate of modern Delhi to the ancient city of that name.

Lahore under the Patháns.

But there is not only a total absence of the old Hindu architectural remains. With the exception of two small mosques in the heart of the city, the *Nimiwála masjid* and *Shiranwála masjid*, and the ruins of one or two shrines, there are no architectural relics of an earlier date than the time of Humáyún. This fact, coupled with the silence of earlier writers, leads to the conclusion that Lahore, at the period of the Pathán dynasties, though a place of considerable importance, was not remarkable for its extent or the beauty of its buildings. Amír Khusrau, at the end of the thirteenth century, alludes to Lahore and the twin city of Kasúr simply as inhabited spots in the midst of a desolate waste. Ibn Batúta, who travelled from Mooltan to Delhi in the middle of the fourteenth, did not think it worth a

* For instance, *Bhairo ka sthán* and the *Chandrát.*

visit; Timúr, at the end of the same century, left it to a sub-ordinate to plunder; the Emperor Bábar, who always took care to see what was to be seen, and in his memoirs has left graphic descriptions of Kábul, Samarkand, and the environs of Delhi, leaves Lahore unnoticed; lastly Amin Ahmad Rázi, author of a work called *Haft Aqlím*, dated A. D. 1624, states that until the time of Akbar, Lahore was nothing more than a number of detached hamlets.

In an architectural point of a view, therefore, Lahore is essentially a Moghal city; and its Muhammadan remains, with a few exceptions, are in the Moghal style; the exceptions being the tomb of Sháh Musa, by the railway station, which is Pathán; and the mosque of Maryam Makáni or Maryam Zamáni by the eastern gateway of the fort, the style of which is transitional between the Pathán and the Moghal. Three localities at Lahore are traditionally connected with the Ghaznivide period, and are looked upon as places of great sanctity,—the tomb of Malik Ayáz, before alluded to, who is said to have built up the walls and fortress of Lahore miraculously in a single night; the tomb of Syad Izhák, in the quadrangle of Wazír Khán's mosque; and lastly, the tomb of Dáta Ganj Bakhsh, a learned divine of Baghdád, the St. Odo of his day, who accompanied the victorious army of Mahmúd of Gházni, in the character of spiritual adviser, and died at an advanced age at Lahore. Whatever may have been his deeds, he has unfortunately had no Robert Wace to chronicle them. He has left a work entitled *Kashful-Mahjúb*, the *Revelation of the Hidden*, but it does not reveal a single fact connected with the history of his time.

To the Moghals we owe the introduction of what now form three striking characteristics of the principal cities of Upper India. In the first place, there grew up with them a new style of architecture, more splendid and elaborate, though less massive than the later Pathán from which it was developed. In the next place, to their love of the picturesque in nature,—a pleasing feature in their character,—we owe the construction of those regularly-planned gardens,* with their dense foliage, fountains and imitative cascades, which have excited the enthusiastic admiration of travellers to the east. Coming from the well-watered valleys and waving foliage of Ush and Indejan, Bábar regarded with almost European disgust the dusty treeless plains of the Punjab. In his memoirs, he bitterly complains of the ugliness of the cities of Hindustán. "They have no walled gardens," he says, "no artificial water-courses;" and he seems to have lost no time in setting them a good example, by laying out a magnificent garden at Agra. "The men of Hind," he continues, "who had never before seen palaces formed on such a plan, or laid out with such elegance, gave the name of Kábul to the side of the Jumna on which these palaces were built."

---

* It is remarkable that there is no Hindi word in common use for a *garden*. *Bágh* and *Chaman* are Persian, and *rouza*, Arabic.

Chapter VI, A.
———
Ancient Lahore.

Lastly, the same appreciation of natural scenery, combined with a solicitude for the preservation of the dead, characteristic of Tartar races, led to the erection of the numerous garden-enclosed tombs, which form a picturesque feature of the environs of every Moghal city.*

Remains of the
Moghal period.

Lahore, with its numerous gardens, tombs and ornamental gateways, must have been, in the days of its splendour, a fine specimen of an Indo-Moghal city; and though no city has perhaps suffered more from devastations and the hand of time, it can still show no mean specimens of architecture. In the old gateways leading to the fort, we have examples of the bold and massive style of Akbar, contrasting remarkably with the elegant but somewhat fantastic architecture of later periods. In the two elaborately carved vestibules, with pillars of red sandstone, supporting a sloping entablature, in the quadrangle of the citadel known as Jahángír's Khwábgáh, we have good specimens of the Hindú-Moslem style of art, usually supposed to have been peculiar to the time of Akbar.

The Khwábgáh of Jahángír consisted of a large quadrangle with a colonnade on three sides † of red stone pillars, intricately carved with bracket capitals, consisting of the figures of peacocks, elephants and griffins. On the centre of the fourth side, which overlooked the Rávi, stood a lofty pavilion, in the Moghal style of architecture, and on either side at the point of contact of the colonnade with the outer wall were two chambers with verandahs of elaborately carved pillars supporting a sloping entablature, in the Hindu style. In the quadrangle was a garden, with a chabútra or platform, of marble mosaic, and beneath the pavilion and colonnades were underground chambers to serve as a refuge from the heat. Sikh and European disfigurements have completely destroyed the effect of this beautiful quadrangle. The pavilion has been transmogrified into a mess room ; the colonnades have been walled in and cut up into quarters, but the two chambers remain in tolerable preservation, and are fine specimens of the Hindu-Moslem style of art usually supposed to be peculiar to the time of Akbar. In the tomb of Jahángír, at Sháhdara ; the Mosque of Wazír Khán, on the south side of the city ; the Pearl Mosque ; the throne-room and marble pavilion in the citadel ; the tomb of Asaf Khán ; the Gardens of Shálámár ; the Gulábi bágh or "Garden of Rose-water ; " the Gateway of Zeb-ul-Nissa, and the Imperial Mosque of Aurangzeb, we have examples of the

———

* The practice of building their own monuments seems at first sight to imply a distrust on the part of the Turki nobles of the piety of their heirs. It must rather, perhaps, be ascribed to the uncertainty under an Eastern despotism, of transmitting wealth to posterity, and the certainty, under any circumstances, of its being minutely subdivided. Most large incomes were the result either of personal favour or peculation ; in either case, the fortune generally died with the possessor. We can understand, therefore, why a man who had been successful in his generation should be anxious to secure for himself a suitable monument,—that "necessary adjunct of a Tartar's glory,"—before the means to do so had been dissipated.

† Usually called the Moti Mandar.

Indo-Moghal style proper, with its usual characteristics of bulb-like domes, supported on elaborate pendentives, ogee arches, with feathered edgings, marble lattice windows, and brilliantly enamelled walls. As works of art, none of them can perhaps bear comparison with the *chefs dœuvre* of Delhi, Agra, or Fatehpur Síkri ; but there is one special feature in the Moghal buildings at Lahore which cannot fail to strike observers, namely, the profusion and excellence of the coloured tiling and enamelled frescoes used as an external decoration. By it the architects of the day were enabled to compensate, to some extent, for the want of stone material and the consequent impossibility of sculpture, and to give to brick walls that appearance of costliness and durability which, in an aesthetic point of view, is essential to success. The native name of this species of decoration is *kási* or *káshi*. Its use is common all over Persia ; and Bábar, writing in the 16th century, speaks of a mosque at Samarkand " covered with porcelain of China" as a novelty to him. It appears to have been introduced, in the form in which it is found in this part of India, from China, through Persia, by the Moghals. Tradition attributes its introduction to the influence of Tamerlane's Chinese wife. However that may be, the earliest instance, according to Ferguson, is the celebrated mosque of Tabríz, built about the end of the thirteenth or beginning of the fourteenth century of our era, just after the conquest of Persia by the Moghals. The next is the tomb of Muhammad Khudábandan, at Sultánia, built by the successor of Ghazan Khan, the builder of the mosque at Tabríz. From this date the use of glazed tiles became common in Persia ; but it was not till upwards of two centuries from this time that it came to be so in Hindústán. The earliest instance of this mode of decoration at Lahore is the tomb of Sháh Músa, built in the reign of the Emperor Akbar. The colours of this, the oldest specimen, are as vivid, and the decoration is as perfect, as in any of the later ones ; but the art did not come into general use until the time of Sháhjahán, when it took a new form. Encaustic tiles were, to a great extent, disused, and the designs were executed on a hard kind of cement. This process, being probably cheaper, led to the almost universal adoption of *káshi* designs as an architectural ornament. There is hardly a mosque, or a tomb, or a gateway, built during this period, the walls of which are not covered with them. Strange to say, after the reign of Sháhjahán, it became almost entirely disused, and the art may now be said to be lost in the Punjab. Coloured tiles are still manufactured in Lahore and Mooltan ; but the colouring is very poor, and the process of executing coloured designs upon plaster is altogether unknown.

The finest existing specimens of *káshi* work are to be found in the mosque of Wazír Khán, built in A.D. 1634 by Hakim Ali-ud-dín Wazír Khan, a native of Chiniot, who, although a Punjabi by birth rose, during the reign of the liberal-minded Sháhjahán to be Governor of Lahore, as well as Court physician. In gratitude for his unlooked for prosperity under the rule of a stranger, he

Chapter VI, A.
—
Ancient Lahore.
Remains of the Moghal period.

Káshi work, or encaustic tiles.

Chapter VI, A.
———
Ancient Lahore.
Káshi work, or
encaustic tiles.

erected the mosque, which bears his name, at a great expense, over the remains of an old Ghaznivide saint. Artists, it is said, were sent for expressly from China to execute the *káshi* work, and the mosque was pronounced, according to a writer of the day,* "a mole on the cheek of the city of Lahore." Dr. Center, the Chemical Examiner to the Punjab Government, made a careful analysis of specimens of *káshi* work, and the results of his analysis are here given :—

"It consists essentially of a layer of glass spread on a hard kind of plaster,— sometimes on a material porcelaneous in structure. On analysis the glass was found to be an ordinary silicate coloured by metallic oxides. The plaster was found to be composed of a mixture of lime and siliceous sand, the hardness being due to silication, which accounts for its bearing the heat required to fuse glass. It is remarkable that an old Buddhist cast was found to be composed of a similar material. I got specimens made at the laboratory by an old man who practises the art at Lahore, but the work was very inferior. The glaze wanted purity and polish, and he made his plaster as hard as stone. The finest specimens in Lahore are to be seen on Wazir Khan's *masjid*, where the glazing is very fine, but the plaster is easily broken, so that it has been destroyed in many places. The work consists of three parts—1st, the plaster called *khamír*; 2nd, the glass called *kanch*; and 3rd, a material called *astar* put between them. The first operation is to make an easily fusible glass by melting powdered siliceous sandstone with carbonate of soda. Portions of the glass are pounded, mixed and fused with metallic oxides to produce glasses of various colours. Considerable skill was shown in producing the oxides from the metals or from the raw materials of the *bázár*. In particular, a species of black sand got from Ajmer is used to furnish three colours—black, green and blue. It contains sulphuret of copper and magnetic iron sand. These were separated by washing according to their specific gravities, and were reduced to oxides in the furnace. The *khamír* is made by mixing siliceous sand, lime and a quantity of the pounded glass first prepared, and according to the quantity of glass used it turns out a hard kind of mortar, or has a porcelaneous structure. It is made into a paste with rice water, and cut into pieces suitable for the pattern. It is then dried at a gentle heat, and afterwards covered with the *astar*, which consists of lime or pounded glass containing a large quantity of lead. This is suspended in a viscid fluid and painted on the plaster, and its use is to cover small inequalities and to act as a medium to unite the glass and the plaster. The coloured glasses are then pounded, suspended in a viscid fluid, made from mucilaginous plants and painted over the *astar*, and the whole is placed in the furnace till all the glass on the surface is fused. The pieces of the pattern are then put in their places and fixed by cement."

But although the art, as practised in India and Persia, seems to have been derived from China at the end of the thirteenth century, it has, doubtless, existed in other forms among Semitic nations from far more ancient times ; and it is remarkable that the term *káshi* is said to be neither Hindi nor Tartar, but of Arabic origin, and akin to the Hebrew *kos*, a cup. The art was imported into Europe by the Arabians at the end of the ninth century, and adopted by the Italians under the name of *majolica*, in the manufacture of earthenware, in the fourteenth. The art thus introduced was rapidly developed, and gave birth, in time, to the porcelain wares of Palissy, Limoges Sevres, and Dresden. Thus, while the nations of India and Persia, ap-

———

* Suján Singh, who, however, makes no allusion to the story about the Chinese artists. The employment of Chinese is improbable in itself, as there are no traces of Chinese style in the designs or their execution : on the other hand, the origin of the tradition is easily accounted for by the fact that *káshi* is popularly known as "China-work."

preciating as deeply as ourselves the æsthetical value of the art, employed it largely, but almost solely, as an architectural ornament, those of the West at once applied it to articles of every-day utility; and the result is that, while the art is well-nigh lost in India, in Europe it has made, and is still making, rapid strides in improvement.

Prince Kámrán, brother of the Emperor Humáyún, when Viceroy of the Punjab, seems to have given the first impulse to the architectural adornment of Lahore by building a palace and garden near the suburb of Naulakha, and extending thence to the river Rávi. The place was afterwards occupied by Asaf Khan. It was here probably that Humáyún on his retreat from Sher Sháh, the Afghán claimant of the throne, was entertained by his perfidious brother just before his temporary expulsion. A story is told that, as the Royal *cortége* was crossing the Rávi in flight for the west, his counsellors suggested to Humáyún the advisability of then and there despatching the brother whose faithlessness was one great cause of his misfortunes; but the Emperor indignantly rejected the proposal. A *bárádari*, said to have been built by Prince Kámrán, is now used as a toll-house at the bridge of boats. This is the oldest specimen of Moghal architecture in Lahore, but has undergone considerable alterations. All that remains of the palace is a large gateway, now used as a private house, in the vicinity of Lehna Singh's *cháuni*. But the period of Lahore's greatest splendour were the reigns of Akbar, Jehángír, Shábjahán, and Aurangzeb. Gardens, tombs, mosques, palaces, sprang up in every direction; the population increased, suburbs arose, until the city became, in the words of Abul-fazl, "the grand resort of people of all nations."

Akbar, as we have seen, made Lahore his capital for some fourteen years, during which time he repaired and enlarged the fort, and surrounded it and the city with a wall, portions of which still remain, though it was almost rebuilt at the commencement of the present century by Ranjít Singh. In the fort, up to within a few years, there were left some good specimens of the peculiar style of architecture adopted by Akbar; but they are nearly all destroyed; the *Akbari mahal*, or chamber of Akbar, has been razed to the ground, and the smaller throne-room has been so altered by modern additions that it is hardly recognisable as an antique building. Other architectural remains of the period are the tomb of Sháh Chirágh, used as a Government office; the tomb of Kásim Khan, once the trysting-place of the Lahore wrestlers, and now the residence of the Lieutenant-Governor of the Punjab; the tomb of Sháh Músa; and a mosque called the mosque of Kála Khán, on the right hand of the road from Lahore to Mian Mir.

During the reign of Akbar, Lahore, as might have been expected, increased greatly in size and opulence. Up to this

Chapter VI, A.
—
Ancient Lahore.
Remains of the Moghal period, continued.

period, according to a native writer,[*] Lahore consisted of a number of detached hamlets; it now grew into an extensive city. The city, *par excellence*, was that portion surrounded by the wall and covered the same area as the present city; but outside the walls were long *bázárs* and thickly populated suburbs which no longer exist; but some idea of their extent may be formed from the fact that at the time Nizám-ud-dín Ahmad wrote his work—that is, the latter part of Akbar's reign—the most populous quarter of Lahore was the quarter of Langar Khán [†]; this quarter was situated between the present site of the Civil Station of Anárkali and the village of Mozang, upwards of a mile from the *enceinte* of the present city. The following is the description of Lahore during the reign of Akbar, given by Abul-fazl in the *Ain Akbari* :—

"Lahore is a very large and populous city. The fort and palace are of brick and lime, and when this city was for some time the seat of Government, many other capital buildings were erected, and gardens laid out with taste and elegance; it became the grand resort of people of all nations, and their manufactures were brought to the highest pitch of perfection. Through His Majesty's (Akbar's) encouragement, gardeners were brought from Irán and Túrán, who cultivated the vine and various kinds of melons. The manufacture of silk and woollen carpets was introduced, together with that of brocades. In short, here could be obtained the choicest productions of Irán and Túrán."

The Emperor Jahángír built but little, but there are specimens of his architecture in the greater *Khwábgáh*, or sleeping palace; the *Moti masjid*, or Pearl mosque, formerly the Chapelle Royal for the imperial harem, but now used as the Government Treasury; and the tomb of Anárkali, which after having served a variety of secular purposes was then adopted for use as a Station Church and now serves as the depository of the Secretariat Records. The following account of Lahore as it was in the reign of Jahángir, taken from a narrative of the travels of Richard Still and John Growther, [‡] two Englishmen, who found their way to the Punjab, "in search of trade," in 1626, will be of interest :—

"Lahore," they say, " is one of the best cities of India, plentiful of all things or, in Master Coryat's words, 'such delicate and even tract of ground as I never saw before.' A row of trees extends itself on both sides the way from the town's end of Lahore, twenty days' journey, to the town's end of Agra, most of them bearing a kind of mulberry. The way is dangerous by night for thieves; by day secure. Every five or six course (*kos*) there are fair *saráis* of the kings or nobles, beautifying the way, and useful for entertainment of travellers, where you may have a chamber and a place to get your horse, with a store of horse-meat; but, in many of them, little provision for men, by reason of the Banian superstition. Merchants resort to this city out of all parts of India, embarking their goods for Tatta, the chief city in Sind. Twelve or fourteen thousand camels laden yearly pass from hence to Persia by Kandahár."

During the reign of Sháhjahán, Lahore, though no longer the *dár-ul-hukúmat*, or capital, was still a place of importance.

---

[*] Amín Ahmad Rází, author of a work called *Haft Iqlím*, dated A.H. 1032 A.D. 1624.

[†] Langar Khán distinguished himself as Governor of Mooltan in the reign of Humáyún, who, in recognition of his services, assigned him a residence at Lahore in the locality which still bears his name.

[‡] "Purchas, his Pilgrimage."

It lay on the route of the imperial marches to Kashmír, and was the arsenal and rendezvous of the armies despatched to Balkh and the north-west frontier. It therefore, continued to increase in size and splendour. The palace was enlarged and beautified under the superintendence of Asaf Khán, and the entire frontage covered with brilliantly coloured designs in porcelain work. The beautiful tomb of Jahángir, at Sháhdara ; the mosque of Wazír Khán, on the south side of the city ; the gardens of Shálámár ; the gateway of the Gulábi Bágh ; the *Idgah* ; the tomb of Mian Mir ; the summer house of Wazír Khán, now used as the Station Library ; the gateway of Zeb-ul-Nissa : and lastly, the tombs which line the road between Anárkali and the Shálámár gardens, are among the works of the period. A smaller *Khwábgáh* was erected adjoining the western side of that built by Jahángir. It consisted of a quadrangle, enclosed on three sides by an arcade, in the Moghal style of architecture, the centre of the fourth side being occupied by a light marble pavilion with lattice windows looking towards the river. In the inner space was a garden, with fountains flowing into marble receptacles inlaid with flowers wrought in precious stones. The arches and the chambers into which they led have suffered the same fate as those in the *Khwábgáh* of Jahángír ; even the marble slabs upon the walls have received the usual coating of white-wash, but the pavilion remains in tolerable preservation, and is an elegent specimen of the palatial architecture of the time. In front of this pavilion, outside the palace walls, was a platform raised on arches,* called the *arz begi,* where the *Omra* assembled every morning to receive the commands of his Imperial Majesty who showed himself at the lattice window immediately above to the multitude assembled beneath.

To the left of the *Khwábgáh* was erected the range of buildings with octagonal towers, the largest of which is called *par excellence,* the Saman Búrj and contains the small though costly marble pavilion, inlaid with flowers wrought in precious stones and known by the significant name of Naulakha, or the pavilion which cost nine lakhs ; and the celebrated Shísh mahal, used by Ranjít Singh as a reception room, and historically interesting as the place where the sovereignty of the Punjab was formerly made over to the British Government. A new gateway was opened into it for the Emperor's private use, called the Háthipáun gateway, which is now the only entrance into the fort. A winding flight of steps, sufficiently broad to allow of an elephant's ascending—hence the gateway's name—led to this portion of the palace, through a garden which covered the space now occupied by the fort magazine, and suggested a comparison with the hanging gardens of Babylon. Opposite the pavilion in Jahángir's *Khwábgáh* a *hammám* or suite of bathing rooms was erected, which served not only for the purpose indicated by the name, but also as a cabinet council chamber ;

Chapter VI, A.
——
Ancient Lahore.
Remains of the Moghal period continued.

---

* It is now used as a stable.

Chapter VI, A.

Ancient Lahore.

Remains of the Moghal period, continued.

and in the centre of the fort enclosure, the once stately building, known as the *Takht* or Throne-room of Sháhjahán, now vandalized into a barrack ; this was the Diwán A'm or Hall of Audience ; where the Emperor daily sat in state to transact business.

The palace was now, in size and interior magnificence, worthy of an Imperial residence ; its front extended some five hundred yards along the banks of the river, which then flowed near its base ; but the dull red brick of which it was built was unsuited to the Imperial taste ; the whole palace front was accordingly covered with brilliantly coloured designs in *káshi* or porcelain work, executed upon hard cement so as to resemble mosaic. These designs are not simply confined to pattern, but include, in defiance of Muhammadan orthodoxy, the figures of men, horses and elephants, engaged in scenes chiefly of a sporting character, and also symbolical representations of zodiacal signs and of the angels, who according to old Persian mythology, presided over each month and each day of the year. Among them we recognize the dragon-form *Hastabar*, representing the constellation of that name, and *Jadí* the oriental Capricorn. But most conspicuous perhaps are four figures of the rising sun over the arched compartments in front of Jahángír's palace. These would appear intended to represent the divine *mihr*, or genius of the Sun, in whose honour two important festivals, that of the *nauroz*, at the vernal equinox, and *mihrgán* at the autumnal, were held. In like manner the frequently recurring ornament of salvers filled with fruit and flowers would appear to be suggested by the offerings presented on those festive occasions ; and the vessels of water and baskets of viands, which form a common decoration of the walls of Moghal tombs,—that of Jahángir's for instance,*—are perhaps referable to the same origin ; for we know that it was an old Persian custom to place offerings of food and drink on the tops of houses and high places to conciliate the spirits of departed friends.

The designs are thus interesting for two reasons,—first, as exhibiting the open contempt in which the strict rules of Muhammadanism forbidding the representation of living beings were held : and, in the second place, as indicating a strong recurrence to old Persian superstitions and mithraic symbolism at the period of their construction. They further completely corroborate the statements of contemporary writers, such as Abd-ul-Kádir, Abul Fazl and the Portuguese Missionaries, who all notice the assiduous worship paid to the sun and heavenly bodies by the earlier Moghal Emperors. This tendency to mithraism was not, however, confined to the Emperors of Hindústán. A mithraic emblem adorns the Hall of Audience at Udepore ; the Lion and the Sun have from a remote period been the heraldic emblems of the Persian empire; and in the title

---

* J. Albert de Mandelslo, a gentleman, belonging to the embassy sent by the Duke of Holstein to the Grand Duke of Muscovy and the King of Persia, in 1683.

Sáhib-i-Qirán, or *Lord of propitious Constellations*, assumed originally by Tamerlane and afterwards adopted by Sháhjahán, and inscribed by him upon the entrance into his palace, at Lahore, we have similar relics of the religion of Zoroaster. The route from Agra to Lahore, in the early part of the seventeenth century, is described by a European traveller : "One continued alley, drawn in a straight line, and planted on both sides with date-trees, palm-trees, cocoa-trees, and other kinds of fruit trees."

An interesting account of Lahore as it was in the period of the Emperor Shájahán is given in the accompanying translated extract from the Itinerary of Fra Sebastain Manrique, a Spanish monk, who visited Lahore in 1641 :

"On the 21st day from our departure from Agra, at sunrise, we came in sight of the city of Lahore, which is large and capacious : but, large as it appeared, there were not houses enough for the accommodation of the people, who were encamped for half a league outside the city. It is a handsome and well-ordered city, with large gateways and pavilions of various colours. I entered the city—a very difficult undertaking on account of the number of people who filled the streets, some on foot, some on camels, some on elephants and others in small carts. jolting one against the other as they went along. Those who best could, passed on first. This being the receiving hour at court, many of the gentry were proceeding there, accompanied by as many as 500 followers on horse-back.

" Finding it difficult to proceed on account of the concourse of people, we decided to change our route, and returned about a musket's shot from the crowd and took our stand under some trees outside the city, where were a number of people selling and preparing food for the multitude, who were moving about—some eating, some selling and others looking on. I was one among the latter, and my curiosity prompted me to proceed still further, until at last I arrived at the principal bázár, where the odour from without prepared you for what you were to see inside—a great many shops, or, more properly speaking, kitchens, in which were sold meats of various kinds, animals, domestic and wild. In place of the pig, which is never used, horseflesh is supplied you instead. Some shops contained fowls of all kinds ; in others might be seen things of all descriptions suited to the taste of all classes, such as butter, oil, scents, *brinjals*, mangoes, plantains, &c. Neither was there wanting in this bázár the most simple commodity, such as rice, herbs, and vegetables. The common bread is made of a mixture of all kinds of flour baked on sheets of iron and in earthen pots, and is known by the name of *apás*. People who travel in caravans use a second kind of bread, named *culchás*, which is made of white flour. This bread is also used by the better classes. A third bread, named *rojanis*, is a finer bread made of the best flour and purified butter. Besides what I have already enumerated, there is a great deal more to be seen in these bázárs ; but I think I have mentioned enough to satisfy the curious reader. But what I most admired was the moderate price at which these things might be had. A man might eat abundantly and royally for two silver reals (five pence) per day. The abundance of the provisions and cleanliness of the streets surprised me much ; also the peace and quietness with which everything was conducted, as well as the justness and rectitude of people towards each other ; so that merchant and merchandise remains perfectly secure from thieves.

" The city of Lahore is beautifully situated, commanding agreeable views, having on one side a river with crystal waters which descends from the mountains of Kashmír and continues its course moistening and fertilizing the ground, till it arrives at the city of Mooltan, where it pays its tribute to the famous Indus. Lahore, the second city of the Moghal Empire (as well on account of riches as its size) is ornamented with fine palaces and gardens, also tanks and fountains. As to the abundance of provision, it would be unnecessary here to describe it. The riches of the principal street (known as the *Bázár del Choco*), if shown to advantage, would equal the richest European mart."

At the date of the accession of Aurangzeb, A.D. 1658, Lahore must have fallen off in wealth and populousness from what it was in the days of his predecessors. The absence of the court, and the foundation of Sháhjahánábad or New Delhi, had drawn away the bulk of the artificers and trading population to that more favoured locality; and when Bernier passed through it in 1664 the houses had begun to look dilapidated, and the long streets of the city to be disfigured with ruins. It was still, however, the capital of the most important province of the Empire, and was benefited by the occasional presence of the Emperor during his march to Kashmír at the beginning of the hot season. In the fourth year of his reign, the city having suffered much from the encroachments of the river, Aurangzeb had a massive quay of masonry constructed for upwards of three miles along the river's bank. The quay, it is said, was faced with lead; flights of steps, at intervals, led down to the water's edge; and rows of Persian wheels, projecting over the side, made the waters of the Rávi available for irrigating the gardens which lined its banks. The work is compared by a contemporary writer to the " rampart built by Sikandar Zulkarnain against the incursions of Gog and Magog; " and as a rampart, indeed, it proved most effectual, for it not only effected the object of saving the city from destruction, but scared away the river altogether. The remains of the quay, or *Band of Alamgir*, as it is called, are still traceable between the north-eest and of the fort and the village of Bhogíwál. But the great work of the period is the Jáma Masjid, or Musalmán Cathedral, the most striking building at Lahore, whose white marble domes and almost colossal minarets may be seen for miles,—a building said by some to have owed its origin to the Emperor's pious remorse for the murder of his brother, Dárá Shikoh, and by others to a desire to eclipse the beauties of the mosque of Wazír Khán. Its architect was Fidáe Khán Khokah, who held the post of Master of Ordnance to His Majesty. The completion of this mosque may be said to close the architectural history of Lahore. Later attempts, such as the Golden Mosque of Bikhári Khán, and the Palace and Tomb of Khán Bahádur, at Begampúra, only prove how architectural taste fell with the fall of the Empire, and became a mongrel style—half-Muhammadan and half-Hindu.

From this time, until the establishment of a Sikh kingdom by Ranjít Singh, Lahore was subject to periodical invasion, pillage and depopulation, and was thus reduced from a mighty city to little more than a walled township in a circle of ruinous waste. Quarter after quarter became deserted. The wealthy residents of Guzar Langar Khán relinquished their extra-mural palaces, and retired for safety within the city walls; the merchants and traders fled in numbers to Amritsar; the artificers were dispersed, some following the invading armies on their return march to Kábul, others finding their way to Hindústán. At length, the inhabited portion of the city was confined to the

area surrounded by the wall of Akbar; outside was ruin and
devastation. The only signs of life were two Sikh forts, built
to overawe the country round about, and a few scattered hamlets,—one peopled by the descendants of a hardy clan of Biloches
who settled at Lahore in happier times, and another by a few
peasants who clung to the site of the old Hindu city. Such was
the state of Lahore when it came into the possession of Ranjít
Singh, and its aspect of desolation is thus graphically described in the following extract from the diary of an English
officer, who visited the Sikh capital in the year 1809 :—

" *24th May.*—I visited the ruins of Lahore, which afforded a melancholy
picture of fallen splendour. Here the lofty dwellings and masjids, which, fifty
years ago, raised their tops to the skies, and were the pride of a busy and active
population, are now crumbling into dust, and in less than half a century more
will be levelled to the ground. In going over these ruins, I saw not a human
being,—all was silence, solitude and gloom."

As might have been expected, no great improvement upon
this state of things was effected during Sikh *régime.* The do-
mination of a peasant race, of martial habits, under a sovereign
ignorant of the alphabet, is not encouraging to the development
of architectural taste ; nevertheless Ranjít Singh, unlettered and
unpolished as he was, had an idea that architecture was a good
thing. Accordingly, he stripped the Muhammadan tombs of their
marble facings, and sent them to adorn the Sikh temple at
Amritsar. He restored the Shálámár Gardens, which had gone
to ruin during the troublous times of Ahmad Sháh ; but at the
same time laid ruthless hands upon the marble pavilions by the
central reservoir, and substituted structures of brick and plaster
in their stead. He turned the *sarái* which separated the fort
and palace from the *Jáma Masjid* into a private garden, and
placed therein the marble edifice which remains to this day
the architectural *chef-d'œuvre* of his reign—an example of
judicious spoliation and hybrid design.* Besides the above, a
few unsightly temples to Siva, erected in honour of a favourite
wife or dancing girl, and some tasteless additions to the fort,
comprise all the architectural works of Ranjít Singh at Lahore.
One of the latest specimens of Sikh architecture is the mausoleum of Ranjít Singh himslf, his son and grandson. The building
is, as usual, in design substantially Hindu, overlaid with
Muhammadan details, and does not bear close inspection ; but
the effect at a distance is not unpleasing. Within, a lotus,
carved in marble, set beneath a canopy, mark the spot where
the ashes of the Lion of Lahore are laid ; around it are eleven
smaller ones, in memory of those who burned themselves upon his
funeral pyre.† The palaces of the Sikh nobility show the same

---

* The building was the joint production of a Muhammadan and a Hindú.
The materials were taken from the tombs of Asaf Khán and Jehángir at Shahdara, and that of Zebinda Begam, at Nawákot.

† The last occasion on which the rite of *suttee* was practised at Lahore was
at the burning of the remains of the murdered Dhyán Singh. But in Kashmír
an attempt at *suttee* was made as late as 1857, on the death of Dhyán Singh's
brother, Mahárája Guláb Singh. Thousands of persons had assembled, and the
victims were ready, but the energetic remonstrances of the Civil Commissioner,
Captain Urmston, prevented its being carried out.

blending of Hindu and Muhammadan design, and are further disfigured by small angular chambers perched on the highest part of the building, to catch the breeze in the hot weather and rains. The walls of the chambers are gaudily but roughly painted with scenes, sometimes of a religious, sometimes of a warlike or sportive character. The former are generally taken from the life of Krishn or of Bába Nának; the fighting scenes relate chiefly to conflicts with the Afgháns of the north-west frontier, but none are remarkable as works of art.

This is not the place to follow the history of the new administration. In Lahore itself, the years that have followed the eventful 29th of March have been years of material progress. The environs of the city in 1849 were "a dreary expanse of crumbling ruins," remains of the ancient city of the Mughals. The houses and offices of the first residents were confined to the neighbourhood of the old cantonments, which occupied a strip of alluvial soil to the south of the city, and running parallel with an old bed of the Rávi. Gradually, however, as the European population increased in numbers, the station spread eastward, making steady inroads upon the less inviting region which lay further from the river. And thus year by year the ruins and graveyards of old Lahore passed under the humanizing influence of western civilization. Metalled roads have pierced the *débris* of former days, and bungalows and gardens have succeeded to ruins and rough jungle. Much still remains to be done, but the scene has already assumed a garb of life and trimness not discreditable to the Punjab capital.

SECTION B.—MODERN LAHORE.

Modern Lahore.

Lahore, the capital of the province and head-quarters of the district, is situated on a slightly rising ground about a mile from the left bank of the river Rávi at its nearest point in 31° 34' north latitude, and 74° 21' east longitude. The river, as might be supposed, once flowed by the city, and in A. D. 1662 made such encroachments that a massive quay or embankment was built for some four miles along its bank to protect the city from destruction. Almost immediately after the completion of this costly work and perhaps, indeed, in consequence of it, the river deserted its old channel and turned to the north, leaving the brick embankment ignominiously high and dry. Since that date the main stream of the Rávi has never returned to its old bed, though occasionally an arm of the river has wandered into its old course; and at the time of annexation there was a small stream flowing under the fort walls.

The city, as already noticed, is in shape an irregular trapezium with its longest side looking northward, and contains an area of 640 acres. The soil is alluvial, but the *débris* of ages has raised the site of the city to a considerable height above the river. The city is built on several mounds rising to a height of fifty feet and under, with innumerable depressions. Its extreme length is one mile and a quarter; its extreme breadth, including the citadel, a little more than three quarters of a mile.

The south-west and east sides were formerly surrounded by a brick wall, originally thirty feet high, afterwards reduced to fifteen feet for sanitary purposes; recently however the Municipal Committee has decided to remove this wall gradually, and the principal gate on the west side standing nearest to the fort has already been demolished and removed. Outside the wall was formerly a deep moat which in more modern times has been filled in and the space reclaimed has with the aid of canal irrigation been turned into gardens or orchards of fruit trees. The north side of the city looking over the Rávi towards Shahdara is occupied by the fort and palace, the Jáma Musjid, and Ranjít Singh's tomb, which with Wazír Khán's mosque are the only buildings in the city of which any detailed accounts need here be given. The descriptions that follow are those given in the 1882-83 edition of the Lahore Gazetteer.

The frontage of the fort and palace extends on this side from east to west for about 500 feet. It was the work of four Emperors. To the extreme east are the foundations of the Akbari Mahal, or palace of Akbar; next comes a portion ascribed to Jahángír, flanked by two towers like abutments; and, lastly, a curtain wall between two hexagonal towers of unequal size is said to have been built by Sháhjahán, with additions by Aurangzeb and the Sikhs. The greater part of the frontage is covered with designs in inlaid enamelled tiles, including, in defiance of Muhammadan orthodoxy, the figures of men, horses, and elephants engaged chiefly in sporting, and symbolical representations of zodiacal signs and of the angels who, according to old Persian mythology, preside over each day and each month of the year. In spandrels over arcaded compartments in front of Jahángír's Palace are four represent-ations of the rising sun. Other spandrels show winged cherubs, exactly resembling those of Christian art, and pos-sibly borrowed from decorations or pictures in the Jesuit Church established at Lahore by Portuguese missionaries which existed at the time of the execution of these designs. This is the more probable from the fact related by Bernier that an image of the Blessed Virgin was placed by Jahángír in a prominent position as a compliment to the missionaries.

The general scheme of the wall decoration is simple, and resembles that of many Italian fronts, consisting of a series of arcaded panelling of flat projection, broken by horizontal bands of mixed enamelled and carved fret-work of geometrical design, the spandrels and some of the panels filled in with procelain work, but most of the latter left in bare plaster, while some have been painted with fruits, flowers, &c., in fresco. Besides the symbols noticed, which may be a faint echo of the ancient mithraic worship of the East, there is a great variety of subjects comprising birds, processions of loaded camels, demons with duly cloven hoofs, conjurors, dancing girls, dragons, horsemen, and some beautiful pieces of geometrical ornament. Rising about half way up the Palace front there is in this enclosure a ruined building on arches immediately beneath a marble pavilion with perforated lattice work. This was the *Arz Begi,* where the *Omra* or nobles of the court assembled in the morning to receive the Emperor's commands.

Returning to the Fort entrance and then to the left the visitor passes under a second gateway of marble, called the *Hathi-paun,* or Elephant's Foot Gate, because the elephants taking the court ladies out for airing went through it: the approach to the harem formerly lay to the left, up a staircase of broad steps, now destroyed. Over the gateway is a Persian inscription dated 1041 Hij, of which the following is a translated extract :—" The King (Sháhjahán) ordered a tower to be erected which in height should be beyond measurement and conception, like unto the highest Heaven. In beauty, loftiness, and excellence such a tower never has been and never will be seen under the sky." The road to the right by which the Fort is now reached is English work. On reaching the top the aspect of the Fort resembles an ordinary barrack square. The barrack in the centre however was formerly the *Takht,* or Throne-room of Sháhjahán. In this *Diwán-i-Ám,* or Hall of Audience, the Emperor daily sat in State ; and as he took his seat the musicians stationed in the *naqár khanah* opposite struck up a martial strain, while a glittering pageant of men, horses and elephants, graphically described by Bernier, passed in review before him ; but meanwhile there issued from an empty tomb immediately in front, which has now disappeared, the voice of a *mulla* reminding the Sháh-an-Sháh from time to time that he too must die like other men. The daily procession, according to Bernier, lasted from upwards of an hour, but, notwithstanding the time wasted on these displays, a large amount of business was got through, and the Emperor, with all his love of show and splendour, never remitted his vigilance over the internal Government. Of Aurangzeb, indeed, it is said that " the appointment of the lowest revenue officer of a district or the selection of a clerk in an office was not beneath his attention, while he planned each campaign, issued instructions during its progress, fixed on points of attack, and regulated the movements of every detachment or convoy ". The work of Akbar, at the extreme east of the Fort, has disappeared ; the quadrangle of Jahángír however can be traced. It is remarkable for the purely Hindu character of the details especially of the red stone consoles supporting the entablature which are of elephants and other conventional animals, precisely similar to those to be found in Hindu temples.

The *Khwábgah* of Sháhjehán is an elegant little pavilion of marble arches and open lattice work immediately over the *Arz Begi* already noticed. In this pavilion, protected by curtains hanging from rings in the walls, the Emperor slept, and on rising showed himself at the marble windows to the nobles gathered below. Like the rest of the buildings in the Fort this has been made to serve a British purpose, and at one time did duty as a garrison church, the font used for baptisms remaining in evidence. The upper frieze is an inlay of corne-jian, &c., and gracefully designed.

Returning westward through the barracks, and passing the *Takht* the visitor sees an archway in which is posted a guard of soldiers of a Native regiment. This is the entrance to the Government Treasury, once known as the Moti Masjid, a small mosque with marble domes, half hidden by surrounding walls which was formerly the private chapel of the ladies of the imperial harem. Between this and the *Takht* is a building, now transformed into a hospital or sleeping quarters, without any distinctively oriental character. This was a *hammám* or suite of bathing-rooms, and it was also used as a cabinet council chamber.

The stern necessities of English military life have had no reverence for the relics of departed greatness, and there is only one part of the Fort and Palace which is not put to some practical modern use. This is the Samman Burj. *Saman* is an abbreviation of *musamman*, octagonal. It is by no means certain that the building which, turning to the left, after passing the Moti Masjid, the visitor has now entered is that to which the name was originally applied. Report says that there was another lofty tower, detached from the main building which was so called ; and unless the language of the inscription on the Háthi-páun gateway is inordinately hyperbolical, it seems to point to some such conclusion. But although the Summan Burj does not merit the extravagant eulogy of the inscription, an examination of its parts will be found interesting. There is the small, though costly, marble pavilion, inlaid with flowers, wrought in precious stones, and known by the significant name of Naulakha, or the building which cost nine lakhs. This delicate and beautiful work belongs to the time of Aurangzeb, and it is distinguished from other architectural forms near it by the curvilinear roof. The inlay, much of which has unfortunately been destroyed, is remarkable for excessive minuteness and finish of execution. In this, as in the later work of most styles of art, mechanical virtuosity (to employ an expressive Germanism) was beginning to usurp the place of originality and purity of design. Still as a specimen of later Mughal work, this little pavilion is full of interest, and it is a pity that it has not been more intelligently repaired.

The Shish Mahal, or Palace of Mirrors, is a much more striking object, and the iridescent sheen of its myriad frag-

Chapter VI, B.
———
Modern Lahore.
The Shísh Mahal.

ments of looking-glass of different colours set in arabesque patterns of white cement, at once attracts the visitor's attention. This is the work of both Shábjahán and Aurangzeb, and the more gaudy and vulgar portions are due to the Sikhs. It is historically interesting as the scene of the formal transfer of the sovereignty of the Punjab to the British Government. There too Ranjít Singh held receptions, and from the lofty vantage point of the upper tower could survey at ease the movements of his troops on the plain below, the stores in his arsenal in the court of the Jáma Masjid, and the varied bustle and life of the Fort and city. The effect of the *shish* or mirror work, though brilliant, narrowly escapes the charge of vulgarity, especially when contrasted with the marble inlay of the Naulakha and of the spandrels of the marble arches on the inner side of the Shísh Mahal itself. Much of the painting has been recently restored, and, compared with other contemporary work, especially that in the house of Kharak Singh, now unfortunately demolished, it must be confessed, somewhat coarsely. In the small rooms leading to the upper tower are fair specimens of the wooden ceilings made in geometrical patterns, gaily painted and gilt, which produce a remarkable effect of intricacy and richness. The principle on which these elaborately panelled ceilings are constructed is identical with that of many examples at Cairo and in other places all over the East. Small pieces of wood of suitable geometrical forms, frequently hexagonal, are cut out and painted separately. They are afterwards joined together on the ceiling, and the process is by no means so slow and costly as the finished result would lead one to imagine. From these chambers the visitor should proceed to the roof of the building and ascend to the summit of the small chamber erected thereon, as from this point the finest view of Lahore and the surrounding country is obtained including the minarets of Shahdara, the river Rávi, the broad plain in front of the citadel, the mausoleum of Ranjít Singh, the Jáma Masjid, the city, and, in clear weather, a distant glimpse of the Hymalayas. Up to quite recently, some relics of Muhammad, which are said to have been brought into India by Tamerlane, were kept in the Fort. They have now been made over to the Anjuman i-Islamia at Lahore for custody on behalf of the Muhammadan community and deposited in the Bádsháhi Masjid or Imperial mosque.

The armoury.

Opposite the Shísh Mahal, in an arcade closed in with glazed windows and doors, is the armoury, which contains a heterogeneous assortment of the weapons and uniforms worn by the Sikh army. Mediæval and modern times are here curiously blended; the round brass bassinet with neck-guard of chain mail, the mace and battle-axe similar to those depicted in the Bayeux tapestry being side by side with modern muskets and rifles and the cuirasses emblazoned with the Gallic cock which the "French guard" of Ranjit Singh wore in emulation of the French cuirassiers. The silver-plated helmets and breast-plates of the Italian and French officers employed by the Sikh ruler are here shown. Here are also specimens of revolving rifles made many years before the perfection of the principle in Europe. Here too is the battle-axe of Guru Gobind Singh, the first warrior *Guru*. Besides these, there is a number of matchlocks, the barrels of some of which are fine examples of intricate and ornamental twisting, and many varieties of sword and dagger. The most important of these are the *talwár*, the ordinary curved sword of the East ; and the *kirch*, a long straight sword. Many of those exhibited here with iron and brass hilts were worn by the Sikh artillerymen. A curious weapon is also displayed, consisting of a huge blade with a basket hilt of steel and a steel arm-guard, which could only have been used for thrusting. Accurate models of this mediæval implement are still made in tin with blades of lath, and are used in the mummeries of the Moharram and other Muhammadan festivals. The long and deadly Afghán knife is here ; the smaller *pesh-kabz*, a straight dagger, sharp on one side, similar to a hunting-knife, and of Persian orgin ; the *bicchuá*, a venomous looking two-edged and serpentine curved blade, which in some varieties is forked like a flame ; and the Hindu *katár*, a straight triangular and heavy-bladed *langue de bœuf* dagger, which branches at the hilt into a fork, in which is set a cross-bar at right angles with the blade, by which it is wielded. The bows are nearly all made in three pieces, like the classic bow of antique sculptures. The *chakra*, or war quoit, has not been used in recent times, but the Akálísor Nihangs still wear these weapons on their fantastic headdresses. There is a great variety of carbines and bell-mouthed weapons, between a pistol and a blunderbus, known by the expressive name of *sher-bacha*. Among the guns are examples of the *zamburahs*, small bore iron cannons mounted on the wooden saddles of camels, and heavy matchlocks, supported on two legs in front like the arquebus of mediæval Europe. Larger than these are the *jazail*—huge musket barrels, roughly mounted, and used like the Chinese jingal, which they much resemble, in protecting forts. The curious light guns mounted on apparently inefficient wheels or castors were invented by Guláb Singh for hill warfare, and were drawn by a man or a goat.

The Jama Masjid is the latest specimen of the architecture of the Moghal dynasty worthy of the name, the mausoleum of Humáyún at Delhi being the earliest. It is the most striking building in Lahore, and its white domes and lofty *minárs* may be seen for miles round. Late as it undoubtedly is, it is far removed from the degenerate forms exhibited in Lucknow and other places as Muhammadan art. The inscription in front of the gateway shows that it was built in the year 1084 of the Hijri, or A.D. 1674, for the Emperor Aurangzeb, by Fidáe Khán Khokah, whom Bernier mentions as the Great Moghal's master of ordnance. The gateway, already noticed, opens on a

The Jama Masjid.

Chapter VI, B.
Modern Lahore.
The Jama Masjid.

large quadrangle paved with brick and overshadowed by two rows of *pipal* trees, a feature of very rare occurrence in this position, the quadrangle of a mosque being usually without vegetation of any kind. The general effect of the building is somewhat bold, but the ornamental white marble inlaid in the red sandstone central arch and arcade is so coarse and recent in design as to dwarf its really fine proportions.

As a work of art, it is not to be compared with the Imperial mosque at Dehli, though at first sight it has some resemblance to it. The absence of side entrances and the position of the minarets at the four corners of the quadrangle give the building a very stiff appearance, and we miss the graceful subordination of part to part, which is so pleasing in the Delhi mosque. There is, moreover, a poverty of detail; the *rawaq*, or colonnades at the side, are plain in the extreme, and *minárs*, divested of their cupolas, which were so shattered in the earthquake of A.D. 1840 that they had to be removed, have some resemblance at a distance to certain unpoetic structures common in manufacturing towns in England. At the same time the effect of the arcade of red sandstone adorned with marble tracing, with the tall semi-domed arch in the centre, seen through the elegant gateway resting on a broad flight of steps, which meets the eye of the spectator from the Hazúri Bágh, is very fine; and in defence of the architect it may be remarked that many of the defects may be ascribed rather to the "orthodoxy" then to the bad taste of the designer. The arrangement of the mosque is in fact a recurrence to that of the exemplar mosque of Al Walid at Mecca, from which that of the Delhi mosque is a tasteful departure. It has already been mentioned that the building was turned into a magazine by the Sikhs, and only restored to the Muhammadans, who, however, to a certain extent, shun it as an *Akeldama*. An archway known as the Roshnái Gateway leads from the north side of the garden, and it was near here that Nau Nihál Singh, the grandson of Ranjít Singh, and son of the imbecile Kharak Singh, met his death by the fall of a portion of an archway (since destroyed) while on his way from his father's funeral pyre to the Saman Burj, where he was to be invested with the dignity of Mahárája.

Ranjít Singh's
Mausoleum.

Ranjít Singth's mausoleum, adjacent to the Hazúri Bagh, is a curious mixture of Hindu and Muhammadan notions, being a compromise between a Hindu *samádh* and a Muhammadan tomb, but there is none of the dignity of the latter style in its comparatively petty details. The door jambs of the shrine itself were originally a very finished example of inlaid work of the same delicate character as that in the palace above. The ceilings are elaborately decorated with tracery in stucco inladi with small convex mirrors. The marble arches of the interior were in a dangerous state, when Sir Donald McLeod, then Lieutenant-Governor of the Punjab, had them strengthened with brick and *chunam* and clamped with iron. The visitor will generally find priests reading the *Granth*, or Sikh scriptures,

a huge volume over which a *chauri* is reverentially waved; or
chanting to the accompaniment of the *sitár*. In the centre
is a raised stone platform on which is a marble lotus flower,
surrounded by eleven smaller ones. The central flower covers
the ashes of the Mahárája, the other those of four wives and
seven slave girls who perished on his funeral pyre. In small
niches in the side walls are to be seen images of the ordinary
Hindu gods, to abolish which was one of the original objects
of the Sikh faith. On the further side of the Mausoleum are
two other domed buildings containing similar but less costly
memorials of Kharak Singh and of Nau Nihál Singh. Below
the mausoleum of Ranjít Singh by the side of the road leading
from the Roshnái Gate to the external plain, is the Shrine
of Arjun Dass, the fifth Sikh Guru, and the compiler of the *Adi
Granth* which now forms the principal portion of the Sikh
scriptures. Here, according to Sikh tradition, the sage miraculously disappeared beneath the waters of the Rávi, which in
the time of Jahángír flowed under the fort walls. A more
prosaic legend says that the holy man committed suicide to
escape the enmity of Chandu Sháh, the Prime Minister of
the Emperor. There is nothing architecturally interesting in
the building itself. Close by Arjan's shrine is the fort entrance.
To the right on entering lies a temple to Síta, now in ruins,
which is said to have stood on the edge of the Rávi before the
fort '. was built, marking the spot where Síta, wife of Ráma,
while in exile, brought forth Láhu and Kusu in the house of
Válmík, the author of the Rámáyána. Passing through the
outer gate, guarded by sentries of an English regiment, there
is, turning to the left, a space of about 50 yards between the
outer walls and the Palace front, where can be examined the
exceedingly curious and interesting decorations in coloured *káshi*
work on enamelled pottery which decorate the facade.

The mosque of Wazír Khan was built on the site of the
tomb of an old Ghaznivide saint in A.D. 1634 by Hakím Alí-ud-
dín, a Pathán of Chiniot, who rose to the position of *Wazír* in
the reign of Sháhjahán. It is remarkable for the profusion
and excellence of the inlaid pottery decorations in the panelling
of the walls. Local legend says that artists were sent for
expressly from China to execute the work; but there is no
historical authority for this, nor is there any trace of Chinese
style in either the design or the execution. Its origin is mani-
festly Persian, and the descendants of the draftsmen employed
to this day pride themselves on their Persian origin. It will
be observed that in these arabesques each leaf and each detached portion of the white ground is a separate piece of pot or tile,
and that the work is strictly inlay and not painted decoration.
The panels of pottery are set in hard mortar. In the mosque
itself are.some very good specimens of Perso-Indian arabesque
painting on the smooth *chunam* walls. This work, which is very
freely painted and good in style, is true fresco painting, the
buono fresco of the Italians, and, like the inlaid ceramic work,

is now no longer practised, modern native decoration being usually *fresco'secco* or mere distemper painting. The reason of this is that there has been no demand for this kind of work for many years. Though the builder was a native of the Punjab, the style is more Perso-Moghal and less Indian than that of any other building in the city. Two chronograms inscribed on the walls give the date of the foundation of the mosque. One —*Sijda-gáh-i-Ahl-Fazl* "The Worshipping Place of the Sons of Grace." Another—*Báni Masjid Wazír Khan*—"The founder of the mosque is Wazír Khan." From the *minárs* of this mosque the best view of the city proper is obtained.

Proceeding to the left of the building along a street which is remarkable from the overhanging balconies carved with a profusion of geometrical tracery and ornament, the visitor will observe the gilt melon-like domes of the *Sunahri Masjid* or Golden Mosque, which was built in A.D. 1753 by Bikhári Khan, a favourite in the court of the widow of Mír Mannu, a lady who governed Lahore for some time after the death of her husband, the gallant opponent of Ahmad Shah. It is said that having incurred the displeasure of his mistress, he was beaten to death with shoes by her women. The domes are pretty, and the situation at the junction of two roads, is picturesque ; but there is nothing of architectural interest in the mosque itself.

Behind the mosque is a *báoli* or large well, with steps de-scending to the water's edge. The well is said to have been dug by Arjan, the fifth Sikh Guru ; the superstructure was built by Ranjít Síngh. Passing along the narrow winding street the open space known as Híra Mandi is reached. Here, the ground being cleared for a space round the massive walls of the fort, is a fine view of the fortress and Jama Masjid. Turning to the right the visitor passes under a gateway between the two, and finds himself in a pleasant garden, the *Hazúri Bágh*. In the buildings adjoining the gateway the Normal School is now located ; on the right is a high crenellated wall, and in the centre a massive gateway of somewhat ruinous appearance, the Akbari Darwáza, which was made by Akbar, and was the ancient entrance to the citadel. The visitor cannot fail to note the elegant design of the towers of this building.

To the left is the quadrangle of the Jama Masjid, raised on a lofty platform set on arches with an imposing archway of red sandstone and marble. The flight of steps is paved with a beautifully variegated stone from Kábul, known as *abrí*. This stone is also found in the Kowagár hills in the Ráwalpindi dis-trict, and was a favourite material with Muhammandan builders for inlaid floors. In the centre of the garden is an elegant marble pavilion of two stories, and, looking further on, the hybrid orna-mentation of the mausoleum of Ranjít Singh is visible. The place is fraught with historical associations. In the days when the Jama Masjid was daily resorted to by crowds of worshippers, and the power of the Moghal Emperors was in its golden prime, this garden—now in spite of the care bestowed on it wearing a deserted air—was a *sarái* thronged with vast retinues of armed men exhibiting all the noisy pomp and glitter of Eastern sovereignty.

Ranjít Singh, who was not generally moved by æsthetic considerations, for once in his life showed some taste in converting it into an ornamental pleasure-ground; and, although it is hard to forgive the ruthless vandalism he displayed in tearing away the material for the marble edifice in the centre from the tombs of Asaf Khán and the Emperor Jahángir at Shahdara, it must be confessed that the pavilion is architecturally a success. Here the Sikh ruler used to sit and transact business of State, or, in official parlance, held *katcheri*. The Jama Masjid was then a magazine, and the place of prayer of the faithful was covered with his munitions of a war. Here, too, a few years later, stood Sher Singh, watching the effect of the cannonade of the fort gateway during the four days' siege that ended in his accession to the throne. The marks of the shot fired on this occasion are still visible on the east walls of the pavilion.

The general aspect of the city from without excepting on its northern front is not imposing. The Hindu temples are small and poor in outline, and neither they nor the cupolas of the mosques sufficiently break the monotonous horziontal lines, which are the chief features of the view. Within the city the streets are narrow and winding, but some of them from their overhanging balconies of wood curiously carved and coloured, the striped awnings over the shop fronts, and the streamers of bright coloured clothes hung at intervals across from balcony to balcony, present much that is picturesque to a stranger's eye.

In the immediate vicinity of the city the country is tolerably well wooded; but the trees are deficient in size and variety, consisting chiefly of the *acacia Arabica*, here called *kíkar*, and the *tanariz Orientalis* or *farás*. But here and there groups of trees of denser foliage and taller growth, such as the mango, *pipal*, and datepalm, indicate the sites of ancient gardens and pleasure grounds.

Some of these are still kept up, chief among which are those of Shahdara and Shálámár, lying four miles or so from the city, one on either side.

The Shahdara gardens owe their existence to the tomb of Jahángir raised by the devoted widow Núr-Jehán in memory of her husband. The gardens probably grew up gradually around the tomb. The tomb itself is still a very striking building and its four high minarets with their graceful cupolas of white marble are visible for miles round : from all accounts however it was a very much grander edifice as originally constructed, having since then received very rough treatment both from Muhammadans and Sikhs.

According to the hereditary *khádims* or attendants, there was once in the centre of the terrace roof a marble cupola supported upon an octagonal basement of perforated marble ; above this was an awning made of cloth of gold, and above this another awning stretched from the upper portions of the four towers. The central dome and the awnings were, it is said, removed by Bahádur Sháh, the son of Aurangzeb ; the carved doorways of the chambers below by Ahmad Sháh Duráni ; while Ranjít Singh carried off the marble lattice parapet which surrounded the roof and the galleries of the towers. The building was not benefited when it was occupied for a time after annexation by British soldiers, but, by way of amends, the marble cupolas have been put in thorough repair by the British Government. The tomb is approached by four corridors leading from the garden, three of which are closed by perforated marble screens. The sarcophagus is of marble decorated with coloured inlay. On two sides are inscribed the 99 attributes of God, and on the top is an extract from the Korán. At the head is a Persian inscription, of which the following is a translation :— " The illumined resting-place of His Majesty, the asylum of pardon, Núr-ud-dín Jahángír Bádsha, A. H. 1037 " (A. D. 1628), giving the date of the erection of the sarcophagus, and —" Reason said Jahángír hath departed from the world, A. H. 1036 " (A. D. 1627), giving the date of the emperor's death.

Both the tomb and surrounding garden had been greatly neglected for many years, partly because vested interests threw difficulties in the way of improvements being taken in hand. A few years ago, however, all such interests were bought up by the Government, and since then much has been done to improve both the tomb and the garden. On the former a sum of nearly Rs. 15,000 has been spent since the year 1882 in executing such repairs as were considered necessary for the preservation of the building round the tomb and in restoring the ancient designs on all the more prominent parts of the edifice. The garden is supported entirely out of the sale proceeds of the produce.

The Shálamár gardens were laid out in A. D. 1667, by order of the Emperor Sháhjehán. Local legend says that the Emperor once spending a night at Shahdara, then just completed by the widowed Empress Núrjahán, had a wondrous dream of a garden like that of Paradise, bright with fruits of gold, marble fountains, cool pavilions, and every variety of foliage. Awaking he sent for Ali Mardán Khan and for Náwáb Fazal Khan, and commanded them to reproduce for him his fleeting vision. They accordingly laid out the garden in seven divisions, representing the seven degrees of the Paradise of Islám. Of these four have been destroyed, and three only are included in the present area, which covers 39 acres, more or less. The actual meaning of the word Shálamár is doubtful. " Hall of Desire " (*Shál-i-már*) and " Royal Edifice " (*Sháhi-imárat*) are conjectural derivations, but neither is satisfactory. *Sho'lah máh*

Persian for " light of the moon," is another, and has this in its favour, that in Kashmír the name of the garden is spelt without a final " r."

The garden itself has the stately formality and symmetry usual in the east :—

> No pleasing intricacies intervene,
> No artful wildness to perplex the scene,
> Grove nods at grove, each alley has a brother,
> And half the platform just reflects the other.

The parallelogram bounding all is subdivided into squares and in the centre is a reservoir bordered by an elaborately indented coping and studded with pipes for *jets d'eau.* A cascade falls into it over a slope of marble corrugated in an ornamental carved diaper. During the troublous times of Ahmad Sháh the gardens were neglected, and some of the decorative works were defaced and removed. Ranjít Singh restored them, but at the same time he laid ruthless hands upon the marble pavilions by the central reservoir, using them to adorn the Rámbágh at Amritsar, and substituting structures of brick and whitewash in their stead. The Shálamár gardens are a favourite resort for fêtes and picnics, and the luxuriant foliage of the mango and orange trees lends itself with admirable effect to illuminations. These famous gardens having suffered much from injudicious cultivation and over-irrigation— the water frequently flooding the terraces—the level of the beds was lowered, the ornamental channels and masonry works in connection with the fountains were properly repaired and sundry other improvements carried out. Altogether of late years upwards of Rs. 13,000 have been expended in restoring kiosks, and the central *bárádari* which commands all the lower part of the garden. The fountains and staircases, the roofs and walls of other buildings, have all been put in repair. The garden is kept up under the control of the District Committee, which in consideration of its expenditure thereon receives the income of the garden, and three-quarters of the land revenue of the Bághbánpura estate within the limits of which the garden is situate.

On the south and east of the city are the civil station, of which the older part generally known as Anárkalli lies to the south, the Naulakha or Railway portion to the east, and the newer houses of general European residents are on the south-east. This latter portion used to be called Donald Town on account of its proximity to Government House, which was first inhabited by Sir Donald MacLeod, Lieutenant Governor of the Punjab in the years 1865-70 : the name Donald Town has, however, now fallen somewhat into disuse, and this part is generally spoken of as the Charing Cross end of the civil station after the name of the Road-crossing on the Upper Mall between the Punjab Club and Nedou's Hotel. The Anárkalli portion derives its name from a large tomb erected by the Emperor

Jahángír in memory of a favourite slave girl : this was for a long time used as the Station Church, but since the opening of the Lahore Cathedral it has been abandoned as a church, and is now used as a depository for Punjab Secretariat records. Anárkalli was the first site of cantonments, and here the first European houses were built in 1847-48. The cantonments were deserted in 1851-52 on account of their unhealthiness, but Anárkalli continued for many years after that to be the principal European quarter of the civil station, and even now some of the best as well as the oldest, houses are to be found there ; also the Secretariat Offices, conevrted from the old residency which adjoined the Anárkalli tomb, and the Financial and Executive Offices are still maintained there. A splendid road known as the old Mall connects Anárkalli with the Lahore city : at the end towards the city are the School and College buildings on either side, then comes the District Court-house on the right hand side : and nearly opposite are the Anárkalli gardens, the oldest in the station. A little below them on the left is the newly built Jubilee Town Hall described further on ; beyond that to the right are the Secretariat and Financial offices mentioned above. From that onwards for some distance the right hand side of the road is occupied by European built bungalows, and on the left are several open *maidáns*, part of which are used as recreation grounds under municipal management, and part are reserved for encamping grounds. That part of the road, which lies beyond the houses and between two large encamping grounds, is rendered most attractive by the fine shady trees it has on either side. For general aspect undoubtedly Anárkalli is the pleasantest part of the civil station to reside in, but it has never had the name of being healthy. It lies at a considerable distance from the Railway Station, Government House, and the Lawrence Hall and gardens, all these being situated two miles or more to the east. Also the building space in Anárkalli was insufficient to meet the requirements of a rapidly increasing European population : thus gradually much of the rough broken ground lying between Anárkalli and the Railway Station has been levelled and built upon. Near the Sadr Bázár, which is a purely native quarter wedged in between Anárkalli, the city and the newer portion of the civil station, a great clearance of over-crowded residences and rubbish mounds has been effected here and there, so that now most of the land between the Railway Station and Government House on the east and the old Rávi bank south of the city which fringes Anárkalli on the west is taken up with various public or private houses and enclosures. Here and there are to be seen some unkept looking banks or patches of coarse uneven ground and an occasional mound of rubbish from the old brick kilns which formerly disfigured all this part ; and between some of the bungalows one comes across small plots of land not yet taken up for building and still under cultivation. Otherwise the civil station conveys a fairly pleasing impression of municipal order and neatness. The chief street or road through the station is the

Upper Mall running almost due east from Anárkali, past Government House on the left and the Lawrence gardens on the right, after which the Mall ends, the continuation being merely the main trunk road to Mián Mír. The Mall being under the Public Works Department is always kept in excellent order. Of recent years it has been widened at considerable expense so as to leave room for a raised pathway to one side and an avenue walk on the other ; the centre roadway being intended for wheeled vehicles. It is on the Mall that all the best European shops of Lahore are to be found. These extend as far as the crossing of the Mall with the principal roads from the Railway and upper part of the civil station ; the crossing is marked by a red brick cylindrical pillar : beyond this along the Mall the Lawrence gardens on the right hand face the Punjab Club compound and the Government House grounds on the left. The roads to the left from Charing Cross lead to the most closely built over portion of all the European civil quarter, and beyond that again between it and the Railway Station is the small village settlement of Kila Gujar Singh, which with the rough piece of open ground facing it from across the railway road makes this the most unsightly part of the whole civil station. With the exception of the Mall roads, which as already mentioned are under the Public Works Department, the remaining roads of the civil station are maintained by the Municipal Committee. The traffic on these is heavy, and there is considerable difficulty in procuring good metalling for them. Consequently the civil station roads are not often in the best condition : in dry weather they are disagreeably muddy and in wet weather they are thick with mud. From a distance Lahore gives the impression of being excellently wooded, but outside the Anárkali quarter, the Government House grounds and the Lawrence gardens, the trees are poor in class and deficient in size and variety. The soil is by no means favourable to vegetation containing as it does much carbonate of lime below and large quantities of soluble salts and carbonate of soda near the surface. Of late years, however, the necessity for supplementing existing avenues with improved varieties of trees under culture has been kept in view and favourable results are already beginning to show.

At the north-east corner of the civil station grouped round the Railway Station, is a colony of Railway officials, sometimes spoken of as the Naulakha settlement ; this being the name of the land revenue estate in which most of the bungalows are situate. An account of the Railway buildings and working and of the arrangements made for the comfort of the Railway staff has been kindly furnished by Lieutenant-Colonel Boughey, R.E., Manager of the North-Western system ; and is given below :—

" The Railway station is the principal junction of the North- " Western system, which comprises the Punjab Northern Railway " with its terminus at Pesháwar, the Mooltan, Indus Valley, and

Chapter VI, B.
—
Modern Lahore.

The Railway Station.

"Sindh-Peshín sections terminating at Karáchi and Quetta and "the Delhi section of the Sindh, Punjab and Delhi line, all now "worked by Government under one management with head-"quarters at Lahore."

"It has connection with all the railways and all the princi-"pal places in India. It is therefore a busy centre, and the "building itself (a castellated structure) is a fine piece of "modern brick-work which cost nearly five lakhs of rupees. It "has been so constructed as to serve as a defensive work in case "of need. During heavy traffic as many as 80 trains pass in "and out of the Lahore station in the 24 hours."

Railway Workshops and quarters.

"Lahore being the centre of the North-Western Railway "system, extensive workshops are here located, which, together "with the station, cover an area of about 126 acres ; the railway "workshops afford constant employment to considerably over "2,500 men, of whom a small percentage are Europeans, Eura-"sians or Parsis. They are capable of maintaining 150 locomo-"tives and 4,000 vehicles in repair. The buildings cost over 15 "lakhs of rupees, and the machinery another 12 lakhs. The "latter is occasionally being added to by the latest and most im-"proved types from England. Among these may be mentioned "a shearing machine for cutting steel and iron which is able to "divide a bar of cold metal five inches square, and hydraulic "rivetters which at one stroke perform perfecty work which "without them would take three men five minutes. One portion "of the machinery shop is lighted by a 6-Brush Electric "Light by means of which work is carried on at night. A well "appointed printing office, with steam presses, is also maintained, "and the Railway possesses an oil-mill which turns out from two "to three tons of pure castor oil each working day at a much less "cost than the impure product can be obtained from the bazár."

"The aptitude of the natives for the mechanical arts is well "known, and during the 30 years the Railway workshops have "been in operation, they have exercised a most beneficial influ-"ence on the craftmanship of the province. On the whole this "busy factory presents one of the most interesting and sugges-"tive spectacles that the Punjab has to show. The tourist or "stranger who has only seen the natives in passing through the "bazárs may here notice them under a new aspect, busily employ-"ed in the care of machines which require constant vigilance "and intelligent adjustment, working with an accuracy formerly "undreamed of, and handling heavy weights with something "approaching the muscular vigour of the Englishman."

"The Railway has not been unmindful of the comfort and "social enjoyment of its large staff: the community of Foreman, "Drivers, Guards, Firemen, and Mechanics are comfortably "housed in quarters built in the vicinity of the station, north and "south of the line. They have their own Institute, Library, "Swimming Bath, Theatre and Co-operative Stores. Water from "the Municipal water-works is laid on to all the quarters, and

" canal water is also supplied for purposes of irrigation. There
" is a church provided and fitted at the Railway's expense, and
" a house given rent free to a Chaplain connected with the Church
" Missionary Society. This Church is a " ci-devant " Musalmán
" tomb, and provides accommodation for 80 persons. The station
" plot encloses a mosque known as the Mosque of Dái Angna,
" the nurse cf the Emperor Sháhjahán by whom it was erected
" in A. D. 1621. After being used as a dwelling-house, it became
" the office of the Traffic Department of the Railway. In the
" interior are fine arches decorated with excellent and perfectly
" preserved specimens of the *káshi* work elsewhere referred to."

The Lahore civil station is still extending on the east side,
the last building in that direction being the Aitchison College for
Punjab chiefs founded within the last eight years. It seems
probable that more building land will be taken up in that direction for private houses, as the present rents in the civil station are
quite high enough to attract this form of money investment on a
more extended scale. The station is included within the limits
of ten land revenue estates : all land already built upon pays five
rupees an acre inclusive of cesses, and any land hereafter
taken up for building is to pay the same. It was not found
advisable to form a separate estate out of the civil station, partly
because its limits are not yet fixed and also because to separate it off from its constituent estates might have trespassed on
various landowner's rights of pre-emption and otherwise produced administrative inconvenience. The cantonments of Mián
Mír, including of course the houses of all military officers attached to the various regiments are distant about three miles from
the Aitchison College. These cantonments were established in
1851-52 when the Anárkali cantonments were abandoned. The
general aspect of the military station, which was formerly most
dreary, has of late years been immensely improved by rapid
extension of arboriculture with the aid of canal irrigation. It
has, however, always been found unhealthy for troops and is
said to keep up its reputation for this still. The name of the
station is taken from the tomb and shrine, situated to the west
of the cantonment close to the canal, which was erected to a
famous Pír, called Mián Mír, a contemporary of Bába Nának,
the first Sikh Guru. The Mausoleum is a domed building of
white marble and red Agra sandstone with a mosque in the
courtyard. The Church at Mián Mír is considered one of the
most beautiful in the Punjab.

Principal build-
ings of the civil
station.

The buildings of principal interest in the civil station are
the new Lahore Cathedral, the new Chief Court, the Municipal Town Hall, the Victoria Jubilee Institute, the Mayo School
of Art, the Lahore Government College, the Aitchison College
for Punjab Chiefs, the Mayo Hospital, Government House and
the Lawrence and Montgomery Halls.

Cathedral.

The Cathedral Church of the Resurrection, begun shortly
after the consecration of the late Dr. Thomas Valpy French as

Chapter VI, B.

——

Modern Lahore.

Cathedral.

first Bishop of Lahore, in 1877 was consecrated on January 25th, 1887. It is a magnificent building in the "decorated early English style," 226 feet in length, and 152 feet in breadth. A good deal of the ornamentation of the interior stone work has yet to be completed, and the two large "saddleback" western towers which are included in the architect's design have yet to be built. Each of these, it is computed, will cost about Rs. 30,000. Up to the present the expenditure on the building has been slightly over four lakhs.

Chief Court.

The new buildings for the Punjab Chief Court were commenced in 1881, and completed in March 1889, for a total cost of Rs. 4,19,724, including out-buildings. They are in Indo-Saracenic style. The main structure is of solid red brick, Nowshera marble also being largely employed for decorative purposes: the mouldings, cornices, and projections were mostly filled in with specially moulded bricks in the place of cut brick work; and the arch fillings are of terracotta tullis work. The front arches of the Judges' verandah and the porch outside and portions of the main towers are built of Nowshera marble with marble tullis work. The floor of the central hall also is of marble. The roof timbers are of deodar wood and the doors of teakwood with carved devices on the stiles as well as on the frames. Spacious verandahs run all round the building, those of the principal front showing a massive cornice of the old Arabic honeycomb pattern. The height of the two central towers is 95 feet, and that of the two at the end 72 feet. The latter contain circular staircases leading to the top. In front of the building between it and the Mall is a fine enclosure laid out with ornamental flower beds and grass lawns, through which lie the main approaches to the Court. A marble fountain stands in the middle and close by one entrance from the Mall is a bronze statue of John afterwards Lord Lawrence, the first Lieutenant-Governor of the Punjab, standing on a pedestal of Nowshera marble.

The Town Hall.

This building was commenced in the year of Her Majesty the Queen-Empress' Jubilee. The foundations were laid by Sir Charles Aitchison, Lieutenant-Governor of the Punjab, in February 1887, and the completed building was opened by His Royal Highness Prince Albert Victor of Wales on the 3rd of February 1890. The Hall which is built on the oriental principle is 80 feet in length and 40 feet in breadth: it cost Rs. 72,000 to build. The ground storey is taken up with the offices of the Municipal and District Board; on the upper storey is a fine large room, the floor of which is laid with teak planks. Here the District and Municipal Committee meetings are held, and the room is also available on occasions for dances, concerts, and other public meetings.

The Victoria Jubilee nsitute.

This was built from a fund raised throughout the Province as a permanent memorial of the Jubilee of Her Majesty the Queen-Empress celebrated in February 1887. The object was to provide a Provincial Institution containing a museum, library and lecture rooms with a sufficiently instructional staff ; and capable in connection with the School of Art of gradual expansion into a Technical College. The foundation stone was laid by the late Prince Albert Victor, Duke of Clarence and Avondale, on February 3rd, 1890, and the building was completed in 1893. At the end of that year the Institute was utilized for the Punjab Exhibition opened in December 1893. The following account of the building has been furnished by Mr. F. H. Andrews, *sub. pro-tempore* Principal and Curator of the Central Museum.

" The building stands near the Anárkali gardens and " adjoins the each side of the Mayo School of Art. The general " style may be described as late Mughal, adapted to suit the " requirements of a museum. Entering by the main entrance on " the north side, the first room is a vestibule directly under the " dome. From the mosaic floor to the painted roof, the height is " about 65 feet, broken at intervals by two *pinjra* work wooden " galleries. Passing from the vestibule under a moulded and " carved plaster archway the central gallery is reached—a room " measuring 96′ 6″ × 26′ 6″ and 39′ in height. The south " wall has been decorated in Persian style by the students and " masters of the Mayo School of Art under the direction of " the Vice-Principal, by whom also the whole of the decoration " work in paint, wood and plaster have been designed. At the " northern end is a small but well proportioned *pinjra* work " gallery, communicating by three small arches with the first " gallery in the vestibule. On either side of the central gallery " run two others parallel with the length of the building, each " measuring 100′ × 60″ and covered by a " saw-tooth " roof " supported on two rows of iron columns."

" Across the further end of the eastern of these two galleries " and parallel to the central one, runs another of slightly larger " dimensions than the first ; and beyond that again is a " smaller room, containing three iron safes built into the wall " for the reception of the valuable coin collection. The building " is lighted almost entirely from the north, with a well diffused " light, and being free from sunlight is comparatively cool in " the summer months. Precautions have been taken to ensure " ventilation while excluding dust. "

" Adjoining the museum on the western side is the Technical " Institute ; consisting of a lecture hall, 60′ × 30′, having a " gallery running around it ; and three class rooms attached."

" The entire area measures about 27,850 square feet. The old " central museum, which this building is designed to replace was " erected in 1864 for the temporary purposes of a provincial exhibi- " tion, and was altogether unsuited for the use it was for so long " put to. It has been purchased by the Lahore Municipality " with a view to turning it into a market as soon as the contents " can be transferred to the new building. These contents may " be briefly described as Greek, Bactrian, Buddhist, Jain,

Chapter VI, B.

Modern Lahore.

" Brahminical, Sikh and Muhammadan remains and monuments;
" the modern artistic and manufacturing industries, the agri-
" cultural mineral and forest products, the natural history and
" ethnology of the Punjab and its borders."

Mayo School of Art.

" Adjoining the Jubilee Institute are the buildings of the
" Mayo School of Art, which institution has been already describ-
" ed on page 221. The school as originally built in 1880 consisted
" of 5 rooms on the ground floor and a lecture room 62 feet by 24
" on the upper. The design is described as late Mughal. It first
" came into use for the Punjab exhibition of 1881, when some
" temporary additions were made to increase the accommodation.
" From the spring of 1882 the entire building has been in use
" for the School of Art. In 1891 it was decided to replace the
" temporary additions of 1881 by permanent buildings. These
" were designed by the Principal of the School and completed
" in the autumn of 1892. The new portion consists of four
" large well-lighted ateliers in which the technical work of the
" school is carried on, Also a good kiln house was built with
" pottery and plaster kilns."

**The Lahore Go-
vernment College.**

The Lahore College was started in 1864, with Dr. G. W.
Leitner as Principal. As no other building was available, the
College course of instruction was pursued in a large building
situate in the city, the property of Rája Dhián Singh. The
present building was commenced in 1872 and completed in
1877 at a cost of Rs. 3,30,000. It stands nearly opposite the
District Court house, near the Anárkali gardens: attention
is attracted to it by its large clock tower. The College consists
of twelve large class rooms and four small ones, eight
of which are in the lower and eight in the upper storey.
Besides these the attached buildings include a library and
examination hall, rooms for the Principal and Assistant Principal and other necessary accommodation. The structure is
said to be in Gothic style. All the exposed faces of the superstructure are of large well-shaped bricks carefully dressed; the
mouldings and ornamentations are also neat enough. Close by
a new boarding house has recently been constructed, the rooms
of which are arranged in the form of a quadrangle enclosing
a spacious yard 160 feet by 170 feet. In front of the building is an imposing gateway with quarters for the Superintendent on the top. The students' quarters are capable of
accommodating nearly 100. This building was completed in
1892 at a cost of Rs. 57,000.

**The Aitchison Col-
lege.**

Arrangements for the establishment of a Punjab Chiefs
College at Lahore were completed in 1885, part of the scheme
being the inclusion of the Wards School at Umballa. Liberal
contributions were made by Native Chiefs of the Province, supplemented by grants from Provincial Funds, and a contribution
from the Imperial revenues. A favorable site was selected
to the east of Government House, between the Civil and

military stations. The foundation-stone was laid in November 1886 by His Excellency the Viceroy in the presence of a very large and representative assemblage, European and Native, including the Duke and Duchess of Connaught, the Countess of Dufferin, Sir Charles Aitchison, the Lieutenant-Governor of the Province, and many of the Ruling Chiefs of the Province. The students of the late Wards College, at Umballa, were brought to Lahore to form the nucleus of the College, and they were accommodated in temporary school buildings and in houses in the civil station. At the request of His Excellency the Viceroy the College was named the Aitchison College after the Lieutenant-Governor of the Province, who had been mainly instrumental in maturing the project. The College buildings were under construction up till 1889, but some of the boarding quarters were ready in 1888. General Black, the first Principal, moved into the house appointed for him in the autumn of 1888, and several of the students entered into residence at the same time. The completed buildings cost a little short of $5\frac{1}{2}$ lakhs. They include some exceedingly fine class rooms, a library, reading room, laboratory, play room, theatre or speech room and office rooms. Also spacious playing grounds are attached to the building, the maintenance of which and of the gardens round the various buildings connected with the College is greatly facilitated by an abundant supply of canal water.

Mayo Hospital.

The Mayo Hospital is a large double storied building situated to the south of the Sháhálmi Gate of the city of Lahore. It consists of a central block with two wings placed slightly in echelon; its total length is 468 feet, and its breadth 51 feet. The tower in the central block rises to a height of 120 feet. The central block contains the dispensary, operating room, offices, and small wards for special cases: four large wards occupy the wings; the number of beds available is 115. The hospital is named after the late Earl of Mayo, who when Viceroy visited it shortly after it was opened in 1871. The out-patient department of the hospital was at first located in the basement storey of the central block of the main building, but in 1891 owing to the rapidly increasing attendance of patients it was found necessary to provide a separate building for this purpose.

Attached to the Mayo Hospital is the Albert Victor Memorial Hospital, built in commemoration of the visit of late Prince Albert Victor to the Punjab in 1890. This was opened in 1892. It is built on the same plan as the Mayo Hospital: on the ground floor it has accommodation for 20 patients, and in the upper storey 8 private rooms for paying patients, as well as an operating room, a dispensary, and nurses' rooms.

Government House.

Govrenment House faces the Lawrence Gardens on the left side of the Mall, on the road to Mián Mír. It was originally the tomb of Muhammad Kásim Khán (a cousin by the mother's side of the Emperor Akbar), who died in the reign of Sháhjehán Muhammad Kásim Khán was a great patron of wrestlers

Chapter VI, B.
Modern Lahore.
Government House.

and even up to the Sikh times the tomb was known as the *kushti-wála gumbaz*, or wrestler's dome. It was subsequently occupied as a residence by Khushál Singh, uncle of Tej Singh, the Sikh General, from whom it was obtained by Sir Henry Lawrence for public offices in exchange for a confiscated house belonging to Diwán Hákim Rái. The incised and moulded decoration of the alcoves in the central hall has been coloured with good effect, and the walls have been decorated with fresco designs after those of the Mosque of Wazír Khán under the superintendence of Colonel Hyde, R. E. The grounds have some fine trees, and there is a good swimming bath.

The Lawrence and Montgomery Halls.

These are in the Lawrence Gardens, the former fronting the Mall and the latter facing the central avenue of the garden. They are joined by a covered corridor. The Lawrence Hall was built as a memorial of Sir John Lawrence, chiefly by the contributions of the European community, in 1861-62, from designs by Mr. G. Stone, C.E., and the Montgomery Hall, in 1866, by contributions by Native Chiefs, whose names are inscribed on a marble tablet in the building, in honor of Sir Robert Montgomery, from designs by the late Mr. Gordon, C.E. The style is frigidly classical, but the general effect is not without dignity. Here are the Lahore and Mián Mír Institute and Tennis Club and Station Library. A commodious reading-room has recently been added leading into the corridor between the two halls. The Montgomery Hall was re-roofed and thoroughly repaired just before the visit of His Royal Highness the Prince of Wales to the Punjab in 1876, and a splendid teak floor for rinking and dancing was then laid down. The Lawrence Hall is sometimes used as an assembly room for public meetings. On its walls are hung portraits of the successive Lieutenant-Governors of the Punjab and other officers of note. The names of those whose portraits are hung are given below. Both buildings are under the care of the Municipality, which holds them in trust for the Government :—

(1). Colonel Sir Henry M. Lawrence, R.A., K. C. B., President of the Board of Administration, 1849-53.

(2). John Laird Mair Lawrence Baron, G.C.B., G.C. S.I., Baron Lawrence of the Punjab. First Lieutenant-Governor, 1859.

(3). Sir Robert Montgomery, G.C.B., G.C.S.I., Lieutenant-Governor, 1859-65.

(4). Sir Donald F. McLeod, G.C.B., G.C.S.I., Lieutenant-Governor, 1865-70.

(5). Major-General Sir H. M. Durand, K.C.S.I., Lieutenant-Governor, 1870.

(6). Sir Robert Henry Davies, K.C.S.I., C.I.E., Lieutenant-Governor, 1871-77.

(7). Sir Robert Eyles Egerton, K.C.S.I., C.I.E., Lieutenant-Governor, 1877-82.

(8). Sir Charles Umpherston Aitchison, K.C.S.I., C.I.E., Lieutenant-Governor, 1882-87.

(9). Sir James Broadwood Lyall, K.C.S.I., C.I.E., Lieutenant-Governor, 1887-92.

(10). Field Marshall Lord Napier of Magdala, Commander-in-Chief in India, 1870-76.

(11). Sir Herbert B. Edwardes, K.C.B., Commissioner of Peshawar, 1857.

(12). General John Nicholson. Born 1821 ; killed at the capture of Delhi, 1857.

(13). Frederick Cooper, C.B., Commissioner of Lahore, 1864. Built the Montgomery Hall.

(14). Arthur A. Roberts, C.B., First Judge of the Chief Court, 1866.

(15). Colonel Sir Williams G. Davies, K.C.S.I., Financial Commissioner of the Punjab, 1883 to 1887.

Anárkali's tomb, once used as the station church and Pro- Cathedral, and now the store house for Secretariat records, derives its name from Anárkali, the title given to Nádira Begam or Sharíf-ul-Nissa, a favourite slave girl of the Emperor Akbar, who, being suspected of the offence of returning a smile from Jahángír his son, was buried alive. The edifice was erected by Jahángír in A. D. 1600, and the marble tomb which once stood beneath the central dome, but is now in a side chamber, bears the following Persian inscription :— *Anárkali's tomb or the Pro-Cathedral.*

> Ah gar man báz bínam rúe yár-e-Khesh rá.
> Tá qayámat shukr goyam Kirdigár Khesh rá.
>
> Ah ! could I behold the face of my beloved once more
> I would give thanks unto my God unto the day of resurrection.

This picturesque building, the four cupolas of which are prominent objects in Anárkali, near the Museum and Post Office, is a good example of the favourite Muhammadan form of *bárádari* or garden-house, in which, as the name imports, there are twelve arches—three on each side of the square plan. It has served several purposes in its time, and was once the home of the Museum, and after that of the Library and Reading Room of the Book Club till the latter was removed to the Montgomery Hall. It is now utilised as the Punjab Public Library. *The Bárádari of Wazír Khan.*

The other public buildings requiring mention are the Civil Secretariat, formerly the Residency, erected in 1845, adjoining Anárkali's tomb ; the Public Works Secretariat, formerly a barrack, erected in 1854 ; the Financial Commissioner's Offices erected in 1867, adjoining the Civil Secretariat ; and the old *Other buildings within the civil station.*

Chapter VI, B.

Modern Lahore.

Other buildings within the civil station.

Chief Court buildings which have been converted into use as Secretariat Offices since the Chief Court moved into its new buildings near the Mall; the Accountant-General's Office (Chirágh Shah) adapted in 1860 and again improved in front in 1890; the District Court-houses completed in 1870 in Anárkali across the old Mall and nearly facing the Anárkali Gardens; the Senate Hall, the Punjab University and Government College buildings also in Anárkali and near the District Court-house. Mention of these latter has already been made under Education in Chapter V A.

Lawrence Gardens.

The Lawrence Gardens—the Kensington Gardens of Lahore —cover 112 acres on the right hand side of the Mall between Anárkali and the Lawrence and Montgomery Halls. In 1860 the land now occupied by them was a desolate wilderness. In that year a portion of the ground was laid out as a garden, and in 1868 the portion on the further side of the mounds was added, having been purchased from the proceeds of the sale of an old Government garden near the fort known as the *Badámi Bágh*. That part of the gardens which was formerly styled the Agri-Horticultural Society Gardens is now known as the Government Agri-Horticultural Gardens, the Society having ceased to exist since 1883-84 when Government took over the management. Part of the grounds are occupied as a menagerie, which of late years has been immensely improved owing to the interest taken in it by Lady Lyall, donations for the erection of buildings and other accommodation for animals having been received from Rájás, Raises, and European residents of the civil station. Part of the grounds are used for public recreation purposes; and the remainder of the gardens is applied to botanical purposes under the superintendence of the Professor of Botany.

The garden is watered by a cutting from the Lahore branch of the Bári Doáb Canal, and contains nearly 80,000 trees and shrubs of 600 different species,—including, in addition to the trees usually met with in the plains of India, the *chíl* (*Pinus longifolia*), the Australian gum tree (*Eucalyptus globulus*), and the carob tree of Syria and the South of Europe.

The average income of the garden for the past five years has been Rs. 14,677, and the expenditure has averaged Rs. 23,536, the difference being met by the yearly Government grant-in-aid of Rs. 9,000 which is not fully expended. The gardens do good work by distributing fruit and ornamental trees, shrubs, European vegetable and flower seeds. Experiments are made with various crops with a view to their introduction into the agriculture of the Province. The existing hot house has been enlarged from 24 to 96 feet and fitted with hot water pipes in lieu of the old flue arrangement. The drainage of the garden has been greatly improved by the construction of a fresh escape cut. Of the irrigation water-courses 5,071 feet are lined with masonry. A deer park enclosure now stands on what was a very insalubrious pond, this having recently been filled in. The actual work of the garden is carried on under a

European Superintendent, under the management of a Committee consisting of a President with three *ex-officio* members and four non-official members.

The Anárkali Gardens, known also as the "Gulbágh" are maintained by the Municipal Committee at a cost of about Rs. 1,300 ; of which the chief item is the head gardener's salary at Rs. 30 per mensem. The land is *nazúl* and comprises about 16 acres. The police band plays here occasionally and at such times the gardens are largely frequented by natives from the city.

Anárkali Gardens.

The Central Museum is near the Anárkali Gardens, and adjoins the premises of the General Post Office. The building was hastily constructed for the Punjab Exhibition of 1864, and was not intended to be permanent; now that a more suitable building has been provided in the new Jubilee Institute, the old building has been sold to the Municipal Committee who intend to utilise it as a market, the site being central and well adapted for the purpose. At present in front of the entrance to this building there stands on a raised platform the famous gun, Zamzamah, known by the Sikhs as the *Bhangián-wáli Top.* The gun is one of the largest specimens of native casting in India, and was made in A. D. 1761 by Shah Wali Khan, Wazír of Ahmad Shah Duráni, by whom it was used at the battle of Pánipat. After the departure of Ahmad Shah the gun was left in the possession of the Sikh Sardárs of the Bhangi *misl* (whence its name, *Bhangián-wáli Top*), and came to be regarded by them as a talisman of supremacy. Ranjít Singh eventually possessed himself of it and it was employed by him at the siege of Mooltan in A. D. 1818. From that date until removed in 1860 it was placed at the Delhi gate of the city of Lahore: it is still regarded by many as an incarnation of Mahádeo. The inscription on the gun opens as follows :—

The Central Museum.

> By order of the Emperor (Ahmad Sháh) Dur-i-Durán Sháh Wali Khan, the Wazír, made this gun named *Zamzamah,* the taker of strongholds.
>
> The work of Sháh Nazr.

Then follow a number of verses, the translation of which will be found at pages 60-61 of Dr. Thornton's Guide Book. The last lines give the date of the gun as 1174 A. H. or 1761 A. D.

At the end of the old Mall, on the right hand side of the Mooltan road, is a fine gateway commonly called the *Chauburji,* once the entrance into the garden of Zebinda Begam, a learned daughter of Shahjehán, and an authoress, who, in her shady retreat on the banks of the Rávi, composed a volume of mystical poems which are still read and admired in the Punjab and Hindustán under the title of *Diwán-i-Makhti.* Urgent repairs have recently been made to its broken masonry, and it has been railed in.

The Chauburji.

The name f the institution formerly known as the Roberts Institute after Mr. Roberts, at one time Judicial Commis-

Social institutions Roberts Institute.

Chapter VI, B.

Modern Lahore.

Roberts Institute.

sioner of the Punjab, who founded it for the benefit of the European subordinates of the Government offices, has recently been changed to the " Roberts Volunteer Club," the building having been converted into a Club for the 1st Punjab Volunteer Rifle Corps.; the class for whom Mr. Roberts intended it having long ceased to take an interest in it. The band plays here every Monday evening, and concerts and dances are periodically given. Tennis courts and billiard rooms are available.

Freemasonry.

Since 1869 Lahore has been the head-quarters of Freemasonry in the Punjab. The District Grand Lodge has a commodious and handsomely furnished hall, situated between the Agra Bank and the Boys' High School in Anárkali, popularly known as the Jádughar or " witchcraft " house. There are 21 (twenty-one) subordinate Lodges in the Punjab with a total membership of 693 masons.

Besides the usual Fund of Benevolence maintained at above Rs. 6,700, there is attached to the District Grand Lodge the Punjab Masonic Institution, supported entirely by voluntary contributions, which educates, clothes, and maintains at present 43 children, orphans of indigent masons. In 1893 it had a funded capital of Rs. 84,900, the interest of which with two-thirds of the yearly contributions helps to defray the expenditure.

The members of the Society are chiefly Europeans, but include Parsis, Muhammadans, Theist, Sikhs and a few Jews.

There is a District Grand Chapter of Royal Arch Masons and 10 Chapters working under it.

European cemetery.

The European cemetery is on the Peshāwar road facing the western wall of the city. This is an exceedingly pretty and well kept enclosure. The walls are all carefully prepared and scrupulously clean, with flowers growing along the sides. The tombs and monuments, of which there are a very large number, are regularly washed and dusted. Its present condition reflects the greatest credit on the management. Recently, owing to the ground being almost entirely occupied with graves, it was found necessary to take in fresh land. This was done at considerable cost, new ground to the south being bought at a cost of Rs. 1,500 an acre or more. The cemetery now covers an area of 9·3 acres, including the recent extensions, and is bounded by a 6 foot masonry wall all round. Separate portions are allotted to Protestants, Roman Catholics and Non-Conformists according to the requirements of each community.

Banks.

The Agra Bank, Bank of Bengal, and Alliance Bank of Simla are all in close proximity between Anárkali and the Upper Mall ; the two latter occupy handsome buildings recently constructed near the Accountant-General's Office.

Hotels.

Lahore possesses only two hotels worthy of the name namely the Sindh and Punjab Hotel, known as Mr. Nedou's and the Charing Cross Hotel under Mrs. Kennelly's management.

There are besides these some three or four hotels kept by natives; but these drag on a very precarious existence and are constantly being removed from one house to another.

The principal European shops are—

Messrs. Gillon & Co., General dealers, having also a Medical Hall.

Messrs. Plomer & Co., Chemists and Druggists.

„   Ranken & Co., Tailors, &c.

„   Phelps & Co., Tailors, &c.

„   Ball, Moody & Co., Tailors.

Mrs. Kavanagh, Dress-maker.

„   Russell,   „

Miss Knoll,   „

Messrs. Cutler, Palmer & Co., Wine Merchants.

„   Max Minck & Co., General dealers.

„   Watts & Co, Saddlers.

„   Griffin & Co.,   „

Mr. Bevan,   }
„   Steiert   } Dealers in musical instruments.

The cantonments of Mián Mír are situated some three miles to the east of the civil station. They were established in 1851-52 on account of the unhealthiness of the former cantonments at Anárkali. They stand on an open and exceedingly dreary arid plain, originally bare of trees, but now gradually growing greener as canal irrigation extends and the trees planted by the roadside and assidously fostered spring up. Here is a church which is considered the most beautiful in the Punjab. Mián Mír has been from the first a conspicuously unhealthy station. The garrison has already been noticed in Chapter V, pages 239 and 240.

The soil in the neighbourhood of Lahore is a kind of clay mixed with vegetable mould, and containing in many places irregular masses of carbonate of lime, termed *kankar*, the whole forming a layer varying in thickness from ten to twelve feet, and below this is a bed of sand in which water is found. The superficial layer of the earth is remarkable for the large quantity of soluble salts contained in it, which in many parts are so abundant as to render the country quite barren or only able to produce plants in the organization of which soda forms a large part. To such an extent does this impregnation occur that an efflorescence appears on the surface of the ground which is called *reh*, and is composed principally of sulphate of soda and chloride of sodium; but in the neighbourhood of Lahore it also contains carbonate of soda. This efflorescence appears in the largest quantity in the cold weather, giving the country the appearance of being covered with hoar frost. It occurs most at this season, probably because the water contained in the

Chapter VI, B.

Modern Lahore.

superficial layer is then unable to hold so much of these salts in solution, even if it does not freeze at the low temperature which then prevails. Consequently the saline substances first form crystals and afterwards effloresce in a white powder.

Lahore Municipality.

The Municipality of Lahore is of the first class and was first constituted in 1867. It lies within the limits of the following villages :—

(1). Mozang.
(2). Killa Gujar Singh.
(3). Shísh Mahal.
(4). Rájgarh.
(5). Killa Hakimán.
(6). Sanda Kalán.
(7). Gunja Kalán.
(8). Jía Músa.
(9). Khokhar.

(10). Garhi Shahu.
(11). Achintgarh.
(12). Begampura.
(13). Kot Khoja Said.
(14). Bhamman.
(15). Khoi Mírán.
(16). Lahore.
(17). Naulakha.
(18). Bela Basti Rám.

The population according to the census of 1891 was 159,362.

The existing Municipal Committee is composed of 20 elected and 10 nominated members, of whom 7 are Christians, 12 Hindús, and 11 Muhammadans. Among the members are 10 officials and 20 non-officials, only three being appointed ex-officio, viz., the Deputy Commissioner, Civil Surgeon, and Executive Engineer. The Deputy Commissioner is President of the Committee by election.

There are but two taxes in the Municipality, these being the octroi and water tax. The latter has been in force since 1890, and yields a revenue of about Rs. 6,000 a year. Octroi forms the main source of income and yields about Rs. 3,00,000 a year.

Other sources of income are a large jágir grant of land revenue derived from the estates lying within municipal limits amounting under the recent assessments to Rs. 21,989 ; sale of sweepings and manure ; water charges for supply of municipal water ; sale of land and rents ; and various other miscellaneous items. The following table shows the income derived from the chief sources during the past five years :—

1	2	3	4	5	6	7	8	9	10
Year.	Octroi collections.	Wheel and dog taxes.	Sale of sweepings and manure.	Water charges.	Sale proceeds of land.	Nazúl and other rents.	Jágír and other Government contributions	Other items.	Total.
	Rs.	Rs.	Rs.	Rs.	Rs.	Rs.	Rs.	Rs.	Rs.
1888-89 ...	2,46,096	...	8,630	12,378	28,081	10,740	17,371	39,012	3,62 307
1889-90 ...	3,01,267	...	7,807	14,456	5,314	10,627	27,010	42,300	4,08,781
1890-91 ...	2,84,859	...	8,509	13,871	2,010	12,312	26,626	41,884	3,90,071
1891-92 ...	3,14,961	4,171	7,839	19,117	302	12,637	17,070	28 189	4,04,286
1892-93 ...	2,94,601	5,779	6,242	23,604	7,119	12,581	14,017	18,704	3,82,647
Average for five years...	2,88,357	1,990	7,805	16,685	8,565	11,779	20,419	34,018	3,89,618

Year.	Cost in rupees.
1888-89	3,69,330
1889-90	3,73,491
1890-91	3,97,200
1891-92	3,86,683
1892-93	4,21,013

The expenditure in each of the last five years has been as shown in the margin. The principal heads under which expenditure occurs may be gathered from the following statement of expenditure in 1892-93 :—

Civil charges.	Rs.
Office establishment	18,118
Octroi collection establishment	10,858
Water-works	19,821
Conservancy	46,033
Gardens	18,690
Schools	8,778
Lighting	17,243
Medical	15,991
Refund of octroi duty	19,262
Repayment of loan	95,000
Police	45,699
Miscellaneous	13,642
Total Civil Charges ...	3,29,135

Public Works Charges.	
Establishment	7,376
Original Works	43,874
Repairs to station roads and drains	27,358
Other repairs	13,280
Total Public Works Charges ...	91,888
Total Charges ...	4,21,023

The heaviest items of expenditure appear to be repayment of loan; police, conservancy, and original works.

The civil station contains 36 miles of metalled roads within municipal limits, while inside the city there are 10 miles of metalled roads and 28 miles of paved streets. The amount of traffic on these roads has become so heavy that the very inferior *kankar* obtainable at Lahore is no longer suitable for

Roads.

Chapter VI, B.

Modern Lahore.

Roads.

road metal. Stone metal is therefore being tried, though very much more expensive than *kankar*. The Municipal Committee has also decided to try wood paving in the city, and this is at the present time being laid down in the Lahori Mandi as an experiment. The wood being used is *kikar*.

Meanwhile the roads of the civil station are left for the most part in very indifferent repair, and in the dryer seasons of the year the dust on these roads makes walking or driving on them a penance.

Water.

Until 1881 Lahore was chiefly dependent on well water for drinking purposes, but in June of that year the water-works were formally opened for public supply. At first there was a good deal of caste prejudice against using the water, but this has long ago broken down, and the people fully appreciate the pure water, with as genuine a feeling as those who are considered more advanced in modern civilisation. The supply is drawn from four wells sunk in a strip of land left by the river Rávi when it changed its course, a little to the north of and below the fort and the North-Western Railway line. The wells are all connected by an under-ground trench made of square blocks sunk about 27 feet below water level, and the water is pumped by two engines (working alternately) each capable of raising the full estimated daily supply, calculated at 10 gallons per head of population, and forcing it through a twenty-inch main 3,200 feet in length to a height of 80 feet into service reservoirs and over a high pressure stand pipe direct into the supply system, which adds another 10 feet of head. There are nearly 29 miles of pipes, and for distributing purposes the area supplied has been divided into five separate districts, each having its own main and system of street service piping supplied directly from the reservoir or high service stand pipes. The service pipes of each district also join the main, supplying the adjoining district, so that in case of a stoppage of one main, the service pipes can be supplied from the main of the adjoining district.

The site fixed upon for the reservoir was the highest part of the city, to the south-east of the fort. This was found to be the only site which would allow water to be delivered under an average head of about 40 feet of pressure throughout the entire system. There were, however, certain other high points within the city where this pressure would only admit of a street service ; and in order to supply the houses in the highest parts and to secure an efficient fire service, stand pipes were erected to the north of and close to the reservoir of such a height that the water thrown over them would reach 90 feet. The reservoir, a masonry building, gave way owing to a settlement in its foundation, which had been laid on the *débris* and foundations of old buildings—the accumulations of centuries—and as soon after the accident as possible, arrangements were made to maintain the water-supply by making use of the high service stand pipes, the height of which was reduced, for the sake of economy in working, to nearly the same level as the ordinary pressure of the reservoir. The reservoir is constructed of iron in four separate compartments in order to guard against failure, each compartment holding 250,000 gallons, or 1 million gallons in all. To supply persons who cannot have connections laid to their houses, 180 street stand posts have been erected at convenient intervals; 210 street fire hydrants have also been provided for use in cases of fire and for sanitary purposes. In laying the mains through the city it was found absolutely necessary to widen the streets ; but to avoid taking up more land than was absolutely necessary, only the side of the street on which the pipes would be laid was re-aligned. The pipe-laying was a work of great difficulty owing to the narrow and tortuous nature of the streets and lanes and the bad soil. The whole of the civil station including the railway colony are supplied with this water as well as the city. Lately it has been extended to Mozang village as well. The following tables furnish an analysis of the water :—

Qualitive analysis.

1	2	3	4	5	6
Physical qualities.	Re-action.	Free carbonic acid.	Chlorides.	Sulphate.	Nitrates.
Clear, transparent, odourless, colourless.	Neutral.	Present small amount.	Present very small amount.	Present small amount.	Trace.
7	8	9	10	11	12
Sulphuretted hydrogen.	Nitrites.	Lime.	Magnesia.	Iron.	Ammonia.
No sign.	No sign.	Present small amount.	Trace.	No sign.	Trace.

Quantitative analysis.

Total hardness.	Permanent hardness.	Total solid grains per gallon.	Free ammonia grains per gallon.	Albumenoid ammonia, grains per gallon.	Chlorides as Na Cl, grains per gallon.	Amount of oxygen, grains for easily oxidizable matter per gallon.	Oxidised nitrogen as nitric acid grains per gallon.
6°	3·1	13·72	·0058	·0022	·82	·002	·86

An analysis of the river, canal and well water of Lahore was made by Dr. Burton Brown, Principal of the Lahore Medical College, the results of whose inquiries are given in extenso, as they are not only interesting in themselves, but have an important bearing upon other subjects :—

" The composition of the river water," he writes, " varies somewhat at different times of the year, but when last examined it contained 12·44 grains of solid substances in a gallon, of which 11·89 grains were composed of salts consisting chiefly of chlorides of sodium and potassium, with the sulphates of soda and lime and the carbonates of lime and magnesia ; there were also ·89 of a grain of organic matter. The water, therefore, is of a moderately pure character,

Chapter VI, B.
———
Modern Lahore.
Water.

and would be useful for irrigation could it be raised to a suitable level. It holds in suspension at all times in the year a large quantity of sediment which is composed chiefly of silicate of lime and alumina, and carbonate of lime, with a little organic matter and sesqui-oxide of iron.

"The canal is a branch of the main Bári Doáb Canal, which derives its water from the river Rávi, near Mádhopur (about 100 miles from Lahore). The water is similar in character to that of the river itself, but is rather more free from saline admixture. This is probably caused by the fact that the canal water passes over a solid bed, and does not receive much admixture from drainage from the land in its course. It contains in a gallon only 8·23 grains of solid contents, of which 6·82 are composed of salts and 1·41 of organic substances : of the former, 0·36 of a grain are composed of alkaline chlorides, 0·5 of a grain of alkaline sulphates, and 5·96 grains consist of sulphate of lime, together with carbonates of lime and magnesia, and silica. The canal water is, therefore, very pure in comparison with other natural waters, and it contains only 0·86 of a grain of alkaline salt. Notwithstanding this, it has been accused of causing an important deterioration of the soil by impregnating it with that base.

"The average depth of wells about Lahore is from 45 to 50 feet. In the dry weather, they often contain only two or three feet of water, but after the rainy season from 25 to 30 feet. The wells near the river partake of the character of the stream, as they probably derive part of their contents by infiltration from the above source. But those wells which are at a distance from the river differ from it greatly in the character of their water, as they have, for the most part, a decidedly alkaline reaction, owing to the presence of a quantity of carbonate of soda ; at the same time, they contain a larger quantity of salts than either river or canal water does.

"One of the wells examined at the Lahore Central Jail contained in a gallon 33·48 grains of solid constituents, of which 2·91 grains were composed of chloride of sodium, 6·31 grains of sulphate of soda, and 3·41 grains of carbonate of soda, making in all 12·63 grains of salts of soda. Besides this 19·07 grains consisted of carbonate of lime and magnesia and silica, and 1·83 of organic matter. Many wells, however, contain a much greater porportion both of solid constituents and of alkaline salts of soda ; thus one well, which was examined at Mián Mír, contained no less than 83·43 grains of solid substances dissolved in a gallon, and of this 63·21 grains were composed of salts of soda."

Drainage.

It was originally intended to carry out a complete system of drainage for the city of Lahore simultaneously with that of water-supply, but chiefly owing to financial reasons an underground outfall sewer, two miles in length, and discharging into the Rávi, was alone constructed in the first instance. During the financial year 1882-83, however, the drainage work of the city was energetically pushed on under Mr. Bull, the Assistant Secretary of the Municipality ; and before the end of the year the guttering and metalling of streets were completed, and the only portions remaining unfinished in the remodelled intercepting sewer were the connecting bridges at the Delhi and the Akbari gates. These were completed in 1883, and the whole sewage of the city now finds its way into the outfall sewer, and is discharged into the Rávi. The system adopted is one of open side gutters of a circular form, capable of carrying off sewage and relieving the streets as much as possible of ordinary storm waters. The gutters discharge at all points into an intercepting sewer from the Bháti to the Masti gate, which leads into the outfall sewer. The intercepting sewer, before it was remodelled, had an outlet near the Khizri gate, intended to take sewage into the back channel of the Rávi ; but this it never did, as the sewage was taken up by cultivators, who spread it upon their lands. In the dry months this had less deleterious effects, but after heavy rain and high floods of the Rávi it became a dangerous nuisance. In order to get rid of this long standing evil, and to relieve the soil near and about the water-works wells from its contaminating influence, it was decided to reverse the levels of the sewer from the Akbari to the Masti gate to suit the continuation from the Akbari to the Bháti gate, and make it discharge towards its original head at the Akbari gate. This has now been done, and arrangements completed for flushing it from the water-works to make it as quick discharging as possible. In order to dispose of storm waters, overflows have been fixed facing the drainage outlets of the city at the Masti, Kashmíri, Khizri, Yakki and Delhi gates, from whence the rain waters run down to the back channel of the Rávi. The gutters are all coated with Portland cement, and very little absorption of sewage is possible, and they become perfectly clean and sweet when flushed from the water-works. The construction of the gutters and the alterations which have been effected in the levels of many of the streets have relieved some parts of the city of the flooding to which they were always liable after heavy rain. The magnitude of the work may be estimated from the following abstract of the improvements effected :—

58,837 feet, or	...	11·14 miles	of streets guttered.
34,933 ,, ,,	...	6·61 ,,	of streets metalled.
109,031 ,, ,,	...	20·65 ,,	of gutters.
2,508 ,, ,,	...	0·47 ,,	of cross gutters.

The result of these improvements has been satisfactory and the sanitary condition of the city has been materially improved by them. There is, however, much to be done before the drainage can be considered to be on a satisfactory basis. Meanwhile the municipal expenditure on drainage constitutes a heavy burden on the Committee's funds.

When the water-supply and sewage drainage schemes were being designed, the widening of some of the principal streets was considered one of the objects to be held in view. There were, however, many difficulties to contend against—amongst the greatest being the prejudice of the inhabitants against any attempt to alter the existing state of things. By far the most serious, however, was the question of taking up land in the streets. The houses were huddled close together, and each house occupied a very small base area, although built many stories high ; and in any street requiring widening, the great number of tenements to be taken up and the many inhabitants thus left houseless became a serious consideration. The Government and the Municipality, however, recognized the fact that the introduction of water-supply and of drainage schemes made it imperative to do something towards widening the streets. In making a re-alignment where the principal mains had to be laid, the following streets were widened :—From the reservoir to the Bháti gate ; Lohári gate bázár ; Shah Alami gate bázár ; Patoli bázár ; Híra Mandi ; from the reservoir to the Delhi gate ; from the reservoir to the Yakki gate ; Mochi gate to Rang

Mahal; Rang Mahal to Shamsher Singh's gali ; Mochi gate to Wazír Khán's chauk; Lohari Mandi to Híra Mandi ; Said Mitha to Kasera bázár ; Gumti bázár to Chakla bázár ; Chakla *bázár* to Pápar Mandi and Kucha Shamsher Singwála.

Conservancy
arrangements.

The municipal arrangements for removing nightsoil are not even yet as satisfactory as they should be, though a considerable improvement has been effected on the system in force in former days, when the Committee's servants had nothing to do but to collect the nightsoil in heaps, its removal being left to the cultivators of the estates around Lahore, who had gradually acquired strong prescriptive rights in the valuable manure they thus obtained. The times and methods of its removal were of course uncertain and incomplete. In 1880 the Committee took steps to terminate this unsatisfactory condition of things. They broke down the cultivators' rights by leasing out the business of collecting manure to a contractor, who paid them so much a year. Now again the Committee has partially reverted to the former system, allowing the cultivators to carry off the sweepings subject to definite rules and times after the conservancy establishment has done their early morning work of collecting the stuff from houses and alleys and have deposited it at certain fixed places. The cultivators pay so much a month for the right of keeping a cart at a manure station : the monthly payment varies from 5 to 15 rupees a month. In addition to these carts the Committee maintains an establishment of donkeys which are kept at work throughout the day taking off any nightsoil or sweepings collected after the carts have gone. The system, however, is said not to work satisfactorily ; unfortunately there are no funds available to introduce any improvements nor will there be until the drainage has been established on a more satisfactory and less expensive basis.

Income from li-
quid sewage.

The Committee derives an income of Rs. 8,000 or so a year from the charge of Rs. 4 a *bigah* on any land irrigated from the large underground outfall sewer, which as noticed above was constructed in 1881, to carry off the principal sewage of the city. The irrigation is done generally by water lifts. If the land is situated low enough for irrigation by direct flow, then Rs. 8 per *bigah* is charged. At present about 251 *bigahs* are irrigated by sewage.

Hired carriages.

There are five classes of carriage for hire ; these and their present rates of hire are regulated by the Municipal Committee and at present are as follows :—

Class I.—Including both open Landaos and shut carriages on four wheels. Hire is one rupee for the first hour, and eight annas for each succeeding hour, a fixed charge of four rupees being allowed for a day of nine hours.

Class Intermediate.—Closed carriage on four wheels. Twelve annas for the first hour, six annas for each succeeding hour three rupees and twelve annas being the charge for a day of nine hours.

Class II.—Closed carriages on four wheels. Eight annas for the first hour, and four annas for each succeeding hour, the charge for a whole day of nine hours being two rupees and eight annas.

Class III.—*Tumtums.*—Four annas for the first hour and two annas for each succeeding hour. One rupee and four annas for a whole day of nine hours.

Class IV.—*Ekkás.*—Two annas for the first hour and one anna for each succeeding hour, up to a maximum of twelve annas for the whole day.

The total number of licensed conveyances, including *ekkás*, is 600.

It is much to be regretted that statistics are not forthcoming of the import and export trade of Lahore. For some years past the Municipal Committee has discontinued registering imports and exports of articles not taxable with octroi. A statement is appended of the trade so far as it can be ascertained from the octroi records for the years 1889-90 to 1892-93.

————

Chapter VI, B.

Modern Lahore.

Trade of Lahore.

1889.

Serial No.	NAMES OF ARTICLES.	IMPORT.	
		Amount of duty.	Weight or value.
	CLASS I. *Articles of food or drink for men and animals.*	Rs.	
1	Grain of all kinds (parched included), rice in husk and dál.	45,772	975,353 Mds.
2	Rice, flour (maida), súji, rawa and dál arhar...	2,334	24,896 ,,
3	Indian-corn (bhutta) and green gram...	202	8,743 ,,
4	All kinds of atta, wand included	8,943	143,086 ,,
5	Sugar (misri and khand) { Misri ...	7,919	7,919 Rs.
	{ Khand ...	23,499	26,856 Mds.
6	Taloncha and molasses of sugar and honey ...	1,547	4,125 ,,
7	Shakkar and gur ...	8,050	32,202 ,,
8	Sweetmeats of all kinds ...	70	226 ,,
9	Molasses of gur ...	1,959	20,895 ,,
10	Pickles, chatnis, jams, jellies, preserves and conserves of all sorts.	80	128 ,,
11	Milk ...	2,885	36,933 ,,
12	Ghi and butter ...	28,972	23,177 ,,
13	Cheese, cream and khoa...	133	267 ,,
14	Tea, coffee, sago, barley and arrowroot	990	5,840 Rs.
15	All kinds of vinegar, lime and other juices ...	84	336 Mds.
16	Fish (fresh and dried) ...	437	855 ,,
17	Oilman's stores and other provisions, and pre-parations of food and drink.	2,214	47,232 Rs.
18	Betel-nut, katha and pán	473	473 Mds.
19	Sparkling wines ...	341	682 Gals.
20	Other wines or spirits ...	12,480	* 12,616 Mds.
21	Beer and Porter ...	2,617	2,350 ,,
22	Vegetables, including potatoes...	1,906	30,497 ,,
23	Garlic, ginger and green chillies ...	474	5,422 ,,
24	Sugar-cane of all kinds ...	841	6,629 ,,
25	Eggs ...	239	383 ,,
26	DRIED FRUITS. Kernels of almonds, walnuts, cocoanuts, pista and khasta.	73	39 ,,
27	Almonds ...	673	1,197 ,,
28	Dates (khajúr) ...	381	2,440 ,,
29	Walnuts and dates (chhoaráh) ...	198	792 ,,
30	All other fruits not specified ...	1,623	25,979 ,,
31	FRESH AND GREEN FRUITS. All kinds of fruits, fresh and green, ripe and unripe.	9,634	25,690 ,,
32	FODDER FOR CATTLE. Grass, bhúsa and all other kinds of fodder dried and green, including bran, gram shells and wand.	6,242	266,321 ,,
33	Oil-cake of all kinds and cotton seed (banaula)	212	4,192 ,,
	CLASS II. *Animals for Slaughter.*		
34	Oxen, cows, buffaloes, camels, &c., including calves.	6,807	1,02,105 Rs.
35	Sheep, goats, &c., including their young ...	25,275	4,04,406 ,,
36	Poultry of all kinds and game birds and animals	1,080	17,287 ,,
	CLASS III. *Articles used for Fuel, Lighting and Washing.*		
37	Wood fuel ...	11,051	530,437 Mds.
38	Upla ...	514	98,697 ,,
39	Charcoal, coal and coke ...	6,807	54,467 ,,

* 49,920 gallons.

90.		1890 91.			
EXPORT.		IMPORT.		EXPORT.	
Amount of duty.	Weight or value.	Amount of duty.	Weight or value.	Amount of duty.	Weight or value.
Rs.		Rs.		Rs.	
2,007	42,826 Mds.	36,932	787,890 Mds.	999	20,992 Mds.
...	...	2,846	30,360 ,,	49	557 ,,
...	...	198	8,439 ,,	...	...
...	...	9,344	149,510 ,,	65	1,045 Mds.
172	172 Rs.	22,397	22,397 Rs.	147	147 Rs.
22	25 Mds.	13,229	15,118 Mds.	128	147 Mds.
...	...	1,678	4,476 ,,	...	...
12	48 Mds.	6,883	27,533 ,,	17	68 Mds.
...	...	71	28 ,,	...	...
...	...	2,096	3,157 ,,	...	...
...	...	36	97 ,,		
...	...	2,923	37,410 ,,	...	...
110	88 Mds.	30,176	24,140 ,,	183	146 Mds.
...	...	102	204 ,,	...	...
2,970	47,627 Rs.	143	2,288 ,,	141	2.255 Rs.
3	13 Mds.	54	216 ,,	...	...
...	...	588	784 ,,	...	...
1,278	27,270 Rs.	2,078	42,992 Rs.	902	19,249 Rs.
...	...	246	245 Mds.	...	...
...	...	689	1,378 Gals.	80	161 Gals.
8,145	32,580 Gals.	10,518	42,032 ,,	7.091	28,364 ,,
2,000	16,003 ,,	1,961	5,618 ,,	785	6.280 ,,
...	...	3.129	100,128 Mds.	2	64 ,,
...	...	576	4,606 ,,	...	...
...	...	1.167	2,375 ,,	...	...
...	...	391	117 ,,	...	...
...	...	96	48 ,,	17	270 Gals.
...	...	513	913 ,,	29	52 Mds.
...	...	266	1,706 ,,	...	...
...	...	132	528 ,,	19	76 Mds.
...	...	759	2,024 ,,	22	351 Rs.
...	...	10,936	29,163 ,,	2,015	32,236 ,,
...	...	6,605	201,821 ,,	...	...
...	...	197	3,154 ,,	...	...
...	...	6,872	1,02,840 Rs.	...	...
...	...	22,068	4,70,944 ,,	...	...
..	...	861	13,780 ,,	...	...
...	...	11,744	501,080 Mds.	...	...
...	...	392	75,295 ,,	...	...
...	...	6,064	48,512 ,,	10	82 Mds.

Chapter VI, B.

Modern Lahore.

Trade of Lahore.

			1889.
Serial No.	NAMES OF ARTICLES.	IMPORT.	
		Amount of duty.	Weight or value.
	CLASS III.—*concluded.* *Articles used for Fuel Lighting and Washing—* concluded.	Rs.	
40	Linseed oil, castor oil, cocoanut and poppy seed oils, máwa, kasúmba, cotton seed and chil oils.	177	354 Mds.
41	Lamp-oil of all kinds	4,565	10,435 „
42	Oil-seeds	2,126	17,012 „
43	Tallow, wax and candles	188	201 „
44	Soap	569	758 „
45	Reh, soap-nuts, kishta, starch (kalaf) and sajji	691	7,376 „
46	Alum	68	362 „
47	Lamps, chandeliers and their fittings	597	83 „
	CLASS IV. *Articles used in the Construction of Buildings.*		
48	Shísham (black), tun, walnut, teak and chikri, deodár and sá!, sawn and unsawn.	13,800	1,47,197 Rs.
49	Chil, kail, rai, shísham (white) and all other woods, sawn and unsawn.	3,912	31,296 „
50	Door and window frames, &c., and planks ...	6	252 „
51	Bamboos, glue and glass	399	8,505 „
52	Sirki, kul, sarkanda and thatching straw ...	166	665 „
53	Marble	168	3,360 „
54	Stone and slate	808	16,157 „
55	Bricks (large)	2,628	47,315 „
56	Small bricks	443	14,175 „
57	Patrah, pinjrah	71	2,887 „
58	Girdah, chauka, tiles, kolába and patnála of all kinds.	175	4,215 „
59	Kankar-lime	1,313	35,006 „
60	Stone-lime	2,161	51,861 „
61	Portland cement	84	3,042 „
62	Wall paper	...	..
63	Turpentine, tar, puttey, varnish and paints of all kinds, including colouring earths.	395	7,103 Rs.
64	San	115	5,692 „
65	Munj rope	238	10,168 „
	CLASS V. *Drugs, Gums, Spices and Perfumes.*		
66	All drugs, medicines, gums, spices and perfumes.	6,648	1,06,378 „
	CLASS VI.—*Tobacco.*		
67	Tobacco, 1st quality, such as Kandhári, Púrbi, Hazro, &c.	2,270	2,269 Mds.
68	Tobacco, 2nd quality (country)	751	1,502 „
69	Cheroots, cigars, cigarettes and imported tobacco (European).	921	737 „
70	Snuff	61	30 „
	CLASS VII. *Piece-goods and other Textile Fabrics and all manufactured Articles of Clothing and Dress.*		
71	All piece goods and other textile fabrics, and all manufactured articles of clothing and dress and gold lace.	22,278	14,85,244 Rs.
	CLASS VIII.—*Metals and Articles of Metal.*		
72	All metals and articles of metal, except gold and silver bullion, and other prohibited articles.	6,376	4,25,054 „

90.		1890-91.			
EXPO RT.		IMPORT.		EXPORT.	
Amount of duty.	Weight or value.	Amount of duty.	Weight or value.	Amount of duty.	Weight or value.
Rs.		Rs.		Rs.	
...	...	90	179 Mds.	7	13 Mds.
...	...	2,924	6,683 ,,	4	10 ,,
77	827 Mds.	2,396	19,169 ,,	4	22 ,,
31	615 Rs.	293	626 ,,	14	283 Rs.
16	356 ,,	469	626 ,,	8	181 ,,
...	...	409	4,361 ,,	...	...
...	...	77	409 ,,	...	...
38	600 ,,	497	79 ,,	123	1,971 Rs.
130	696 ,,	9,227	98,424 Rs.	50	271 ,,
55	443 ,,	1,590	12,718 ,,	29	237 ,,
...	...	2	82 ,,	...	...
...	...	420	448 ,,	5	104 Rs.
...	...	191	4,587 ,,	...	...
...	...	216	4,335 ,,	...	...
...	...	404	8,080 ,,	...	...
...	...	2,700	48,604 ,,	...	...
...	...	552	17,660 ,,	...	...
...	...	31	1,023 ,,	...	...
...	...	132	3,165 ,,	237	1,89,000 Rs.
...	...	909	24,240 ,,	...	...
...	...	1,705	20,457 ,,	...	...
...	...	160	3,195 ,,	...	...
2	50 Rs.	533	11,365 ,,	2	31 Rs.
...	...	310	7,848 ,,	...	...
...	...	282	7,017 ,,	...	...
114	1,823 Rs.	6,839	1,09,424 ,,	148	2,363 Rs.
...	...	5,212	5,212 ,,	3	3 Mds.
...	...	1,978	3,955 Mds.	...	...
323	5,046 Rs.	911	729 ,,	186	2,272 ,,
...	...	36	18 ,,	...	...
86	5,741 Rs.	19,934	13,29,982 Rs.	571	38,100 Rs.
241	16,075 ,,	5,517	3,67,800 ,,	194	8,711 ,,

Serial No.	NAMES OF ARTICLES.	1891.	
		IMPORT.	
		Amount of duty.	Weight or value.
	CLASS I.	Rs.	
	Articles of food or drink for men and animals.		
1	Grain of all kinds (parched included), rice in husk and dál.	41,083	876,454 Mds.
2	Rice, flour (maida), súji, rawa and dál arhar...	2,931	31,800 ,,
3	Indian-corn (bhutta) and green gram	517	22,155 ,,
4	All kinds of atta, wand included	12,787	24,599 ,,
5	Sugar (misri and khand) ... { Misri ...	24,362	24,662 Rs.
	{ Khand ..	11,549	13,199 Mds.
6	Taloncha and molasses of sugar and honey ...	2,363	6,302 ,,
7	Shakkar and gur	13,191	52,763 ,,
8	Sweetmeats of all kinds	66	212 ,,
9	Molasses of gur	2,446	26,092 ,,
10	Pickles, chatnis, jams, jellies, preserves and conserves of all sorts.	106	283 ,,
11	Milk	2,540	32,511 ,,
12	Ghi and butter	31,350	25,080 ,,
13	Cheese, cream, and khoa...	73	143 ,,
14	Tea, coffee, sago, barley and arrowroot ...	303	4,848 Rs.
15	All kinds of vinegar, lime and other juices ...	16	64 Mds.
16	Fish (fresh and dried)	5,033	853 ,,
17	Oilman's stores and other provisions, and preparations of food and drink.	2,960	63,143 Rs.
18	Betel-nut, katha and pán	465	532 Mds.
19	Sparkling wines	245	490 Gals.
20	Other wines or spirits	9,638	38,552 ,,
21	Beer and Porter	2,101	16,808 ,,
22	Vegetables, including potatoes	3,056	97,799 Rs.
23	Garlic, ginger and green chillies	526	4,210 ,,
24	Sugar-cane of all kinds	1,205	38,560 ,,
25	Eggs	364	291 Mds.
	DRIED FRUITS.		
26	Kernels of almonds, walnuts, cocoanuts, pista and khasta.	161	129 ,,
27	Almonds	657	1,168 Rs.
28	Dates (khajúr)	236	1,512 ,,
29	Walnuts and dates (chhoaráh)	427	709 Mds.
30	All other fruits not specified	1,409	2,255 ,,
	FRESH AND GREEN FRUITS.		
31	All kinds of fruits, fresh and green, ripe and unripe.	10,750	34,401 ,,
	FODDER FOR CATTLE.		
32	Grass, bhúsa and all other kinds of fodder, dried and green, including bran, gram shells and wand.	6,772	288,930 ,,
33	Oil-cake of all kinds and cotton seed (banaula)	192	3,069 ,,
	CLASS II.		
	Animals for Slaughter.		
34	Oxen, cows, buffaloes, camels, &c., including calves.	6,050	60,500 Rs.
35	Sheep, goats, &c., including their young ...	22,907	488,684 ,,
36	Poultry of all kinds and game birds and animals	875	14,009 ,,
	CLASS III.		
	Articles used for Fuel, Lighting and Washing.		
37	Wood fuel	12,613	605,413 Mds.
38	Upla	542	104,132 ,,
39	Charcoal, coal and coke	8,995	71,961 ,,

92.		1892-93.			
EXPORT.		IMPORT.		EXPORT.	
Amount of duty.	Weight or value.	Amount of duty.	Weight or value.	Amount of duty.	Weight or value.
Rs.		Rs.		Rs.	
3,284	70,067 Mds.	48,188	1,028,030 Mds.	514	10,914 Mds.
56	599 „	3,860	41,175 „	14	152 „
...	...	172	7,327 ,.	...	...
655	10,888 Mds.	13,252	212,033 „	...	...
446	446 Rs.	10,752	10,752 Rs.	203	203 Rs.
86	95 Mds.	19,467	22,248 Mds.	151	173 Mds.
16	43 „	1,708	2,954 „	7	19 „
30	122 „	7,696	30,784 ,.	49	195 „
...	...	81	259 „	...	...
...	...	2,295	24,477 „	...	...
7	109 Mds.	76	101 „	...	...
...	...	2,870	36,740 „	...	...
1,488	1,190 Mds.	27,024	21,619 „	1,947	1,078 Mds.
9	18 „	73	146 „	...	...
89	1,421 Rs.	150	2,400 Rs.	83	1,336 Rs.
..	...	14	58 Mds.	...	...
...	...	233	465 „	...	...
1,018	21,717 Rs.	3,281	48,663 „	1,980	42,236 Rs.
...	...	386	386 Mds.	14	226 „
69	137 Gals.	279	558 Gals.	41	82 Gals.
6,478	25,914 „	10,309	41,236 „	7,726	30,905 „
386	3,090 „	2,302	18,416 .,	553	4,428 „
...	...	2,245	71,845 Mds.	57	1,640 Rs.
...	...	525	4,200 „	...	...
...	...	1,503	24,056 „	...	...
...	..	248	198 „	...	...
...	...	557	557 „	...	...
...	...	552	991 „	..	...
...	...	315	2,016 „	...	...
...	...	255	1,022 „	2	8 Mds.
...	...	23	75 „	...	...
626	10,018 Rs.	10,986	35,155 „	426	6,821 Rs.
2	83 Mds.	7,030	299,946 „	...	...
...	...	152	2,440 „	...	...
...	...	5,146	51,460 Rs.	...	...
...	...	20,622	441,220 „	...	...
...	...	878	14,058 „	...	...
26	1,266 Mds.	12,244	585,459 Mds.	380	82,012 Mds.
...	...	421	80,991 „	...	...
...	...	5,750	46,001 „	81	650 Mds.

Serial No.	NAMES OF ARTICLES.	1891.	
		IMPORT.	
		Amount of duty.	Weight or value.
	CLASS III—*concluded.* *Articles used for Fuel, Lighting and Washing*—concluded.	Rs.	
40	Linseed oil, castor oil, cocoanut and poppy seed oils, máwa, kasumba, cotton seed and chil oils.	192	287 Mds.
41	Lamp-oil of all kinds	2,623	5,996 ,,
42	Oil-seeds	2,902	23,936 ,,
43	Tallow, wax and candles	254	542 ,,
44	Soap	521	694 ,,
45	Reh, soap-nuts, kishta, starch (kalaf) and sajji	480	5,114 ,,
46	Alum	69	367 ,,
47	Lamps, chandeliers and their fittings	1,406	450 ,,
	CLASS IV. *Articles used in the Construction of Buildings.*		
48	Shísham (black), tun, walnut, teak and chikri, deodár and sál, sawn and unsawn.	10,969	73,061 Rs.
49	Chil, kail, rai, shisham (white) and all other woods, sawn and unsawn.	1,709	10,254 ,,
50	Door and window frames, &c., and planks ...	25	538 ,,
51	Bamboos, glue and glass	562	11,984 ,,
52	Sirki, kul, sarkanda and thatching straw ...	133	2,127 ,,
53	Marble	125	2,505 ,,
54	Stone and slate	1,110	17,760 ,,
55	Bricks (large)	3,683	66,294 ,,
56	Small bricks	383	10,656 ,,
57	Patrah, pinjrah	41	650 ,,
58	Girdah, chauka, tiles, kolába and patnála of all kinds.	294	9,420 ,,
59	Kankar-lime	1,249	33,933 ,,
60	Stone-lime	2,321	27,858 ,,
61	Portland cement	214	6,427 ,,
62	Wall paper	1	17 ,,
63	Turpentine, tar, puttey, varnish and paints of all kinds, including colouring earths.	252	5,983 ,,
64	San	101	2,580 ,,
65	Múnj rope	316	16,875 ,,
	CLASS V. *Drugs, Gums, Spices and Perfumes.*		
66	All drugs, medicines, gums, spices and perfumes.	7,787	1,24,597 ,,
	CLASS VI.—*Tobacco.*		
67	Tobacco, 1st quality, such as Kandhári, Púrbi, Hazro, &c.	1,635	1,635 Mds.
68	Tobacco, 2nd quality (country)	1,816	3,632 ,,
69	Cheroots, cigars, cigarettes and imported tobacco (European).	1,061	566 ,,
70	Snuff	33	16 ,,
	CLASS VII. *Piece-goods and other Textile Fabrics, and all manufactured Articles of Clothing and Dress.*		
71	All piece-goods and other textile fabrics, and all manufactured articles of clothing and dress and gold lace.	24,086	16,05,018 Rs.
	CLASS VIII.—*Metals and Articles of Metal.*		
72	All metals and articles of metal, except gold and silver bullion, and other prohibited articles.	7,114	4,74,218,, ,,

92.		1892-93.			
EXPORT.		IMPORT.		EXPORT.	
Amount. of duty.	Weight or value.	Amount of duty.	Weight or value.	Amount of duty.	Weight or value.
Rs.		Rs.		Rs.	
6	12 Mds.	218	437 Mds.	34	68 Mds.
...	...	2,857	6,530 ,,		
...	...	5,204	41,633 ,,	286	1,523 Mds.
19	407 Rs.	193	275 ,,	...	...
33	712 ,,	427	1,566 ,,	18	401 Rs.
...	...	679	7,239 ,,	4	47 Mds.
..		40	215 ,,		
164	2,632 Rs.	1,490	477 ,,	154	2,468 Rs.
231	1,232 ,,	7,738	51,586 Rs.	505	2,696 ,,
42	336 ,,	1,597	9,581 ,,	6	51 ,,
		26	1,500 ,,	...	...
44	937 Rs.	373	1,554 ,,	13	290 Rs.
...		153	2,453 ,,	...	...
...	...	203	4,065 ,,	5	20 Mds.
...	...	631	12,630 ,,		
644	12,88,000 Rs.	2,837	53,562 ,,	2,048	9,941 Rs.
...	...	250	7,995 ,,	...	...
...	...	44	1,760 ,,	9	379 Rs.
237	1,90,000 Rs.	342	10,963 ,,	...	...
134	17,816 ,,	1,463	38,835 ,,	657	87,566 Rs.
		1,862	28,620 ,,	...	
...	...	205	9,834 ,,	20	40 Casks.
...	...	2	33 ,,	...	...
...	...	258	5,518 ,,	2	44 Casks.
...	...	139	3,552 ,,	...	...
...	...	297	15,849 ,,	...	...
280	4,488 Rs.	7,823	1,25,170 ,,	787	12,597 Rs.
73	73 Mds.	4,935	4,935 Mds.	404	863 ,,
		2,025	4,051 ,,	...	...
307	4,913 Rs.	913	730 ,,	...	...
		52	26 ,,	...	...
237	15,828 ,,	20,975	13,97,345 Rs.	586	30,109 Rs.
344	22,955 ,,	5,095	3,39,647 ,,	85	5,695 ,,

Chapter VI, B.

—

Modern Lahore.

Commercial enterprise.

Considering its situation at the junction of three Railway lines, Lahore is not remarkable for its commercial enterprise. Mr. Robson had established extensive workshops in proximity to the Railway, but these did not succeed ; and were closed on Mr. Robson's death. The only factories of importance in Lahore city are the Punjab Oil and Flour Mills Company and Cotton Ginning Factory in Dhobi Mandi, Anárkali Bazár.

Punjab Oil and Flour Mills.

The Punjab Steam Mills Company was started in September 1881 with a capital of Rs. 1,00,000 of which Rs. 81,000 had been paid up. The machinery consisted of four hydraulic presses with five chambers each and three pairs of flour mills driven by steam power. In 1890 the mills were purchased by Messrs. Scrofton & Co. The oil and flour mills were remodelled and started afresh in July 1890. The capital now stands at Rs. 1,70,000.

The oil mills can turn out about 80 maunds of oil per diem. Castor oil is manufactured for medical, burning and lubricating purposes. Also til, linseed and rape oils and oil-cake for which there is a large demand both in the Punjab and abroad are manufactured in large quantities on the latest modern principles. Shipments of oil and oil-cake made by this firm are despatched from Bombay, Calcutta and Karáchi, it is said, to the amount of one thousand tons or so annually.

The flour mills have been set up with modern plant and the owners say they can turn out about 400 maunds of flour and *atta* daily. Contracts are made to supply the Commissariat Department with flour, and *atta* is sold in the different markets of the Punjab. The number of workmen employed vary from 50 to 70 according to the press of work.

Cotton Ginning Factory.

The Cotton Ginning Factory in Anárkali Bazár belongs to a man of the name of Bhagat Singh. At present it is worked by an eight horse-power engine ; but the proprietor has lately sent orders to England for an engine of twenty-five horse-power. The factory at present employs only 10 looms, and during the working season (from November to April) it turns out 100 maunds of cleaned cotton daily. This is all exported to Karáchi where it fetches from Rs. 18 to Rs. 20 per maund.

Brick burning.

Mr. F. Atkinson, C. E., started an establishment some three years ago for the manufacture of a superior class of bricks and lime. He invested in expensive machinery for the purpose and established himself in the vicinity of the Thaggi School. Subsequently the business was taken over by a Company styling itself the Brick, Tile and Lime Manufacturing Company. It was soon discovered that there was but little demand for a class of brick better than that supplied from the ordinary native *paja-wahs*, and the only business done now by the Company is in *kankar* lime and to a limited extent in roofing tiles. The lime is ground by engine power and is of very superior quality. It is sold to the public at Rs. 27 per 100 maunds.

Chapter VI, B.

Modern Lahore.

A tramway was laid down in 1886 commencing from Mr. J. Robson's workshops, and traversing the Landa Bazár, the city circular road to Lohári Gate and the Anárkali Bazár on to the Telegraph Office. The Company met with nothing but misfortune from the commencement. The cars were made too heavy and the management was inefficient. The end came very soon and after vain attempts to induce English capitalists to purchase the concern, the property of the Company was put up to auction by the Civil Courts and was bought in by the Alliance Bank of Simla for a sum that fell considerably short of the Bank's advances on the property. The unfortunate shareholders lost all their money. The Bank seeing no prospect of making the tramway pay, eventually in the summer of 1893 decided to sell the materials for what they would fetch. A considerable portion of the line had been pulled up when an enterprising Contractor of Mooltan, Bhai Gurdit Singh, came forward and purchased the remainder as it lay. His attempts to work the line have not proved successful so far.

Tramway.

The following is a statement of the Printing Presses at work in the Lahore District during the year 1892-93.

Printing Presses.

Locality.	Names of Presses.	Names of Proprietors.	PUBLICATIONS THEREAT.	
			Newspapers.	Periodicals.
LAHORE.	Government Press ...	Government, Punjab ...	...	1
	Central Jail Press ...	Do. do. ...	...	...
	North-Western Railway Press.	Do. do. ...	...	...
	Civil & Military Gazette Press.	The Hon'ble W. H. Rattigan and others.	2	3
	Albert Press ...	Pohlo Mal ...	...	...
	New Albion Press ...	Lal Din ...	...	...
	Tribune Press ...	Sardár Dyal Singh, Majithia	2	...
	New Imperial Press ...	Sayad Rajab Ali Shah ...	1	...
	News Press ...	Muncherji Manakji ...	1	...
	Anglo-Sanskrit Press ...	Ram Chand ...	1	...
	Sri Wahi-Guru Press ...	Nihal Singh ...	1	1
	Empress Press ...	Rája Ram ...	...	...
	Islamia Press ...	Karm Bakhsh ...	...	...
	Sidiqi Press ...	Abdul Rahman and Muhammad.	...	...
	Caxton Press ...	Chiragh Din ...	...	1
	Public Advocate Press ...	Hukam Chand ...	1	...
	Gulzar Mahamdi Press ...	Gulzar Bakhsh ...	1	...
	Qanún-i-Hind Press ...	Budha-Mal ...	...	1

Chapter VI. B.

Modern Lahore.

Printing presses.

Locality	Names of Presses.	Names of Proprietors.	Publications thereat.	
			News-papers.	Periodi-cals.
	Rafiq-i-Hind Press	Muharram Ali Chisti ...	1	...
	Aftab-i-Punjab Press ...	Dewan Buta Singh ...	1	1
	Saifi Press ...	Mir Nadir Saifi ...	1	...
	Virja Nand Press ...	Durga Parshad ...	...	1
	Koh-i-Núr Press ...	Jagat Narain ...	1	1
	Qiblat-ul-Matabia ...	Feroze Din ...	2	...
	Fakhr-ud-din Press ...	Fakhr-ud-din ..	1	...
	Mitter Vilas Press ..	Pandit Mokand Ram ...	3	...
	Mufid-i-Am Press ...	Munshi Gulab Singh ...	...	...
	Shahab-i-Saqib Press ...	Shahab-ud-din ...	1	...
	Ghamkhar-i-Hind Press ...	Pandit Máháraj Kishen,	1	...
	Dev Bidban Press ...	S. N. Agnihotri ...	1	...
	Jafri Press ...	Sayad Jawad Ali Shah ...	1	...
	Delhi Punch Press ...	Fazl-ud-din ...	1	...
	Niwal Kishore Press ...	Munshi Niwal Kishore ...	...	...
	Victoria Press ...	Muhammad Jan and Muhammad Husain ...	...	...
	Ganesh Parkash Press ...	Harsukh Rai ...	...	...
LAHORE—concluded.	Khadim-ul-talim Press ...	Mahbub Alam ...	1	4
	Kishen Chander ...	Pritam Dás ...	1	...
	Grishan-i-Hind Press ...	Imam Din ...	...	...
	Gulshan-i-Punjab ...	Mirza Iwaz Beg ...	...	...
	Presidency Press ...	Mul Chand ...	...	...
	Fazal Ilahi Press ...	Fazal Din ...	...	...
	Khatri Samachar Press ...	Hari Lal Kapur ...	2	...
	Dilkushai Hind Press ...	Muhammad Bakhsh ...	...	...
	Hari Parkash Press ...	Jagat Singh, son of Komedan Bakhshish Singh,	...	...
	Benazir Press ...	Mirza Imdad Ali Rasá ...	...	...
	Gul Bahar Press ...	Chuni Lal ...	...	...
	Qanún-i-Punjab Press ...	Mahtab Din ...	...	...
	Rahmani Press ...	Malik Pir Bakhsh ...	1	...
	Guru Granth Parkash Press,	Rup Lal ...	...	...
	Lahore Gazette Press ...	Sheikh Didar Bakhsh ...	...	...
	Economical Press ...	Suraj Bhan ...	...	1
	New Lyall Press ...	Mirza Imdad Ali and Haji Ilahi Bakhsh.	...	2
	Mercantile Press ...	Ghulam Moy-ud-din ...	...	...
	Vidya Parkash Press ...	Thakar Dás ...	...	...
	Gur Parkash Press ...	Sham Dás ...	...	...
	Subhani Press ...	Abdur Rahman ...	1	...
	Khair Andesh ...	Piddu Jogi ...	...	...
	Kadir Press Kasur ...	Kadir Bakhsh Khan, Honorary Magistrate ...	1	...
	Aror Bans Press ...	Salig Rám ...	2	...

The following is a list of the newspapers, English and Vernacular at present published in Lahore:—

Serial No.	Name of paper	Place of publication.	Subject matter.	Language.	Period of publication.	Circulation.
1	Civil and Military Gazette	Lahore	General news	English	Daily.	1,400
2	Punjab Patriot	Do.	Do.	Do.	Weekly.	600
3	Tribune	Do.	Do.	Do.	Bi-weekly.	600
4	Arya Patreka	Do.	Religious	Do.	Fortnightly.	425
5	People's Journal	Do.	General news	Urdu	Weekly.	40
6	Aftáb-i-Punjab	Do.	Do. and political news	Do.	Bi-weekly.	400
7	Arorbans Parkásh	Do.	Do. and social news	Do.	Monthly.	175
8	Bhárat Sudhár	Do.	Do. news and religions	Do.	Weekly.	300
9	Durbín	Do.	Do. news	Lo.	Do.	400
10	Ghamkhár-i-Hind	Do.	Political and general news	Do.	Do.	175
11	Imperial Paper	Do.	General news	Gurmukhi	Do.	300
12	Khálsa Parkásh	Do.	Do. and political news	Do.	Do.	400
13	Khalsa Akhbár	Do.	Do.	Urdu	Do.	175
14	Lahore Punch	Do.	General news	Hindi	Do.	400
15	Mitra Vilasa	Do.	Political and Literary	Urdu	Do.	500
16	Toifa-i-Punjab	Do.	General news	Do.	Do.	300
17	Sada-i-Hind	Do.	Political and general news	Do.	Bi-weekly.	244
18	Rahber-i-Hind	Do.	Do.	Do.	Daily.	2,358
19	Akhbar-i-'Am	Do.	Do.	Do.	Weekly.	5,100
20	Paisa Akhbár	Do.	General news	Do.	Do.	1,000
21	Wafadár	Do.	Do.	Do.	Do.	250
22	Sultan-i-Hind	Do.	Local and general news	Do.	Do.	400
23	Khatri Sama-char	Do	Social	Do.	Bi-weekly.	200
24	Mukhbar-i-Sádik	Kasúr	Local and general news	Do,	Weekly.	

SECTION C, MINOR TOWNS.

At the census of 1891 all places were classed as towns which had been constituted municipalities, civil stations, or cantonments, and also all those containing a population of over 5,000 souls, provided that they were possessed of some real urban characteristics such as a bázár or the like. Under this rule the following places were returned as towns in the Lahore district :—

Tahsíl.	Towns.	Persons.	Males.	Females.
Lahore	Lahore	159,597	92,835	66,762
	Mián Mír Cant. ...	17,257	11,875	5,382
Chúnián	Chúnián (M) .	10,339	5,532	4,807
	Khudian (M) ...	2,921	1,526	1,395
Kasúr	Kasúr ...	20,290	10,596	9,694
	Khem Karan (M) ...	5,935	3,215	2,720
	Patti (M) ...	7,495	3,816	3,679
Sharakhpur ...	Sharakhpur (M) ...	4,924	2,541	2,383

The distribution by religion of the population of these towns and the number of houses in each are shown in Table No. XLIII, while further particulars will be found in Tables III and IV attached to the Census Report for 1891. The city of Lahore has already been fully described in the preceding pages.

Mián Mír.

Mián Mír is the principal military station and the head-quarters of the General Commanding the Lahore Division, it is situated above four miles to the east of the civil station and six miles from the Fort of Lahore.

Kasúr.

Kasúr is the most important town in the district after Lahore. It is built upon the high bank which marks the termination of the Mánjha and looks down upon the lowlands of the Sutlej Hithár. It stands just to one side of the Grand Trunk Road to Ferozepore, 34 miles south of Lahore and 16 miles north of Ferozepore. The town is an aggregation of fortified hamlets, called *kots*, small in themselves, but together forming a considerable town. They are quite close together, four of them being actually contiguous. Their names are : Kot Khwája Hussain ; Kila Pukhta ; Kot Ghulám Mohi-ud-dín ; Kot Murád Khán ; Kot Usmán Khán ; Kot Badar-ud-dín Khán ; Kot Bakar-ud-dín Khán ; Kot Azam Khan ; Kot Hakim Khán ; Kot Fatehdín Khán ; Pirán ka Kot and Kot Abdul Ghani Khan.

About a mile-to the east of the town, situate on the other side of the Trunk-Road and quite close to it are the Tahsíl and Police Station buildings. Here also is the Court-house of the Assistant Commissioner in charge of the subdivision which embraces the Kasúr and Chúnián tahsíls.

The building in which his court is held also has a rest-house for civil officers on tour which is occupied permanently by the Assistant in charge when he happens to be a European as is the case at present. A little further up the road is another bungalow, the property of the Public Works Department.

Within historical times, Kasúr has been in the possession of a remarkable colony of Patháns, perhaps the most remarkable on this side of the Indus. There is little doubt, however, that the site was occupied by a Rájpút town long before the period of the earliest Muhammadan invasions. Its name is probably a corrupted form of Kasháwar, in the same way as Lahore is said to be a shortened form of Laháwar. Tradition refers the foundation of the town to Kush, a brother of Loh or Lav, son of Ráma, who is said to have founded Lahore. However this may be, Kasúr does not appear in history until far on in the Muhammadan period. The colony of Patháns was located at some time during the 15th century, according to the account during the reign of Bábar, but more probably in 1560, during the reign of his grandson Akbar. The colony is said to have numbered 3,500 souls. Among the colonists were certain Hasanzais, whose descendants became the chiefs of the colony and founded a considerable principality, including territory on both banks of the Sutlej. When the Sikhs rose to power, they experienced great opposition from the Patháns of Kasúr. In 1763 and again in 1770, however, the chiefs of the Bhangi *misl* succeeded in storming the town, and eventually overran and subdued the whole Kasúr territory. Large numbers of Patháns were slaughtered on those occasions. The two brothers, Nizám ud-dín Khán and Kutb-ud-dín Khan who at the time represented the family, at first entered the service of their conquerors. But they were energetic and brave, and a few years later (in 1794) again expelled the Sikhs from Kasúr, and, re-establishing the Pathán rule, held their own against repeated attacks of the Sikhs until 1807, when at last Kutb-ud-dín Khan was forced to give way before Ranjít Singh and retire to his property at Mamdot beyond the Sutlej. The town of Kasúr was then incorporated in the dominions of the conqueror. Since then the town has declined in importance and at present is nothing more than the centre of a local trade in country produce. Since the extension of the Kasúr and Ferozepore railway there has been a brisk exportation of wheat, gram, rape-seed and cotton from the local railway station, the annual value of which on the average exceeds ten lakhs at present and is no doubt on the increase. There are three or four cotton gins working now in the town, the largest of which cleans about a hundred maunds of cotton per diem. The only manufacture of Kasúr worth noticing

Chapter VI, C.

Minor Towns.

Kasúr.

is that of leather, especially country harness and shoes, for which it has a considerable reputation. A school of industrial art was founded there in 1876 of which mention has been made in Chapter V, A.

The Kasúr Municipality was established in 1867 and at present consists of three *ex-officio* members and 12 non-official members, of whom 2 are nominated and 10 elected. Last year they held 18 meetings. The municipal income has averaged Rs. 42,000 in the last three years, and is derived mainly from octroi duty on various articles, principally of food and drink, from rents and taxes, and from sale of the town manure. In the same period the expenditure averaged annually about Rs. 30,000, the chief items being maintenance of schools, the pay of octroi and conservancy establishment and of police, refunds of octroi duty averaging over ten thousand rupees and the cost of keeping roads in repair. The situation of the town affords considerable facilities for drainage. The main streets are paved and furnished with side drains and a sufficient conservancy establishment is maintained. The population in 1881 was 17,336. At the recent census it was found to have increased to 20,290. The distribution by religions is shown in Table No. XLIII, from which it will be seen that more than three-fourths the inhabitants are Musalmáns. The number of births and deaths which occurred in Kasúr during the last ten years are shown in Table No. XLIV. The annual birth and death-rates per *mille* of population since 1881 are given below, the basis of calculation being in every case the figures of the most recent census :—

1	2	3	4	5	6	7
	BIRTH-RATES.			DEATH-RATES.		
YEAR.	Males.	Females.	Persons.	Males.	Females.	Persons.
1881	30	30	30	29	29	29
1882	32	32	32	19	19	19
1883	35	27	36	20	24	22
1884	41	39	40	33	33	33
1885	32	30	31	23	20	21
1886	40	33	37	24	22	23
1887	35	35	35	40	37	38
1888	37	35	36	38	36	37
1889	37	33	35	40	42	41
1890	34	30	33	41	42	42
1891	40	38	39	27	29	28
Average	36	34	35	30	30	30

The lands belonging to the township of Kasúr were confiscated by the Sikh Government when the city of Kasúr was taken from the Patháns and had not been disposed of by them when the government passed from the hands of the Sikhs to the British. The present occupation of the land has already been noticed in Chapter V, B.

Chunián is a small town situated like Kasúr upon the high bank of the old bed of the Beás, on the road from Ferozepore to Mooltan, distant 38 miles from Lahore and ten miles from the Chánga Manga Railway Station on the Lahore and Mooltan Railway. The town was formerly divided into three separate fortified hamlets, one of which is now entirely in ruins while the other two have completely coalesced. At present its only importance consists in its being the head-quarters of the tahsíl and the centre of all the local traffic in wheat, gram and cotton. Also much through traffic passes it on its way to Chánga Manga Railway Station.

It has a police station and a rest-house for civil officers on tour, a school and a dispensary. It was constituted a Municipality in 1866. The committee at present consists of three *ex-officio* members and nine non-official, of whom one is nominated and eight elected. Last year the committee met thirteen times. The income of the Municipality during the last three years averaged annually between thirteen and fourteen thousand rupees, derived principally from octroi duty on imported articles, mainly cloth, food and drink. The expenditure in the same time was slightly over Rs. 11,000 a year, the principal items being charges for police, schools, conservancy and octroi establishment.

The population has increased during the last ten years from 8,122 as enumerated in 1881 to 10,339, the figure recorded in 1891. Slightly more than half the number are Musalmáns. Many are agriculturists owning the land included in Chunián estate. The birth and death-rate per mille of population during the last eleven years is shown below, the basis of calculation being the figure enumerated at the later census :—

	1				2	3	4	5	6	7
					BIRTH-RATES.			DEATH-RATES.		
	YEARS.				Males.	Females.	Persons.	Males.	Females.	Persons.
1881	...	...	...	...	...	...	...	20	11	19
1882	...	...	...	...	...	...	...	17	15	16
1883	...	...	...	...	...	...	...	13	12	13
1884	...	...	...	...	...	...	...	13	9	11
1885	...	...	...	...	30	37	33	18	15	17
1886	...	...	...	...	34	36	35	16	14	15
1887	...	...	...	...	31	28	30	25	21	23
1888	...	...	...	...	32	41	36	15	17	16
1889	...	...	...	...	40	36	38	27	24	25
1890	...	...	...	...	37	31	34	35	32	34
1891	...	...	...	...	36	31	34	24	24	24
	Average	...	...		34	34	34	15	18	17

Chapter VI, C.
———
Minor Towns.
Chunián.

There is very little trade in Chunián, and no manufactures to speak of. Of late years two or three cotton gins have been established in which a considerable amount of cleaning business is done. The canal-irrigated lands in the neighbourhood of Chunián produce a large quantity of cotton.

Khudián.

The town of Khudián is situated about 16 miles east of Chunián, close to the border of Kasúr and Chunián tahsíls, and just to one side of the Mooltan and Ferozepore road. It is an old town surrounded by a brick wall; many of the houses are large and well built. In the neighbourhood is the remnant of an old mud fort now in ruins. At Khudián the Katora Canal which has its outlet from the Sutlej river at Gunda Singhwála on the Kasúr and Ferozepore road, breaks up into three large distributaries carrying its waters right across the Chunián Hithár. The population was found to be 2,917 at the census of 1881, and in the recent census was enumerated at 2,921 ; most of the people are agricultural, cultivating the lands attached to the estate. There are, however, a fair number of money-lenders and petty shop-keepers in the bazár. Seven of these have been assessed to income-tax on incomes in excess of Rs. 1,000, and these pay altogether the sum of Rs. 169. The town was declared a Municipality in 1874. The committee includes one *ex-officio* member, the Tahsíldár of Chunián, and eight non-official members, of whom two are nominated and six elected. The income of the committee has averaged during the last three years less than Rs. 1,800, derived chiefly from octroi duty. Its expenditure averages about Rs. 1,500, being chiefly on police, conservancy and octroi establishment. A small police station is kept up and there is a rest-house for civil officers on tour.

Patti.

Patti is a very old town situate 38 miles south-east of Lahore and 28 miles east of Kasúr. It stands on the road to Haríke Ferry, which used to be an important line of communication between the Lahore and Ferozepore districts. The town is walled and the houses are built to a large extent with brick masonry. It has a good bazár with a paved street. About 200 yards from the town on the north-east is an old masonry built fort, which under the Sikh rule was used by Mahárája Ranjít Singh as a horse-breeding establishment, and now contains the police station and one or two rooms as a rest-house for civil officers on tour. The population consists principally of Mughals, and is largely agricultural; deriving their living from the produce of the land included in the estate. There are in the bazár 16 traders, who pay tax on incomes over Rs. 1,000 and their aggregate income-tax is Rs. 924.

Patti was constituted a Municipality in 1874 and there are at present nine members, of whom the Tahsíldár is one *ex-officio* : of the remaining eight two are nominated and six elected. The income of the Municipality during the last three years has averaged slightly over Rs. 4,400, derived almost entirely from octroi duty on articles of food and drink and on cloth : the annual expenditure generally exceeds their income apparently, education being the heaviest item and police, conservancy and octroi establishment being also proportionately heavy. The total population was enumerated at 6,407 in 1881 and as 7,495 at the late census.

Khem Karan is a small town in the Mánjha Tract of Kasúr tahsíl, distant 7 miles from Kasúr with which it is connected by a metalled road. The town is surrounded by a thick well-built masonry wall buttressed at intervals : it has some good straight bazár roads all paved. There are some large houses in the town and a fine *baoli* well, with steps leading down to the water's edge. It must at some former time have been a larger and more important place than at present, as there are a number of ruins scattered round its present site. The public buildings are the Municipal Committee house, school-house and police post. The Kasúr branch of the Bári Doáb Canal passes Khem Karan and there is a canal rest-house situate somewhat over a mile from the town on the road to Kasúr. The Municipality was constituted in 1869 and at present there are nine members, of whom the Tahsíldár of Kasúr is one *ex-officio*, and of the eight others, two are elected. The municipal income during the last three years has averaged slightly over Rs. 4,000 annually, of which at least half is derived from octroi duty or articles of food and drink. The expenditure in the same time has averaged Rs. 4,400, of which the heaviest items are on account of police, education and octroi establishment. The population according to the census of 1881 was 5,516, and by the results of the recent census has increased to 5,935. This increase is very small compared to that shown under other towns. Khem Karan is largely agricultural. The Kamboh land owners are well-to-do and having much more land on their hands than they can cultivate themselves, nevertheless do not use their tenants well. Consequently the condition of the agriculture is not nearly so good as it might be. Their are a considerable number of money-lenders and petty traders in the bazár. The number of those paying tax on annual incomes over Rs. 1,000 is 11, and their total payments amount to Rs. 325.

The town of Sharakpur is situated in latitude 31° 28′ north and longitude 74° 8′ east about three miles north of the Ravi ; its distance from Shahdara is a little over 15 miles and beyond that to Lahore city is two miles. Sharakpur is the head-quarters of a tahsíl and police station. It is surrounded by a high and thick mud built wall against which some of the houses are built. It is a poor-looking place and hardly deserves the name of town. The tahsíl and police buildings stand a little distance from the settlement, and opposite them is an excellent rest-house lately built for civil officers on tour. A school and hospital are also maintained here. It is the only large place of any importance in the district on the north

Chapter VI, C.

Minor Towns.

Sharakpur.

of the Rávi, and consequently most of the local trade is centred here. The population, however, is chiefly agricultural, dependent on the produce of the land included within the estate. The number of traders paying tax on incomes in excess of one thousand rupees is ten, and the total amount they pay as income-tax is Rs. 296. The population was ascertained to be 4,595 in 1881 and 4,924 in the recent census of 1891. The people are nearly all Musulmáns, chiefly Aráins and Khojás. The low rate of increase in population is due to the depressed condition of the cultivating portion of the community. They are heavily embarrassed with debt to the money-lenders.